Environmental, Social, and Governance (ESG) Integration for Green FinTech

Dharmendra Singh
https://orcid.org/0000-0002-3892-8299
Modern College of Business and Science, Oman

Garima Malik
https://orcid.org/0000-0002-3892-8299
Birla Institute of Management Technology, India

Rene Ymbong Paquibut
Modern College of Business and Science, Oman

IGI Global
Scientific Publishing
Publishing Tomorrow's Research Today

Vice President of Editorial Melissa Wagner
Director of Acquisitions Mikaela Felty
Director of Book Development Jocelynn Hessler
Production Manager Mike Brehm
Cover Design Jose Rosado

Published in the United States of America by
IGI Global Scientific Publishing
701 East Chocolate Avenue
Hershey, PA, 17033, USA
Tel: 717-533-8845 | Fax: 717-533-7115
Website: https://www.igi-global.com E-mail: cust@igi-global.com

Library of Congress Cataloging-in-Publication Data

LCCN: 2025031496 (CIP Data Pending)
ISBN13: 9798337354378
Isbn13Softcover: 9798337354385
EISBN13: 9798337354392
British Cataloguing in Publication Data
A Cataloguing in Publication record for this book is available from the British Library.

Table of Contents

Detailed Table of Contents

As financial institutions increasingly adopt ESG principles, sustainable finance emerges as a powerful tool for economic growth and environmental stewardship.

Sustainability is the most important aspect for businesses, organizations, and companies of all types in current scenario. Scaling sustainable practices is becoming increasingly important, and the financial industry is no exception. Environmental concerns have led to a number of innovative technological and financial advancements. In the framework of digital revolution and sustainable finance, fintech has appeared as a competitive alternate to traditional financial institutions. Fintech has the potential to accelerate the growth of green finance, which tackles climate change and environmental preservation and has emerged as a means for developed nations to attain sustainable development. The achievement of "17 Sustainable Development Goals" set out by the UN will depend largely on the digital change of the financial structure and sustainable growth of economy. The chapter discusses the Fintech solutions to enable a switch toward a "low-carbon", "green", and "resilient economy". It focuses on diverse areas of association between Fintech and sustainable finance.

As the world accelerates toward sustainable development, the financial sector plays a pivotal role in driving environmental and social responsibility. Green Digital Payment Systems (GDPS) a new frontier in financial technology are redefining how transactions can align with Environmental, Social, and Governance (ESG) compliance standards. This chapter explores the emergence, evolution, and impact of green digital payment systems that not only facilitate cashless economies but also embed sustainability into their core design and functionality. These innovative platforms leverage technologies such as blockchain, carbon footprint tracking, AI-driven ESG analytics, and eco-friendly payment infrastructures to promote green consumer behavior, ethical investing, and climate-conscious financial decisions. From biodegradable payment cards to platforms that reward low-emission purchases, GDPS are reshaping the landscape of responsible finance.

This chapter explored workforce planning in Quick Commerce through a FinTech lens. It demonstrated how digital payments, performance incentives, and embedded financial tools not only magnify demand volatility but also influence workforce behaviour and heighten managerial trade, offs. By adopting a contingency, based approach, firms can more effectively tailor their workforce strategies to fit changing conditions, while also safeguarding human sustainability. The chapter concludes that the future of Quick Commerce lies not in accelerating delivery speeds indefinitely, but in the intelligent integration of FinTech systems with realistic, human, centred workforce design.

The transition to digital platforms is a significant trend in the contemporary retail sector, as numerous companies embrace a customer-centric methodology by employing omnichannel tactics to facilitate cohesive shopping experiences across online and offline channels. This study examines the factors, obstacles, and effects of this change, concentrating on electrical retailers within the Indian market. Omnichannel retailing amalgamates diverse shopping channels to deliver a cohesive and convenient client experience. An efficient omnichannel approach enables customers to seamlessly transition between onlineand in-store encounters, potentially enhancing customer expenditure. The retail sector is experiencing a digital revolution, propelled by the necessity to improve consumer experiences and operational efficiency.

This chapter explains how digitalization is a cornerstone of economic sustainability, which strikes the balance between economic growth and environmental and social well-being. The final frontier of the digital revolution is the assets & commodities industry, and here, big data, blockchain, artificial intelligence, and IoT are changing

The objective of this research paper is to examine the Circular Economy (CE) strategies adopted by companies by applying established frameworks and predefined indicators from existing literature. The study aims to analyze how these strategies generate social and economic benefits and contribute to overall sustainability. To achieve this, the research used a qualitative methodology and specifically content analysis of published sustainability reports. This approach involved collecting and analysing data on companies' efforts to provide goods sustainably. By reviewing these reports, the research identifies CE initiatives implemented by companies and evaluates how these strategies align with sustainability goals, including their contribution to reducing environmental footprints, promoting resource efficiency and fostering social equity. This analysis provides a deeper understanding of the intersection between Circular Economy practices and sustainable development outcomes.

One of the primary objectives of the BRICS countries has been to promote technology-facilitated financial inclusion. The increasing utilisation of the internet and mobile technology is diverting the attention of the BRICS nations. The governments and regulatory authorities of the BRICS nations have initiated several measures to foster FinTech adoption, establish a robust, accountable, and supportive digital financial ecosystem and infrastructure, and develop a regulatory framework that enhances consumer and data protection while promoting digital and financial literacy. These initiatives have resulted in substantial advancements in digitisation across all BRICS countries. Digital retail payment transactions have experienced a significant transformation following the implementation of the Unified Payment Interface (UPI) in India. This article describes how the BRICS countries have lessened the risks by implementing a sensible framework that protects consumer rights and privacy.

Preface

The accelerating convergence of Environmental, Social, and Governance (ESG) principles with financial technology is redefining the future of sustainable finance. As governments, businesses, financial institutions, and investors increasingly recognize the urgency of addressing climate change, social equity, and responsible governance, digital innovation has emerged as a critical enabler of this transformation. Green FinTech, through technologies such as artificial intelligence, blockchain, digital payments, big data analytics, and Internet of Things (IoT) applications, is creating new opportunities to improve transparency, expand financial inclusion, enhance investment decision-making, and support environmentally responsible economic growth.

Environmental, Social, and Governance (ESG) Integration for Green FinTech brings together scholarly perspectives that examine the evolving relationship between sustainability and financial innovation. The volume provides a comprehensive exploration of contemporary research, emerging technologies, governance frameworks, and practical applications that are shaping sustainable financial systems across developed and developing economies. The contributions highlight both the opportunities and challenges associated with integrating ESG principles into digital financial ecosystems while emphasizing the importance of interdisciplinary collaboration, sound policy frameworks, and responsible technological adoption.

The chapters collectively examine a broad range of themes, including climate finance, ESG integration, green finance, sustainable investment, corporate governance, digital payment systems, circular economy, sustainable energy, financial inclusion, risk management, green marketing, responsible business models, and artificial intelligence. Through bibliometric analyses, literature reviews, conceptual discussions, empirical investigations, and case studies, the contributors present valuable insights into how financial innovation can support long-term environmental sustainability and inclusive economic development.

A distinguishing feature of this volume is its global perspective. While many chapters focus on emerging economies, particularly India and other developing regions, the discussions also incorporate international experiences that broaden understanding of sustainable finance across diverse institutional and regulatory contexts. The collection underscores that technological advancement alone cannot achieve sustainability objectives; rather, meaningful progress depends upon effective governance, transparent reporting, ethical business practices, and stakeholder collaboration.

The volume is intended to serve researchers, academicians, policymakers, financial professionals, industry practitioners, regulators, and postgraduate students interested in ESG, FinTech, sustainable finance, corporate sustainability, and digital transformation. By bringing together current research and practical perspectives, the book seeks to stimulate further academic inquiry while supporting informed decision-making in both public and private sectors.

Chapter Overview

1. Presents a bibliometric analysis of climate finance research in developing countries, examining publication trends, collaboration networks, thematic evolution, and future research directions.
2. Reviews recent literature on ESG integration, FinTech innovation, and sustainable finance in developing economies, highlighting opportunities, challenges, and emerging research priorities.
3. Examines green finance instruments and corporate sustainability strategies, emphasizing environmentally responsible investments and their contribution to organizational and societal goals.
4. Explores how financial institutions balance profitability with environmental responsibility through sustainable finance frameworks, regulatory developments, and ESG-focused investment approaches.
5. Discusses the role of FinTech in advancing sustainable finance by enabling green finance, supporting climate action, and facilitating the transition toward a low-carbon economy.
6. Investigates the emergence of green digital payment systems and their alignment with ESG objectives through technologies such as blockchain, artificial intelligence, and carbon footprint tracking.
7. Examines workforce planning in the quick commerce sector through a FinTech perspective, focusing on human sustainability, digital financial tools, and organizational resilience.
8. Analyzes the digital transformation of retail businesses and its implications for sustainable economic development through omnichannel strategies and digital innovation.

9. Explores how digitalization, artificial intelligence, blockchain, and the Internet of Things contribute to reducing carbon footprints while promoting sustainable economic development.
10. Investigates the relationship between corporate governance, financial performance, transparency, and investor perceptions within the Indian corporate sector.
11. Evaluates the effectiveness of corporate social responsibility initiatives in Omani companies and their relationship with financial performance and investor confidence.
12. Examines how circular economy strategies contribute to environmental sustainability, resource efficiency, and broader sustainable development objectives.
13. Analyzes digital financial risk mitigation strategies within BRICS economies, emphasizing financial inclusion, consumer protection, and secure digital financial ecosystems.
14. Presents a thematic analysis of green marketing and sustainable supply chain research, identifying key trends, stakeholder influences, and opportunities for future investigation.
15. Explores responsible business models founded on environmental, social, and economic sustainability through conceptual discussion and illustrative organizational case studies.
16. Examines the AI–productivity paradox by analyzing the relationship between artificial intelligence adoption, employee productivity, organizational adaptation, and long-term performance outcomes.

As the global financial landscape continues to evolve, the integration of ESG principles with digital innovation will remain central to achieving sustainable and inclusive economic development. It is our hope that this volume will contribute meaningfully to the growing body of knowledge in Green FinTech, inspire future research, and encourage the development of innovative, ethical, and resilient financial systems that support the well-being of both present and future generations.

Dharmendra Singh
Modern College of Business and Science, Oman

Garima Malik
Birla Institute of Management Technology, India

Rene Ymbong Paquibut
Modern College of Business and Science, Oman

Chapter 1
A Bibliometric Study on the Transformation of Climate Finance in Developing Countries

Poonam Singh
http://orcid.org/0000-0003-1113-6096
Manav Rachna International Institute of Research and Studies, India

Ishrat Rasool
http://orcid.org/0000-0002-0873-635X
Jamia Millia Islamia University, India

Kanhaiya Singh
G.L. Bajaj Institute of Technology and Management, India

Jitin Gambhir
K R. Mangalam University, India

Mohd Shamshad
http://orcid.org/0000-0001-9859-5337
Galgotias University, India

ABSTRACT

This chapter provides a bibliometric analysis of climate finance research from 2010 to 2024, emphasizing developing nations. A total of 246 studies from journals and edited volumes were analyzed using Three-Field Plots, TreeMap visualizations, and Co-word Network analysis to examine authorship, collaboration, thematic trends, and temporal shifts. Publications steadily increased, peaking in 2022, with

DOI: 10.4018/979-8-3373-5437-8.ch001

notable contributions from key scholars. Research evolved from foundational environmental and policy concerns to sustainability and carbon markets, and more recently to empirical analyses in developing nations. Persistent gaps in adaptation and climate justice highlight the need for broader participation, interdisciplinary collaboration, and a diversified research focus to advance equitable and effective climate finance globally.

INTRODUCTION:

Climate finance has grown significantly, particularly since adoption of the Paris Agreement in 2015, reflecting the increasing importance of financial mechanisms (green bonds, carbon markets, public-private partnerships, and international climate funds like the Green Climate Fund (GCF) in addressing climate change, especially in the context of developing countries for achieving climate goals linked to sustainable development goals (SDGs)(Incerti & Barnett, 2024; Michaelowa et al., 2020).

The OECD (2022)[1] reported that developed countries met and exceeded this target for the first time. They collectively provided and mobilized $115.9 billion in climate finance to help developing nations mitigate and adapt to climate change. In previous years, it was only $1000 billion. This goal is critical for supporting global efforts to combat climate change, particularly in more vulnerable regions with fewer resources(Bowen et al., 2017; Jin & Kim, 2017). This indicates that developed nations are taking steps ahead to help developing nations through substantial financial support to address climate finance hurdles in nations (Halimanjaya, 2015; Mumuni & Hamadjoda Lefe, 2023).

Research in the climate finance domain is robust and rapidly evolving, with a growing body of literature addressing various aspects of financing climate action (Jin & Kim, 2017; Li et al., 2022). This calls for an urge to find out the answer to research questions that this present study seeks, the following questions are raised:

1. How has the publication of climate finance research studies evolved, and what are the trends in their distribution across different countries and academic journals?
2. What are the key areas of focus within the field of climate finance, and who are the most prominent contributors driving research and innovation in these areas?
3. What past themes have been underexplored in climate finance research within developing nations, and what emerging themes should be prioritized in future studies to address the unique challenges and opportunities in these regions?

The above research questions will be answered with the help of the research objectives given below:

1. To analyze published climate finance research studies distributed over time, across different countries, and among various journals.
2. To identify specific key areas and prominent contributors within the research field of climate finance.
3. To explore the past and future themes unexplored or less explored in climate finance in developing nations.

To achieve these research objectives, a bibliometric analysis was conducted on a dataset of 246 research papers sourced from various journals within the Scopus database. This study design highlights the most cited research papers, journals, and authors within the field. Additionally, an in-depth analysis was performed to explore the co-occurrence of keywords, bibliometric coupling, and co-citation patterns, focusing on country, author, source, and publication year. This approach enables the identification of interconnections and relationships within the literature (Li et al., 2022; Lyeonov et al., 2023; Shah et al., 2023). Furthermore, conceptual analysis was employed to extract insights and address the research questions specifically related to climate finance in developing nations.

RESEARCH METHODOLOGY

The present study aimed to discuss various key areas of climate finance, the evolution of research over time, and the identification of underexplored themes, particularly in developing nations, by analyzing prominent contributors, publication trends, and interconnections within the literature.

The study adopts the most appropriate research process based on its requirements and nature. The research process is explained below:

Figure 1. Research Process of the Study

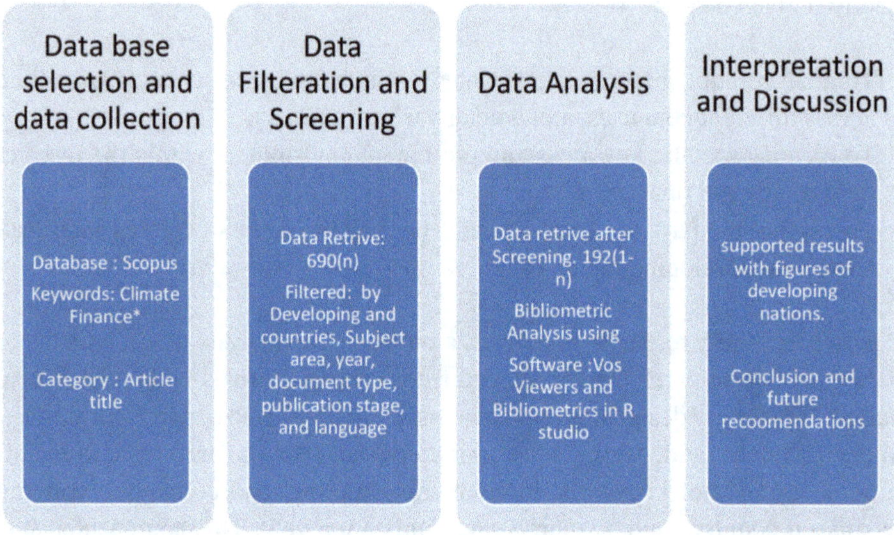

The research process illustrated in the above Figure 1 begins with selecting an appropriate database for collecting research papers. The initial step involves choosing the right data source for extracting relevant literature. The Scopus database, known for consistently providing quality journals, was selected for this purpose (Halsnæs et al., 2020; Muchiri et al., 2022). The chosen keyword for the research paper search was "Climate Finance," specifically targeting the Research Article category. This search yielded approximately 635 research papers. The next step involved filtering these retrieved papers to align with the specific requirements of the present study. Filters were applied based on criteria such as "developing countries," "subject area," "document type," "time span," "language," and "publication stage." Following this filtration process, 246 research papers relevant to the study were extracted.

Keywords used while searching:

```
(TITLE (climate AND finance)) AND (developing AND countries) AND (LIMIT-TO (SUBJAREA, "envi") OR LIMIT-TO (SUBJAREA, "soci") OR LIMIT-TO (SUBJAREA, "econ") OR LIMIT-TO (SUBJAREA, "busi")) AND (LIMIT-TO (DOCTYPE, "ar") OR LIMIT-TO (DOCTYPE, "ch")) AND (LIMIT-TO (PUBSTAGE, "final")) AND (LIMIT-TO (SRCTYPE, "j") OR LIMIT-TO (SRCTYPE, "b")) AND (LIMIT-TO (LANGUAGE, "english"))
```

The subsequent step in the research process involves selecting the appropriate tools for analysis, a critical phase in any study. For this research, we opted for Bibliometric Analysis, employing software such as VOSviewer and the Bibliometrics package in R Studio. The choice of these tools is aligned with the nature of the study, as it involves bibliometric analysis, necessitating the use of specialized bibliometric software. The Bibliometrics package in R Studio offers comprehensive insights into the research papers, enabling an extensive analysis. These tools have been utilized by various researchers to identify future research gaps(Muchiri et al., 2022; Shah et al., 2023) While both studies provide valuable precedents, the present chapter advances beyond them in three important respects: it focuses exclusively on developing countries as a geographical boundary condition; it draws from the Scopus database across a broader 2010–2024 timespan; and it deploys a richer suite of visualisation tools — Three-Field Plots, TreeMap analysis, and Co-word Network analysis — to map not only publication trends but also thematic gaps, including the underrepresentation of adaptation finance and climate justice in the scholarly literature. Following the analysis of the Scopus database in Bibliometrics, we have meticulously detailed the descriptive information summarized in the table 1 given below.

Table 1. Descriptive Information of Specific Results of the Search / Research Process

Description	Results
MAIN INFORMATION ABOUT DATA	
Timespan	2010:2024
Sources (Journals, Books, etc)	142
Documents	246
Annual Growth Rate %	22.93
Document Average Age	4.53
Average citations per doc	18.18
References	13137
DOCUMENT CONTENTS	
Keywords Plus (ID)	671
Author's Keywords (DE)	632
AUTHORS	
Authors	567
Authors of single-authored docs	57
AUTHORS COLLABORATION	
Single-authored docs	70
Co-Authors per Doc	2.8
International co-authorships %	32.11
DOCUMENT TYPES	

continued on following page

Table 1. Continued

Description	Results
article	202
book chapter	44

The table above presents the search results, focusing on documents within the selected time span of 2010-2024. Of the 246 documents identified, 142 sources were attributed to Journals (202) and Books (44). The content analysis of these research papers included both general and author-specific keywords, with a total of 632 keywords retrieved and analyzed using specialized software. The average number of co-authors per document was calculated at 2.8. Notably, the rate of international co-authorship stands at 32.11%, significantly surpassing the average co-authorship rate. Additionally, the average citation per document was found to be 18.18%.

NO OF DOCUMENT BY YEAR

In this section, the researcher inspects the number of documents published on climate finance.

Figure 2. Number of Documents

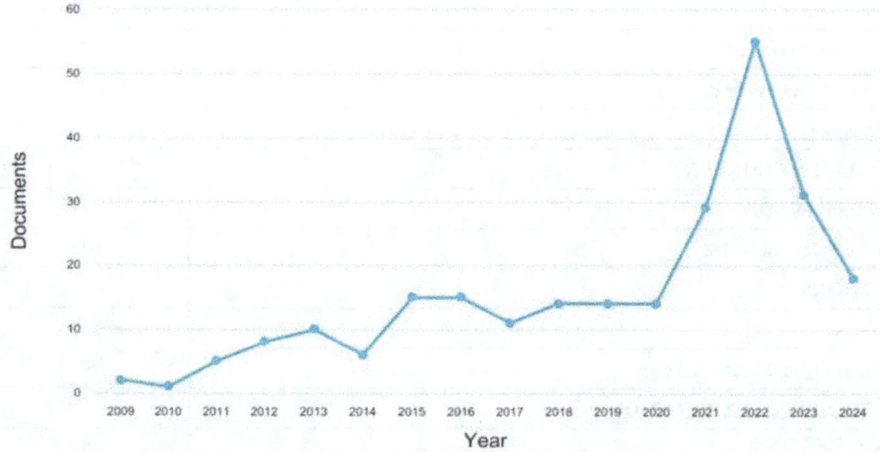

The figure 2 clearly illustrates a significant increase in the number of documents in this field, beginning in 2020 and reaching its peak in the year 2022. This suggests that the highest volume of publications on climate finance in developing countries occurred in 2022, indicating that it is an emerging area of interest for researchers. However, following 2022, there is a slight decline from 2023 to 2024, as depicted by the graph, suggesting that fewer articles were published in this area, or that researchers may have shifted their focus to other aspects of climate finance in developing nations. Additionally, it would be valuable to examine which prominent researchers contributed a substantial number of papers on climate finance in developing countries.

Figure 3. By Authors

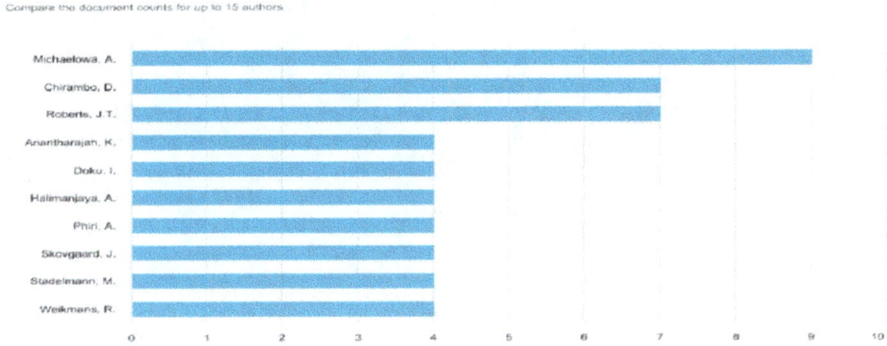

The Figure 3 indicates that Michaelowa, A. has authored the highest number of papers in this domain, with a total of 9 publications, followed by Chirambo, D., and Roberts, J.T., each contributing 7 papers. This suggests that these authors have extensively explored and addressed various aspects of climate finance in their research. Additionally, authors such as Anantharajah, K., Doku, Halimanjaya, A., Phiri, A., Shovgaard, J., Stadelemann, M., and Weikmans, R. have each contributed 4 papers on climate finance. Further analysis will be conducted to gain deeper insights into this body of work, utilizing tools such as VOSviewer and Bibliometrix from R Studio for more comprehensive analysis.

THEMATIC ANALYSIS

1. Three Field Plot Analysis (Keyword, Source, and Country) on Climate Finance

A three-field analysis can be conducted to synthesize the connections among three dimensions by selecting keywords, sources, and countries. By exploring the relationships between these dimensions, researchers can gain valuable insights into the structure and trends within the field of climate finance. The primary focus of this study is to examine the research conducted on climate finance in the context of developing countries, thereby providing a deeper understanding of the geographical focus, thematic emphasis, and publication sources that dominate this area of study.

Figure 4. 3-Plot Dimension analysis

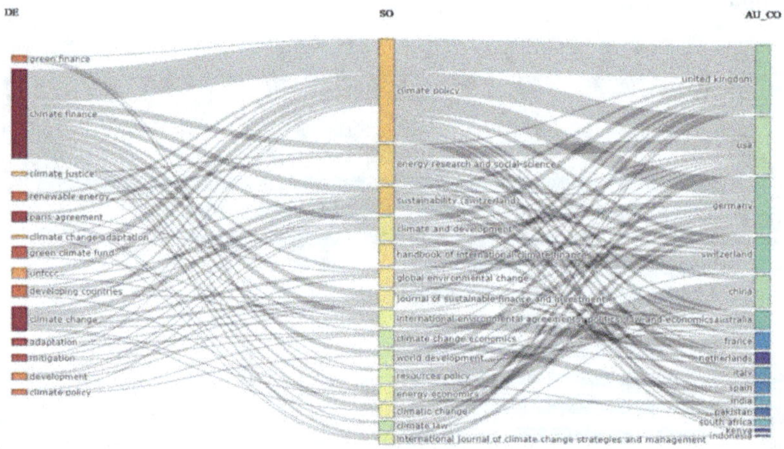

As illustrated in Figure 4, climate finance research is predominantly concentrated in countries such as the United Kingdom, the United States, Germany, and Switzerland. Notably, fewer studies have been conducted in China, and even fewer in Indonesia, Pakistan, Italy, South Africa, and Kenya, which are classified as developing nations. This disparity highlights an opportunity for researchers to focus more on climate finance studies in developing countries. The prevailing sources contributing most to climate finance research include Climate Policy, followed by Energy Research & Social Science, Sustainability, and Climate & Development. In contrast, sources such as Climate Law, Climate Change, Energy Economics, and Climate Change & Economies have made the least contributions. The majority of these sources have concentrated more on studies related to developed nations, with less attention given to developing countries. Additionally, an analysis of keywords revealed that terms such as "climate finance," "climate change," and "Paris Agreement" had the highest frequency, while terms like "climate change adaptation," "climate justice," "climate policy," and "development" appeared less frequently. This suggests a need for increased research attention on climate finance in the context of developing nations.

Citation analysis Country-wise

Citation analysis by country involves examining citations in academic literature based on their country of origin. This analysis helps to understand the impact and influence of research from different countries, identify leading nations in a specific field, and observe collaboration patterns between countries.

Figure 5. Citation Analysis as Per Country.

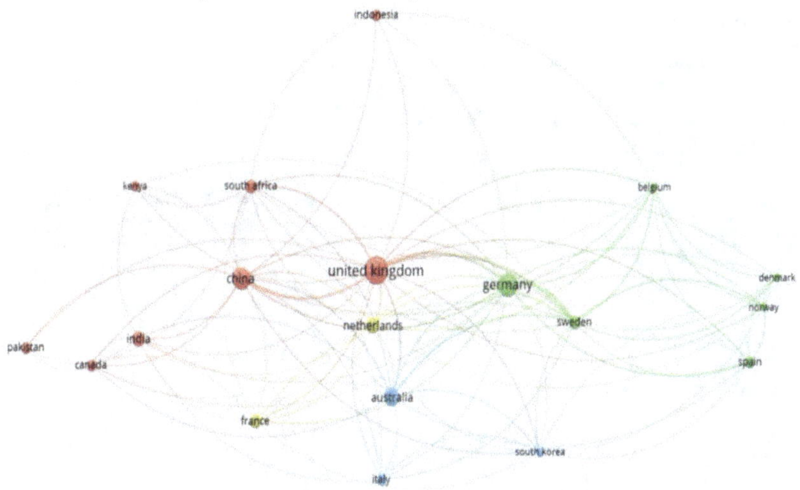

The selection of citations per country was aimed at identifying which nations are predominantly engaged in climate finance or green finance research. As illustrated in Figure 5, several clusters of countries are formed, distinguished by different colors. The prominent red cluster represents developing nations, while the green cluster corresponds to developed nations. The blue cluster includes Australia and Italy, and the yellow cluster consists of the Netherlands and France. These clusters reflect the citation patterns of climate finance or green finance research by other authors. While both developed and developing nations are similarly represented, the red cluster of developing nations is more prominent in terms of citations in climate finance research.

When relating Figure 5 to Figure 4, it is evident that in the recent past, research from developed nations was more frequently cited. However, more recently, research from developing nations has also gained recognition, though there is a need for further work in this area to be cited by other authors. This section of the study also assesses the core keywords that are more or less frequently used in the context of climate finance.

2. Tree map (frequency of keywords used)

This tree map analysis facilitates the rapid identification of prominent trends, key contributors, and the overall structure within a specific field of study. Each rectangle represents a distinct category, such as authors, institutions, or keywords, with the size and color reflecting metrics like publication volume, citation count, or other relevant data.

Figure 6. Tree map

Figure 6 presents a TreeMap visualization that captures the repetition and thematic grouping of keywords within the climate finance literature. The visualization operates on the principle that the size of each "leaf" represents the frequency of keyword occurrence: larger leaves correspond to terms that appear more frequently across the dataset, while smaller leaves indicate keywords of relatively lower frequency. Importantly, both large and small leaves retain analytical significance, as they collectively illustrate the interconnectedness of research themes and the relative balance between dominant and emerging topics in the field.

The color coding of the TreeMap groups keywords into thematic categories, demonstrating associations irrespective of their frequency. Thus, keywords belonging to the same cluster are represented with the same color, providing insight into their conceptual linkages. For instance, the repeated occurrence of larger leaves such as "climate change" and "financial provision"—both displayed in blue—reflects the centrality of financial mechanisms in addressing climate change and highlights their strong thematic association. This suggests that a substantial body of literature situates climate finance within the broader challenge of mobilizing financial resources to confront climate change.

Similarly, the red grouping associates "environmental policies" with "climate finance," revealing the degree to which policy-oriented discussions intersect with financial considerations in the scholarly discourse. The relative sizes of these leaves suggest that while "climate finance" dominates in terms of frequency, "environmental policies" continues to provide an important contextual framework for understanding financial flows. This association underscores the recognition that climate finance cannot be meaningfully separated from the policy environment in which it operates.

The TreeMap further displays an orange cluster that links "finance" with "greenhouse effect," indicating that a segment of research explicitly connects financial instruments to the mitigation of emissions. Meanwhile, a grey grouping encompasses keywords such as "mitigation," "vulnerability," "green economy," "climate," and "risk assessment." The clustering of these terms reflects an integrated thematic orientation that combines environmental risk, adaptive capacity, and the promotion of low-carbon economies with financial strategies. This grey cluster is particularly noteworthy as it bridges both environmental and economic domains, suggesting that research in this area emphasizes the dual role of climate finance in reducing vulnerability and supporting systemic transition toward greener economic models.

Smaller leaves within the TreeMap, such as "adaptation" and "panel data," though less frequently represented, carry interpretive significance. Their limited size implies that fewer studies directly engage with these themes, pointing toward underexplored areas within the climate finance literature. For example, the relatively modest representation of "adaptation" suggests that scholarly attention has been disproportionately concentrated on mitigation and financing mechanisms, leaving adaptation finance comparatively underexamined despite its critical importance for developing nations. Similarly, the appearance of "panel data" reflects a growing but still limited application of advanced econometric methods in empirical studies of climate finance, signaling potential for further methodological expansion in future research.

In summary, Figure 6 demonstrates not only the relative prominence of recurring keywords but also the structural associations between them. Larger leaves emphasize dominant areas of scholarly engagement—particularly climate change, finance, and policy linkages—while smaller leaves reveal gaps and emerging domains, such as adaptation finance and econometric analysis. The thematic color groupings highlight the multidimensional nature of the field, where environmental, economic, and policy concerns converge. Taken together, this visualization underscores both the concentration of research in certain domains and the opportunities for further scholarly exploration in underrepresented areas of climate finance.

3. Co-words and Co-occurrence network analysis

In this section, "co-words" refers to the process of identifying author-supplied keywords from a range of articles within a database to construct a graphical network depicting the topics and their interconnections within the literature. The fundamental principle of keyword co-occurrence is that the frequent appearance of two or more keywords within a document signifies contextual and conceptual similarity.

Figure 7. **Co-Occurrence Network Analysis**

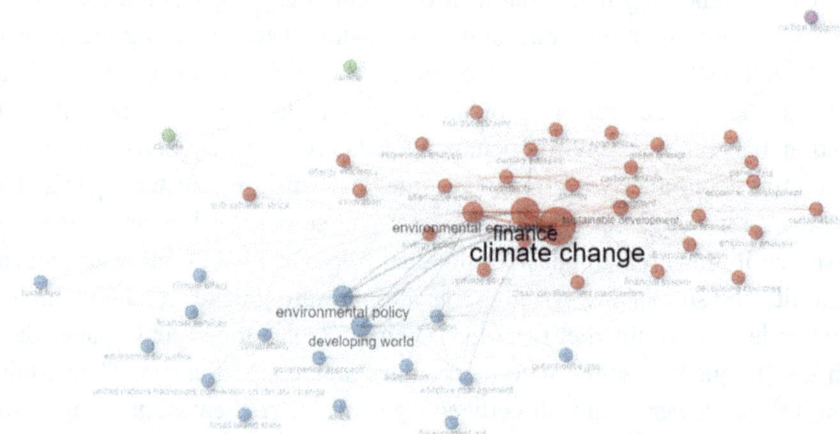

Figure 7 presents the keyword co-occurrence network, which illustrates the formation of distinct clusters within the body of climate finance literature. Each cluster reflects the thematic orientation of research over the study period and offers valuable insights into the intellectual structure of the field.

The largest and most prominent cluster, represented in blue, groups together keywords such as "Environmental Policies," "Developing World," "Greenhouse," "Fossil Fuel," "Africa," "Climate Effect," and "Adaptation Management." This cluster highlights a body of scholarship concentrated on the environmental and developmental dimensions of climate finance. The recurring emphasis on developing nations, particularly Africa, suggests a research trajectory that explores the consequences of fossil fuel dependency, greenhouse gas emissions, and the resultant climate effects on vulnerable regions. The inclusion of "adaptation management" further signals an applied orientation, wherein studies are increasingly concerned with designing and evaluating strategies to mitigate adverse climate impacts and strengthen resilience in the developing world.

The red cluster, which emerges as the second dominant grouping, includes keywords such as "Finance," "Climate Change," "Investment," "Sustainable Development," "Green Finance," "Panel Data," and "Regression." This cluster demonstrates the field's growing preoccupation with financial and economic mechanisms in addressing climate change. The prominence of terms like "investment" and "green finance" indicates a shift toward market-based instruments and capital mobilization strategies for advancing sustainability goals. Meanwhile, the methodological keywords "panel data" and "regression" reveal the increasing reliance on quantitative and econometric approaches, underscoring a trend toward empirically grounded research that evaluates the effectiveness of financing mechanisms and policy interventions.

In contrast, the green cluster contains only two keywords, "Climate" and "Article," while the purple cluster is represented by a single keyword, "Carbon Footprint." Although comparatively smaller in scale, these clusters are noteworthy as they reflect the presence of emerging or niche domains within the broader discourse. The isolated representation of "carbon footprint," for instance, suggests a specialized but growing concern with measuring and reducing emissions at the micro level—potentially linking climate finance to behavioral, corporate, and sector-specific studies. Similarly, the generic keywords within the green cluster may indicate preliminary or less developed streams of inquiry that have yet to coalesce into a fully defined thematic direction.

Taken together, the clusters depicted in Figure 7 reveal both the breadth and differentiation within climate finance research. While the blue cluster underscores the environmental and developmental challenges of fossil fuel dependency and adaptation in the developing world, the red cluster signifies the rise of financial, investment-oriented, and quantitatively driven analyses. The smaller green and purple clusters, though limited in size, point toward areas of emerging scholarly interest that may evolve into significant research themes in the future.

The co-occurrence network reveals a structurally divided field. The dominance of the red cluster — grouping finance, investment, sustainable development, and quantitative methods — indicates that mainstream climate finance scholarship has adopted the logic of capital markets and econometric evaluation. This is analytically coherent but carries a political implication: it tends to privilege interventions that are measurable and financeable, while rendering structurally difficult problems — such as adaptation for small island states or loss and damage compensation — comparatively invisible. The blue cluster's emphasis on developing nations and adaptation management, though substantial, remains secondary in terms of citation density. This asymmetry between the two clusters should prompt researchers to ask not simply what is studied, but whose problems are treated as tractable. The persistence of the

North–South knowledge imbalance evident in the country-level analysis (Figure 5) is reproduced here at the conceptual level: investment and finance dominate; justice and vulnerability remain peripheral. Broadening this conceptual map — by engaging with frameworks of climate justice, epistemic equity, and decolonial approaches to development finance (Islam, 2022; Falzon et al., 2023) — represents the most important scholarly frontier for this field.

4. Trend Topics

Figure 8. Trending Keywords

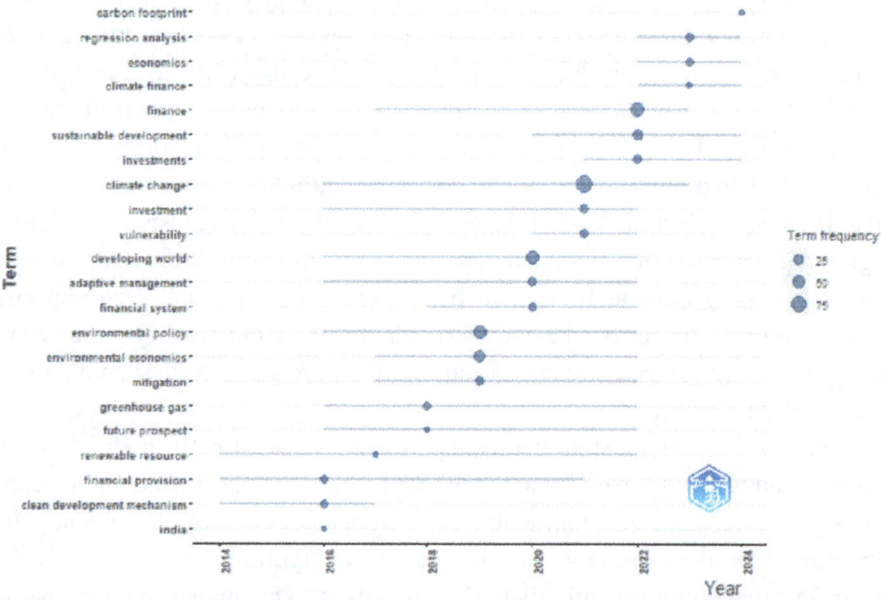

Figure 8 illustrates the temporal evolution of trending keywords in climate finance research pertaining to developing nations, categorized across three distinct periods. This chronological mapping provides important insights into how the scholarly discourse has expanded and shifted over time, reflecting broader global debates as well as methodological and thematic advancements in the field.

In the early phase (2014–2018), the dominant keywords included "Greenhouse Gas," "Prospects," "Environmental Economies," and "Environmental Policies." This cluster of terms indicates that research during this period was primarily rooted in environmental concerns, with scholars focusing on the implications of greenhouse gas emissions and the prospects for policy frameworks to address them. The prominence of "environmental economies" highlights an initial effort to integrate ecological perspectives with economic structures, laying the groundwork for understanding the role of financial mechanisms in climate governance. The repeated occurrence of "environmental policies" suggests that much of the scholarship was conceptual or policy-oriented, reflecting global momentum following the Kyoto Protocol and preceding the adoption of the Paris Agreement in 2015.

The mid-phase (2018–2020) marks a discernible shift toward a more finance-oriented and development-focused discourse. Trending keywords during this period included "Climate Finance," "Developing World," "Investment," and "Financial Systems." The emphasis on "climate finance" as a recurring keyword indicates that the concept had matured into a central research theme, coinciding with intensified debates around the operationalization of the Paris Agreement's financing commitments. The presence of "developing world" underscores the growing recognition of differentiated needs and challenges faced by emerging economies and vulnerable regions. Simultaneously, terms such as "investment" and "financial systems" point to a research focus on mobilizing capital, building institutional capacity, and exploring the role of financial architecture in supporting climate-related projects. This period represents a transitional phase where climate finance moved from being primarily a conceptual concern to becoming a practical and operational agenda.

In the most recent phase (2020–2024), the trending keywords shifted further toward empirical and measurement-oriented themes, with "Climate Finance," "Finance," "Carbon Footprint," "Regression," and "Sustainable Development" emerging as central. The recurrence of "climate finance" and "finance" signifies the consolidation of financial flows as the core axis of scholarship, with increasing attention to both international and domestic mechanisms for resource mobilization. The inclusion of "carbon footprint" highlights the growing importance of quantification and accountability in assessing the impact of financial interventions, particularly in terms of emissions reduction. The appearance of "regression" as a keyword reflects the methodological evolution of the field, with researchers employing econometric and statistical tools to generate evidence-based insights on the effectiveness of financial policies and investment strategies. Meanwhile, the persistent visibility of "sustainable development" demonstrates the continued alignment of climate finance research with the global development agenda, reinforcing its role as a key enabler of the Sustainable Development Goals (SDGs).

Taken together, the temporal progression delineated in Figure 8 illustrates a clear transformation in the orientation of climate finance research. What began as a predominantly environmental and policy-centered discourse (2014–2018) gradually evolved into an agenda emphasizing finance, institutional systems, and investment in developing nations (2018–2020), before finally consolidating into a mature phase characterized by empirical rigor, methodological sophistication, and strong linkages to sustainable development objectives (2020–2024). This trajectory not only demonstrates the dynamic and adaptive nature of the field but also reflects the increasing demand for actionable, evidence-driven knowledge to guide global and national responses to climate change..

DISCUSSION:

RO1. To analyse published climate finance research studies distributed over time, across different countries, and among various journals.

The objective of the bibliometric study on climate finance was to systematically identify and elucidate the various studies conducted across different nations and published in a range of journals. The research commenced with a comprehensive search in the Scopus database using the keyword "Climate Finance," specifically targeting the Research Article category. This initial search yielded approximately 635 research papers.

Subsequent filtration based on criteria such as "developing countries," "subject area," "document type," "time span," "language," and "publication stage" refined the dataset to a final selection of 246 relevant papers. The scope of the analysis spanned from 2010 to 2024. Among the 246 documents, 142 were sourced from journals, and 44 were from books. A total of 632 keywords were examined, with an average of 2.8 co-authors per document. The rate of international co-authorship was notably high at 32.11%, and the average citation count per document was 18.18.

The analysis revealed a significant increase in publications on climate finance in developing countries, beginning in 2020 and reaching its zenith in 2022(Ervine, 2014; Warren, 2020) . This trend indicates a burgeoning interest in the field. However, a slight decline in the number of publications from 2023 to 2024 suggests either a potential shift in research focus or a possible saturation of the topic.

Identifying key contributors to this body of work is essential. Prominent researchers who have significantly advanced the study of climate finance in developing countries were noted.

The bibliometric analysis has revealed several prominent contributors to the field of climate finance, reflecting the dynamic nature and growing interest in this area. Michaelowa, A. emerges as the most prolific author with a total of nine publications. This high volume of research underscores Michaelowa's significant and sustained engagement with various facets of climate finance. His extensive work likely covers a broad spectrum of topics and methodologies, contributing to a deeper understanding of the field's complexities(Michaelowa et al., 2020).

Following Michaelowa, Chirambo, D. and Roberts, J.T. have each authored seven papers on climate finance. Their considerable output indicates substantial contributions to advancing knowledge in the domain. The research produced by these authors is expected to offer valuable insights into different dimensions of climate finance, such as policy implications, financial mechanisms, and their effects on developing countries(Chaudhury, 2020; Hofisi et al., 2013; Leal et al., 2023; Li et al., 2022).

Additionally, authors including Anantharajah, K., Doku, Halimanjaya, A., Phiri, A., Shovgaard, J., Stadelemann, M., and Weikmans, R. have each published four papers. This level of contribution highlights their focused exploration of specific aspects within climate finance, enriching the literature and providing diverse perspectives on the subject.

The findings of this study highlight a marked surge in research on climate finance in developing countries, particularly evident in 2022. Despite the recent decrease in publication numbers, the field remains of considerable scholarly interest, characterized by high levels of international collaboration and citation impact(Hoffart et al., 2024).

RO2. To identify specific key areas and prominent contributors within the research field of climate finance.

This objective is examined using three distinct strategies under the thematic analysis approach, incorporating Three Field Plot Analysis, Tree Map visualization, and Co-word and Co-occurrence Network analysis for a comprehensive evaluation.

Three Field Plot Analysis:

The analysis presented through the three-field plot and citation analysis by country offers a detailed examination of the geographical and thematic trends within climate finance research, particularly focusing on the distinction between developed and developing nations.

In the three-field analysis, the synthesis of connections among keywords, sources, and countries reveals the dominance of research originating from developed countries such as the United Kingdom, the United States, Germany, and Switzerland. These countries not only lead in the volume of publications but also influence the thematic focus of climate finance research, as indicated by the frequent use of keywords like "climate finance," "climate change," and "Paris Agreement." In contrast, developing countries like China, Indonesia, Pakistan, South Africa, and Kenya are underrepresented, both in terms of research output and thematic emphasis. This disparity underscores a critical gap in the literature, suggesting that climate finance in the context of developing nations has not received adequate scholarly attention. The research sources contributing most to this field, including Climate Policy, Energy Research & Social Science, and Sustainability, predominantly focus on issues relevant to developed nations, leaving a void in the discourse surrounding the unique challenges faced by developing countries.

The citation analysis by country further complements these findings by highlighting the impact and influence of research from various nations. The clusters of countries, distinguished by colors in Figure 5, illustrate the citation patterns within climate finance research. The red cluster, representing developing nations, stands out in terms of citations, indicating a growing recognition of research from these regions. However, the prominence of developed nations in earlier citations, as reflected in the green and blue clusters, suggests that historically, research from developed countries has been more influential. The emergence of the red cluster indicates a positive trend towards increased citation and acknowledgment of research from developing countries, although it remains evident that further efforts are needed to enhance the visibility and impact of climate finance research in these regions.

When comparing Figure 4 and Figure 5, a clear pattern emerges: while developed nations have historically dominated the field of climate finance research, there is an encouraging shift towards greater inclusion and citation of studies from developing nations. This shift is crucial, as it reflects a growing recognition of the importance of addressing climate finance in contexts where it is most urgently needed. However, the relatively lower frequency of keywords related to "climate change adaptation," "climate justice," "climate policy," and "development" signals that the discourse is still skewed towards global frameworks like the Paris Agreement, with less focus on the specific needs and challenges faced by developing nations (Anantharajah & Setyowati, 2022; Islam, 2022; Leal et al., 2023) .

To conclude, the three-field plot and country-wise citation analysis together highlight both the progress and the gaps in climate finance research. While there has been an increase in the visibility of research from developing countries, the thematic and geographical imbalances in the literature suggest that more targeted efforts are required to ensure that climate finance research adequately addresses the needs of these regions. Enhancing the focus on underrepresented themes such as adaptation, justice, and policy in the context of developing nations could lead to a more equitable and comprehensive understanding of climate finance globally.

Tree Map:

The tree map analysis presented in Figure 6 provides a detailed visualization of the key trends, contributors, and structural elements within the field of climate finance research. This analysis offers a clear overview of how certain themes, authors, and institutions are interlinked and where the research focus has been most intense.

In this tree map, the size and color of each rectangle, or "leaf," serve as indicators of the frequency and thematic connections among the keywords. Larger leaves represent keywords that appear more frequently in the literature, highlighting the dominant themes in climate finance research. For instance, keywords like "climate change" and "financial provision" are prominently featured, indicating their central role in the discourse. The association between these keywords, as represented by their similar coloring, suggests a strong thematic link, underscoring the importance of financial strategies in addressing climate change.

On the other hand, smaller leaves in the tree map correspond to keywords that are less frequently used, such as "adaptation" and "panel data." The smaller size of these leaves' points to areas where fewer studies or publications are available, indicating potential gaps in the literature(Bhandary et al., 2021, 2022; Calliari et al., 2022). These less frequent keywords, although not as dominant, are still crucial as they represent emerging or underexplored areas within the field. The relative scarcity of research on these topics may suggest opportunities for future studies to delve deeper into these areas, contributing to a more comprehensive understanding of climate finance.

The grouping of keywords by color further enhances the analysis by indicating thematic connections across different research areas. For example, the blue group linking "climate change" and "financial provision" reflects the integration of financial mechanisms in climate change mitigation strategies. Meanwhile, the red group associating "environmental policies" with "climate finance" highlights the role of policy frameworks in shaping financial approaches to climate change(Hariharan et al., 2022; Lyeonov et al., 2023; Román et al., 2018). The orange and grey groups, representing associations between "finance" and "greenhouse effect" and between "mitigation," "vulnerability," "green economy," "climate," and "risk assessment," respectively, illustrate how different aspects of climate finance are interconnected.

These groupings not only show how various keywords are linked within the field but also reveal the diversity of research topics and the complexity of climate finance as a multidisciplinary field(Böhm & Sullivan, 2021; Economy, 2017; Michaelowa et al., 2020). The presence of multiple thematic clusters suggests that climate finance research spans a broad range of issues, from policy and economics to environmental science and risk management.

The TreeMap findings carry interpretive weight that extends beyond keyword enumeration. The dominance of "climate change," "financial provision," and "environmental policies" signals that the field has consolidated around the nexus of finance and macropolitical frameworks, while the marginal presence of "adaptation" points to a systematic underinvestment in research that addresses the lived realities of climate-vulnerable communities. This pattern is not incidental: it reflects broader structural asymmetries in who sets the climate finance research agenda. Institutions in developed countries — which dominate publication output — have historically prioritised mitigation and capital-market mechanisms over the adaptation needs of Global South communities most exposed to climate risk (Anantharajah & Setyowati, 2022). The relative absence of adaptation finance research is therefore not simply a gap in scholarly coverage; it mirrors the systematic underfunding of adaptation relative to mitigation in international climate finance flows themselves. Future research should address this imbalance by centring adaptation, community resilience, and equity outcomes alongside financial mechanism design.

Co-words and Co-occurrence Network Analysis:

The analysis of co-words in Figure 7 offers a valuable perspective on the thematic structure and interconnections within the climate finance literature. By examining the co-occurrence of keywords supplied by authors across a range of articles, the graphical network depicted in this figure reveals how different topics are conceptually related within the field. The principle underlying this analysis is that when two or more keywords frequently appear together in a document, they likely share contextual and conceptual similarities, indicating a close relationship between the topics they represent.

The network is divided into several clusters, each representing a group of related keywords that reflect distinct themes within climate finance research.

PROMINENT CLUSTERS AND THEIR IMPLICATIONS

Blue Cluster: *Environmental Policies and Developing World Focus*

Keywords: "Environmental Policies," "Developing World," "Greenhouse," "Fossil Fuel," "Africa," "Climate Effect," and "Adaptation Management."

Discussion: The blue cluster stands out as a significant thematic area within the literature, focusing on the intersection of environmental policies and the unique challenges faced by developing nations. The presence of keywords such as "Fossil Fuel" and "Climate Effect" highlights the concern with the environmental impact of fossil fuel emissions, particularly in the context of developing regions like Africa. This cluster also includes keywords related to adaptation strategies, indicating a research focus on how these nations are managing and adapting to the adverse effects of climate change. The prominence of this cluster suggests that there is substantial research interest in understanding the implications of climate policies and the need for tailored adaptation strategies in the developing world (Locatelli et al., 2016) .

Red Cluster: *Financial Aspects and Sustainable Development*

Keywords: "Finance," "Climate Change," "Investment," "Sustainable Development," "Green Finance," "Panel Data," and "Regression."

Discussion: The red cluster emphasizes the financial dimensions of climate change, including investment strategies and the pursuit of sustainable development. Keywords like "Green Finance" and "Sustainable Development" indicate a focus on the economic mechanisms that support environmentally friendly investments and practices. The inclusion of "Panel Data" and "Regression" points to the use of empirical methods in climate finance research, suggesting that quantitative analysis plays a significant role in understanding and modeling the financial aspects of climate change. This cluster reflects a broad interest in exploring how financial tools and investments can be leveraged to address climate change challenges (Kotchen & Costello, 2018; Phiri & Doku, 2024).

Green and Purple Clusters: *Emerging and Niche Interests*

Green Cluster Keywords: "Climate" and "Article."

Purple Cluster Keyword: "Carbon Footprint."

The green and purple clusters are notably smaller, with only a few keywords, indicating that these areas represent more specialized or emerging topics within the field. The green cluster's keywords, "Climate" and "Article," might suggest a focus on general climate-related publications, possibly reflecting broad thematic overviews or reviews. The purple cluster, with "Carbon Footprint" as its sole keyword, points to a niche interest in the environmental impact of human activities, particularly in relation to carbon emissions (Grieshop et al., 2017; Hourcade et al., 2021). While these clusters are less prominent, they nonetheless contribute to the diversity of topics being explored in climate finance research.

RO3. To explore the past and future themes unexplored or less explored in climate finance in developing nations.

The Figure 8 provides a valuable longitudinal perspective on the evolving trends in climate finance research within developing nations by categorizing trending keywords across distinct temporal periods. This analysis not only highlights the shifting focus of academic inquiry but also underscores the dynamic nature of the research field as it adapts to emerging challenges and priorities.

Past Period (2014-2018): Foundational Concerns:

In the earlier period of 2014-2018, the dominant keywords include "Greenhouse Gas," "Prospects," "Environmental Economies," and "Environmental Policies."

This phase reflects a foundational concern with understanding the environmental and economic implications of climate change. The emphasis on "Greenhouse Gas" suggests a focus on quantifying and managing emissions, a critical issue for both global climate strategies and national policy frameworks. Similarly, "Environmental Economies" and "Environmental Policies" indicate an interest in the intersection of environmental challenges and economic systems, exploring how economies can be structured or restructured to mitigate environmental impacts(Chelminski, 2022; Falzon et al., 2023; Halimanjaya, 2015).

The keyword "Prospects" may imply an exploration of future scenarios and possibilities within the context of climate change and finance, indicating a forward-looking approach in the early stages of research within this domain(Buchholz & Rübbelke, 2021). This period set the groundwork for subsequent inquiries by establishing a comprehensive understanding of the environmental and economic dimensions of climate change, particularly as they pertain to developing nations.

Mid-Period (2018-2020): Expanding Focus on Finance and Development:

The mid-period of 2018-2020 marks a significant shift in research focus, with keywords such as "Climate Finance," "Developing World," "Investment," and "Financial Systems" taking prominence (He et al., 2022; Hilbrandt & Grafe, 2022; Hourcade et al., 2012; Muchiri et al., 2022; Román et al., 2018). This shift indicates a growing recognition of the crucial role that finance plays in addressing climate change, particularly in the context of developing nations. The keyword "Climate Finance" itself suggests that research during this period began to more explicitly address the mechanisms and strategies for funding climate-related initiatives.

The inclusion of "Developing World" highlights a targeted focus on the specific challenges and opportunities faced by these nations, reflecting a nuanced understanding of how climate finance must be tailored to the unique contexts of developing countries(Clark et al., 2018; Gomez-Echeverri, 2013; Hofisi et al., 2013). Keywords like "Investment" and "Financial Systems" point to an exploration of the financial instruments, strategies, and institutional frameworks necessary to mobilize resources effectively for climate action (Calliari et al., 2022). This period represents a maturation of the field, where the theoretical foundations laid in the earlier period are increasingly applied to practical financial considerations.

Current Period (2020-2024): Emphasis on Sustainable Outcomes and Measurement:

In the most recent period of 2020-2024, the research focus has further evolved, with "Climate Finance," "Finance," "Carbon Footprint," "Regression," and "Sustainable Development" emerging as key keywords. This evolution signals a continued emphasis on the financial aspects of climate action but with a more refined focus on sustainability and empirical measurement.

The persistence of "Climate Finance" and "Finance" as dominant keywords underscores the ongoing centrality of financial considerations in the discourse. However, the appearance of "Carbon Footprint" suggests a growing interest in quantifying and managing the environmental impacts of various activities, reflecting a more granular approach to assessing climate-related outcomes(Ervine, 2014; Matsuo & Schmidt, 2017; Shawoo et al., 2022).

The inclusion of "Regression" indicates a methodological focus, likely pointing to the use of statistical and econometric techniques to analyze relationships between variables within climate finance(Doku et al., 2021; He et al., 2022; Phiri & Doku, 2024; Rashid et al., 2023). This methodological rigor is essential for producing robust and actionable insights that can inform policy and investment decisions.

Finally, "Sustainable Development" as a prominent keyword highlights the overarching goal of aligning financial practices with long-term sustainability objectives (Chaudhury, 2020; Grijalvo & García-Wang, 2023). This reflects a broader trend in the field towards integrating economic development with environmental stewardship, particularly in the context of developing nations where the balance between growth and sustainability is often most challenging.

CONCLUSION

The bibliometric study of climate finance research reveals a nuanced landscape characterized by significant growth in scholarly interest, particularly in developing countries. From 2010 to 2024, the number of publications increased substantially, peaking in 2022, reflecting the rising importance of climate finance as a response to global climate challenges(Calliari et al., 2022; Gomez-Echeverri, 2013; Islam, 2022; Li et al., 2022). The analysis underscores the importance of international collaboration, with a notable 32.11% rate of co-authorship across borders, highlighting the global nature of climate finance discussions(Baatz, 2018; Bhandary et al., 2021, 2022; Fang et al., 2021; Vanderklift et al., 2022). Despite the recent decline in publications, this area remains vibrant and influential, with high citation impact, suggesting a continued recognition of the importance of climate finance.

However, the study also identifies critical gaps and imbalances. Research output has been predominantly concentrated in developed countries, leaving developing nations underrepresented in both thematic focus and research volume. Key areas such as climate change adaptation, justice, and specific policy frameworks for developing nations need more exploration to create a comprehensive understanding of climate finance. The thematic clusters identified in the co-word and co-occurrence network analysis show an established focus on financial mechanisms and sustainable development, while areas like carbon footprint analysis and niche climate topics indicate emerging interest(Halsnæs et al., 2020; Hoffart et al., 2024; Hourcade et al., 2012; Kelp et al., 2018; Larralde, 2008; Ryan Hogarth, 2012). Addressing these gaps and diversifying research efforts will be essential for developing equitable and effective climate finance strategies that cater to the needs of both developed and developing nations (Grijalvo & García-Wang, 2023; Halsnæs et al., 2020; Hourcade et al., 2021; Leal et al., 2023; Mekonnen, 2014; Muchiri et al., 2022).

These gaps invite three deeper theoretical questions that this field must begin to engage. First, why does the North–South knowledge imbalance in climate finance research persist, and what structural conditions sustain it? Institutional concentration in European and North American universities, unequal access to research funding, language barriers in international publishing, and the dominance of Global North editorial frameworks collectively shape which voices define the field. Addressing this requires deliberate investment in Southern-led research capacity and journal representation, not merely calls for "more research from developing nations." Second, what do the identified thematic gaps — particularly in adaptation finance and climate justice — reveal about the politics of knowledge production in climate finance? The field's orientation toward measurable, market-compatible mechanisms reflects the priorities of dominant funders and institutions, not necessarily the needs of the most climate-vulnerable populations (Islam, 2022). The relative invisibility of adaptation and justice in the bibliometric landscape is not a scholarly oversight; it mirrors the systematic under-allocation of adaptation finance relative to mitigation in international climate flows, and the continuing marginalisation of loss and damage in multilateral negotiations (Falzon et al., 2023). Third, how do these findings relate to emerging debates about epistemic justice and the decolonisation of climate research? A growing body of scholarship argues that climate finance governance — and the research ecosystem that legitimises it — tends to reproduce colonial asymmetries by privileging technocratic, financialised solutions designed and evaluated in the Global North (Anantharajah & Setyowati, 2022). A genuinely equitable climate finance scholarship would centre the knowledge, priorities, and governance frameworks of communities most exposed to climate risk, treating them as co-producers of research rather than objects of study. Engaging these questions will not only enrich the field intellectually; it is essential to ensuring that climate finance research contributes to outcomes that are just, inclusive, and adequate to the scale of the crisis.

Across the three temporal periods (2014–2018, 2018–2020, 2020–2024), the analysis confirms a progressive shift from foundational environmental concerns toward empirically sophisticated, finance-centred inquiry (Muchiri et al., 2022).

The longitudinal analysis of climate finance research trends in developing nations reveals an evolving focus from foundational environmental concerns to more complex financial mechanisms and sustainable development (Bhandary et al., 2021; Ryan Hogarth, 2012). Initially, research centred on understanding the environmental impacts of climate change and the economic policies needed to address them. Over time, the emphasis shifted towards the role of finance in climate action, exploring specific strategies and instruments to support climate-related initiatives in developing countries. More recently, the research has focused on empirical measurement, sustainability, and the integration of financial practices with long-term environmental goals(Anantharajah, 2019; Anantharajah & Setyowati, 2022; Brunner & Enting, 2014; Ervine, 2014; Grijalvo & García-Wang, 2023; Incerti & Barnett, 2024; Skovgaard et al., 2023; Suroso et al., 2022). These evolving trends highlight a growing sophistication in climate finance research, demonstrating a progression from broad foundational inquiries to more targeted, actionable insights that address the unique challenges of developing nations.

Overall, this analysis reveals that while climate finance research in developing nations has expanded significantly, it continues to evolve in response to emerging challenges and priorities. The increasing sophistication and methodological focus in recent years suggest a field that is not only growing in importance but also in its capacity to contribute to meaningful climate action(Chaudhury, 2020; Gomez-Echeverri, 2013; Ryan Hogarth, 2012; Skovgaard et al., 2023). However, the identified gaps in thematic and geographical representation highlight the need for continued efforts to ensure that research adequately addresses the diverse and complex realities of developing nations(Anantharajah, 2019; Anantharajah & Setyowati, 2022; Gomez-Echeverri, 2013; Halsnæs et al., 2020; Locatelli et al., 2016). This will be crucial for advancing a more equitable and effective global response to climate change.

IMPLICATIONS AND FUTURE DIRECTIONS

The co-occurrence network confirms that climate finance research is structured around two poles: environmental and developmental concerns (blue cluster) on one side, and financial mechanisms and quantitative analysis (red cluster) on the other. The blue and red clusters together capture the dominant research interest in environmental aspects and sustainable development, particularly in relation to developing nations.

However, the presence of smaller clusters like the green and purple ones also highlights areas that may be underexplored, suggesting opportunities for future research. Scholars might consider investigating why certain topics, such as carbon footprint analysis or general climate-related publications, have not yet gained as much traction as others. These areas could represent emerging fields that may grow in importance as the global response to climate change continues to evolve.

The progression of keywords illustrates a clear trajectory: from environmental and economic theory toward applied finance, investment, and sustainable outcomes, supported by increasingly sophisticated methodologies.

This evolution points to two priorities for future research. First, continued refinement of financial mechanisms for climate action in developing nations, with attention to how instruments can simultaneously achieve environmental and economic goals. Second, development of metrics and models that can accurately assess the distributional and equity impacts — not only the aggregate financial flows — of climate finance initiatives.

The persistence of "climate finance" as a dominant keyword across all three periods signals that while methodological sophistication has grown, the core challenge — mobilising finance equitably and effectively in developing nations — remains unresolved and central.

Understanding these thematic clusters and their interconnections allows researchers to contribute to both well-established and underexplored areas of climate finance.

REFERENCES

Anantharajah, K. (2019). Governing climate finance in Fiji: Barriers, complexity and interconnectedness. *Sustainability (Basel), 11*(12), 3414. Advance online publication. DOI: 10.3390/su11123414

Anantharajah, K., & Setyowati, A. B. (2022). Beyond promises: Realities of climate finance justice and energy transitions in Asia and the Pacific. *Energy Research & Social Science, 89*, 102550. DOI: 10.1016/j.erss.2022.102550

Baatz, C. (2018). Climate adaptation finance and justice. A criteria-based assessment of policy instruments. *Analyse & Kritik, 40*(1), 73–105. DOI: 10.1515/auk-2018-0004

Bhandary, R. R., Gallagher, K. S., Jaffe, A. M., Myslikova, Z., Zhang, F., Petrova, M., Barrionuevo, A., Fontaine, G., Fuentes, J. L., Karani, P., Martinez, D., Seitlheko, L., Staicu, D., Ullah, N., & Yimere, A. (2022). Demanding development: The political economy of climate finance and overseas investments from China. *Energy Research & Social Science, 93*(September), 102816. DOI: 10.1016/j.erss.2022.102816

Bhandary, R. R., Gallagher, K. S., & Zhang, F. (2021). Climate finance policy in practice: A review of the evidence. *Climate Policy, 21*(4), 529–545. DOI: 10.1080/14693062.2020.1871313

. Böhm, S., & Sullivan, S. (2021). Negotiating climate change in crisis. *Negotiating Climate Change in Crisis*, 1–402. DOI: 10.11647/OBP.0265

Bowen, A., Campiglio, E., & Herreras Martinez, S. (2017). An 'equal effort' approach to assessing the North–South climate finance gap. *Climate Policy, 17*(2), 231–245. DOI: 10.1080/14693062.2015.1094728

Brunner, S., & Enting, K. (2014). Climate finance: A transaction cost perspective on the structure of state-to-state transfers. *Global Environmental Change, 27*(1), 138–143. DOI: 10.1016/j.gloenvcha.2014.05.005

Buchholz, W., & Rübbelke, D. (2021). Overstraining international climate finance: When conflicts of objectives threaten its success. *International Journal of Climate Change Strategies and Management, 13*(4–5), 547–563. DOI: 10.1108/IJCCSM-06-2021-0071

Calliari, E., Castellari, S., Davis, M., Linnerooth-Bayer, J., Martin, J., Mysiak, J., Pastor, T., Ramieri, E., Scolobig, A., Sterk, M., Veerkamp, C., Wendling, L., & Zandersen, M. (2022). Building climate resilience through nature-based solutions in Europe: A review of enabling knowledge, finance and governance frameworks. *Climate Risk Management, 37*(July), 100450. DOI: 10.1016/j.crm.2022.100450

Chaudhury, A. (2020). Role of intermediaries in shaping climate finance in developing countries-lessons from the green climate fund. *Sustainability (Basel), 12*(12), 5507. Advance online publication. DOI: 10.3390/su12145507

Chelminski, K. (2022). Climate Finance Effectiveness: A Comparative Analysis of Geothermal Development in Indonesia and the Philippines. *Journal of Environment & Development, 31*(2), 139–167. DOI: 10.1177/10704965211070034 PMID: 35557746

Clark, R., Reed, J., & Sunderland, T. (2018). Bridging funding gaps for climate and sustainable development: Pitfalls, progress and potential of private finance. *Land Use Policy, 71*(February), 335–346. DOI: 10.1016/j.landusepol.2017.12.013

Doku, I., Ncwadi, R., & Phiri, A. (2021). Determinants of climate finance: Analysis of recipient characteristics in Sub-Sahara Africa. *Cogent Economics & Finance, 9*(1), 1–17. DOI: 10.1080/23322039.2021.1964212

. Economy, T. H. E. D. (2017). *World Investment Report 2017 - INVESTMENT AND DIGITAL ECONOMY.*

Ervine, K. (2014). Diminishing Returns: Carbon Market Crisis and the Future of Market-Dependent Climate Change Finance. *New Political Economy, 19*(5), 723–747. DOI: 10.1080/13563467.2013.849672

Falzon, D., Shaia, F., Roberts, J. T., Hossain, M. F., Robinson, S. A., Khan, M. R., & Ciplet, D. (2023). Tactical Opposition: Obstructing Loss and Damage Finance in the United Nations Climate Negotiations. *Global Environmental Politics, 23*(3), 95–119. DOI: 10.1162/glep_a_00722

Fang, Z., Xie, J., Peng, R., & Wang, S. (2021). Climate finance: Mapping air pollution and finance market in time series. *Ekonometria, 9*(4), 43. Advance online publication. DOI: 10.3390/econometrics9040043

Gomez-Echeverri, L. (2013). The changing geopolitics of climate change finance. *Climate Policy, 13*(5), 632–648. DOI: 10.1080/14693062.2013.822690

Grieshop, A. P., Jain, G., Sethuraman, K., & Marshall, J. D. (2017). Emission factors of health- and climate-relevant pollutants measured in home during a carbon-finance-approved cookstove intervention in rural India. *GeoHealth, 1*(5), 222–236. DOI: 10.1002/2017GH000066 PMID: 32158989

. Grijalvo, M., & García-Wang, C. (2023). Sustainable business model for climate finance. Key drivers for the commercial banking sector. *Journal of Business Research, 155*(PB), 113446. DOI: 10.1016/j.jbusres.2022.113446

Halimanjaya, A. (2015). Climate mitigation finance across developing countries: What are the major determinants? *Climate Policy, 15*(2), 223–252. DOI: 10.1080/14693062.2014.912978

Halsnæs, K., Bay, L., Dømgaard, M. L., Kaspersen, P. S., & Larsen, M. A. D. (2020). Accelerating climate service development for renewable energy, finance and cities. *Sustainability (Basel), 12*(18), 7540. Advance online publication. DOI: 10.3390/su12187540

Hariharan, R., Arumugam, S. K., & Seranmadevi, R. (2022). Perception of Climate Finance: An Empirical Approach. *Environment and Ecology Research, 10*(2), 284–293. DOI: 10.13189/eer.2022.100218

He, C., Li, A., Li, D., & Yu, J. (2022). Does Digital Inclusive Finance Mitigate the Negative Effect of Climate Variation on Rural Residents' Income Growth in China? *International Journal of Environmental Research and Public Health, 19*(14), 8280. Advance online publication. DOI: 10.3390/ijerph19148280 PMID: 35886132

Hilbrandt, H., & Grafe, F. J. (2022). URBAN VISIONS OF GLOBAL CLIMATE FINANCE: Dispossessive Mechanisms of Futuring in the Making of Groy. *International Journal of Urban and Regional Research, 46*(5), 896–905. DOI: 10.1111/1468-2427.13106

Hoffart, F. M., D'Orazio, P., Holz, F., & Kemfert, C. (2024). Exploring the interdependence of climate, finance, energy, and geopolitics: A conceptual framework for systemic risks amidst multiple crises. *Applied Energy, 361*(February), 122885. DOI: 10.1016/j.apenergy.2024.122885

Hofisi, C., Chigavazira, B., Mago, S., & Hofisi, M. (2013). "Climate finance issues": Implications for climate change adaptation for food security in Southern Africa. *Mediterranean Journal of Social Sciences, 4*(6), 47–53. DOI: 10.5901/mjss.2013.v4n6p47

Hourcade, J. C., Dasgupta, D., & Ghersi, F. (2021). Accelerating the speed and scale of climate finance in the post-pandemic context. *Climate Policy, 21*(10), 1383–1397. DOI: 10.1080/14693062.2021.1977599

Hourcade, J. C., Perrissin Fabert, B., & Rozenberg, J. (2012). Venturing into uncharted financial waters: An essay on climate-friendly finance. *International Environmental Agreement: Politics, Law and Economics, 12*(2), 165–186. DOI: 10.1007/s10784-012-9169-y

Incerti, N., & Barnett, J. (2024). Following the money: Climate adaptation finance in the Marshall Islands. *Environmental Research Letters*, *19*(5), 054010. Advance online publication. DOI: 10.1088/1748-9326/ad383e

Islam, M. M. (2022). Distributive justice in global climate finance – Recipients' climate vulnerability and the allocation of climate funds. *Global Environmental Change*, *73*(March), 102475. DOI: 10.1016/j.gloenvcha.2022.102475

Jin, I., & Kim, Y. (2017). Analysis of the impact of achieving NDC on public climate finance. *Journal of Sustainable Finance & Investment*, *7*(4), 309–334. DOI: 10.1080/20430795.2016.1275934

Kelp, M. M., Grieshop, A. P., Reynolds, C. C. O., Baumgartner, J., Jain, G., Sethuraman, K., & Marshall, J. D. (2018). Real-time indoor measurement of health and climate-relevant air pollution concentrations during a carbon-finance-approved cookstove intervention in rural India. *Development Engineering*, *3*(May), 125–132. DOI: 10.1016/j.deveng.2018.05.001

Kotchen, M. J., & Costello, C. (2018). Maximizing the impact of climate finance: Funding projects or pilot projects? *Journal of Environmental Economics and Management*, *92*, 270–281. DOI: 10.1016/j.jeem.2018.08.009

Larralde, A. S. & B. (2008). Electronic copy available at : Electronic copy available at. *Grou*, *23529*(2), 1–45.

Leal, P. H., Marques, A. C., & Shahbaz, M. (2023). Does climate finance and foreign capital inflows drive de-carbonisation in developing economies? *Journal of Environmental Management*, *347*(May), 119100. Advance online publication. DOI: 10.1016/j.jenvman.2023.119100 PMID: 37776791

Li, N., Shi, B., Wu, L., Kang, R., & Gao, Q. (2022). Climate-Related Development Finance, Energy Structure Transformation and Carbon Emissions Reduction: An Analysis From the Perspective of Developing Countries. *Frontiers in Environmental Science*, *9*(January), 1–19. DOI: 10.3389/fenvs.2021.778254

Locatelli, B., Fedele, G., Fayolle, V., & Baglee, A. (2016). Synergies between adaptation and mitigation in climate change finance. *International Journal of Climate Change Strategies and Management*, *8*(1), 112–128. DOI: 10.1108/IJCCSM-07-2014-0088

Lyeonov, S., Toušek, Z., Bozhenko, V., & Kérmárki-Gally, S. E. (2023). The impact of corruption in climate finance on achieving net zero emissions. *Journal of International Students*, *16*(1), 142–159. DOI: 10.14254/2071-8330.2023/16-1/10

Matsuo, T., & Schmidt, T. S. (2017). Hybridizing low-carbon technology deployment policy and fossil fuel subsidy reform: A climate finance perspective. *Environmental Research Letters, 12*(1), 1–9. DOI: 10.1088/1748-9326/aa5384

Mekonnen, A. (2014). Economic costs of climate change and climate finance with a focus on Africa. *Journal of African Economies, 23*(SUPPL.2), 50–82. DOI: 10.1093/jae/eju012

Michaelowa, K., Michaelowa, A., Reinsberg, B., & Shishlov, I. (2020). Do multilateral development bank trust funds allocate climate finance efficiently? *Sustainability (Basel), 12*(14), 5529. Advance online publication. DOI: 10.3390/su12145529

Muchiri, M. K., Erdei-Gally, S., Fekete-Farkas, M., & Lakner, Z. (2022). Bibliometric Analysis of Green Finance and Climate Change in Post-Paris Agreement Era. *Journal of Risk and Financial Management, 15*(12), 561. Advance online publication. DOI: 10.3390/jrfm15120561

Mumuni, S., & Hamadjoda Lefe, Y. D. (2023). Greening the environment: Do climate-related development finances and renewable energy consumption matter? An African tale. *Carbon Management, 14*(1), 2251934. Advance online publication. DOI: 10.1080/17583004.2023.2251934

Phiri, A., & Doku, I. (2024). Is climate finance aiding food security in developing countries? A focus on Sub-Sahara Africa. *Cogent Economics & Finance, 12*(1), 2312777. Advance online publication. DOI: 10.1080/23322039.2024.2312777

. Rashid, S., Khan, M. R., & Haque, N. (2023). Does climate finance enhance mitigation ambitions of recipient countries? *Earth System Governance, 17*(December 2022), 100188. DOI: 10.1016/j.esg.2023.100188

Román, M. V., Arto, I., & Ansuategi, A. (2018). Why do some economies benefit more from climate finance than others? A case study on North-to-South financial flows. *Economic Systems Research, 30*(1), 37–60. DOI: 10.1080/09535314.2017.1334629

Ryan Hogarth, J. (2012). The role of climate finance in innovation systems. *Journal of Sustainable Finance & Investment, 2*(3–4), 257–274. DOI: 10.1080/20430795.2012.742637

Shah, S. B., Sopin, J., Techato, K. A., & Mudbhari, B. K. (2023). A Systematic Review on Nexus Between Green Finance and Climate Change: Evidence from China and India. *International Journal of Energy Economics and Policy, 13*(4), 599–613. DOI: 10.32479/ijeep.14331

Shawoo, Z., Dzebo, A., Funder, M., & Dupuy, K. (2022). Country ownership in climate finance coordination: A comparative assessment of Kenya and Zambia. *Climate Policy*, *22*(9–10), 1266–1280. DOI: 10.1080/14693062.2022.2098227

Skovgaard, J., Adams, K. M., Dupuy, K., Dzebo, A., Funder, M., Fejerskov, A. M., & Shawoo, Z. (2023). Multilateral Climate Finance Coordination: Politics and Depoliticization in Practice. *Global Environmental Politics*, *23*(2), 125–147. DOI: 10.1162/glep_a_00703

Suroso, D. S. A., Setiawan, B., Pradono, P., Iskandar, Z. S., & Hastari, M. A. (2022). Revisiting the role of international climate finance (ICF) towards achieving the nationally determined contribution (NDC) target: A case study of the Indonesian energy sector. *Environmental Science & Policy*, *131*, 188–195. DOI: 10.1016/j.envsci.2022.01.022

Vanderklift, M. A., Herr, D., Lovelock, C. E., Murdiyarso, D., Raw, J. L., & Steven, A. D. L. (2022). A Guide to International Climate Mitigation Policy and Finance Frameworks Relevant to the Protection and Restoration of Blue Carbon Ecosystems. *Frontiers in Marine Science*, *9*(July), 1–14. DOI: 10.3389/fmars.2022.872064

Warren, P. (2020). Blind spots in climate finance for innovation. *Advances in Climate Change Research*, *11*(1), 60–64. DOI: 10.1016/j.accre.2020.05.001

ENDNOTES

1 https://www.oecd.org/en/topics/sub-issues/climate-finance-and-the-usd-100-billion-goal.html#:~:text=Released%20on%2029%20May%202024,goal%20for%20the%20first%20time.

Chapter 2
Literature Review on ESG Integration, FinTech Innovations, and Sustainable Finance in Developing Economies

Siriyama Kanthi Herath
http://orcid.org/0000-0002-6443-9739
Clark Atlanta University, USA

ABSTRACT

In this chapter, recent developments of ESG integration, FinTech adoption, and sustainable finance in developing economies are discussed. A paradigm shift in the world scenario focuses on sustainable generation of values rather than the blind maximization of profits and is of the utmost importance related to financially weak countries that are fragile, socially divided, and struggling to maintain themselves. The findings suggest that ESG frameworks are gaining traction as instruments of transparency and risk allocation crucial for attracting valuable foreign investments. Fintech has become a powerful driver, promoting financial inclusion, clarity of data, and the regulation of capital to green and socially responsible projects. These convergences present unheralded possibilities of sustainable growth, but the challenges ahead still seem to be numerous such as the quality of data, inconsistencies in regulations, greenwashing and effective cybersecurity. Filling these gaps has been important to developing interdisciplinary research and strategic interventions.

DOI: 10.4018/979-8-3373-5437-8.ch002

1. INTRODUCTION

The world is experiencing a radical paradigm transformation where the relationship between the performance of economies, the management of the environment and social equity is gaining increased attention. The culture of the traditional paradigm (which focused on profit maximization) is giving way to models that emphasize the creation of sustainable value (Porter & Kramer, 2011). During economic development, especially in developing economies, which are described as being fragile environment-wise, strapped financially, and have a high social and economic divide, such change is critical. To attain sustainable development, new strategies that combine economic growth with social fairness and environment security are required. The objectives of such measures are to enhance the positive social and environmental impacts in addition to ensuring the sustainability of organizations in terms of benefits and competitive edge. Climate change takes a toll on these developing countries more than other states in the world. Thus, investing finances taking environmental implications into consideration is not only cost-effective but is an ethical way of doing it, particularly in helping the developing countries to act on climate. The relatively low level of adaptation finance received by such countries in question highlights the necessity to make the international funds flow stronger (UNEP, 2023). Such a changing environment has resulted in the creation of new forms of corporate performance measurement, like sustainability reports and Environmental, Social, and Governance (ESG) performance systems. Such systems enable firms to monitor developments towards the sustainability objectives and evince responsibility to stakeholders.

Environmental, Social and Governance (ESG) have evolved to form significant corporate responsibilities and sustainability. Compared to traditional financial indicators, ESG provides a multi-dimensional lens that examines long-term sustainability sustainability and ethical outcomes (Gillan et al., 2021). The increasing interest can be explained by the fact that more investors, regulators, and consumers are coming to know that non-financial qualities can have a significant impact on the long-term value of a firm and its risk exposure (Amel-Zadeh & Serafeim, 2018). The penetration of ESG is increasingly becoming popular in developing economies as a means of attracting foreign investment, improving corporate governance and averting the risks of operations related with such risks as socially and environmentally embedded risks (Broadstock et al., 2021). This tendency is also boosted by the demand of international investors on the transparent and responsible investment opportunities (Goel & Sahay, 2024). Besides these predetermined structures, technology has now been providing new tools to catalyze this transition.

At the same time, there is also an advent of Financial Technology (FinTech) which involves financial systems that offer new alternatives to engage with financial inclusion, enhanced transparency, and access to green finance (Arner et al., 2021; (Fan et al., 2025). Recent FinTech discoveries like mobile banking, peer-to-peer lending platforms, and blockchain technologies are leveling the accessibility to financial services, in previously underserved communities, which is a vital element of the ESG S (Lule Yawe et al., 2022). What is more is that FinTech may strengthen the process of collecting and evaluating ESG data and thus enhancing the quality and transparency of sustainability reporting, which is one of the major issues in most developing economies (Gao et al., 2024). Sustainable finance and FinTech are leading to the formation of new channels through which capital can be redirected to climate friendly projects and socially responsible enterprises, through digitalizing the matching of investors to impactful investments. The key objective of the chapter is to discuss the interconnections of these concepts.

The chapter provides a systematic literature review of the research topic in the connections of ESG integration, FinTech innovation, and sustainable finance in developing economies. Its structure is based on observing tendencies, challenges, and gaps through the synthesis of recent empirical studies and industry reports to provide a guide as to future research and practice. The chapter will endeavor to give an increasingly broad view of how the three interrelated domains are leading to the transformation of a more sustainable and inclusive financial environment in the Global South.

2. METHODOLOGY OF THE LITERATURE REVIEW

This systematic literature review was based on the rigorous approach that enabled depth, transparency, and replicability. The search strategy consisted in locating the appropriate academic databases (Scopus, Web of Science, Google Scholar, and particular industry report databases, such as reports of the IFC, UNEP, World Bank, and other large financial institutions with sustainable finance departments). The search terms that were used in combinations were ESG integration, FinTech innovation, sustainable finance, developing economies, emerging markets, financial inclusion, green bonds, sustainable sukuk, blended finance, regulatory sandbox, green taxonomy, and data quality.

The inclusion criteria centered around peer-reviewed articles, chapters of books, and well-known industry reports released mostly in 2015 and mid-2025 with a slight emphasis on research related to developing countries. The exclusion criteria were the studies that failed to explain the convergence between the three key themes and the studies that concentrate only on the experience of developed economies that cannot be generalized. The first search resulted in a wide literature, which was carefully filtered using titles, abstracts and a full-text assessment, to determine the most relevant literature. The data were extracted through identifying key findings, methodologies, challenges, opportunities and the policy implications of selected studies. The synthesis procedure included thematic analysis, the detection of recurrent patterns, contradictions, and gaps in the literature to create a logical sequence of events and theoretical models. Such methodical approach puts the validity of the identified trends, challenges, and future research directions on basis in this chapter.

2.1 Objectives of the Literature Review

The key objectives of this chapter are:

1. To systematically review literature on the adoption and integration of the ESG in developing economies with a view toward identifying the motivators and challenges and the observed outcomes. This goal will explore the exact factors encouraging the adoption of ESG, including regulatory forces, investor interest as well as improved brand fame and at the same time analyzing the peculiarities of the issue profile of firms within these regions. Such obstacles sometimes involve the unavailability of standardized ESG data, poor governance, and excessive implementation cost (Glova & Panko, 2025; Amel-Zadeh & Serafeim, 2018). The analysis will pertain to the way in which companies are adapting to these challenges and how increased incorporation of ESG is affecting financial performance, volatility reduction, and stakeholder outreach.
2. To determine the capacity of FinTech to realize the ESG objectives and to empower sustainable finance with the help of financial inclusion, data transparency and democratization of investors. In this section, how various FinTech applications, such as mobile payment, artificial intelligence and blockchain are simplifying the process of achieving the ESG objectives are discussed. As an illustration, blockchain application can be used to improve traceability and transparency of supply chains thereby creating certainty on social and environmental standards compliance (Kouhizadeh et al., 2021; Tyron, 2024). The review will also evaluate the democratization of investment available through FinTech platforms allowing retail investors to engage with sustainable finance activities and on how it is creating a more open investment landscape (Gao et al., 2024).
3. To evaluate the design and effectiveness of green bonds sustainable sukuk and blended finance models. This is on the practical aspect of sustainable finance within the context of developing economies. The review will examine the development pattern of green bonds and other emerging products such as sustainable sukuk, which are especially applicable in areas with a huge number of Muslims (Lule Yawe et al., 2022). It will also discuss how blended finance the tactical

application of public or charitable funds to appreciate private capital benefits large-scale sustainable development initiatives, specifically in such activity areas as renewable energy or sustainable farming (UNEP, 2023). The success of these instruments in meeting their announced targets with respect to environment and social preservation will be measured in the chapter.

4. To analyze policy, regulatory frameworks that either support or oppose ESG integration and sustainable financial practices. This chapter examines changes in the regulatory environment of the developing economies. It will compare various strategies, including mandatory and voluntary ESG disclosures, or reporting and their success in facilitating sustainable finance (Broadstock et al., 2021). The interaction of the international organizations and regional bodies in the development of these policies and enhancing cross-border cooperation and similar ones in the sustainability standards will also be reviewed.
5. To be able to point out the serious empty areas of the current research and offer directions in which research may be developed in the future. In this chapter, gaps in the literature will be described based upon a systematic review of existing literature. To illustrate, one can raise the requirements to examine the long-term financial implication of ESG implementation on branches of the economy in the realm of developing economies and the efficiency of the various FinTech variations to achieve the real deliverance of the case of financial inclusion and sustainability. This chapter will suggest a research agenda on these gaps, including giving a roadmap to scholars and practitioners on how to further develop the knowledge and practice of sustainable finance in these important regions.

Based on these goals, the next part contains the description of the systematic approach that was to be used to implement this literature review and organize the upcoming analysis.

3. THE CONNECTION OF ESG, FINTECH, AND SUSTAINABLE FINANCE IN DEVELOPING ECONOMIES

3.1 Introduction: Sustainable Development in Developing Economies

Developing The emerging economies must juggle between the industrial development run and sustainable growth. Their susceptibility to climate change, the high extractive industries, and informal sectors increase the need to embrace sustainability framework. Assessment on ESG and green financial innovations can be considered as such transformative tools, so that these countries could adjust the rise of their national economics to the sustainability targets as a global country (United Nations, 2015). This alignment requirement has taken ESG to the center stage of financial discussion within these regions.

Although ESG is a mainstream in developed countries, the concept is difficult to apply in developing countries. The issues, like poorer regulation environments and other cultural priorities, demand more subtle treatment. Technological advances increase and overcome this complexity. FinTech makes this image more complicated and sophisticated. FinTech can be used as an enabler of sustainable finance by digitalizing financial services which make them more universal and provides more people with access to credit, saving and investment opportunities.

3.2 ESG Integration in Developing Economies: Drivers, Challenges, and Performance

3.2.1 ESG Adoption Drivers

The need to attract international investment, access foreign finance, regulatory incentives, and reputational advantages are causing firms in developing economies to increasingly implement ESG frameworks. Moreover, the institutional interest can be explained by increased convergence with risk management and sustainable value creation (Barker et al., 2020; Gillan et al., 2021). Such pressures on the globe often also attain local implementation obstacles.

The most frequent ESG standards with global scope, like Sustainability Accounting Standards Board (SASB), Global Reporting Initiative (GRI), or the Task Force on Climate-related Financial Disclosures (TCFD), are commonly referred to, yet their implementation usually is not compatible with the local environment and data availability (LSEG, 2022). Which is now taken up more recently by the development of the International Sustainability Standards Board (ISSB), especially its IFRS S1 and S2, which is likely to have a profound effect on worldwide minimum reporting. Although implemented by their own choice, their incorporation by jurisdictions, particularly those in emerging markets, has a potential of facilitating reporting and cross blistering (IFRS Foundation, 2024). The difference between international aspiration and local situation creates a few issues.

3.2.2 ESG Integration Challenges

Data Availability and Quality: The availability and quality of data (i.e., reliable ESG metrics) for many firms are low, because standards are not consistent, there are minimal data-gathering infrastructure and the expensive cost of third-party verification (Bao et al., 2024; GRESB, 2024). Such scarcity of data makes meaningful analysis and oversight a challenge. The most recent research has emphasized the pre-existing problem of data fragmentation and insufficient interoperability amid various standards of reporting, which has resulted in the inability of the investors to compare the ESG performance between various companies in emerging economies (KPMG, 2023).

Capacity and Expertise: The limited supply of ESG-trained professionals, particularly within SMEs and the public sector, not only hinders effective activity and integration but also contributes significantly to the common challenges SMEs face when implementing ESG reporting practices, notably limited resources and a lack of expertise (Sustainability Directory, 2025). It is also through human capital that even the purest of the initiatives might not turn out to be a success. This is coupled with the absence of ESG advantages knowledge among a certain number of local stakeholders, which blocks the overall purchase (Pawar et al., 2025).

Greenwashing: Without strict regulatory monitoring, certain companies pretend to make advancements in ESG when they have no, which also destroys stakeholder trust. According to Mu & Lee (2023), certain businesses, to portray a positive image to the world and under pressure to do so by the stakeholders, report information and data that is either inflated or outright false concerning their CSR (including ESG aspects). This results in growing distrust among the consumer base, and depending on the brands affected this may undermine brand recognition and trust to a point of no return.

This inability to hold leaders to count makes the whole movement lose its credibility. This is being tried to solve by the emergence of advanced FinTech-enabled greenwashing detection tools, but their success and usefulness in less developed regulatory jurisdiction is still undecided (Sun et al., 2024).

Short-Term Financial Pressures: The nature of ESG investments has some long-term returns that could not fit well with the short-term profitability concerns in cash-strapped settings (Liu et al., 2024). This poses a trade-off that is sharp especially to business firms operating in the developing economies that tend to prioritize survival and short-term benefits.

Policy Gaps: Ineffective enforcement mechanisms in addition to weak or patchy ESG regulation further gives the industry an issue to meaningful adoption. Such regulatory gaps set a kind of an atmosphere of uncertainty on the part of companies and investors. Although developing economies are taking steps in that direction, most of them must deal with the lack of a framework of the ESG disclosure that is both detailed and mandatory, resulting in inconsistent reporting and other problems associated with it (OECD, 2023).

Generally, these difficulties are further exacerbated by structural problems like fragmentation, little resources, cultural complexities and governance issues that exist in most developing economies including India, Brazil and other countries of Africa.

3.2.3 ESG and Financial Performance

Empirical research supports the idea that there is a positive relationship between the ESG performance and financial performance with regards to minimizing volatility and increasing the loyalty of stakeholders (Whelan et al., 2021; Narula et al., 2024). Nevertheless, it is hard to justify the causality because of institutional differences depending on the country and different methods of measuring (Acquah et al., 2023; Liu et al., 2024). More recent meta-studies affirm that this association is positive, although researchers note that it varies greatly in its intensity and that a stronger ESG performance still correlates with stronger financial resilience of a firm and to its survival during adverse economic environments (Friede et al., 2015; Chen et al., 2023; Fettahoglu et al., 2025). Such results are encouraging, but show that more fine-grained, context-based research is necessary. As an example, the effect of certain ESG pillars (E, S, or G) can vary between sectors and regions in developing economies and, therefore, should be thoroughly investigated.

3.3 FinTech Innovations and Sustainable Finance: A Catalyst for Green Growth

3.3.1 Financial Inclusion and ESG

FinTech can provide funds to unbanked communities, promote the entrepreneurial sector, and decentralize green initiatives. Financial services such as mobile banking, peer-to-peer lending, and crowdfunding are increasingly capital democratizing by means of aligning financial services with Sustainable Development Goals (SDGs) (UNDP, 2025a). Democratization stretches to ESG data accumulation and approval. A good example is in Southeast Asia, where FinTech applications such as digital wallets, peer-to-peer loans have sought to address the unavailability of basic financial services in countries like the Philippines, Indonesia, Vietnam, and Cambodia and achieved financial inclusion. In the same light, India and Brazil have recorded extensive developments in digital payment systems, which aid financial inclusion and green finance (Nagrale & Chandnani, 2025). In addition to basic financial services (e.g. microlending to small companies), FinTech is becoming a means to access micro loans to go green (e.g., solar panels to switch rural households' and to fund sustainable agriculture (direct contribution to the E and S of ESG (UNDP, 2025a).

3.3.2 ESG Data and Transparency

AI and big data analytics are used more often to validate ESG claims, simplify reporting and spot anomalies. These technologies are used to increase transparency, lower the costs, and instill trust in the ESG reporting (Shukla et al., 2025; Liu et al., 2025). Based on data analytics, machine learning, and blockchain, FinTech solutions are smashing the emergence of green finance by offering solutions to evaluate sustainability risks, to create investment plans, and to monitor environmental situations. They can improve ESG scoring and investing because they analyze big data, unstructured, and structured information. As another instance, natural language processing enabled by artificial intelligence may be used to scan numerous corporate reports and news outlets to detect possible cases of greenwashing or ESG risks that are not reported (Saxena, 2024). Blockchain is also being actively pursued to generate unalterable records of carbon credits, renewable energy certificates, sustainability supply chain provenance, and enhance the integrity of green claims and associated traceability manyfold (Brears, 2024; Bassi et al., 2025; Mohamed et al., 2023). Investment markets are also experiencing the above benefits of these technologies.

3.3.3 Retail Participation in Green Investment

Digital Retail investors also can enjoy ESG-compliant financial products and vehicles, including green ETFs and impact-centered mutual funds, gaining access to them digitally, which diversifies investment and attracts more capital to sustainable growth (Fan et al., 2025). Reher & Sokolinski (2024), discuss the influence of robo-advisor access to less wealthy investors on their financial investment and welfare. It notes that robo-advisors have increased accessibility; that is, they lower the account minimums thus bringing more middle-class investors into the industry. Mohapatra et al., (2025) explore the influence of factors on the behavioral intention of investors to use robo-advisors to conduct sustainable investments. It implies that those robo-advisors are popular as they limit the complexity, increase awareness, and make sustainable investing more affordable.

This does not only open access in a more democratic way, but it educates the general population about sustainable finance, too. Nevertheless, technological advancement also has its risk.

3.3.4 Risks and Contradictions

Regardless of its advantages, FinTech has also several risks such as cyber-attacks, digital inequality, and heavy usage of electricity such as blockchain mining that conflicts with sustainability strategies (Dunbar et al., 2023). Such conflicts should very well be handled to keep perceiving the overall effects of technology to be positive. Moreover, although FinTech has great potential to facilitate the process of data collection and processing, it is limited in its ability to eliminate the problem of data quality and availability, especially when it comes to social and governance indicators in emerging markets. The data of ESG is unstructured, inconsistent and incomplete, and several companies may apply different reporting frameworks that cannot be combined. An accuracy issue, along with the possibility of greenwashing, is also associated with self-reported data. With their power, AI algorithms can reify preexisting biases, resulting in biased (or even discriminatory) decisions in ESG scores in case they are deployed based on biased data. Some AI models are also a so-called black box, which introduces an issue of a lack of transparency and explainability that further undermines trust in AI-based ESG analysis. All these challenges underline that FinTech is an effective tool, yet not a remedy to all the problems of ESG data and governance. The exploration of these risks needs powerful cybersecurity frameworks, digital literacy, and creation of a green FinTech solution that generates the lowest possible environmental impact on its own (Simanungkalit et al., 2025).

3.4 Sustainable Finance Instruments in Developing Economies

3.4.1 Green Bonds and Sustainable Sukuk

Green bonds and sukuk instruments turned out to be a prime instrument to finance environmental projects in emerging markets. Greener Islamic finance has been pioneered by the two countries, Malaysia and Indonesia, through the issuance of sovereign sukuk and the use of incentive taxes (UNDP, 2025b). These novel tools are usually combined with the new financing forms. Green bond issuance in developing economies has been evidenced by municipal green bonds in Mexico City and Cape Town whose cost of certification and reporting may be higher but focus on sustainable economic growth. The international market in green, social, and sustainability (GSS) bonds has also been growing fast with the developing economies contributing an important percentage of the volumes to finance their climate and development targets (World Bank, 2025). Of interest as well is the prospect of transition bonds, which can enable decarbonization journeys of industries with high greenhouse gas emissions in the emerging economies to put up finance (ICMA, 2023).

3.4.2 Blended Finance and Sustainable Lending

Commercial banks and development finance institutions are engaging in the use of blending concessional and market-rate finance to risk-free investment in climate resilience, renewable energy, and sustainable agriculture (Azam et al., 2024). This process is also reinforced with increasing levels of socially conscious investment trends. The necessity of blended finance models is especially important in securing the investment of the private sector in the projects that would be otherwise disregarded as being not profitable enough or too risky, filling the gap between financing and the construction of large-scale sustainable infrastructure in developing countries (World Bank, 2023).

3.4.3 Impact Investing and ESG-focused Venture Capital

Impact investing revolves around the private equity being ventured in endeavors that have quantifiable low-carbon and social returns. The increasing FinTech-based platforms also target startups to focus on the healthcare, education and clean tech sectors with the mission of ESGs (Liu et al., 2025; Shukla et al., 2025). An effective policy environment is needed to make such initiatives a success. The financial environment in Latin America is experiencing a significant transformation, with sustainable financial instruments, such as green, social, and sustainability-related bonds, increasingly becoming an ordinary feature of debt markets (World Bank, 2025). This move has been attributed to a strategic plan to tackle climate change impacts and advance development goals in the region. In addition to the traditional instruments of debt financing, such as the above-mentioned IFACC Responsible Commodities Facility, the strategic ideas of climate smart finance investment are manifested in the form of more sustainable farming in areas of significant ecosystems such as Amazon, Cerrado, and Chaco (IFACC, n.d.). Other scholars concluded that FinTech has the potential of boosting economic growth due to attainment of higher productivity, sustainable growth through diversification, technological upgrading, entrepreneurship, creativity and innovation (Hasan et al., 2024).

3.5 Policy and Regulatory Frameworks for Sustainable Finance

3.5.1 Central Banks and Public Policy

Developing economies have a trend to support ESG utilizing central banks by means of regulatory mechanisms, green taxonomies, and subsidies. Participation in international platforms such as the Network for Greening the Financial System (NGFS) gives policy advice and coordinating (Carbon Tracker Initiative, 2025). Central banks are very important to maintain financial stability and provide invariable market signals concerning risks/opportunities affected by climate. Worldwide cooperation is vital in normalization of practices. There has been an increase in the number of central banks in developing economies to adopt climate stress testing in their supervision frameworks, which has amplified pressure on financial institutions to understand and report exposures to threats of climate-related financial risks (NGFS, 2023).

3.5.2 Global Institutions and Standards

Such bodies as the International Finance Corporation (IFC) and United Nations-supported Principles of Responsible Investment (UNPRI) are contributing to the standardization of the ESG practice and the capacity-building (Climate Policy Initiative, 2021). Nevertheless, there are local setbacks to the implementation of these international standards. The common pressure that international organizations exercise on the introduction of mandatory climate-related financial disclosures, within the framework of such entities as TCFD and ISSB, is affecting policy trends in developing economies in the context of providing more transparency and accountability (UNEP FI, 2024).

3.5.3 Implementation Challenges

The incoherence of both policy and the limited financial regulator capacity, as well as the lack of the correlation between the global standard and the local realities remain hindering factors. Implementing good ESG involves a national development policy and international sustainable initiatives (Gazi et al., 2024). These issues explain why focused studies are necessary. Some of the challenges that surround the implementation of sustainable finance taxonomies, to give an example, include its inability to be integrated within regulatory environments, leadership, and its ability to be harmonized and standardized across the various national jurisdictions. Moreover, the fact that a lot of current frameworks are voluntary may restrict the availability of data and the evaluation of alignment between taxonomies. An emerging concept is the so-called double materiality that acknowledges the existence of financial materiality and impact materiality; however, it is also associated with implementation challenges, particularly in the developing economies where impact data may be limited (Dunfjäl, 2025).

3.5.4 Policy Recommendations

To support faster integration of ESG and sustainable finance in developing economies, several policy interventions are advised:

Develop Clear Regulatory Frameworks and Green Taxonomies: Government and central banks should provide robust regulatory frameworks and clear green taxonomies that effectively define, distinguish, and register green and sustainable activities government and central banks should provide robust regulatory frameworks, and clear green taxonomies describing what is meant by green activities and sustainability activities and what registry requirements there shall be. This also involves harmonizing national taxonomies with the international taxonomy (e.g., ISSB) and leaving the space to the local practices with a transition roadmap.

Foster Innovation through Regulatory Sandboxes and Innovation Hubs: Introduce special regulatory sandbox or digital banking license framework to give a test environment to implement new FinTech innovations in green finance. Countries such as Brazil, Colombia, the UK, and Singapore have been able to establish such sandboxes, which can enable responsible data flows and exchanges, inclusive of across boundaries. Furthermore, to facilitate development and take-up, it is possible to create FinTech innovation hubs that should also focus on sustainable solutions.

Incentivize Sustainable Investments with Differentiated Support: Provide differentiated support to encourage sustainable investments by offering incentives including tax breaks, subsidies, and certification programs to players in the private equity and venture capital market to invest in FinTech and green projects. This would de-risk the private capital and utilize government funds in the green programs. This may also mean performance-based incentives attached to objective ESG outcomes.

Enhance Data Infrastructure and Standardization: Invest in an ESG data collection, verification and reporting infrastructure, which may include such FinTech tools as AI and blockchain to make it more accurate and transparent. Encourage the standardized ESG reporting framework to be more flexible to the abilities of domestic firms, which may involve a tiered system of reporting (e.g. simplified version of reporting to SMEs). Back the emergence of free-source ESG information sites.

Promote Financial Literacy and Capacity Building: Launch Impose education campaigns to improve financial literacy in sustainable finance and ESG investing by customers and investors. Undertake capacity-building programs of ESG-trained professionals to financial sector, SMEs and regulatory agencies. This is accompanied by Academic institution partnerships and Vocational training.

Align Public and Private Financial Instruments Strategically: Encourage more closely coordinated interaction between public financing mechanisms (e.g., multilateral development banks) and flows of private investment to marshal resources to fund major projects in sustainable development. This may include increasing the blended finance instruments and coming up with catalytic capital funds that can be used in the high-impact and early-stage green enterprises.

Strengthen Cross-Border Cooperation and Regional Harmonization: Foster the cross-border investment in sustainable projects and harmonize international rules to minimize market friction and distribute international funds to green development. Regional organizations (e.g. ASEAN, ECOWAS, Mercosur) may be important in standardizing ESG reporting, green taxonomies to establish bigger and more desirable regional markets of sustainable finance.

4. OPERATIONALIZING ESG AND SUSTAINABLE FINANCE: PRACTICAL IMPLEMENTATION CHALLENGES

While although the foregoing pages have described the macro motivators, technological facilitators, and policy considerations, the reality of establishing ESG integration and sustainable finance in developing economies deals with different and mostly insurmountable operational realities. Such obstacles are not confined to data or regulatory shortages, but they relate to the core of business, market frameworks, and domestic abilities.

4.1 Capacity Building and Skill Gaps

The lack of special expertise in local financial institutions, corporations, and regulatory bodies is a serious hindrance. Deploying advanced ESG standards, carrying out rigorous impact analysis, or designing complicated environmental financial instruments may not only entail a thorough grasp of environmental science, social indicators, governance principles, and creative financial engineering. Most developing economies do not have an adequate supply of such interdisciplinary professionals. Curriculum acceleration due to these emerging needs is often slow to respond in their universities and vocational training programs which results in a bottleneck in effective adoption. An example is that although a large bank in a developing country may profess an interest in green lending, it may not be educated on how to evaluate the environment risks and merits of a project or how to evaluate its overall long-term sustainable consequences. The result of this gap in capacity may be shallow compliance or excessive use of expensive outside consultants, and this may be prohibitive to smaller firms.

4.2 Cost of Compliance and Disclosure

ESG compliance and disclosure can be very pricey to businesses especially the Small and Medium-sized Enterprises (SMEs). Aligning to a global reporting standard such as GRI or SASB, contracting third party intervener, or investing in software as well as human resources to capture and analyze data translates into a serious investment of money. In those economies where profit margins tend to be thinner and access to capital is more limited these sorts of forward investments can be seen as an unpleasant albatross instead of a strategic opportunity. This barrier to entry may outweigh local firms, who work in a potential duopoly: bigger operators with a global focus are willing to pursue and comply with ESG, as opposed to small companies that cannot afford to remain agile in meeting the marks, and the divide in sustainability grows in the economy.

4.3 Supply Chain Complexity and Traceability

Most developing economies form part of the global supply chains and are specialized in extraction of raw materials or in performing labor-intensive production. It is very challenging to secure ESG compliance before and after these convoluted, oft times perilous, supply chains. Such concerns as child labor, poor work safety, and deforestation, as well as water pollution can be rooted deeply. Although there is potential in such FinTech solutions as blockchain, their broader application is limited by the number of participants as well as the level of technological preparedness, in addition to the absence of unified protocols of data transfer across jurisdictions. Both due diligence and measuring impact are extremely challenging due to a lack of visibility of companies around direct suppliers. Such intricacy is also applicable to the scope 3 emissions reporting which is both time-consuming and involves extensive efforts on the value chain.

4.4 Cultural Context and Stakeholder Engagement

ESS organizational areas, such as the Social and Governance areas of ESG, are strongly interconnected with local traditions and cultural norms, legal practice, and the expectations of stakeholders. The definition of good governance or social equity may differ a lot among the various developing economies. Inclusion of various stakeholders such as indigenous groups, workers in the informal sector, and local non-governmental organizations cannot be addressed through mere top-down instructions but rather only by referring to culturally sensitive measures and true participatory actions. Other sustainable finance projects, no matter how well-intentioned, may have unanticipated adverse social consequences, or they may be put off schedule, or even produce a bad reputation, due to insurgence of local settings. Trust-building and making sure that all stakeholders have the true buy-in is a complex task that should be approached with time flexibility.

4.5 Risk Perception and Investment Appetite

There is an increase in interest, but a basic issue is the view that sustainable investments in the developing economies come with an increased sense of risk.

The investor might receive projects in other industries such as renewable energy projects or sustainable agriculture as riskier due to the perceived political stability, currency movement, poorer legal systems, or lack of substantiated track records. This increased perception of risk frequently translates into increased capital expenses and sustainable schemes are even more costly than those that are traditional and that emit lots of pollution. To move past this, it is not just a case of de-risking interventions such as blended finance, but also ensuring there is a fund of bankable, sustainable projects and development of a successful precedent which can help incite greater investor interest.

These operational difficulties point to the fact that mere presence of policies or technologies does not suffice; proper on-ground implementation needs the investment of much human capital, financial resources, capacity-building of systems, and understanding of the local dynamics thereof.

Even though the nexus of ESG, FinTech, and sustainable finance in emerging economies has received the growing academic and practical interest, it still leaves several critical knowledge gaps, which leads to promising future research directions. Filling these gaps is most important when planning theoretical frameworks into relevant and successful solutions that are scalable and equitable in the Global South.

5. DEEPER CAUSAL ANALYSIS OF ESG INTEGRATION ON FIRM PERFORMANCE AND DEVELOPMENT OUTCOMES

Although the relationship between the adoption of ESG and financial performance is shown as being positively related in the developed markets according to the available literature, the same is not so clear and one sided in so far as developing economies are concerned. Future studies should be able to get beyond correlation and see causal relationships. This requires:

Rigorous Econometric Modeling: Use of advanced econometric tools (e.g., natural experiments, quasi-experimental designs, instrumental variables) to estimate the causal effect of ESG measures or sustainable finance efforts being driven by FinTech on firm valuation, cost of capital, risk management and long-term profitability in a diverse range of developing country situations.

Sector-Specific and Country-Specific Studies: ESG materiality varies significantly by industry and local context. Research should delve into specific sectors (e.g., agriculture, mining, renewable energy, manufacturing, tourism) within developing economies to understand how ESG integration uniquely affects their operations, supply chains, and market access. Similarly, country-specific case studies can offer granular insights into the effectiveness of national ESG policies and frameworks.

Impact on Broader Development Indicators: Future research must advance a critical discussion of whether sustainable finance and FinTech have a causal effect on the overall development indicators, like poverty alleviation, income disparity, education and healthcare provision, biodiversity protection, and climate resistance on the national or regional scale. This requires the cooperation of the development of economists and social scientists.

5.1 Nuanced Understanding of FinTech's Transformative Potential and Risks

FinTech is an effective enabler, yet the use of FinTech on the grounds of sustainable finance in the developing economies needs to be explored more coarsely:

FinTech and Climate Change Adaptation and Resilience: Although a lot is focused on financing the mitigation of climate change, little is known about how FinTech can play a specific role in financing adaptation to climate change brought on by climate change and ramping up resilience. This involves the study of the place of micro-insurance, blockchain-powered parametric insurance, online infrastructure financing platforms, and FinTech tools that support mitigation of disasters.

Addressing the Digital Divide and Financial Inclusion for ESG: Though FinTech has potential to include, studies must be conducted on how to eliminate the ongoing digital divide in some of the distant or untapped locations of third world countries. In what ways can FinTech technologies be inclusive of populations with low levels of digital literacy or poor internet connectivity or without means of identity documentation? They should also examine how FinTech may engage directly with the marginalized (e.g., to women, the indigenous, smallholder farmers) and enable access to sustainable finance to fund their livelihoods and ESG-related projects.

Measuring the environmental impact of FinTech: Some of the FinTech technologies, especially blockchain and artificial intelligence, encompass a high energy consumption and, therefore, threaten the environment. To sustainably finance future studies ought to measure in a systematic manner the carbon footprints of different FinTech applications used in finance quantitatively and recommend the ways (e.g. green data centers, energy-efficient algorithms) deemed effective to offset these effects so that FinTech can make a positive contribution to sustainability.

Cybersecurity, Data Privacy, and Ethical AI in ESG: Since FinTech works with SORE data in massive volume, the dangers of cyberattacks and data breaches, data privacy issues, and ethical AI are gaining paramount importance. Work should be done to ensure that they devise strong cybersecurity models to support sustainable finance FinTech, that they deploy ethical AI to ESG ratings and investment choices, and that data on vulnerable people is safe.

5.2 Developing Context-Specific and Actionable Policy Frameworks

While although universal structures are in place, they usually do not work well in developing economies due to the existence of unique issues. In future, research should be done on the following:

Effectiveness of Policy Instruments: A comparative analysis to determine effectiveness of various policy tools (e.g., green taxonomies, mandatory ESG disclosure, carbon pricing, blended finance incentives, regulatory sandboxes of Green FinTech) in catalyzing sustainable capital mobilization and generating real change in a variety of developing regions should be conducted.

Regional Integration and Harmonization: Investigating the opportunity to make stronger region integration and unification of the regional sustainable finance policies and regulations of FinTech in such regional organizations as ASEAN, ECOWAS, or the African Union. This would help to lessen fragmentation, develop bigger markets, and enable cross-border sustainable investments.

Role of Public Finance and Multilateral Development Banks (MDBs): How public finance and MDBs can strategically de-risk sustainable investments, catalytic capital and local capacity to lure the private sector into climate and SDG-compliant projects in developing economies. These include consideration of new monetary products and risk sharing arrangements.

Addressing Greenwashing and Accountability: Creating more advanced instruments and governmental bodies to prevent greenwashing in less developed markets, where the ability to oversee the process might not be sufficient. This might include an investigation into the utilization of FinTech as a tool to greater transparency and real-time influence checks.

5.3 Behavioral Aspects and Stakeholder Dynamics

Sustainable finance conversion is not a strictly technical change; it can be related to behavioral changes and complicated stakeholder relations.

Investor Behavior in Developing Markets: The motives of domestic investors and foreign investors, as well as their level of risk-taking and their decision making in taking up the ESG and sustainable finance opportunities in the developing markets. What motivates them to make other decisions other than the conventional financial returns?

Corporate Adoption Barriers and Enablers: Greater qualitative and quantitative research is required to provide a comprehension of the organizational obstacles and facilitating factors (e.g., the absence of leadership buy-in, resistance to change, short-term outlook), to adopt ESG in developing economic companies.

Community Engagement and Social License: Studies on the best practices meant to achieve meaningful stakeholder engagement, especially in directing the capabilities of local communities and civil society organizations, to ensure that the sustainable finance efforts will truly appeal to community about the social equity issues and attain a so-called social license to operate.

These lines of research should be followed with great enthusiasm and determination by academic and practitioners to imbue the financial systems with greater resilience, inclusive, and environment-friendly value that can translate the sustenance development goals of the Global South.

The synchronization of the ESG principles, FinTech innovations and sustainable finance can be described as essential innovation of the financial environment of developing economies. In this literature review, massive opportunities and complicated elements of such nexus stand highlighted. Although global structures and digital instruments present new opportunities that have never been realized before, their effectiveness in the Global South is limited and determined by the existence of targeted policy-driven measures, strong institutions, as well as inclusive designs of technologies. In the future, financial systems should be designed to be pliable and adaptive and the current and future generations should ensure that systems should be designed to balance the profit against planet and society's health. The Beyond Profit perspective dimension of this chapter highlights how these financial systems are more than ever needed to sustain not only economic development but also real social justice and ecological sustainability.

Based on this thematic analysis, the next section will provide visual images and quantitative summary addressing the market growth and regional readiness that is outlined in the literature.

6. VISUAL REPRESENTATIONS AND QUANTITATIVE OVERVIEW

This chapter provides a graphical description of the trends and interdependencies that will be raised in the previous literature review. Despite the elaboration of the scope of the intersection of ESG, FinTech, and sustainable finance using a conceptual framework based on a qualitative basis, these examples provide a data-based glimpse into the transformation of the market at the level of developing economies.

Table 1 displays the complex and visual connections between the key drivers and outcomes, with the issues also being portrayed in the following tables regarding specific quantitative metrics of the problem. Table 2 presents a comparative picture of the circumstances of the four major regions of the world to be ready to process sustainable finance since the perspective of the readiness is realized in terms of strengths and challenges of a policy and regulatory environment, FinTech infrastructure and innovation, and the quality of ESG data and reporting. The fact that these visual aids and quantitative indicators are also efficient tools to supplement empirical observations and theoretical discussions gives a comprehensive and practical idea of the modern landscape. Between these interrelations, the chapter seeks to deepen the understanding of the reader of the practical relevance and the regionalities of impacts of ESG, FinTech, and the connection with sustainability in a structured framework.

Table 1. Conceptual Framework of ESG-FinTech-Sustainability Linkages

Component	Key Elements	Interdependencies / Linkages
ESG Drivers	1. Investor Demand: International & domestic investors seeking sustainable portfolios.	→ Sustainability Outcomes: Drives long-term value creation, reduced volatility, and enhanced stakeholder loyalty.
	2. Regulatory Pressure: Evolving green taxonomies, mandatory disclosures (e.g., ISSB standards).	← FinTech Enablers: FinTech provides tools (e.g., data analytics) that help firms meet these demands and pressures.
	3. Corporate Reputation & Risk: Enhanced brand value, reduced operational risks.	
FinTech Enablers	1. Financial Inclusion: Mobile banking, peer-to-peer lending for the unbanked, micro-green loans.	→ ESG Drivers: Improves data quality and reporting, making ESG more credible and attractive to investors.
	2. Data & Transparency: AI, blockchain, and big data for verifying ESG claims, greenwashing detection.	→ Sustainability Outcomes: Directly contributes to financial inclusion (a social outcome) and better resource allocation.
	3. Retail Participation: Digital platforms for easy access to green investments (e.g., green ETFs, impact funds).	→ Sustainable Finance: Creates the platforms and tools necessary for issuing and managing green bonds and impact investments.
Sustainable Finance Instruments	1. Green Bonds & Sukuk: Capital for environmental projects, transition bonds.	→ Sustainability Outcomes: Channels capital towards achieving specific environmental and social goals (e.g., renewable energy, climate resilience).
	2. Blended Finance: Combining public/private funds to de-risk projects, catalytic capital.	← FinTech Enablers: FinTech platforms are used to manage, track, and democratize access to these instruments.
	3. Impact Investing: Equity for social and environmental ventures, FinTech-driven impact platforms.	
Sustainability Outcomes	1. Green & Inclusive Growth: Economic development aligned with SDGs.	← ESG Drivers: The ultimate goal and result of effective ESG integration.

continued on following page

Table 1. Continued

Component	Key Elements	Interdependencies / Linkages
	2. Environmental Resilience: Investment in climate adaptation and mitigation.	← FinTech Enablers: A direct result of FinTech's ability to facilitate financial inclusion and data transparency.
	3. Social Equity: Improved financial access and social well-being.	

Table 2. Regional Sustainable Finance & ESG Readiness Indicators

Region	Policy & Regulatory Environment	FinTech Infrastructure & Innovation	ESG Data & Reporting Quality	Overall Readiness
Southeast Asia	Strong, with regional cooperation (e.g., ASEAN Green Finance Taxonomy) and clear green taxonomies in key countries (e.g., Singapore, Malaysia). Increasing alignment with ISSB.	Highly developed, with rapid FinTech adoption and supportive regulatory sandboxes. Significant investment in RegTech for compliance.	Improving, but with persistent data gaps and a lack of unified standards. Growing adoption of digital reporting tools.	**High:** A leader in policy and FinTech, positioning it for rapid growth and innovation.
South Asia	Growing, with national-level green finance policies and central bank initiatives (e.g., RBI's green finance push). Emerging green taxonomies.	Rapidly expanding FinTech adoption, particularly in mobile payments and financial inclusion. Strong potential for AI/ML in financial services.	Lagging, with limited mandatory disclosures and fragmented reporting. Challenges with data verification persist.	**Medium-High:** Strong on FinTech and policy intent but needs to improve data quality and enforcement.
Latin America	Emerging, with increasing regulatory focus on climate risk and a growing sustainable bond market. Some countries adopt voluntary ESG guidelines.	Moderate, with established digital banking but slower integration of advanced ESG tech. Growing FinTech for financial inclusion.	Fragmented, with significant variation between countries (e.g., Brazil vs. smaller economies). Data availability is a key hurdle.	**Medium:** Making progress, but with wide disparities and a need for stronger, harmonized policy frameworks and data infrastructure.
Sub-Saharan Africa	Nascent, with some countries showing leadership (e.g., South Africa) but overall policies are fragmented, and implementation capacity is limited.	A global leader in mobile money and financial inclusion, but with infrastructure gaps and varying digital literacy levels.	Low, facing significant challenges with data collection, verification, and expertise. High reliance on international frameworks.	**Medium-Low:** High potential due to FinTech innovation, but held back by policy fragmentation, capacity gaps, and poor data quality.

Collectively, these tables can be seen as important cornerstones which secure the theoretical framework and the literature review in verifiable data and regional individualities, thus providing a background for exploring future directions and conclusions.

7. FUTURE DIRECTIONS AND CONCLUSION

This chapter reviews recent literature and evidence based on ESG integrations in the context of FinTech innovation and sustainable finance within developing economies and indicates a dynamic but tough environment. In the review, it was highlighted that ESG frameworks are becoming increasingly relevant towards the realization of long-term sustainability particularly in economies that are vulnerable to climate change, conversely, affected by institutional gaps and limited financial capability to withstand climate-related effects (Broadstock et al., 2021). The movement toward abandoning the concept of profit-only metrics across the globe is especially important in the Global South where the cost of environmental and social risks is extremely high (UNEP, 2023). FinTech turns out to be a driver of changes and a catalyst of change as well: it supports financial inclusion, increases transparency, and capital allocation towards more sustainable development. Nonetheless, some fundamental issues exist in terms of data quality, regulatory capability and greenwashing, as well as financial motivation to move urgently towards sustainability.

Moving forward, to achieve the desired sustainable and inclusive financial system in the developing economies, it is important to fill a few research gaps and understand the strategic directions to follow.

7.1 Research Gaps and Future Directions

Although there is an increasing amount of literature, there are still some essential gaps that might be explored in the future:

Longitudinal Causal Studies on ESG Impact: Although there is a growing number of correlations between ESG integration and financial performance, there is an urgent need to study causality of this long-term study. A step forward to answering this question should be to attribute causality to finding out that there exists a correlation between ESG adoption and its subsequent development of consequences on various outcomes e.g., renewable energy, sustainable agriculture, manufacturing, in different developing economies, long-term results on them are to be explored. This should be accompanied by strong econometric models on which it will be possible to conduct checks to control the influence of institutional, economic and cultural factors that are country specific.

Localized ESG Taxonomies and Cultural Nuances: There is little literature on the impact of varying cultural values, local economies, and native practices and how they affect the perception, adoption, and success of ESG frameworks in different developing regions. The future research opportunity might include the valuable experimentation of designing ESG taxonomies, globally consistent (e.g., matched to the ISSB) and locally contextual (considering specific developmental priorities and social norms). It would also be of great value to have comparative analysis on how effective mandatory and voluntary ESG reporting is across various regulatory landscape conditions in emerging markets.

Interdisciplinary Methodologies: To Future research ought to be interdisciplinary, integrating the expertise of both finance and data science, as well as environmental studies and social science, to foster a complete picture of this nexus. By taking advantage of modern data science to process big, unstructured ESG data sets, such as satellite imagery of environmental impact, sentiment analysis of social data and AI analysis of governance data, deeper and more granular information can be obtained. Combining financial risk models and climate science models also play a very important role in providing imminent information on climatic related financial risks and opportunities.

FinTech's Role in Informal Economies and SMEs: The mechanisms through which FinTech platforms can best facilitate the adoption of ESG and financial inclusion in informal economies and Small and Medium-sized Enterprises (SMEs), are not well understood. The paper would benefit those studies further to test its capability in particular activities, like micro-lending green ventures, digital payment systems of impact tracking, simplified FinTech tools of ESG reporting among SME. It is important to explore issues in data collection, trust-development, and proper regulation in such settings.

Addressing FinTech's Contradictions and Biases: Further studies will be necessary to measure the environmental impact that energy intensive FinTech solutions (e.g., blockchain mining) have and to find strategies aimed at reducing the associated impacts. Moreover, research ought to address the possibility of algebraic bias in AI-powered ESG-ratings, namely, the social measure under various cultural conditions, thus present equitableness and justice in FinTech algorithms to adopt sustainable money-making.

Effectiveness of Policy Interventions and Blended Finance Models: Comparative It is necessary to analyze comparatively which types of policy incentives (e.g., preferential taxation, subsidies, green-bond frameworks, regulatory sands boxes) have proven to be the most effective in mobilizing privately sourced capital on a sustainable development basis in diverse developing regions. It might also be interesting to investigate in more detail the structure and performance of new blended finance instruments as well as funds for catalytic capital and their role in de-risking and mobilizing investment into large, high-impact sustainable projects.

These areas of research provide a guidebook to academics and practitioners to develop the testing and cultural emergence of sustainable finance within these critical areas in a more informed and effective direction

7.2 Conclusion

ESG principles and FinTech innovations combined with sustainable finance is the breakthrough in the sphere of finance in developing economies. This literature review highlights the massive potential and intricate challenges in this junction. Although there are unprecedented opportunities in the Global South presented by global structures and digital technologies to support and promote green and inclusive growth, the effective implementation of such tools requires well-defined policy interventions, institutional arrangements, and inclusive technological designs.

Making the "Beyond Profit" vision of finance in developing economies a reality is not just a goal, it is a growing need. It demands a combined, global effort by the policy formulators who need to design easy-to-understand, facilitating rules and incentives, financial bodies who maintain to integrate sustainability into their fundamental methods and technology gurus who need to create something strong by being easy-to-use. Finally, constructing flexible, resilient economies, which truly balance profits with the needs of the planet and our human communities will be the cornerstone of opening a door to sustainable economic progress, creating tangible social justice, and establishing environmental resilience in the Global South. The lessons for this review are very vital in this common effort.

REFRENCES

Acquah, E., Carbonari, L., Farcomeni, A., & Trovato, G. (2023). Institutions and economic development: New measurements and evidence. *Empirical Economics*, *65*(3), 1693–1728. DOI: 10.1007/s00181-023-02395-w

Amel-Zadeh, A., & Serafeim, G. (2018). Why and how investors use ESG information: Evidence from a global survey. *Financial Analysts Journal*, *74*(3), 87–103. DOI: 10.2469/faj.v74.n3.2

Arner, D. W., Buckley, R. P., Dahdal, A. M., & Zetzsche, D. A. (2021). Digital finance, COVID-19 and existential sustainability crises: Setting the agenda for the 2020s. (University of Hong Kong Faculty of Law Research Paper No. 2021/001; UNSW Law Research Paper No. 21-16; University of Luxembourg Law WPS 2021-003). *SSRN*. https://ssrn.com/abstract=3783605

Azam, M., Hunjra, A. I., & Hassan, M. K. (2024). The role of financing in achieving sustainable development goals: Economic and legal implications. In *Green Finance and Sustainable Development Goals* (pp. 299–316). World Scientific., DOI: 10.1142/9781800614482_0011

Bao, X., Sadiq, M., Tye, W., & Zhang, J. (2024). The impact of environmental, social, and governance (ESG) rating disparities on corporate risk: The mediating role of financing constraints. *Journal of Environmental Management*, *371*, 123113. DOI: 10.1016/j.jenvman.2024.123113 PMID: 39481154

Barker, R., Eccles, R. G., & Serafeim, G. (2020, December). The future of ESG is accounting. Harvard Business Review. https://hbr.org/2020/12/the-future-of-esg-is-accounting

Bassi, E., Lustenberger, M., & Letina, S. (2025). Blockchain-based voluntary carbon market: Strategic insights into network structure. *Frontiers in Blockchain*, *8*, 1603695. Advance online publication. DOI: 10.3389/fbloc.2025.1603695

Brears, R. C. (2024). How Blockchain Technology is Transforming Climate Change Initiatives: Carbon Credits, Renewable Energy, and Supply Chains. *Medium*. https://medium.com/global-climate-solutions/how-blockchain-technology-is-transforming-climate-change-initiatives-carbon-credits-renewable-9941ca4523eb

Broadstock, D. C., Chan, K., Cheng, L. T. W., & Wang, X. W. (2021). The role of ESG performance during times of financial crisis: Evidence from COVID-19 in China. *Finance Research Letters*, *38*, 101716. DOI: 10.1016/j.frl.2020.101716 PMID: 32837385

Carbon Tracker Initiative. (2025, June 30). New NGFS short-term scenarios for central banks & supervisors [News release]. https://carbontracker.org/new-ngfs-short-term-scenarios-for-central-banks-supervisors/

Chen, S., Song, Y., & Gao, P. (2023). Environmental, social, and governance (ESG) performance and financial outcomes: Analyzing the impact of ESG on financial performance. *Journal of Environmental Management*, *345*, 118829. DOI: 10.1016/j.jenvman.2023.118829 PMID: 37688968

Climate Policy Initiative. (2021). Global Landscape of Climate Finance 2021. https://www.climatepolicyinitiative.org/publication/global-landscape-of-climate-finance-2021/

Dunbar, K., Sarkis, J., & Treku, D. N. (2023). FinTech for environmental sustainability: Promises and pitfalls. *One Earth*, *7*(1), 23–30. DOI: 10.1016/j.oneear.2023.12.012

Fan, J., Wang, D., & Zheng, Y. (2025). Smart Money, Greener Future: AI-Enhanced English Financial Text Processing for ESG Investment Decisions. *Sustainability (Basel)*, *17*(15), 6971. DOI: 10.3390/su17156971

Fettahoglu, S., Allak, S., & Ozcan Turkkan, B. (2025). ESG Scores and Corporate Performance in Emerging Markets: Evidence from E7 Countries. *Sustainability (Basel)*, *17*(19), 8936. DOI: 10.3390/su17198936

Friede, G., Busch, T., & Bassen, A. (2015). ESG and financial performance: Aggregated evidence from more than 2000 empirical studies. *Journal of Sustainable Finance & Investment*, *5*(4), 210–233. DOI: 10.1080/20430795.2015.1118917

Gao, D., Tan, L., & Duan, K. (2024). Forging a path to sustainability: The impact of Fintech on corporate ESG performance. *European Journal of Finance*, •••, 1–19. DOI: 10.1080/1351847X.2024.2416995

Gazi, M., Islam, H., Islam, M. A., Karim, R., Momo, S. M., & Senathirajah, A. R. B. S. (2024). Unlocking sustainable development in East Asia Pacific and South Asia: An econometric exploration of ESG initiatives. *Sustainable Environment*, *10*(1), 2366558. Advance online publication. DOI: 10.1080/27658511.2024.2366558

Gillan, S. L., Koch, A., & Starks, L. T. (2021). Firms and social responsibility: A review of ESG and CSR research in corporate finance. *Journal of Corporate Finance*, *66*, 101889. DOI: 10.1016/j.jcorpfin.2021.101889

Glova, J., & Panko, M. (2025). The Effects of Environmental, Social, and Governance Factors on Financial Performance and Market Valuation in the European Automotive Industry. *International Journal of Financial Studies*, *13*(2), 82. DOI: 10.3390/ijfs13020082

GRESB. (2024). Navigating the evolving ESG data landscape: Challenges, trends, and solutions. GRESB Insights. https://www.gresb.com/nl-en/navigating-the-evolving-esg-data-landscape-challenges-trends-and-solutions/

Hasan, M., Hoque, A., Abedin, M. Z., & Gasbarro, D. (2024). FinTech and sustainable development: A systematic thematic analysis using human- and machine-generated processing. *International Review of Financial Analysis*, *95*(Part C), 103473. DOI: 10.1016/j.irfa.2024.103473

IFRS Foundation. (2024, September). Voluntarily applying ISSB Standards—A guide for preparers. IFRS Foundation. https://www.ifrs.org/content/dam/ifrs/supporting-implementation/issb-standards/issb-voluntary-application-preparers.pdf

Innovative Finance for the Amazon. Cerrado and Chaco (IFACC). (n.d.). Home. Retrieved from https://www.ifacc-initiative.org/home

International Capital Market Association (ICMA). (2023, June). Climate Transition Finance Handbook. https://www.icmagroup.org/assets/documents/Sustainable-finance/2023-updates/Climate-Transition-Finance-Handbook-CTFH-June-2023-220623.pdf

ISSB. (2024). *IFRS S1 General Requirements for Disclosure of Sustainability-related Financial Information and IFRS S2 Climate-related Disclosures*. International Sustainability Standards Board.

Kouhizadeh, M., Saberi, S., & Sarkis, J. (2021). Blockchain technology and the sustainable supply chain: Theoretically exploring adoption barriers. *International Journal of Production Economics*, *231*, 107831. DOI: 10.1016/j.ijpe.2020.107831

KPMG. (2023, September). ESG Assurance Maturity Index 2023. KPMG International. https://assets.kpmg.com/content/dam/kpmg/xx/pdf/2023/09/esg-maturity-report-2023.pdf

Liu, B., Chen, Z., Wang, Y., & Sun, X. (2025). Fintech empowers enterprises to practice ESG: The role of political connections. *Energy Economics*, *142*, 107693. DOI: 10.1016/j.eneco.2025.108183

Liu, X., Huang, N., Su, W., & Zhou, H. (2024). Digital finance and firm green innovation: Evidence from China. *International Review of Economics & Finance*, *95*, 103461. DOI: 10.1016/j.iref.2024.103461

LSEG. (2022). Climate Report 2022. London Stock Exchange Group. https://www.lseg.com/content/dam/lseg/en_us/documents/sustainability/climate-report-2022.pdf

Lule Yawe, B., Ddumba-Ssentamu, J., Nnyanzi, J. B., & Mukisa, I. (2022). Role of Mobile Money and Digital Payments in Financial Inclusion for Sustainable Development Goals in Africa. In IntechOpen. DOI: 10.5772/intechopen.105858

Mohamed, I. D., Haddad, S., Barakat, M., & Rosi, B. (2023). Blockchain Technology Adoption for Improved Environmental Supply Chain Performance: The Mediation Effect of Supply Chain Resilience, Customer Integration, and Green Customer Information Sharing. *Sustainability (Basel)*, *15*(10), 7909. DOI: 10.3390/su15107909

Mohapatra, N., Shekhar, S., Singh, R., Khan, S., Santos, G., & Carvalho, S. (2025). Unveiling the Nexus Between Use of AI-Enabled Robo-Advisors, Behavioural Intention and Sustainable Investment Decisions Using PLS-SEM. *Sustainability (Basel)*, *17*(9), 3897. DOI: 10.3390/su17093897

Mu, H., & Lee, Y. (2023). Greenwashing in Corporate Social Responsibility: A Dual-Faceted Analysis of Its Impact on Employee Trust and Identification. *Sustainability (Basel)*, *15*(22), 15693. DOI: 10.3390/su152215693

Nagrale, A. V., & Chandnani, S. (2025). Digital payment ecosystems and financial inclusion: Comparative analysis of UPI in India and PIX in Brazil. *Global Journal of Engineering and Technology Advances*. DOI: 10.30574/gjeta.2025.23.2.0148

Narula, R., Rao, P., Kumar, S., & Matta, R. (2024). ESG scores and firm performance—Evidence from emerging market. International Review of Economics & Finance, *89*(A), 1170–1184. DOI: 10.1016/j.iref.2023.08.024

Network for Greening the Financial System (NGFS). (2023, July). NGFS Climate Scenarios for central banks and supervisors – Phase IV. NGFS. https://www.ngfs.net/sites/default/files/medias/documents/ngfs_climate_scenarios_for_central_banks_and_supervisors_phase_iv.pdf

OECD. (2023). *Sustainable Finance in Asia: ESG and Climate-Aligned Investing and Policy Considerations*. OECD Publishing., DOI: 10.1787/bde9ec0d-

Pawar, S., Chougule, M., & Channaveer, R. M. (2025). Human capital and stakeholder engagement intervention: A women empowerment pathway to achieve sustainable community development in water, sanitation, and hygiene at Vaijapur Village of Karnataka, India. *Frontiers in Sustainable Cities*, *6*, 1562033. DOI: 10.3389/frsus.2025.1562033

Porter, M. E., & Kramer, M. R. (2011). Creating shared value. *Harvard Business Review*, *89*(1-2), 62–77.

Reher, M., & Sokolinski, S. (2024). Robo advisors and access to wealth management. *Journal of Financial Economics*, *155*, 103829. DOI: 10.1016/j.jfineco.2024.103829

Saxena, S. (2024, November 18). Using Natural Language Processing for detecting greenwashing indicators and constructing impact-focused index portfolio. *SSRN*. https://ssrn.com/abstract=5024113 DOI: 10.2139/ssrn.5024113

Shukla, R., Bagotia, H., Satish, P., Kamath, H. S., Chatterjee, S., Savariah, D., Kaulgud, V., Gobburi, H., & Acharya, S. (2025). Fintech and healthtech synergism: Pioneering a digital healthcare revolution for accessible, affordable, and effective patient-centered care. *Journal of Family Medicine and Primary Care*, *14*(3), 820–824. DOI: 10.4103/jfmpc.jfmpc_999_24 PMID: 40256084

Simanungkalit, R. H. M., Jumono, S., Arrozi Adhikara, M. F., Munandar, A., & Suharna, J. (2025). Integration of Digital Technology in Green Finance: A Systematic Analysis of Green Digital Finance. *Journal of System and Management Sciences*, *15*(1).

Sun, Z., Liu, L., Johan, S., & Zhao, L. (2024). FinTech Adoption and Corporate Greenwashing: A Technology Affordance Perspective. *British Journal of Management*, *36*(3), 978–1002. DOI: 10.1111/1467-8551.12879

Sustainability Directory. (2025, April 1). What are common challenges for SMEs when implementing ESG reporting practices? Sustainability-Directory.com. Retrieved July 31, 2025, from https://sustainability-directory.com/question/what-are-common-challenges-for-smes-when-implementing-esg-reporting-practices

Tyron, L. (2024). How Blockchain Revolutionizes Supply Chain Tracking for ESG and Corporate Accountability. Medium. Retrieved from https://medium.com/@adelstein/how-blockchain-revolutionizes-supply-chain-tracking-for-esg-and-corporate-accountability-0deea5bcc4dc

UNEP. (2024). *Digital Finance for the Planet: Accelerating Climate Action through FinTech.* United Nations Environment Programme.

United Nations. (2015). Transforming Our World: The 2030 Agenda for Sustainable Development.

United Nations Development Programme (UNDP). (2025a) Egypt Accelerator Lab. (2025, July 24). Mapping global signals for fintech in green sectors: agriculture, energy, and sustainable tourism. UNDP. https://www.undp.org/acceleratorlabs/blog/mapping-global-signals-fintech-green-sectors-agriculture-energy-and-sustainable-tourism

United Nations Development Programme (UNDP). (2025b, May 7). THE POTENTIAL GROWTH AND FUTURE TRENDS OF GREEN SUKUK AS A TOOL FOR SUSTAINABLE FINANCING. https://www.undp.org/sites/g/files/zskgke326/files/2025-05/undp-kfh-green-sukuk-tool-for-sustainable-financing.pdf

United Nations Environment Programme Finance Initiative (UNEP FI). (2024). *From Disclosure to Action: Advancing Climate-Related Financial Disclosures in Emerging Markets*. UNEP Finance Initiative.

United Nations Environment Programme (UNEP). (2023). Adaptation Gap Report 2023: Underfinanced. Underprepared. Inadequate investment and planning on climate adaptation leaves world exposed. DOI: 10.59117/20.500.11822/43796

Whelan, T., Atz, U., Van Holt, T., & Clark, C. (2021). ESG and financial performance: Uncovering the relationship by aggregating evidence from 1,000 plus studies published between 2015 – 2020. NYU Stern Center for Sustainable Business & Rockefeller Asset Management. https://www.stern.nyu.edu/sites/default/files/assets/documents/NYU-RAM_ESG-Paper_2021%20Rev_0.pdf

World Bank. (2023). *Blended Finance for Climate Action: A Progress Report*. World Bank Group.

World Bank. (2025, February). Labeled Sustainable Bonds Market Update February 2025. The World Bank. https://thedocs.worldbank.org/en/doc/cd82b4033281dab2cb1a1c71eeb691e4-0340012025/original/Labeled-Bond-Quarterly-Newsletter-Issue-No-10.pdf

Chapter 3
Green Finance and Corporate Sustainability

Sruthi Rajan
http://orcid.org/0000-0002-7019-3632
Christ University, Bangalore, India

ABSTRACT

Green finance instruments, an essential part of the sustainable finance ecosystem, enable the transition to a low-carbon economy and give investors an opportunity to support significant environmental projects. The need for creative financial solutions that might promote sustainable development has increased due to the worsening consequences of climate change and environmental deterioration. To support a culture of responsibility, corporations are modifying their investment plans to include green finance possibilities. The objective of this chapter is to examine the new developments in sustainable finance and corporate green investment strategies. Green finance instruments allow businesses to align their financial goals by offering a specific source of funding for ecologically beneficial projects. By doing this, businesses can take advantage of the numerous opportunities offered by the green finance industry in addition to fulfilling their corporate social responsibility.

INTRODUCTION

Achieving the Sustainable Development Goals (SDG) is by no means an easy or quick process. There are a number of barriers in the way of accomplishing the objectives. A green economy necessitates a shift in our perspective on and approach to economic management. It's not only about cutting waste or carbon emissions; it's also about generating new employment, inventing cutting-edge technology, and upholding social fairness. The United Nations Social Development Goal (UN-SDG)

DOI: 10.4018/979-8-3373-5437-8.ch003

13 makes it abundantly evident how important it is to move to a green economy. The economic model of the green economy prioritises sustainable development. The focus is on the sustainable use of natural resources, reducing waste, reducing environmental risks, enhancing human well-being, protecting against environmental damage and improving inclusive economic growth (Vishnevsky et al., 2021). Inclusive economic growth is the outcome of integrating environmental concerns and social equity. In essence green economy aims to improve human welfare, social equality, and reduce environmental risks (Chaaben et al., 2022).

The need to embrace green economic policies as essential tools for efficient environmental management has been sparked by the growing degradation of the global environment (Heshmati, 2018). Zhang et al. (202) examined the effectiveness of reformations to China's Sustainable Development Goals and economic goals, influencing enterprises' emissions reduction and energy conservation behaviour for a green economic reclamation after COVID-19. The Green technological innovation is the prominent factor enabling separating the environmental degradation from economic growth. The Green Technonological innovation encompasses Green Cities, Carbon Capture, Utilization and Storage (CCUS), Green Architecture/Building, Vertical Farming, Electric Vehicles, Renewable energy sourses, Biomimicry, and plant based packaging etc. However, these initiatives are coupled with challenges namely, high initial costs, market acceptance and consumer preference, resource scarcity, technological limitations, infrastructure deficiencies, and regulatory and policy hurdles. This is considered the basis of eco-innovation and a possible approach for enhancing sustainable development leading to the creation of eco-friendly technologies (Chen et al., 2023a; Popp et al., 2009). Erdogdu et al. (2025) examines strategies to combat climate change through sustainable energy technologies, energy optimization, and circular economy practices. Green technical innovation emphasizes the development of a management model and control mechanism that coordinates the economy, resources, and environment, and is no longer restricted to merely lowering production costs and increasing economic efficiency (Ma et al., 2022).

According to Pliavskyiy et al. (2021), a number of nations are concerned about the transition to a green economy. However, in recent decades, companies started integrating green technologies and sustainable business preparations into their operations as the initial step towards a green economy. The scarcity of funds for environmentally friendly investments is one of these obstacles that sticks out the most, especially in emerging nations (Yoshino et al., 2021; Li et al., 2023). The government's ability to finance all economic endeavours is restricted due to the problem of capital accumulation. As a result, projects with quick returns are frequently prioritised. Xu et al. (2022) examined the role of private investment in green finance for renewable energy expansion in China. Results show that international financial aid, legislative support policies, economic stability, and feed-in tariffs are strong green finance factors for growing renewable energy investment in China. Additionally, this study clarifies that the effects of entrepreneurial contextual factors and private sector investment on spending differ based on the funding source, highlighting the significance of analysing investment spreads in order to completely understand private investment choices in green finance for renewable development. Lack of financial support affects the private sector, since large corporations are reluctant to participate in green initiatives because they believe the investments will be riskier and yield poorer returns. Green projects can lack the appeal of efficiency and financial profitability, despite their significant environmental benefits for nations. Investing heavily in sustainable technologies, infrastructure, and initiatives is necessary to mitigate one of the biggest problems of our time: climate change. Green finance is essential because it directs funds towards projects that lower carbon emissions and aid in the energy transition.

EVOLUTION AND KEY THEMES IN SUSTAINABLE FINANCE

The origins of sustainable finance follow its development from early ethical concerns to its present-day complex incorporation into traditional financial operations. The area advanced to include risk management (Sustainable Finance 2.0) after being initially propelled by ethical reasons and exclusionary screening (Sustainable Finance 1.0) (Busch et al., 2021). The original phase of sustainable finance, known as "Sustainable Finance 1.0," saw financial actors begin to link financial investments and markets to ecological degradation and social issues. The measurement of the environmental, social, and governance performance of business firms, taking into account the rating grades that result when deciding whether to avoid, prioritise, or discount ventures based on that ESG data, was summarised by Sustainable Finance 2.0, which included the coining of the term ESG. Sustainability gained traction in mainstream financial markets by highlighting the idea that ESG data are important from both an ethical and financial standpoint. Sustainable Finance 3.0 is defined as a significant shift in focus toward financial market implications. According to this theory, investors must cause a significant shift in a business's social and environmental performance (Kolbel et al., 2020).

The development of a more thorough understanding of sustainable finance that considers governance, social, and environmental factors is now crucial for long-term value generation (Schoenmaker & Schramade, 2019). This change is a result of public awareness and stronger laws that require businesses and financial institutions to be more accountable and transparent (Behind ESG Ratings, 2025). Going beyond a general classification of sustainable investment, the current chapter investigates the factors that underpin the development of innovative green financial products to examine the unique traits that propel their invention (Monk & Perkins, 2020). This necessitates the critical evaluation of the different ways in which financial markets and institutions can facilitate the shift to a low-carbon economy. Due consideration is given to the financial performance and investment choices related to green assets as opposed to conventional ones (Lichtenberger et al., 2022).

The green finance concept gives due consideration to the social, environmental and governance issues. The problems triggering stakeholder finance and ESG investment are addressed under the governance issues. However, issues on income equality, diversity, labour practices of suppliers, workplace injury rates, and philanthropy comes under the category of social issues and consequences. The climate and green finance exclusively address environmental issues. The derivation of the term sustainable finance comes from responsible investment and ESG investing. Responsible investing was used in the 1990's and 2000's,. The term "ESG investing took place in the 2010s. Although the financial industry proposes a sizable range of investment products, there are substantial discrepancies in integrating ESG considerations (Schoenmaker & Schramade, 2019).

Sustainable finance as one of the prominent pillar of sustainable development that focusses the incorporation of environmental, social, and governance factors into financial decision-making. It is anticipated that when financial sector investment decisions are being made, sustainable finance framework is crucial to the process of considering environmental, social, and governance (ESG) factors. Academia and corporates have shown interest in sustainable finance because of the growing global concerns about social inequality, environmental degradation, and governance failures, along with the growing awareness of sustainability challenges (Jayaram & Singh, 2020; Poyser & Daugaard, 2023). According to Cunha et al. (2021), sustainable finance refers to a broad variety of financial operations, products, and investments that seek to produce both financial returns and favourable social and environmental effects. To tackle sustainability concerns and advance sustainable financial reform, Governments and organisations jointly worked to collect more than $400 billion in capital markets for sustainable development (Refinitiv, 2020; Cunha et al., 2021). Sustainable finance has emerged as an important concept in environmentally friendly development and global sustainability goals and it is essential to creating a robust economy since it directs funds toward sustainable enterprises and projects (Kumar et al., 2022; Ziolo et al., 2019). The urgent need to guarantee ethical business practices, encourage social inclusion, and move toward a low-carbon economy its important to consider sustainable finance.

Today, the previously ignored non-financial aspects are given more consideration. The traditional financial systems have given more importance to economic security and profitability. Now, the traditional financial systems are under growing pressure to change and incorporate non-financial aspects. The continued transition from short-term profitability to a more comprehensive viewpoint, as the long-term value creation is reflected in the development of sustainable finance. The socially responsible investing required vetting investments according to moral or ethical standards was the main association of sustainable finance (Schoenmaker & Schramade, 2019). The phrase "sustainable finance," which encompasses social, environmental, and economic factors, is seen as the broadest.

CORE CONCEPTS IN SUSTAINABLE FINANCE

A system that generates, values, and exchanges financial assets in a way that shapes actual wealth to meet the long-term demands of an ecologically conscious and inclusive economy is said to be sustainable. The related terminologies revealed broad agreement in the distinctions between "sustainable," "green," and "climate" finance, despite the fact that sustainable investment categories are not mutually exclusive. The phrase "sustainable finance," which encompasses social, environmental, and economic factors, is seen as the most broad. Thus, "green finance" refers to any financial instruments whose proceeds are allocated to environmentally friendly projects and initiatives, as well as environmental products and policies, with the sole objective of advancing a green economic transition toward low-carbon, sustainable, and equitable development. There are numerous green finance initiatives undertaken by companies and the Government to promote sustainable development. The Sustainable Supply Chain Finance (SSCF) programme was initiated by Walmart and HSBC in 2019 to promote green finance. Walmart under its Project Gigaton initiative aimed at reducing one billion metric tons of greenhouse gas emissions from its global supply chain before 2030. Walmart suppliers are expected to demonstrate reduced greenhouse gas emissions, improved energy efficiency, or adoption of science-based climate projects. With this they receive financial assistance at lower interest rates. This financial incentive encourages suppliers to invest in sustainable practices while maintaining liquidity. HSBC supported this goal by linking suppliers' access to working-capital finance with their sustainability performance. Larsen & Toubro (L&T) was the first company in India to list an ESG bond under SEBI's new green finance rules. The successful issuance highlighted strong investor appetite. HSBC acted as the sole lead arranger. UltraTech Cement Limited (UltraTech) raised US$500 million through a sustainability-linked loan with participation from six banks. The transaction marks the second sustainability-linked financing raised by UltraTech, subsequent to its inaugural sustainability-linked bond issuance in 2021. The Issuer(s) i.e. Prayatna Developers Private Limited, Parampujya Solar Energy Private Limited and Adani Green Energy UP Limited are committed to generating and provide reliable power in a sustainable manner by optimising the use of renewable energy resources with innovative eco-friendly technologies thereby contributing to the economic development of the nation. The amount raised has been fully allocated for refinancing of "Eligible Green Projects" i.e. for solar electricity generation facilities where 100% of the electricity generated from the facility is derived from solar energy resources. Iberdrola, World Bank, Alphabet, and Apple are considered as the global issueers of green bonds initiative. The Government of India have issued sovereign green bonds to finance green and climate-friendly projects. Indore Municipal Corporation and Vadodara Municipal Corporation were among the first municipal bodies in India

A number of fundamental ideas serve as the foundation for sustainable finance, and each is essential in directing financial flows in the direction of more sustainable results. ESG integration, impact investing, green finance, and social responsibility are some of these ideas.

Integration of ESG: Integrating ESG considerations with standard financial analysis is known as ESG integration. Incorporating ESG principles in business has a major impact on its risk profile and performance. Companies or businesses with robust environmental policies is equipped to deal with the frequent shifting resource shortages and regulations. On the other hand, those with sound governance processes are frequently more stable and open.

Impact Investing: The investment behaviour is influenced by many factors like risk, return, and safety. Financial returns along with positive social or environmental impact is described under impact investing. It focuses on investments that give both financial outcome and a quantifiable, positive social or environmental impact. Industries like agriculture, renewable energy, healthcare, and education have more role to play in impact investing. This kind of investment encompasses a broad range of industries with a sustainability goal to use investment activities to bring about positive change.

Social Responsibility: In finance, how investments and the financial operations of the firms affect society is a matter of concern. This can involve funding companies that support ethical labour practices, community development, and access to basic amenities like education and healthcare. A generic practice in socially conscious investing is to preclude investment in the tobacco or gun sectors.

Green Financing: Financial support and services offered for environmental friendly projects like pollution control programs, renewable energy projects, and energy efficiency improvements are referred to as green financing. To raise money for these kinds of initiatives, governments, financial institutions, or businesses frequently issue green bonds, a well-liked green financing instrument. Thus, "green finance" refers to any financial instruments whose proceeds are allocated to environmentally friendly projects and initiatives, as well as environmental products and policies, with the sole objective of advancing a green economic transition toward low-carbon, sustainable, and equitable development.

Green Finance: Reducing risk perceptions and internalising environmental externalities are two of green finance's primary objectives. Green investments are given precedence over conventional investments that sustain unsustainable growth patterns when green financing is promoted on a broad and financially feasible basis. Green finance encompasses all sustainable development criteria established by the UN Sustainable Development Goals (SDGs) and promotes openness and long-term planning of investments flowing into environmental objectives.

Investment, banking, and insurance goods are just a few of the many financial services and products that fall under the umbrella of green finance. In green finance, debt and equity are the most common financial instruments. New financial institutions, such green banks and green funds, as well as new financial products, like carbon market instruments and green bonds, have been created to satisfy the increasing demand. The most sought-after areas of green financing operations remain green bonds, sustainable infrastructure financing, and investments in renewable energy.

The urgency to solve environmental issues along with promoting economic growth has has become a crucial subject of attention in finance and sustainable development (Gilchrist et al., 2021). Green finance, a subcategory of sustainable finance has become well-known route to direct funds towards projects and activities that benefit the environment. The adoption of renewable energy projects, net-zero carbon emissions proposals, and the conservation of natural resources, is the good solutions to address urgent environmental issues and achieve sustainable economic growth (Guo et al., 2024; Raman et al., 2025). It aids in achieving the United Nations SDG goals. The term green finance refers to a wide range of financial products and services, including green credit, green bonds, green funds, green insurance, and green investment (Liu & Zhu, 2024). The green finance systems are crucial for allocating investments towards pollution avoidance, renewable energy, energy efficiency, and sustainable resource management. This ensures minimum environmental deterioration and fosters ecological balance. The distinguishing feature of green finance compared to sustainable finance is the inclusion of environmental, social, and governance factors into financial decision-making practices, which harmonises financial incentives with sustainability goals (Raman et al., 2025). The ESG factors are becoming more and more important for long-term financial stability and resilience since they take into account opportunities and hazards that traditional financial analysis lacks.

GREEN FINANCE INSTRUMENTS

As a result of the worldwide need for sustainable development, the green finance instruments have become an essential tool that accomplishes the social, economic, and environmental goals (Andreeva et al., 2018). The prominent role of green finance instruments in promoting ecological sustainability and resource conservation necessitates a review on the topic. Thus, the chapter attempts to methodically examine the body of research on conventional green finance instruments and their compatibility with the Sustainable Development Goals of the UN (Gilchrist et al., 2021). The review looks at how different financial products and services, such as sustainable investment funds and green bonds, support climate change adaptation and mitigation, biodiversity conservation, and the shift to a circular economy (Liu & Zhu, 2024; Raman et al., 2025). Furthermore, it outlines the prospects and difficulties of expanding green finance programs while taking both developing and established capital markets into account. Additionally, the comprehensive review incorporating empirical studies and theoretical frameworks will outline the effects of the tools on financial performance and corporate social responsibility (Zhou & Cui, 2019). The growing interest in sustainable finance among industry and academia is reflected in the cutting-edge green financing instruments such as crowdsourcing, green venture capital, carbon offsets, carbon credits, green loans, and sustainable banking (Jayaram & Singh, 2020). This progress shows the relation between ecological well-being and financial systems, highlighting the sustainability criteria (Poyser & Daugaard, 2023).

Ranging from green bonds to sustainability-linked loans, the green finance instruments play a crucial role in channelling capital towards sustainable development and climate goals. These instruments offer a mechanism for investors to support environmental projects while potentially securing financial returns.

Green Bonds: One of the most recognised forms of green finance is green bonds. They are intended to garner money, especially for environmental projects, including renewable energy, sustainable waste management, biodiversity preservation, and energy efficiency. An influential turning point in the progression of green finance was reached in the year 2007 when the European Investment Bank released the first green bond (Flaherty et al., 2017). Green bonds abide by the Green Bond Principles (GBP), as voluntary rules that validate integrity in the growth of the green bond market and advocate for disclosure and openness. The Climate Bonds Initiative reports highlight that the overall number of green bonds issued in 2020 hit a record high, showing the growing demand for these bonds.

Sustainability-Linked Bonds (SLB): SLBs are general-purpose bonds dependent on the issuer meeting specific sustainability goals. The bond's interest rate is correlated with the issuer's performance, as it acts as a direct financial incentive for sustainability performance. SLBs are a cutting-edge strategy for coordinating business funding with more general sustainability objectives. Their adaptability and capacity to draw in a wider spectrum of issuers and investors have won them praise (Zerbib, 2019).

Green Loans: A green loan assists individuals, companies, and governments in obtaining the capital required to support ecologically friendly initiatives and operations. Both households and corporations may find green loans to be a profitable source of funding. Compared to conventional loans, green loans frequently have more lenient interest rates. Green loans give consumers the chance to enhance their quality of life and lower costs (by switching to environmentally friendly practices) over time at low interest rates. They can encourage households to install solar panels, buy electric cars, and construct rainwater tanks. Businesses are frequently hampered by the false belief that switching to green, low-carbon routes invariably results in additional expenses and lower earnings. Instead of making sustainability a yearly ESG obligation, a green loan can assist businesses (particularly MSMEs) in integrating sustainability into the very fabric of their operations. Companies can get a competitive edge in the market and draw in investments from socially conscious investors by using green loans to show both their clients and investors that they are concerned about the environmental impact of their operations. Additionally, a type of green loan is called a sustainability-linked loan (SLL). The parameters of these loans, usually the interest rate, are tied to the borrower meeting pre-established sustainable performance goals. Borrowers are expected to enrich their sustainability run-throughs under this arrangement.

Climate Bonds: Climate bonds are a subgroup of green bonds which is dedicated to climate change-related initiatives. This safeguards financing for renewable energy, sustainable transportation, energy-efficient projects, and other initiatives that reduce greenhouse gas emissions. Climate Bonds Standard and Certification Scheme provides the guidelines and certification for bonds, which is administered by the Climate Bonds Initiative.

Blue Bonds: Marine and ocean-related projects are financed through blue bonds as a means of sustainable initiatives. To fund sustainable fisheries and marine projects, the Seychelles issued the first sovereign blue bond in history in 2018. Among the several, the important tools for directing capital towards the preservation and sustainable use of marine resources is the blue bond.

Green Real Estate Investment Trusts (REITs): Green REITs are a sort of real estate investment trust that invests in properties with sustainability credentials, such as energy-efficient buildings or sustainable real estate developments. Investors can purchase real estate with environmental benefits through green REITs.

Green Private Equity: Green private equity is the practice of private equity firms making investments in businesses that provide eco-friendly goods or services. These investments are frequently made in the form of growth capital for more established businesses that focus on green practices or technology, or venture capital for startups.

Green Venture Capital (VC): In order to combat climate change and promote environmental conservation, green venture capital (VC) can fund initiatives and businesses that are creating sustainable technologies. It can give industries like garbage, energy, and transportation much-needed access to funding for the development of greener technology. Due to the substantial investment risk, technology-based green businesses sometimes struggle to obtain funding from conventional sources; venture capital funding can assist mitigate these risks.

Green Grants: Governments, private foundations, charitable organizations, and green non-governmental organizations that support sustainable development all provide green grants. Universities and research institutes can also receive green subsidies to support studies on sustainable development and climate change. For financially unprofitable initiatives, green grants assist in filling the funding gap. One of the top organizations, Global Greengrants Funds, supports a bottom-up strategy and awards green grants to grassroots initiatives that aim to enable local communities to use traditional knowledge and locally developed climate change solutions. Established under the United Nations Framework Convention on Climate Change (UNFCCC) in 2010, the Green Climate Fund has committed USD 12 billion to managing climate change, with a particular emphasis on approving funds for African governments, small island developing states, and least developed nations.

Green Insurance: Green insurance offers reduced rates to environmentally friendly companies and purchases in an effort to encourage sustainable production and consumption. Following the publication of the Principles for Sustainable Insurance manual by the United Nations Environment Programme Finance Initiative (UNEPFI), which outlines how insurance companies must support the sustainable development agenda by assisting green project insurers in quantifying risks and, consequently, better mitigating climate risks, financial institutions around the world are placing a greater emphasis on sustainability-linked insurance. The absence of a unified definition of what comprises a green product is one of the difficulties in offering green loans; this makes it hard for banks to provide green insurance. For example, EVs have an adverse effect on the environment even though it is widely accepted that they are less polluting than conventional cars that operate on fossil fuels. The disposal of lithium-based EV batteries is challenging, and managing a significant amount of e-waste will become more challenging as the number of EVs on the road rises. The process of recognizing green products is very complicated because, even with green products, there are different hues of green. Banks should supply the green premium after inspection and use caution when implementing insurance policies to avoid fraudulent green claims from organizations.

Carbon Markets: Participating countries decided to establish a global carbon credit trading system at the 2021 Glasgow COP26 Climate Change Summit. A business can release up to one tonne of carbon dioxide into the atmosphere with a single carbon credit. In order to encourage businesses to become more climate-friendly, polluting enterprises are given credits that allow them to pollute up to a specific level (cap), and the credits supplied are decreased annually. A carbon market encourages businesses to sell their unused carbon credits and generate income that may be used to fund research and development of more sustainable technology. At the moment, there are two different kinds of carbon markets: voluntary markets (carbon offsets) and compliance markets (carbon credits). While the latter relates to the voluntary issuance and purchase of carbon credits, the former is established by a sovereign and is a regulatory requirement.

Despite the fact that carbon offsets and carbon credits have separate functions, the phrases are sometimes used interchangeably. A carbon credit may be given for each tonne of CO2 that an activity is able to absorb, prevent, or otherwise lessen. A tradeable permit that permits a polluting corporation to emit one tonne of CO2 is called a carbon credit, and it can be bought or sold based on the amount of CO2 the company emits. When the equivalent of one tonne of carbon dioxide (CO2-e) is taken out of the atmosphere and stored on land, or is kept from being released into the atmosphere, a carbon credit may be issued by the government. Carbon credits and carbon offsets are both products offered for sale on the carbon market.

As they move toward a low-carbon economy, developing nations might use carbon credits to further socioeconomic development. One clever strategy to encourage businesses to switch to better energy systems is to provide carbon credits or offsets. The instrument will have fulfilled its goal even though the supply of carbon credits and offsets will surpass demand after the bulk of businesses have made the switch, making the credits less valuable.

Crowdfunding: Through the practice of crowdfunding, a company or individual can raise money from a large number of interested backers, each of whom contributes a small sum of money directly, without the assistance of a traditional financial middleman. The funder may expect a social or environmental return, or the investment may be entirely charitable. Crowdfunding can help green enterprises get started when they don't have access to traditional finance methods.

However, there are different green finance instrument, Green Bonds is closely associated with Sustainable Development Goals. Alamgir and Cheng (2023) studied Green Bonds as a tool for sustainability. Focusing on clean energy, represented by per capita production of renewable energy and climate action represented by per capita carbon emissions (CO2), the results showed a rise in renewable energy and a decrease in carbon emissions. Furthermore, it was observed that the nations that issue green bonds have an improved chance of achieving the sustainability objectives.

Research shows that green bonds are effective tools for promoting Environmental, Social, and Governance (ESG) frameworks and the Sustainable Development Goals (SDGs). Instigating ownership strategies enhances enterprises' commitment to SDGs and ESG, which in turn expediates the issue of green bonds (Jonsdottir et al., 2021). According to Tolliver et al. (2019), green bond profits from fifty-three organisations in ninety-six countries between 2008 and 2017. The market grew quickly as more money was allocated to renewable energy, clean water, and low-carbon transportation projects that matched the goals of the SDGs and the Paris Agreement. Nonetheless, there are still problems with green bonds' usefulness. Green bond issuance is concentrated in certain industries, such as construction and energy, with different regulatory and investor appeal barriers in different nations (Barokah & Bandiyono, 2025). Although green bonds target seven important SDG sectors, Siswantoro (2018) pointed out that not all issuers set SDG objectives, and the quantitative targets are unclear.

Market pricing, economic and environmental impacts, and institutional concerns are the three primary topics of recent research on green bonds, which have become a significant financial tool for socially conscious investing (Cheong & Choi, 2020). The "greenium," a significant pricing phenomenon, is where green bonds may be more expensive than conventional bonds, although empirical data reveal conflicting findings because of variations in sample selections, methodology, and bond characteristics (Liaw, 2020). While issuers face obstacles such inadequate market growth and a dearth of appropriate green projects, survey data indicates that their top motivations are reputational benefits, market signaling power, and climate change mitigation (Sangiorgi & Schopohl, 2023). In terms of pricing experiences, 42% of issuers claim lower costs, while 48% report funding costs comparable to those of conventional bonds (Sangiorgi & Schopohl, 2023). Although the topic of green finance is still in its infancy and has many study limitations, studies show that environmentally conscious activities increase the value of both shareholders and non-financial stakeholders (Gilchrist et al., 2021).

The sustainable and green finance innovations like green bonds, impact investment, ESG integration, and green fintech solutions have become a transformative strength for accomplishing the Sustainable Development Goals (Raman et al., 2025). Resent research in this field shows that green finance is essential for allocating funds to climate change initiatives, renewable energy projects, and sustainable infrastructure. It also actively supports SDGs, such as clean energy (SDG 7), climate action (SDG 13), and partnerships (SDG 17) (Ali et al., 2023; Raman et al., 2025). Lack of institutional frameworks in underdeveloped nations, high transaction costs, regulatory obstacles, and market difficulties are some of the major obstacles that hinder it's adoption (Raman et al., 2025). Green finance products encompass carbon finance, climate financing, green securities, insurance, and infrastructure bonds, with the

US, UK, and China leading in research collaborations (Ali et al., 2024). In order to mobilise capital flows parallel with Global aspirations, future research paths needs to focus on creating sophisticated analytics, local adaptation, and derisking techniques.

Although green bonds receive the most attention, the other financial tools, including green loans with different features and market dynamics, are equally important for encouraging sustainable development. However, due to the established market presence and quantifiable environmental outcomes, green bonds are emphasised in this article (MacAskill et al., 2021). Their ability to fund initiatives related to green buildings, low-carbon transportation, energy efficiency, and renewable energy highlights how directly they are aligned with a number of SDGs, especially SDGs 7 and 13 (Monk & Perkins, 2020). Furthermore, they support green innovation and infrastructure development, contributing to SDG 9, and they invest in sustainable urban planning and infrastructure, which contributes to SDG 11 (Dong et al., 2024).

The combined effect of carbon credit mechanisms and the United Nations Sustainable Development Goals is a renowned case showing the interconnectedness of global environmental and socioeconomic concerns (Mishra et al., 2023). The literature investigates how carbon credit schemes intended to reduce greenhouse gas emissions help achieve the goals set forth in the 2030 Agenda for Sustainable Development endorsed by 193 United Nations member states (Nerini et al., 2019; Kroll et al., 2019). The carbon budget is anticipated to run out around 2030, which is exactly the time when SDG timeframe is expected to occur. This complex link is urgent, highlighting the need for integrated, successful policies (Pathak et al., 2024). To maximise the affect of carbon credit programs, it is also vital to comprehend the recurrent patterns of SDG interlinkages. Here the advancements in one area either support or jeopardise the advancement of others (Bennich et al., 2023). A universal framework for tackling a wide range of interconnected policy objectives across economic, social, and environmental dimensions is provided by the 2030 Agenda for Sustainable Development. It lays forth 17 Sustainable Development Goals, which range from combating poverty and promoting health to addressing climate change and protecting biodiversity (Goubran & Cucuzzella, 2019).

The current chapter tries to address how well the green finance instruments, namely green bonds, green loans, carbon market instruments, green funds and sustainable equity investments, add value to renewable energy, clean transportation, energy efficiency, sustainable infrastructure, and environmental remediation, which enhance company reputation, attract investors and competitive advantage.

One of the main challenges in building and maintaining sustainable business practices for a sustainable future is finding the sources required to finance vital development, infrastructure and maintenance activities. Green finance, which falls under the umbrella of sustainable finance, centres its attention on investments and financial methods that not only yield economic profits but also contribute to favourable environmental consequences. Green finance is the use of existing capital markets to develop and distribute a variety of financial goods and services that generate returns that may be invested in and have a positive impact on the environment. Green finance can be prioritised over conventional investment, which supports unsustainable development patterns, making current infrastructure investments more environmentally friendly or encouraging new investment in vital fields, including clean energy, environmentally friendly transportation, natural resource management, biodiversity, sustainable tourism, ecosystem services, and pollution prevention and control. Green finance, a crucial aspect of corporate sustainability, involves channelling financial resources into projects that benefit the environment. This includes funding renewable energy, energy-efficient buildings, sustainable infrastructure, and other initiatives that reduce pollution and conserve resources. Corporations are increasingly adopting green finance practices as a means to demonstrate their commitment to environmental responsibility and attract investors.

The broader concept of Green finance is aligned with Green Finance and Environmental sustainability (Chen et al., 2023b; Xu et al., 2023; Yan and Tan 2023; Chu et al., 2023), Green Finance and Investments where they study the study how green and non-green investments affect portfolio strategies, risk management, and the financial environment (Akhtaruzzaman et al., 2022; Song et al., 2023), Green Finance and Innovation (Chen and Xie 2023; Li et al., 2023), Green Credit guidelines (Cheng et al., 2023; Pan and Dong 2023), Green Finance and Economy (Lee et al., 2023; Li et al., 2022), Green Finance and Corporate social responsibility (Zhou and Cui 2019; Li et al., 2022). As part of a green policy drive to promote sustainability, Cui et al. (2020) proposed that green finance acts as a catalyst, encouraging businesses and investors to actively participate in green finance markets, whether by obtaining bonds, obtaining credit, or taking out loans. Ronaldo and Suryanto (2022) emphasised how green financing may improve financial inclusion and raise vulnerable households' purchasing power.

By optimising its financial, social, and environmental value over the long run, a company can prepare for the shift to a more sustainable economic model (Dyllick and Muff, 2016; Tirole, 2017; Schoenmaker and Schramade, 2019). This is known as long-term value generation. Unfortunately, we are still unable to establish inclusive capitalism since existing corporate practices are still overly narrowly focused on short-term financial gains (Cort, 2018). Profit maximisation has been the primary goal of corporate finance for many years. However, new studies (Hart and Zingales, 2017) make the case for a business goal that goes beyond limited shareholder value.

According to Dutta et al. (2016), businesses that practice sustainable corporate management look for green money to invest in environmentally friendly projects and develop plans to lessen negative environmental effects. This leads to fighting against climate change as one of the SDGs goals. The financial sector plays a vital role in fighting against climate change by supporting investors in mitigating the impact of adverse climate events. Diversifying the climate-related risk is possible with catastrophe bonds and indexed insurance basically called as hedging instruments that help insure against increasing natural disaster risk. Further, other financial instruments, namely green stock indices, green bonds, and voluntary de-carbonisation initiatives, help investors to diversify their risk by allocating the finance to green sectors. Environmental protection is the link between the green economy and green finance.

Thus, corporate management is the art of utilising resources, namely capital, labour force, and natural resources, in order to improve environmental quality and achieve financial prosperity which further promotes ESG investing, expands innovation, and digitises businesses to hasten the greening of businesses (Maia et al., 2022; Sanoran, 2023). Therefore, corporate sustainability management is a suitable incentive for business performance (Park, 2023).

For businesses looking to improve their environmental performance and carry out their larger corporate social responsibilities, including green finance methods into corporate frameworks is a strategic necessity (Abuatwan, 2023). This strategy reduces financial risks related to environmental instability and regulatory changes in addition to bringing financial systems into line with sustainability goals (Peng et al., 2025). A subset of sustainable finance, green finance includes a wide range of financial services and products, including as investment funds and green bonds, that are intended to direct funds toward environmentally friendly initiatives (Raman et al., 2025). In addition to providing vital support for projects including clean technology, renewable energy, and energy-efficient infrastructure, this innovative financial method also operates as a tactical tool to lessen the extensive effects of environmental issues (Abuatwan, 2023). In order to promote carbon neutrality and sustainable economic development, this all-encompassing framework includes projects that address pollution, deforestation, and climate change (Bhatnagar et al., 2022). This financial paradigm, which dates back to the 1990s, highlights the importance of taking into account favorable environmental effects at every stage of the production, investment, and financing processes (Zhao et al., 2024). This development marks a significant turn toward combining ecological care with financial viability, reframing business responsibilities beyond generating profits (Abuatwan, 2023). However, there are companies or initiatives that tries to mislead the public by introducing misleading products or claims into their green finance initiative. This is typically referred as Green Washing. This is been considered as typical marketing strategy adopted by companies where a company spends more on advertising itself as environmentally friendly than on actually minimizing its environmental impact, misleading consumers who want to make ethical purchases. These sort of activities highlights minor green initiatives ignoring significant harmful practices, thereby generating profit from growing consumer demand for sustainable goods. Essentially this result in reputational damage and loss of trust, financial and credit risks. Consequently, companies may delay implementing genuine, substantive changes necessary for long-term sustainability. This creates a "backlog of necessary transitional activities," which can lead to higher costs and more significant disruption in the future. Essentially, this results in hindered environmental progress. To reduce this, Initiatives from the government and judicial system are a must for preventing these sorts of activities in society.

CONCLUSION

Although the terms green finance and sustainable finance is used interchangeably, both are different concept. Sustainable finance includes social, environmental, and governance issue, however, green finance is a part of sustainable finance. In the current scenario, it's high time to think about environmental friendly projects, which ensures the sustainability requirements. Apart from corporate social responsibility, corporates are much interested in allocating their funds towards environmental friendly projects. Thereby, companies are transforming from traditional financial instruments to green finance instruments like green bonds, weather bonds, green loans, sustainability-linked bonds, and climate-linked bonds. However, there are some challenges in achieving SDG requirements with green finance. The scarcity of funds for environmentally friendly investments is one of these obstacles that sticks out the most, especially in emerging nations. The government's ability to finance all economic endeavours is restricted due to the problem of capital accumulation. As a result, projects with quick returns needs to be frequently prioritised. Further, the general public needs to more aware about the concept of greenwashing, thus ensuring the proper channelisation of funds for the essential cause. Governments must design supportive regulatory framework, such as green taxonomies, disclosure standards, and ESG reporting norms to ensure transparency and prevent greenwashing. Clear policies help investors identify genuinely sustainable projects. Further incentivising investors in the form of tax benefits, subsidies, and interest-rate support encourage investment in renewable energy, clean technology, and sustainable infrastructure, accelerating progress toward climate goals. The financial sector policies integrating environmental risk into credit assessment and capital adequacy norms improve financial stability by accounting for climate-related risks.

REFERENCES

Abuatwan, N. (2023). The Impact of Green Finance on the Sustainability Performance of the Banking Sector in Palestine: The Moderating Role of Female Presence. *Economies (Basel)*, *11*(10), 247. DOI: 10.3390/economies11100247

Akhtaruzzaman, M., Banerjee, A. K., Ghardallou, W & Umar, Z. (2022). Is greenness an optimal hedge for sectoral stock indices? *Economic Modelling*. . econm od. 2022. 106030DOI: 10. 1016/j

Alamgir, M., & Cheng, M.-C. (2023). Do Green Bonds Play a Role in Achieving Sustainability? *Sustainability (Basel)*, *15*(13), 10177. DOI: 10.3390/su151310177

Ali, E., Anshari, M., Hamdan, M., Ahmad, N., & Surieshtino, Y. (2023). Green Finance for Sustainable Development: A Bibliographic Analysis. *2023 International Conference on Sustainable Islamic Business and Finance (SIBF)*, Bahrain, 46-49, DOI: 10.1109/SIBF60067.2023.10379915

Andreeva, O. V., Vovchenko, N. G., Ivanova, O. B., & Kostoglodova, E. D. (2018). *Green Finance: Trends and Financial Regulation Prospects (world)*. Emerald Publishing Limited., DOI: 10.1108/S1569-375920180000100003

Barokah, I. N., & Bandiyono, A. (2025). *The Dynamics of Green Bond Effectiveness in Achieving Sustainable Development: A Comparative Study with a Scoping Review Approach. JAE*. JURNAL AKUNTANSI DAN EKONOMI., DOI: 10.29407/jae.v10i1.24792

Bennich, T., Persson, A., Beaussart, R., Allen, C., & Malekpour, S. (2023). Recurring patterns of SDG interlinkages and how they can advance the 2030 Agenda. *One Earth*, *6*(11), 1465–1476. 10.1016/j.oneear.2023.10.008. DOI: 10.1016/j.oneear.2023.10.008

Bhatnagar, M., Taneja, S., & Özen, E. (2022). A wave of green start-ups in India - The study of green finance as a support system for sustainable entrepreneurship. *Green Finance*, *4*(2), 253–273. DOI: 10.3934/GF.2022012

Busch, T., Bruce-Clark, P., Derwall, J., Eccles, R., Hebb, T., Hoepner, A., Klein, C., Krueger, P., Paetzold, F., Scholtens, B., & Weber, O. (2021). Impact investments: A call for (re)orientation. *SN Business & Economics*, *1*(2), 33. Advance online publication. DOI: 10.1007/s43546-020-00033-6

Chaaben, N., Elleuch, Z., Hamdi, B., & Kahouli, B. (2022). Green economy performance and sustainable development achievement: Empirical evidence from Saudi Arabia. *Environment, Development and Sustainability, 26*(1), 549–564. Advance online publication. DOI: 10.1007/s10668-022-02722-8 PMID: 36320556

Chen, D., Haiqing, H., & Chang, C. P. (2023a). Green finance, environment regulation, and industrial green transformation for corporate social responsibility. *Corporate Social Responsibility and Environmental Management, 2476*(5), 2166–2181. Advance online publication. DOI: 10.1002/csr.2476

Chen, S., & Xie, G. (2023). Assessing the linkage among green finance, technology, and education expenditure: Evidence from G7 economies. *Environmental Science and Pollution Research International, 30*(17), 50332–50345. Advance online publication. DOI: 10.1007/s11356-023-25625-1 PMID: 36795206

Chen, Z., Hao, X., & Chen, F. (2023b). Green innovation and enterprise reputation value. *Business Strategy and the Environment, 32*(4), 1698–1718. DOI: 10.1002/bse.3213

Cheng, Z., Kai, Z & Zhu, S. (2023c). Does green finance regulation improve renewable energy utilization? Evidence from energy consumption efficiency. *Renewable Energy.* . renene. 2023. 03. 083DOI: 10. 1016/j

Chu, H., Hongjuan, Y., Chong, Y., & Li, L. (2023). Does the development of digital finance curb carbon emissions? Evidence from county data in China. *Environmental Science and Pollution Research International, 30*(17), 49237–49254. Advance online publication. DOI: 10.1007/s11356-023-25659-5 PMID: 36773252

Cort, T. (2018). Incentivizing the direction of multi-capital toward inclusive capitalism. *Journal of Sustainable Finance & Investment, 8*(3), 203–212. DOI: 10.1080/20430795.2018.1423850

Cui, H., Wang, R., & Wang, H. (2020). An evolutionary analysis of green finance sustainability based on a multi-agent game. *Journal of Cleaner Production, 269*, 121799. DOI: 10.1016/j.jclepro.2020.121799

Cunha, F. A. F. D. S., Meira, E., & Orsato, R. J. (2021). Sustainable finance and investment: Review and research agenda. *Business Strategy and the Environment, 30*(8), 3821–3838. DOI: 10.1002/bse.2842

Dong, H., Zhang, L., & Zheng, H. (2024). Green bonds: Fueling green innovation or just a fad? *Energy Economics, 135*, 107660. 10.1016/j.eneco.2024.107660. DOI: 10.1016/j.eneco.2024.107660

Dutta, S., Lawson, R., & Marcinko, D. (2016). A management control system to support corporate sustainability strategies. *Advances in Accounting*, *32*, 10–17. DOI: 10.1016/j.adiac.2015.12.001

Dyllick, T. & Muff, K. (2016). Clarifying the meaning of sustainable business introducing a a Typology From Business-as-Usual to True Business Sustainability.

Erdogdu, A., Dayi, F., Yanik, A., Yildiz, F., & Ganji, F. (2025). Innovative Solutions for Combating Climate Change: Advancing Sustainable Energy and Consumption Practices for a Greener Future. *Sustainability (Basel)*, *17*(6), 2697. DOI: 10.3390/su17062697

Flaherty, M., Gevorkyan, A., Radpour, S., & Semmler, W. (2017). Financing climate policies through climate bonds – A three stage model and empirics. *Research in International Business and Finance*, *42*, 468–479. DOI: 10.1016/j.ribaf.2016.06.001

Fuso Nerini, F., Sovacool, B., Hughes, N., Cozzi, L., Cosgrave, E., Howells, M., Tavoni, M., Tomei, J., Zerriffi, H., & Milligan, B. (2019). Connecting climate action with other Sustainable Development Goals. *Nature Sustainability*, *2*(8), 674–680. DOI: 10.1038/s41893-019-0334-y

Gilchrist, D., Yu, J., & Zhong, R. (2021). The Limits of Green Finance: A Survey of Literature in the Context of Green Bonds and Green Loans. *Sustainability (Basel)*, *13*(2), 478. DOI: 10.3390/su13020478

Goubran, S., & Cucuzzella, C. (2019). Integrating the Sustainable Development Goals in Building Projects. *Journal of Sustainability Research*, *1*(2), e190010. DOI: 10.20900/jsr20190010

Guo, X., Yang, J., Shen, Y., & Zhang, X. (2024). Impact on green finance and environmental regulation on carbon emissions: Evidence from China. *Frontiers in Environmental Science*, *12*, 1307313. Advance online publication. DOI: 10.3389/fenvs.2024.1307313

Hart, O., & Zingales, L. (2017). Companies Should Maximize Shareholder Welfare Not Market Value. *Journal of Law, Finance, and Accounting*, *2*(2), 247–274. DOI: 10.1561/108.00000022

Heshmati, A. (2018). An empirical survey of the ramifications of a green economy. *International Journal of Green Economics*, *12*(1), 53. DOI: 10.1504/IJGE.2018.092359

Jayaram, R., & Singh, S. (2020). Sustainable finance: A systematic review. *International Journal of Indian Culture and Business Management*, *21*(3), 317. DOI: 10.1504/IJICBM.2020.110452

Jonsdottir, G. E., Sigurjonsson, T. O., Alavi, A. R., & Mitchell, J. (2021). Applying Responsible Ownership to Advance SDGs and the ESG Framework, Resulting in the Issuance of Green Bonds. *Sustainability (Basel), 13*(13), 7331. DOI: 10.3390/su13137331

Kolbel, J. F., Heeb, F., Paetzold, F., & Busch, T. (2020). Can Sustainable Investing Save the World? Reviewing the Mechanisms of Investor Impact. *Organization & Environment, 33*(4), 554–574. DOI: 10.1177/1086026620919202

Kroll, C., Warchold, A., & Pradhan, P. (2019). Sustainable Development Goals (SDGs): Are we successful in turning trade-offs into synergies? *Palgrave Communications, 5*(1), 140. DOI: 10.1057/s41599-019-0335-5

Kumar, S., Sharma, D., Rao, S., Lim, W. M., & Mangla, S. K. (2022). Past, present, and future of sustainable finance: Insights from big data analytics through machine learning of scholarly research. *Annals of Operations Research, 345*(2-3), 1061–1104. DOI: 10.1007/s10479-021-04410-8 PMID: 35002001

Lee, C. C., Wang, F., Lou, R & Wang, K. (2023). How does green finance drive the decarbonization of the economy? Empirical evidence from China. *Renewable Energy.* 204:671. . renene. 2023. 01.058DOI: 10. 1016/j

Li, C., Sampene, A. K., Agyeman, F. O., Brenya, R & Wiredu, J. (2022). The role of green finance and energy innovation in neutralizing environmental pollution: empirical evidence from the MINT economies. *Journal of Environmental Management.* 317:115500. . jenvm an. 2022. 115500DOI: 10. 1016/j

Li, G., Jia, X., Khan, A. A., Khan, S. U., Ali, M. A. S., & Luo, J. (2023). Does green finance promote agricultural green total factor productivity? Considering green credit, green investment, green securities, and carbon Finance in China. *Environmental Science and Pollution Research International.* Advance online publication. DOI: 10.1007/s11356-022-24857-x PMID: 36562964

Li, Y., Yan, C., & Ren, X. (2023). Do uncertainties affect clean energy markets? Comparisons from a multi-frequency and multi-quantile framework. *Energy Economics, 121*, 106679. DOI: 10.1016/j.eneco.2023.106679

Liaw, K. T. (2020). Survey of Green Bond Pricing and Investment Performance. *Journal of Risk and Financial Management, 13*(9), 193. DOI: 10.3390/jrfm13090193

Lichtenberger, A., Braga, J. P., & Semmler, W. (2022). Green Bonds for the Transition to a Low-Carbon Economy. *Ekonometria, 10*(1), 11. DOI: 10.3390/econometrics10010011

Liu, W., & Zhu, P. (2024). The impact of green finance on the intensity and efficiency of carbon emissions: The moderating effect of the digital economy. *Frontiers in Environmental Science, 12*, 1362932. Advance online publication. DOI: 10.3389/fenvs.2024.1362932

Ma, N., Liu, P., Xiao, Y., Tang, H., & Zhang, J. (2022). Can Green Technological Innovation Reduce Hazardous Air Pollutants?-An Empirical Test Based on 283 Cities in China. *International Journal of Environmental Research and Public Health, 19*(3), 1611. DOI: 10.3390/ijerph19031611 PMID: 35162639

MacAskill, S., Roca, E., Liu, B., Stewart, R. A., & Sahin, O. (2021). Is there a green premium in the green bond market? Systematic literature review revealing premium determinants. *Journal of Cleaner Production, 280*, 124491. 10.1016/j.jclepro.2020.124491. DOI: 10.1016/j.jclepro.2020.124491

Maia, R., Junior, A., Pessanha, J & Garcia, K. (2022). Methodology for setting corporate sustainability targets. *Journal of Cleaner Production*. 369:133359. . jclepro.2022.133359DOI: 10.1016/j

Mishra, M., Desul, S., Santos, C.A.G. et al. (2023). A bibliometric analysis of sustainable development goals (SDGs): a review of progress, challenges, and opportunities. Environment, Development and Sustainability, *26*, 11101–11143 (2024). DOI: 10.1007/s10668-023-03225-w

Monk, A., & Perkins, R. (2020). What explains the emergence and diffusion of green bonds? *Energy Policy, 145*, 111641. DOI: 10.1016/j.enpol.2020.111641

Pan, Y & Dong, F. (2023). Green Finance policy coupling effect of fossil energy use rights trading and renewable energy certificates trading on low carbon economy: taking China as an example. *Economic Analysis and Policy*. 77:658–679. . eap. 2022. 12. 014DOI: 10. 1016/j

Park, S. (2023). Bringing strategy back in: corporate sustainability and firm performance. *Journal of Cleaner Production*. 388:136012. . 136012DOI: 10.1016/j.jclepro.2023

Pathak, M., Patel, S., & Some, S. (2024). Climate change mitigation and Sustainable Development Goals: Evidence and research gaps. *PLOS Climate*, *3*(3), 1–5. DOI: 10.1371/journal.pclm.0000366

Pliavskyiy, I., Martusenko, I., Molnar, O., Dzyana, H., & Kushniriuk, V. (2021). Modelling ways of improving the green economy and environmental protection in the context of governance. *Business: Theory and Practice*, *22*(2), 310–317. DOI: 10.3846/btp.2021.13336

Popp, D., Newell, R., & Jaffe, A. (2009). Energy, the Environment, and Technological Change. *Handbook of the Economics of Innovation, 2*. DOI: 10.1016/S0169-7218(10)02005-8

Poyser, A., & Daugaard, D. (2023). Indigenous sustainable finance as a research field: A systematic literature review on indigenising ESG, sustainability and indigenous community practices. *Accounting and Finance*, *63*(1), 47–76. DOI: 10.1111/acfi.13062

Raman, R., Ray, S., Das, D., & Nedungadi, P. (2025). Innovations and barriers in sustainable and green finance for advancing sustainable development goals. *Frontiers in Environmental Science*, *12*, 1513204. Advance online publication. DOI: 10.3389/fenvs.2024.1513204

Refinitiv. (2020). Sustainable finance review. Refinitiv. Available at https://www.refinitiv.com/content/dam/

Ronaldo, R., & Suryanto, T. (2022). Green finance and sustainability development goals in Indonesian Fund Village. *Resources Policy*, *78*, 102839. DOI: 10.1016/j.resourpol.2022.102839

Sangiorgi, I., & Schopohl, L. (2023). Explaining green bond issuance using survey evidence: Beyond the greenium. *The British Accounting Review*, *55*(1), 101071. 10.1016/j.bar.2021.101071. DOI: 10.1016/j.bar.2021.101071

Sanoran, K. (2023). Corporate sustainability and sustainable growth: the role of industry sensitivity. *Finance Research Letters*. 53:103596. . 2022.103596DOI: 10.1016/j.frl

Schoenmaker, D., & Schramade, W. (2019). Investing for long-term value creation. *Journal of Sustainable Finance & Investment*, *9*(4), 356–377. DOI: 10.1080/20430795.2019.1625012

Siswantoro, D. (2018). The relationship of the green bond and the Social Development Goals (SDGs) targets: a case study of Vigeo Eiris. *E3S Web Conf.*, *74*, 1003. DOI: 10.1051/e3sconf/20187401003

Song, M., Zheng, H., Shen, Z & Chen, B. (2023). How financial technology affects energy transformation in China. *Technological Forecasting and Social Change*. . techf ore. 2022. 122259DOI: 10. 1016/j

Tirole, J. (2017). *Economics for the Common Good*. Princeton University Press. DOI: 10.2307/j.ctvc77hng

Tolliver, C., Keeley, A. R., & Managi, S. (2019). Green bonds for the Paris agreement and sustainable development goals. *Environmental Research Letters, 14*(6), 64009. DOI: 10.1088/1748-9326/ab1118

Vishnevsky, V. P., Harkushenko, O. M., Zanizdra, M. Y., & Kniaziev, S. I. (2021). Digital and green economy: Common grounds and contradictions. *Science and Innovation, 17*(3), 14–27. DOI: 10.15407/scine17.03.014

Xu, A., Zhu, Y & Wang, W. (2023). Micro green technology innovation effects of green finance pilot policy-from the perspectives of action points and green value. *Journal of Business Research.* 159:113724. . jbusr es.2023. 113724DOI: 10. 1016/j

Xu, N., Kasimov, I., & Wang, Y. (2022). Unlocking private investment as a new determinant of green finance for renewable development in China. *Renewable Energy, 198*, 1121–1130. DOI: 10.1016/j.renene.2022.07.037

Yan, C., & Tan, Q. (2023). Has the level of green finance development improved carbon emission performance?—Empirical evidence from China. *MDE. Managerial and Decision Economics, 3891*(6), 3485–3499. Advance online publication. DOI: 10.1002/mde.3891

Yoshino, N., Rasoulinezhad, E., & Taghizadeh-Hesary, F. (2021). Economic impacts of carbon tax in a general equilibrium framework: Empirical study of Japan. *Journal of Environmental Assessment Policy and Management, 23*(01), 2250014. DOI: 10.1142/S1464333222500144

Zerbib, O. (2019). The effect of pro-environmental preferences on bond prices: Evidence from green bonds. *Journal of Banking & Finance, 98*, 39–60. DOI: 10.1016/j.jbankfin.2018.10.012

Zhang, S., Anser, M. K., Yao-Ping Peng M., & Chen C. (2022). Visualizing the sustainable development goals and natural resource utilization for green economic recovery after COVID-19 pandemic. *Resources Policy.* December 13, 103182. .DOI: 10.1016/j.resourpol.2022.103182

Zhao, X., Benkraiem, R., Abedin, M. Z., & Zhou, S. (2024). The charm of green finance: Can green finance reduce corporate carbon emissions? *Energy Economics, 134*, 107574. 10.1016/j.eneco.2024.107574. DOI: 10.1016/j.eneco.2024.107574

Zhou, X., & Cui, Y. (2019). Green Bonds, Corporate Performance, and Corporate Social Responsibility. *Sustainability (Basel), 11*(23), 6881. DOI: 10.3390/su11236881

Ziolo, M., Bak, I., Cheba, K., & Spoz, A. (2020). Sustainable business models of enterprises - actual and declared activities for ensuring corporate sustainability. *Procedia Computer Science, 176*, 1497–1506. https://creativecommons.org/licenses/by-nc-nd/4.0. DOI: 10.1016/j.procs.2020.09.160

Chapter 4
Sustainable Finance:
Balancing Profitability and Environmental Responsibility

Anshuman Vijay Magar
http://orcid.org/0000-0002-7349-5011
JSPM University, Pune, India

Priyanka Kaskar
http://orcid.org/0009-0000-7144-0351
JSPM University, Pune, India

Pushpalata Shivram Patil
JSPM University, Pune, India

Mohd Abdul Maroof
http://orcid.org/0000-0002-3066-046X
JSPM University, Pune, India

Vineeta Agrawal
http://orcid.org/0000-0002-0252-3134
JSPM University, Pune, India

ABSTRACT

This chapter, delves into the rising significance of sustainable finance and its impact on financial institutions. The key objective is to explore how these institutions reconcile the pursuit of profitability with ESG responsibilities. The methodology involves an analysis of theoretical frameworks, regulatory developments, and case studies, highlighting successful approaches to integrating sustainability in finance. Results demonstrate that sustainable finance is not only viable but also increasingly profitable when paired with innovative models such as green bonds and ESG-focused funds.

DOI: 10.4018/979-8-3373-5437-8.ch004

The chapter identifies major challenges, including short-termism and regulatory inconsistencies, while also exploring growth opportunities in renewable energy and climate finance. The implications suggest that while challenges persist, the integration of sustainability can lead to long-term financial stability and broader societal benefits. As financial institutions increasingly adopt ESG principles, sustainable finance emerges as a powerful tool for economic growth and environmental stewardship.

1. INTRODUCTION

"Sustainability is not a goal to be reached, but a way of thinking that must be integrated into every financial decision."

Sustainable finance has moved steadily from a niche concern to a mainstream institutional priority. In broad terms, it refers to the incorporation of environmental, social, and governance (ESG) factors into financial decision-making, with the purpose of directing capital toward activities that support long-term economic stability and social well-being (Fatemi & Fooladi, 2013). The urgency behind this shift has grown considerably as climate change, resource scarcity, and social inequality have intensified, placing pressure on financial institutions to reconsider what it means to generate value.

Several forces have driven this change. International policy frameworks, particularly the United Nations' Sustainable Development Goals (SDGs) and the 2015 Paris Agreement, have provided a common reference point for aligning investment decisions with broader social and environmental objectives. At the same time, investors and regulators — especially in the European Union — have pushed for greater transparency through instruments such as the EU Taxonomy and the Task Force on Climate-related Financial Disclosures (TCFD). These developments have made ESG integration not merely a question of values, but a regulatory and competitive reality (Zhou & Cui, 2019).

Yet a fundamental tension persists. Traditional finance models continue to reward short-term returns, and the argument that sustainability requires sacrificing profit has not entirely disappeared. The empirical picture is more nuanced: companies with strong ESG profiles have, in a number of studies, demonstrated lower costs of capital, reduced risk exposure, and competitive long-term equity returns (Murau & Thie, 2024; Kumar et al., 2022). But this relationship is neither automatic nor uniform. It depends on the quality of governance, the maturity of the regulatory environment, the reliability of ESG measurement, and — critically — the capacity of institutions to translate ESG commitments into genuine operational change. In developing economies, including India, these conditions are often only partially in place, which complicates the picture further.

This chapter offers a structured and critical analysis of sustainable finance as it operates across these varying contexts. It is positioned as a conceptual and review-based contribution: it synthesises empirical evidence and theoretical frameworks to provide a coherent picture of the current state of sustainable finance, identify where the main gaps lie, and set out what more effective ESG integration would require in practice. The chapter is organised as follows. Section 1 establishes the theoretical framework. Section 2 reviews the literature critically, engaging with both areas of consensus and contested findings. Section 3 examines the profitability–sustainability relationship and the financial instruments through which it is operationalised. Sections 4 and 5 address opportunities and structural challenges, respectively. Section 6 introduces the behavioural and organisational dimensions of ESG adoption. Sections 7 and 8 examine the roles of government policy and corporate governance. Section 9 maps emerging trends, and Section 10 brings the chapter together with a synthesising framework.

1.1 Theoretical Framework of Sustainable Finance

Definition and Scope

Sustainable finance is a broad concept that integrates ESG factors into financial activities — investment decisions, banking practices, and corporate governance — with the objective of supporting long-term economic growth that does not come at the cost of environmental or social integrity. It spans a wide range of instruments and practices: green bonds, sustainability-linked loans, ESG-screened investment funds, climate finance, and social impact investing (Panigrahi & Sukla, 2016). What distinguishes sustainable finance from conventional finance is not simply the addition of non-financial criteria to existing processes, but a recognition that environmental and social risks are, over the long run, material financial risks — ones that affect valuations, credit quality, and portfolio resilience in ways that traditional models often fail to capture.

The scope of sustainable finance extends across industries, asset classes, and geographies. It encompasses direct investment in emission-reducing projects, sustainable infrastructure financing, and the integration of ESG risks into credit assessments. It also has a disclosure dimension: financial institutions and corporations are increasingly required to report on their sustainability practices through standardised frameworks that allow for comparison and accountability (Alim, 2024).

1.2 Key Components: The ESG Framework

The ESG framework is the primary operational structure through which sustainable finance is assessed and implemented. Each dimension captures a distinct but interconnected category of risk and opportunity:

- **Environmental Factors:** These include exposure to climate change, energy efficiency, natural resource management, and pollution control. Financial institutions are increasingly examining the carbon intensity of their loan books and investment portfolios, with exposure to stranded assets — fossil fuel reserves that may become uneconomical under climate regulation — emerging as a material credit risk.
- **Social Factors:** This dimension covers labour standards, human rights, community relations, gender equity, and financial inclusion. Socially responsible investing uses these criteria both to avoid high-risk counterparties and to identify firms that manage stakeholder relationships more effectively.
- **Governance Factors:** Governance evaluates the quality of corporate leadership, board composition, executive accountability, and shareholder rights. Research consistently finds that strong governance structures are associated with lower agency costs and more sustained ESG performance over time.

A practical limitation is worth noting here. ESG scores assigned by different rating agencies frequently diverge, sometimes substantially, reflecting inconsistent methodologies, data sources, and definitions of materiality. Studies have found correlations between major ESG rating providers in the range of 0.4 to 0.6 — far below the near-perfect alignment seen in credit ratings for the same issuer. Pedersen et al. (2021) demonstrate that this measurement divergence is not merely a technical inconvenience: it affects portfolio construction, risk assessment, and the ability of investors to reliably identify genuine ESG leaders. This measurement challenge is a recurring theme throughout this chapter and one that institutional practitioners must actively manage.

1.3 Historical Development

The history of sustainable finance is longer than the current vocabulary suggests. Its roots lie in the socially responsible investing (SRI) movement of the 1960s and 1970s, which operated largely through exclusionary screening — avoiding industries such as tobacco, weapons, and alcohol on ethical grounds. Over the following decades, this evolved as practitioners began to recognise that environmental and social performance could affect long-term financial outcomes, not just investor values.

The launch of the United Nations Principles for Responsible Investment (UNPRI) in 2006 marked a significant formalisation, establishing a common framework for ESG integration and attracting support from major institutional investors globally (KRIPA, 2024).

The 2015 Paris Agreement accelerated the pace of change considerably. By committing signatory nations to emissions reduction targets, it signalled a structural shift in the economics of fossil fuel investment and created both an opportunity and an obligation for the financial sector to redirect capital. Regulatory innovation followed: the EU Taxonomy, introduced in 2020, attempted to provide a science-based classification of environmentally sustainable economic activities, while proposed ESG disclosure rules in the United States indicated growing regulatory convergence across jurisdictions.

1.4 Regulatory Frameworks

Several international frameworks now shape sustainable finance practice in ways that affect institutions across jurisdictions:

- **EU Taxonomy:** A classification system defining which economic activities qualify as environmentally sustainable, providing the criteria for green investment labelling and mandatory disclosure for large institutions operating within the EU.
- **Sustainable Development Goals (SDGs):** The UN's 17 SDGs, adopted in 2015, serve as a global reference for aligning investment priorities with development needs — spanning poverty, health, climate action, and inequality.
- **Task Force on Climate-related Financial Disclosures (TCFD):** Established in 2015, the TCFD encourages institutions to disclose climate-related risks across four domains: governance, strategy, risk management, and metrics and targets.
- **Green Bond Principles (GBP):** Issued by the International Capital Market Association (ICMA), these voluntary guidelines promote transparency and reporting standards for the green bond market, including use-of-proceeds tracking and impact reporting.

The applicability of these frameworks, however, remains uneven across regions. Emerging markets — including India — face real challenges in adopting global standards due to limited regulatory capacity, shallow capital markets, and development priorities that compete with sustainability investment. This gap between international standard-setting and local implementation is a recurring theme in the analysis that follows.

2. REVIEW OF LITERATURE

The academic literature on sustainable finance has grown substantially over the past two decades, and it reflects a genuine evolution in understanding — from initial questions about whether ESG integration is compatible with financial performance, to more nuanced debates about when it works, for whom, and under what conditions. A critical reading of this body of work reveals areas of reasonable consensus alongside significant points of conflict that are important not to paper over.

Kumar et al. (2022), drawing on big data analytics and machine learning across a large corpus of sustainable finance research, identified seven major thematic clusters — including socially responsible investing, climate finance, green financial instruments, and corporate governance — and highlighted persistent gaps around greenwashing, policy coherence, and the practical use of artificial intelligence in ESG assessment. Their work points to a fragmented research landscape and the need for more integrated analytical frameworks that can connect these themes.

On the central question of whether ESG integration improves financial performance, the literature is more divided than popular accounts often suggest. Pedersen et al. (2021) develop the concept of an ESG-efficient frontier — the idea that investors can improve sustainability outcomes without proportionally sacrificing return — but they also show that ESG-constrained portfolios can underperform unconstrained ones in the short run, and that the quality of ESG data significantly affects whether any positive effect materialises. This stands in some contrast to Xu and Solangi (2023), who document a positive causal relationship between green bond investment and renewable energy development in China, and to Katper et al. (2024), who find a positive association between green finance adoption and shareholder wealth in S&P 1500 firms. The divergence is instructive: the ESG–performance link appears to be real in aggregate and over longer time horizons, but it is instrument-specific, context-dependent, and not guaranteed in any individual case.

The question of who should lead sustainable finance — public institutions or private markets — is another area where perspectives diverge. Murau and Thie (2024) argue that private-sector-driven sustainable finance has structural limits, particularly for the large-scale, long-duration investments needed for green infrastructure and climate adaptation. They advocate for a “Public Sustainable Finance” paradigm in which state mechanisms, such as Germany’s Climate and Transformation Fund, provide the anchoring capital that private markets, constrained by short-term return expectations and liquidity requirements, cannot supply. This directly challenges the market-centric framing that dominates much of the mainstream ESG literature.

In the domain of financial technology and innovation, Ren et al. (2023) provide a systematic review of blockchain applications in green finance, including supply chain transparency, smart city financing, and green bond verification. While the potential is real, the authors caution that scaling these solutions requires regulatory standardisation and that blockchain itself introduces governance and energy-use challenges. Edunjobi (2024) finds a similar pattern in sustainable supply chain finance: green bonds and sustainability-linked loans create genuine incentives for ESG compliance, but adoption remains uneven because many firms, particularly in lower-income markets, lack the institutional capacity to engage with these instruments effectively.

Evidence from emerging and developing economies generally tells a more cautious story. Alim (2024), in a study of African banks, finds mixed results: philanthropic CSR activities positively influenced bank profitability, but green credit portfolios showed limited measurable impact. Panigrahi and Sukla (2016) reach a similar conclusion in the Indian context, finding that while CSR activities in Indian banks are widespread, their effects on sustainable outcomes are often limited by weak accountability structures and the absence of credible impact measurement. These findings are particularly relevant given India's position as a major economy with ambitious sustainability commitments but significant institutional constraints.

Two studies shed light on the organisational dynamics of ESG adoption. Lu and Li (2024), analysing Chinese banks, find that ESG performance initially had a neutral or slightly negative effect on environmental responsibility metrics, only improving over longer time periods — a result consistent with the idea that genuine ESG integration involves costly internal restructuring before benefits emerge. Ning and Shen (2024) reinforce this point, showing that regulatory pressure alone does not reliably translate into firm-level environmental investment when access to finance is constrained. Together, these studies highlight a dimension of the sustainable finance challenge that structural analyses often miss: the internal organisational and financial capacity to respond to external ESG mandates matters as much as the mandates themselves.

2.1 Research Gap and Chapter Contribution

The review above reveals four main gaps in the existing literature. First, the ESG–profitability relationship is extensively studied but rarely integrated into a framework that specifies the conditions under which it holds, weakens, or reverses. Second, most empirical work remains concentrated in advanced economies, with the mechanisms through which sustainable finance operates in developing economies — and India specifically — substantially under-examined. Third, the behavioural and organisational factors that determine how deeply institutions embed ESG principles — as distinct from compliance-level adoption — receive disproportionately little attention. Fourth, the practical consequences of ESG rating divergence for investors and policymakers are acknowledged in the literature but rarely addressed in a structured way.

This chapter responds to these gaps by offering an integrative synthesis rather than another descriptive survey. Specifically, it: (i) maps the conditions under which the profitability–sustainability relationship tends to hold, drawing on evidence from both advanced and emerging markets; (ii) gives substantive attention to the Indian institutional context; (iii) introduces the organisational and behavioural dimensions of ESG adoption as a distinct analytical layer; and (iv) concludes with a framework that practitioners and policymakers can apply to their own settings.

3. BALANCING PROFITABILITY AND ENVIRONMENTAL RESPONSIBILITY

3.1 The Profitability–Sustainability Tension

The perceived conflict between profitability and sustainability is, to a significant degree, a product of how financial performance has traditionally been measured. When returns are evaluated over quarterly or annual cycles, investments in renewable energy infrastructure, ESG compliance systems, or community impact programmes look expensive relative to conventional assets that offer faster payback. This short-termism — embedded in performance measurement systems, fund manager evaluation cycles, and incentive structures — creates a systematic bias against sustainability investment, even where the long-run risk-adjusted case is sound (Rasoulinezhad & Taghizadeh-Hesary, 2022).

The empirical record, however, challenges the assumption that sustainability necessarily compromises returns. Meta-analyses across studies from the early 2000s onward find a positive ESG–financial performance relationship in the majority of cases, though with meaningful variation by industry, geography, and measurement methodology (Murau & Thie, 2024). Data from major equity indices over the decade from 2014 to 2024 broadly shows that MSCI ESG Leaders Indices matched or outperformed conventional benchmarks on a risk-adjusted basis, though short-run divergences were common. The more accurate framing, supported by this evidence, is not that sustainability always improves returns, but that the conventional characterisation of sustainability as a financial drag is empirically weak, particularly over the time horizons relevant to long-term institutional investors.

The key insight is that ESG integration changes the risk profile of a firm or portfolio in ways that tend to be favourable over time — reducing exposure to regulatory penalties, reputational damage, and stranded assets — provided that governance quality and the depth of implementation are adequate. The relationship is real but conditional, and those conditions deserve more attention than they typically receive.

3.2 Sustainable Business Models and Financial Instruments

Several financial instruments have emerged that embed sustainability directly into the economics of the transaction:

- **Green Bonds:** Green bond issuances surpassed USD 500 billion in 2023, up from approximately USD 170 billion in 2018. They finance projects with defined environmental benefits, with proceeds tracked and reported against use-of-proceeds standards (Zhou & Cui, 2019). Their growth reflects both genuine investor demand for labelled sustainability instruments and the development of infrastructure — verification, reporting, and market conventions — that gives them credibility.
- **ESG-Focused Investment Funds:** These funds apply ESG screens or tilts to portfolio construction, often combined with active engagement strategies. As of 2023, global ESG assets under management were estimated at approximately USD 35–40 trillion, representing roughly a third of professionally managed assets worldwide. The quality of ESG integration within this category, however, varies considerably.
- **Sustainability-Linked Loans (SLLs):** SLLs tie borrowing costs to the achievement of specific, pre-agreed ESG performance targets — such as measurable reductions in carbon emissions or improvements in gender representation at senior management level. Unlike green bonds, the use of proceeds is not restricted; the incentive operates through the interest rate mechanism.

3.3 Investment Strategies

Three broad investment strategies have developed to operationalise sustainability in finance:

- **Impact Investing:** Directed at generating measurable social or environmental returns alongside financial gains, with particular activity in renewable energy, affordable housing, healthcare infrastructure, and financial inclusion.
- **Responsible Investing:** A broader category in which ESG factors are integrated into portfolio analysis as material risk and opportunity signals, without necessarily imposing exclusionary screens on the investment universe.

- **Climate Finance:** Specifically targeted at mitigation and adaptation activities, climate finance is a critical channel for funding the low-carbon transition across both public and private sectors.

Institutional Case Studies

Two well-known cases illustrate how these instruments and strategies operate in practice. Unilever's Sustainable Living Plan, launched in 2010, embedded environmental and social targets into core business operations and supply chain management. By 2020, the company reported that its sustainability-oriented brands were growing faster than the rest of the portfolio — an indication that ESG integration can create commercial differentiation, not merely reputational benefit.

Goldman Sachs' commitment to deploy USD 750 billion in sustainable finance by 2030, spanning clean energy, sustainable transport, and inclusive growth initiatives, represents one of the largest private-sector pledges in this space. The credibility of commitments of this scale depends on rigorous use-of-proceeds tracking and third-party verification, and the industry is still developing the norms that would make such accountability routine.

4. OPPORTUNITIES IN SUSTAINABLE FINANCE

4.1 Market Growth and New Investment Frontiers

The sustainable finance market has expanded rapidly. Renewable energy represents the most capital-intensive growth opportunity: the International Energy Agency estimates that the global energy transition requires USD 4–6 trillion annually in clean energy investment through 2030. Solar, wind, and grid modernisation projects are attracting significant institutional capital in most major economies. In India specifically, the government's target of 500 GW of non-fossil electricity capacity by 2030 creates a large domestic market for renewable energy finance, drawing interest from development finance institutions and international green bond investors alike.

Sustainable infrastructure — energy-efficient buildings, smart city systems, low-carbon transport — is another growing category. These assets often feature long and stable cash flows that suit the liability profiles of pension funds and insurance companies, making them natural anchor investors in sustainable infrastructure projects.

4.2 Financial Innovation and Technology

Technology is improving both the quality and the accessibility of sustainable finance. Artificial intelligence and machine learning are being applied to process unstructured ESG data from satellite imagery, supply chain databases, social media, and corporate disclosures, enabling more granular and timely assessments than traditional analyst-driven approaches allow. Blockchain applications in green bond verification and supply chain ESG tracking are expanding, though their scaling requires regulatory standardisation and interoperability between platforms (Ren et al., 2023).

Digital investment platforms are widening access to sustainable finance products, enabling retail investors to direct savings toward ESG funds, green bonds, and impact vehicles with a degree of transparency that was previously available only to institutional participants. This broadening of the investor base supports market depth and, in time, pricing efficiency (Hongxuan Yang, 2024).

4.2.1 Long-Term Value Creation

Sustainable finance is increasingly understood as a means of creating durable value for investors, companies, and society — not just an expression of ethical preference. By reducing exposure to climate and transition risks, enhancing governance quality, and building stronger stakeholder relationships, ESG-oriented institutions tend to be more resilient to regulatory and environmental shocks. This resilience is itself a form of financial value that conventional return metrics often undercount.

5. CHALLENGES IN SUSTAINABLE FINANCE

5.1 Short-Termism in Financial Decision-Making

Short-termism remains perhaps the most entrenched structural barrier to the growth of sustainable finance. Fund managers evaluated against quarterly benchmarks have incentives that systematically discount the long-run payoffs of sustainability investments. An asset manager whose fund underperforms its benchmark for two consecutive years faces redemptions regardless of the underlying ESG quality of the portfolio. Until performance measurement frameworks are redesigned to capture long-run, risk-adjusted returns rather than short-run relative performance — a change that requires action by both institutional investors and their boards — this structural tension will persist (Rasoulinezhad & Taghizadeh-Hesary, 2022; Xu & Solangi, 2023).

5.2 ESG Measurement Inconsistency and Greenwashing

The absence of a universally accepted standard for ESG measurement and reporting is a material problem. Empirical studies have documented correlations between ESG ratings from major providers — MSCI, Sustainalytics, and ISS ESG — in the range of 0.4 to 0.6. This degree of disagreement arises from differences in scope, data inputs, weighting schemes, and assessments of what is material for a given sector. The practical consequence is that an investor using one provider's ratings may reach fundamentally different conclusions from one using another's.

Greenwashing exploits this measurement gap. Without robust third-party verification and mandatory disclosure aligned to common standards, investors cannot reliably distinguish genuine ESG leaders from companies that engage in selective disclosure. Pedersen et al. (2021) note that the ESG-efficient frontier they identify depends critically on the reliability of the underlying data; where data quality is poor, the frontier itself may be illusory in practice.

5.3 Limited Capital Allocation Toward Transformative Activities

Despite strong growth in labelled sustainable finance assets, the capital directed toward genuinely transformative sustainability activities remains insufficient at the scale the challenge requires. Much of what is categorised as "ESG investment" in practice involves tilting conventional equity or bond portfolios toward companies with better ESG scores — a meaningful but incremental change rather than a fundamental redirection of capital toward new green activities. Direct financing for early-stage climate technologies, climate adaptation infrastructure in vulnerable regions, and biodiversity protection continues to fall well short of identified needs.

5.4 Global Disparities and the Emerging Market Challenge

The global sustainable finance architecture reflects and often reinforces existing economic inequalities. The European Union has built the most comprehensive regulatory infrastructure in this space. The United States has taken a more fragmented, market-led approach. Emerging markets, by contrast, face structurally different challenges: limited domestic institutional investor bases, weak regulatory enforcement capacity, shallow capital markets, and development priorities — job creation, poverty reduction, basic infrastructure — that compete directly with sustainability investment (KRIPA, 2024).

India illustrates both the potential and the constraints of sustainable finance in an emerging economy. The Securities and Exchange Board of India (SEBI) introduced its Business Responsibility and Sustainability Report (BRSR) framework in 2021, mandating ESG disclosures for the top 1,000 listed companies from 2023. This represents genuine regulatory progress. However, the quality and comparability of disclosures under the BRSR remain variable. The domestic green bond market, while growing, is still nascent relative to India's climate finance needs. And the large public sector banks that dominate the Indian financial system continue to carry significant fossil fuel exposure that constrains the pace of portfolio decarbonisation. The gap between India's stated sustainability ambitions and its institutional realities is not a reason for pessimism, but it does call for a more contextually grounded approach to sustainable finance policy than the frameworks developed in Europe or North America readily provide.

6. BEHAVIOURAL AND ORGANISATIONAL DIMENSIONS OF ESG ADOPTION

Structural and regulatory factors alone do not determine how quickly or how deeply institutions adopt ESG principles. Organisational and behavioural dynamics play a substantial, and often underappreciated, role. Senior leadership commitment, board-level ESG expertise, internal cultural norms, and the design of management incentive systems all influence whether ESG commitments result in genuine operational change or remain at the level of disclosure and marketing (Lu & Li, 2024).

Institutional inertia is a real force. Banks and asset managers with established product lines, client relationships, and risk frameworks built around conventional assets face genuine switching costs — both operational and cultural — in moving toward sustainability-integrated approaches. Research on Chinese firms by Ning and Shen (2024) shows that even where regulatory pressure is clear, financial constraints and internal resistance can delay or dilute the intended response. ESG mandates and incentives that do not account for the organisational capacity of firms to respond may produce compliance on paper without genuine transformation in practice. This has direct implications for how regulators design transition frameworks: phased timelines, capacity-building support, and transparent implementation benchmarks are likely to produce more durable change than headline mandates alone.

The behavioural dimension also extends to investors and fund managers. Loss aversion, herding behaviour, and the asymmetric treatment of short-term underperformance relative to long-term outperformance all create psychological biases that work against the adoption of sustainability-oriented investment strategies. Addressing these biases requires changes not just in incentive structures but in how performance is communicated, benchmarked, and interpreted by investment committees and their principals.

7. ROLE OF GOVERNMENTS AND POLICY INTERVENTIONS

7.1 Government Initiatives and Incentive Design

Governments play an irreplaceable role in creating the conditions for sustainable finance to operate at scale. Beyond setting regulatory standards, they shape the risk-return landscape for sustainable investments through subsidies, tax incentives, concessional loans, and public co-investment vehicles. Sovereign green bonds have become important market-development tools, establishing pricing benchmarks and demonstrating government commitment to sustainability goals (Beschloss & Mashayekhi, n.d.). In emerging markets, the gap between private market returns and the social returns from sustainability investment is often too large for private capital to bridge unaided; in these contexts, public financial intermediation is not a temporary measure but a structural necessity.

Murau and Thie (2024) make a strong case that this is true even in advanced economies for certain categories of investment — particularly long-lived infrastructure, nature-based solutions, and climate adaptation in low-income regions, where private capital will not flow at the required scale without first-loss guarantees or subsidised return structures. The lesson from Germany's Climate and Transformation Fund, and from the US Inflation Reduction Act's investment in clean energy, is that large-scale public balance sheet commitment can catalyse private investment in ways that regulatory standards alone cannot.

7.2 Carbon Pricing and Emission Regulations

Carbon pricing mechanisms — carbon taxes and emissions trading systems (ETS) — represent a critical policy lever for aligning private financial incentives with decarbonisation goals. By putting a price on emissions, they shift the relative economics of fossil fuel versus clean energy investment and provide a continuous incentive for technological innovation. The EU Emissions Trading Scheme covers approximately 40% of EU greenhouse gas emissions and has, particularly as carbon prices have risen above €60–80 per tonne in recent years, demonstrably redirected investment toward cleaner technologies in covered sectors (Cui et al., 2023). The design of carbon pricing matters, however: prices that are too low or too volatile fail to alter investment calculus sufficiently, and jurisdictions without carbon pricing create competitive distortions for businesses that operate internationally.

7.3 International Cooperation and Global Partnerships

Sustainable finance is inherently a global challenge. Capital markets are integrated, environmental problems do not respect national boundaries, and the countries with the greatest sustainability needs often have the least capacity to meet them from domestic sources. Multilateral development banks — including the World Bank, Asian Development Bank, and European Investment Bank — are critical intermediaries for channelling concessional finance to large-scale sustainability projects in emerging markets. The Green Climate Fund, established under the UNFCCC framework, was designed to address this need, though its capitalisation has consistently fallen short of identified requirements (Antoncic et al., 2020). Closing this gap requires both greater political commitment from donor countries and improved project development capacity in recipient countries.

8. CORPORATE SOCIAL RESPONSIBILITY AND CORPORATE GOVERNANCE

8.1 The Evolving Role of CSR in Financial Institutions

Corporate Social Responsibility has evolved considerably within financial institutions — from a largely discretionary activity, associated with charitable donations and community investment programmes, to a strategic governance function that shapes lending policy, product design, and stakeholder communication. For banks and asset managers, CSR now encompasses ethical lending criteria, financial inclusion initiatives, and proactive investment in green or socially beneficial projects. In India, the Companies Act of 2013 mandates CSR spending for qualifying companies, making India one of the few jurisdictions globally where such expenditure is a legal requirement. This creates a large but heterogeneous landscape of sustainability activity whose effectiveness — and whose connection to the core financial strategy of the institution — varies considerably across firms (Panigrahi & Sukla, 2016).

8.2 Governance, Accountability, and ESG-Linked Compensation

The quality of corporate governance is one of the most reliable predictors of long-run ESG performance. Boards with relevant environmental and social expertise, independent oversight structures, and clear accountability for sustainability outcomes consistently produce more substantive ESG results than those treating sustainability as a compliance exercise. ESG-linked executive compensation — tying a portion of bonuses or long-term incentives to defined ESG targets — has become more common among large listed companies, though the credibility of this instrument depends heavily on its design. ESG metrics that are poorly defined, easily gamed, or set at levels that require minimal effort to achieve undermine the governance function they are supposed to serve.

8.3 Stakeholder Engagement

Meaningful engagement with investors, employees, communities, and regulators serves both a governance and a strategic function. On the governance side, it provides accountability mechanisms that complement formal regulatory requirements. Strategically, it enables institutions to identify ESG-related risks and opportunities before they become material financial issues. Public-private partnerships, when structured with clear governance and accountability arrangements, can mobilise capital for sustainability outcomes that neither sector could achieve independently. Adebayo et al. (2024) point to the value of life cycle assessment and shared accountability frameworks in enabling multi-stakeholder collaboration on sustainability goals, particularly in the context of project finance and infrastructure investment.

9. FUTURE TRENDS IN SUSTAINABLE FINANCE

9.1 Regulatory Convergence and Evolving ESG Standards

The current fragmentation of ESG standards is increasingly recognised as untenable. Regulatory bodies — including the International Sustainability Standards Board (ISSB), the European Financial Reporting Advisory Group (EFRAG), and national securities regulators — are working toward greater harmonisation of disclosure requirements. As standards converge and become mandatory in more jurisdictions, the ability of firms to engage in selective disclosure or greenwashing will diminish, and the quality of ESG data available to investors should improve. This will, in turn, make it easier to construct and validate the kind of ESG-efficient investment strategies that the research literature describes in theory but that are difficult to implement reliably in practice (Switzerland, n.d.).

9.2 Technology and Data in Sustainability Assessment

The next decade is likely to see artificial intelligence and real-time data analytics become central to how ESG risks are assessed, monitored, and priced. Satellite data can now track deforestation, carbon emissions, agricultural land use, and physical climate risks with a precision that was impossible a decade ago. As these data streams are integrated into credit and investment models, the pricing of ESG risk will become more accurate and more consistent across institutions. Organisations that invest early in building these analytical capabilities will be better positioned to identify risk and opportunity in the sustainable finance landscape (Hongxuan Yang, 2024).

9.3 Sustainable Finance in Emerging Markets

Emerging markets represent both the greatest need and the most significant barriers for sustainable finance. Sub-Saharan Africa, South and Southeast Asia, and Latin America face the most acute climate vulnerabilities while possessing the least financial capacity to respond. The blended finance model — combining concessional public capital with commercial investment to reduce the risk profile of sustainability projects to a level that private investors can accept — has shown genuine promise in pilot projects but has not yet scaled to the level required. In India, growing interest from sovereign wealth funds, infrastructure investors, and development finance institutions in renewable energy and sustainable agriculture suggests that this is an evolving rather than static picture, and that the conditions for more substantial capital deployment are gradually developing.

9.4 Social Impact as a Core Investment Objective

The boundary between environmental and social finance is increasingly blurred, as practitioners and researchers recognise that climate impacts, poverty, and inequality are deeply interconnected. The concept of a "just transition" — ensuring that the shift to a low-carbon economy does not disproportionately harm workers and communities dependent on carbon-intensive industries — has become an important design criterion for sustainable finance strategies. Financial products that measure and report on both environmental and social outcomes, rather than treating these as parallel but separate considerations, are likely to become more standard over the coming decade.

10. CONCLUSION: TOWARDS AN INTEGRATIVE FRAMEWORK

The central argument of this chapter is that the question of whether sustainable finance is compatible with profitability is, at its core, a question about time horizon, governance quality, and institutional design. The evidence does not support the view that ESG integration necessarily sacrifices financial returns. It does show, clearly and consistently, that the relationship between ESG performance and financial outcomes is conditional, context-specific, and mediated by structural and organisational factors that receive insufficient attention in much of the popular discourse on the subject.

Three enabling conditions appear most consistently across the evidence base. First, governance quality at the firm, market, and regulatory level is the most reliable predictor of whether ESG commitments translate into genuine practice rather than compliance theatre. Second, measurement integrity is essential: without reliable and comparable ESG data, markets cannot efficiently direct capital toward sustainability outcomes, and the greenwashing problem will persist. Third, time horizon alignment between capital providers, financial intermediaries, and the projects or firms they finance is required; where incentive structures push toward short-term returns, sustainability investments will be systematically undervalued regardless of their long-run merits.

For financial institutions in India and other emerging markets, the practical pathway is clear in broad outline, even if the implementation is genuinely difficult: develop internal ESG capacity, engage proactively with evolving regulatory frameworks, invest in sustainability data infrastructure, and use partnerships with public finance institutions to access the concessional capital needed to de-risk early-stage sustainable investments. For policymakers, the priority is creating stable and credible frameworks that reduce long-term uncertainty for investors, while directly addressing the market failures in climate adaptation and nature finance where private capital alone will not suffice.

For researchers, the most productive directions lie in more granular empirical work on the conditions governing the ESG–performance relationship in developing economies; in the organisational and behavioural determinants of ESG adoption depth; and in the effectiveness of specific policy instruments — carbon pricing, green bond mandates, blended finance structures — in mobilising private capital for sustainability at scale. The field has moved well beyond the question of whether sustainable finance is legitimate. The productive questions now are about how to design it, implement it, and evaluate it honestly.

REFERENCES

Adebayo, Y. A., Ikevuje, A. H., Kwakye, J. M., & Esiri, A. E. (2024). Balancing stakeholder interests in sustainable project management: A circular economy approach. *GSC Advanced Research and Reviews, 20*(3), 286–297. DOI: 10.30574/gscarr.2024.20.3.0354

Alim, O. (2024). Sustainable finance and economical profitability in Africa. *International Journal of Finance and Banking Research, 10*(1), 11–19. DOI: 10.11648/j.ijfbr.20241001.12

Antoncic, M., Bekaert, G., Rothenberg, R. V., & Noguer, M. (2020). Sustainable investment: Exploring the linkage between alpha, ESG, and SDGs. SSRN Electronic Journal. DOI: 10.2139/ssrn.3623459

Beschloss, A., & Mashayekhi, M. (n.d.). *A greener future for finance: Green bonds offer lessons for sustainable finance*. UNCTAD.

Cui, Q., Ma, X., & Zhang, S. (2023). Does green finance drive low-carbon economic development? Evidence from China. *Ekonomska Istraživanja, 36*(3), 2183421. Advance online publication. DOI: 10.1080/1331677X.2023.2183421

Edunjobi, T. E. (2024). Sustainable supply chain financing models: Integrating banking for enhanced sustainability. International Journal of Multidisciplinary Research Updates, 7(2), 001–011. DOI: 10.53430/ijmru.2024.7.2.0030

Fatemi, A. M., & Fooladi, I. J. (2013). Sustainable finance: A new paradigm. *Global Finance Journal, 24*(2), 101–113. DOI: 10.1016/j.gfj.2013.07.006

Katper, N., Salman, S. M., & Mohy-ud-Din, K. (2024). Unleashing the mechanism in green finance, corporate social responsibility and shareholders wealth: Insight from quantile GMM. *Global Business Review*, 09721509241276254. Advance online publication. DOI: 10.1177/09721509241276254

Kripa, E.KRIPA. (2024). Sustainable finance and management: Challenges for achieving sustainable finance and management for businesses. *Economicus, 23*(1), 5–6. DOI: 10.58944/yxou8636

Kumar, S., Sharma, D., Rao, S., Lim, W. M., & Mangla, S. K. (2022). Past, present, and future of sustainable finance: Insights from big data analytics through machine learning of scholarly research. *Annals of Operations Research*. Advance online publication. DOI: 10.1007/s10479-021-04410-8 PMID: 35002001

Lu, Z., & Li, Y. (2024). The impact of ESG on banks' sense of environmental responsibility. In *Proceedings of the 3rd International Conference on Big Data Economy and Digital Management (BDEDM 2024)* (pp. 1–11). DOI: 10.4108/eai.12-1-2024.2347202

Murau, S., & Thie, J.-E. (2024). Towards a public sustainable finance paradigm for the green transition. *Finance and Stochastics, 10*(1), 38–50. DOI: 10.1017/fas.2023.15

Ning, Y., & Shen, B. (2024). Environmental regulations, finance, and firm environmental investments: An empirical exploration. *Total Quality Management & Business Excellence, 35*(7–8), 713–738. DOI: 10.1080/14783363.2024.2329691

Panigrahi, A. K., & Sukla, T. N. (2016). Sustainable corporate social responsibility in financial institutions and banks in India. SSRN Electronic Journal. DOI: 10.2139/ssrn.2736814

Pedersen, L. H., Fitzgibbons, S., & Pomorski, L. (2021). Responsible investing: The ESG-efficient frontier. *Journal of Financial Economics, 142*(2), 572–597. DOI: 10.1016/j.jfineco.2020.11.001

Rasoulinezhad, E., & Taghizadeh-Hesary, F. (2022). Role of green finance in improving energy efficiency and renewable energy development. *Energy Efficiency, 15*(2), 14. DOI: 10.1007/s12053-022-10021-4 PMID: 35529528

Ren, Y.-S., Ma, C.-Q., Chen, X.-Q., Lei, Y.-T., & Wang, Y.-R. (2023). Sustainable finance and blockchain: A systematic review and research agenda. *Research in International Business and Finance, 64*, 101871. DOI: 10.1016/j.ribaf.2022.101871

Switzerland, W. (n.d.). Integrating ESG factors into financial models for infrastructure investments: Guidance note. World Economic Forum.

Xu, L., & Solangi, Y. A. (2023). Evaluating the impact of green bonds on renewable energy investment to promote sustainable development in China. *Journal of Renewable and Sustainable Energy, 15*(5), 055901. Advance online publication. DOI: 10.1063/5.0161387

Yang, H. (2024). Advancing sustainable development through financial innovation and investment. The Frontiers of Society. *Science and Technology, 6*(1). Advance online publication. DOI: 10.25236/FSST.2024.060111

Zhou, X., & Cui, Y. (2019). Green bonds, corporate performance, and corporate social responsibility. *Sustainability (Basel), 11*(23), 6881. DOI: 10.3390/su11236881

Chapter 5
FinTech for Sustainable Finance

Bushra Bushra
http://orcid.org/0000-0001-8377-7840
Jagan Institute of Management Studies, Delhi, India

ABSTRACT

Sustainability is the most important aspect for businesses, organizations, and companies of all types in current scenario. Scaling sustainable practices is becoming increasingly important, and the financial industry is no exception. Environmental concerns have led to a number of innovative technological and financial advancements. In the framework of digital revolution and sustainable finance, fintech has appeared as a competitive alternate to traditional financial institutions. Fintech has the potential to accelerate the growth of green finance, which tackles climate change and environmental preservation and has emerged as a means for developed nations to attain sustainable development. The achievement of "17 Sustainable Development Goals" set out by the UN will depend largely on the digital change of the financial structure and sustainable growth of economy. The chapter discusses the Fintech solutions to enable a switch toward a "low-carbon", "green", and "resilient economy". It focuses on diverse areas of association between Fintech and sustainable finance.

INTRODUCTION

The global financial system is facing two powerful pressures at present. One is the urgent need to address environmental and social crises, and the other is the rapid evolution and usage of digital financial technologies. Climate change, biodiversity loss, and widening inequality require large-scale shifts in where and how capital is

DOI: 10.4018/979-8-3373-5437-8.ch005

allocated, yet conventional financial practices have struggled to move money quickly and reliably toward sustainable outcomes (IPCC, 2022; United Nations, 2015). The digital tools and platforms have reshaped financial services, risk assessment, and access to financial products (Arner et al., 2016). This chapter explores the evolution of fintech, its scope and how fintech meaningfully advances sustainable finance. This chapter is a conceptual intervention rather than an empirical study or a policy blueprint. Its goal is to bring together ideas from technology studies, sustainability research, and finance to build a clear, usable framework for rational thinking about Fintech for sustainable finance. Sustainable finance seeks to reorient capital flows by incorporating environmental, social, and governance (ESG) considerations into financial decisions (World Bank, 2020). But even today, putting ESG principles into practice faces challenges like uneven data, costly verification, and emphasis on short-term returns over long-term stewardship. These challenges are leading to doubts about credibility and effectiveness (Kotsantonis & Serafeim, 2019; Delmas & Burbano, 2011). Fintech offers tools that could help address many of these practical obstacles. Technologies such as distributed ledgers, machine learning, and digital platforms can lower transaction costs, increase transparency, and broaden participation (Philippon, 2016; Thakor, 2020). For example, blockchain can create verifiable records for carbon credits and improve traceability in supply chains, which supports trust and accountability (Kouhizadeh et al., 2021). Machine-learning models can process large, complex datasets to identify ESG risks that human might miss, while crowdfunding and mobile finance can open opportunities for small-scale sustainable projects and underserved populations (Fuerst, 2019; Belleflamme et al., 2014; Demirgüç-Kunt et al., 2018). But technological shifts also bring risks like algorithmic bias, cybersecurity vulnerabilities, heavy energy use in some blockchain systems, and the potential to deepen digital exclusion (Narayanan et al., 2016; De Filippi & Hassan, 2016; Eubanks, 2018).

Existing research on the Fintech–sustainability nexus remains scattered. Studies often focus narrowly, either on a technology in isolation or on sustainability concerns without attention to technological affordances. They are leaving conceptual connections underdeveloped (Lee & Shin, 2018; Gomber et al., 2018). Moreover, few researchers treat technology as merely instrumental, ignoring how system designs carry values and power relationships that shape outcomes (Latour, 1992; Winner, 1980). This chapter aims to bridge those divides by offering a synthetic, conceptual clarity that brings technical, institutional, and ethical considerations into conversation. By treating Fintech as both an opportunity and a socio-technical challenge, this chapter seeks to move beyond simple optimism. It argues that Fintech can support sustainable finance, but its promise depends on purposeful design choices, inclusive access, and governance that aligns incentives with long-term public goods (De Filippi & Wright, 2018; European Banking Authority, 2019). In doing so, the chapter aims to equip researchers and decision-makers with a clearer conceptual toolkit to study and shape the emerging field of Fintech for sustainable finance.

CONCEPTUAL BACKGROUND

Fintech refers to cutting-edge technologies applied to create innovative financial products and services. This advanced business model has significant potential for alliances among public and private entities, making it one of the most significant new markets in recent times. Fintech is the use of modern technology and digital innovation to improve, develop, and automate financial services (Zhang-Zhang et al.,2020). It supports investors, industries, and customers in managing their financial activities using high-quality software and applications. Fintech usually draws clients with more automated, transparent, efficient, and accessible products and services (Moro-Visconti et al., 2020). In the financial services industry, Fintech refers more precisely to new applications, actions, and business models that comprise one or more financial services that are mostly or exclusively offered online, "simultaneously by various independent service providers, typically including at least one licensed bank or insurance company." Robo investment advising, credit decisions, asset swapping, digital currencies, automatic transactions, payment settlement, crowdsourcing, P2P transactions, and smartphone wallets are a few examples of the financial services that may be offered. (Kabulova & Stankevičienė, 2020). Fintech 3.0 started in 2008, and its early years were marked by the global financial crisis and a decline in public confidence in the banking system. Subsequently, tech companies started functioning outside of the legal framework on peer-to-peer networks and implementing new technologies in the financial markets, which transformed the nature of business in all economic sectors (Hommel & Bican, 2020). The US primarily created the largest Fintech market, which was followed by the UK, which at the time was the most significant Fintech market in Europe (Haddad, C. and Hornuf, L 2019). The features and history of European and American fintech are different from those of Asian fintech, which specialises in providing solutions for the absence of banking infrastructure (Arner et al., 2016). In developed economies, Fintech establishment is facilitated by the pre-existing infrastructure and market rules. The creation of sustainable, original financial innovation depends on this infrastructure and judiciously valued technology, even though Fintech development often takes place in nations where loan availability is more restricted. Actually, "new financial start-ups depend heavily on scalability, and Fintech's profits stay relatively small until a scalable number of customers has been convinced." Process scalability can be attained by the development of user networks and platforms, which result in economies of scale and subsequently lower costs. Better control over one's personal finances, quick financial decision-making, and the capacity to send and receive money swiftly are among fintech's main benefits; nevertheless, these come at the expense of efficiency and data security. "So, from a regulatory standpoint, the biggest challenges are then to guarantee financial stability and to ensure both investor and consumer protection" (Ozili, P.K 2018).

Fintech "gives flexibility to all actors by enabling business transactions to be performed from anywhere at any time" (al Hammadi & Nobanee, 2019). Businesses that have created Fintech have more creative ways to provide investors and consumers with banking services via smartphone apps; their financial services are more flexible and efficient; and they provide the possibility of time and money savings by utilising digital technologies (Zhang-Zhang et al.,2020). Moreover, by creating the framework for a cutting-edge digital financial ecosystem, Fintech plays a pivotal role in promoting "financial development, inclusion, social stability and integrity, and resulting sustainable development." It signifies the digitalisation of the financial industry by changing the methods in which traditional services are provided and making financial services more efficient, economical, and reachable for clients (Hommel & Bican, 2020). "Fintech, a new industry with distinct characteristics from the traditional financial industry, is also viewed as an engine for sustainable economic growth." Fintech investments have surged globally, driven by high growth expectations. Indeed, according to a KPMG analysis, "between 2013 and 2018, global investment in Fintech has doubled more than six times, from $18.9 billion to $111.8 billion" (Ryu, H.S and Ko, K.S., 2020).

The most pioneering technical advancement in the finance industry is fintech. Fintech can add value in all areas of finance, even though the majority of it focuses on a single market segment. Examples of these include payments, wealth management, crowdfunding, lending, and capital market business models. Peer-to-peer financing (P2P), stock crowdfunding, innovative digital advisory and trading systems, artificial intelligence and machine learning, and mobile payment systems are just a few of the instruments they employ. The most widely used Fintech solutions at the moment are digital payments and mobile banking, which are becoming more and more important as a result of contactless epidemic prescriptions (Deng et al., 2019). Because of its incredible improvements for the financial system and other infrastructure, fintech is extremely disruptive and has an impact on many other areas, including the energy industry, the economy, and society. Fintech also encourages the use of funds for energy and environmental projects, as well as the building of renewable energy and ecological infrastructure, "leading to environmental and ecological development by providing cheap and adequate financing," which has several affirmative effects on social, environmental, and ecological benefits (Deng et al., 2019). Thanks to "technological implementation, related digital economy business models, and integrated services from different areas," fintech provides "offerings beyond the traditional banking boundaries". It opens up new avenues for conducting business in the financial markets. Furthermore, technology is adding value to the financial services industry by decreasing costs significantly and increasing profits due to quicker and anytime-anywhere banking (Moro-Visconti et al., 2020).

FINTECH EVOLUTION AND SCOPE

Pre-1990s: The foundations of modern Fintech were laid in the 1960s with the introduction of technologies like ATMs (Automated Teller Machines), the electronic funds transfer system (EFTS), and credit cards. The development of online banking and electronic trading platforms in the 1980s began to change how financial institutions and individuals interacted with money.

The Internet Age (1990s-2000s): The widespread adoption of the Internet enabled the launch of online banking services. Banks began to offer basic financial services such as account management and bill payments over the web. The advent of PayPal was a significant moment, as it allowed individuals and businesses to conduct transactions online securely, setting the stage for the e-commerce boom.

Fintech Revolution (2010s): The proliferation of smartphones enabled mobile banking applications, making it easy for customers to conduct banking transactions from anywhere. With the launch of Bitcoin (2009), the use of blockchain technology introduced new concepts like decentralised finance (DeFi) and cryptocurrencies, changing the landscape of digital assets. Platforms like Lending Club and Zopa made it possible for borrowers and lenders to connect directly, bypassing traditional financial institutions.

Expanding Frontiers (2020s and beyond): Artificial Intelligence (AI) and Machine Learning are now used to enhance customer experiences (e.g., chatbots and robo-advisors), detect fraud, and improve investment strategies. Governments and regulators are encouraging open banking frameworks, enabling consumers to share their financial data with third-party service providers for better service offerings. As the world shifts toward more environmentally conscious practices, Fintech is playing a critical role in promoting green finance and sustainable investments through innovative tools like carbon footprint tracking apps and green bond issuance.

SCOPE OF FINTECH

Payments: - Digital Payments Platforms like PayPal, Stripe, and Square have transformed how individuals and businesses transfer money globally. "Mobile Payment Apps like Venmo, Google Pay, and Apple Pay" have become essential tools for peer-to-peer payments and contactless transactions. Digital currencies like Bitcoin, Ethereum, and stablecoins (e.g., USDC) are being used for both speculative investment and as a payment method, albeit with volatility concerns.

Lending: Peer-to-peer (P2P) Lending options like "Prosper and Funding Circle" connect individual borrowers with lenders, providing an alternative to traditional bank loans. Digital Lenders like SoFi and Upstart offer personal loans, student loan refinancing, and mortgages using advanced data analytics to assess creditworthiness. "Buy Now, Pay Later (BNPL)" services like "Klarna, Afterpay, and Affirm" let consumers divide payments into parts without using traditional credit cards.

WealthTech: Robo-Advisors, automated investment platforms like Betterment, Wealthfront, and Acorns, use algorithms to provide personalised financial assistance and portfolio management at a fraction of the price of human counsellors. Online Brokerage platforms like Robinhood, E*TRADE, and Charles Schwab provide low-cost or commission-free trading of stocks, ETFs, and other financial instruments. Digital Wealth Management companies like Personal Capital and Ally Invest use data analytics and AI to provide personalised financial planning and asset management solutions.

InsurTech: On-demand insurance platforms like Lemonade and Trov use AI to offer real-time, customizable insurance policies that consumers can purchase instantly via mobile apps. Fintech innovations allow companies to provide flexible insurance plans based on usage or behaviour, such as auto insurance that tracks driving habits via telematics. AI is revolutionising how claims are processed by using data to detect fraud and automate approval processes, making the experience faster and more efficient for customers.

RegTech (Regulatory Technology): Fintech tools like Comply Advantage and Trulioo help financial institutions stay compliant with "anti-money laundering (AML)" regulations, "know-your-customer (KYC)" standards, and other legal requirements. RegTech solutions use AI and big data to monitor and assess risk, ensuring real-time reporting and better governance.

Blockchain and Cryptocurrencies: Decentralised Finance (DeFi) aimed at disrupting traditional finance, DeFi platforms like Uniswap, Aave, and Compound use blockchain technology to provide decentralised lending, borrowing, and trading. Smart Contracts are self-executing deals with the terms transcribed directly into code, used in various blockchain applications to eliminate intermediaries in transactions. There has never been more urgency to combat climate change and reduce environmental hazards. Extreme weather, rising global temperatures, and ecological impacts emphasise the urgency of taking quick action. By offering a framework for coordinating financial decisions with environmental goals, sustainable finance makes sure that economic activity is carried out in a way that respects the planet's natural systems. The following are the urgent points to be considered for sustainable finance: -

Social Responsibility: Sustainable finance acknowledges the social aspect of economic growth in addition to environmental issues. It places a strong emphasis on advancing human welfare, diversity, and social justice. Green finance aims to enhance community resilience, support sustainable livelihoods, and alleviate social inequities by integrating social factors into financial decision-making.

Economic Resilience: Aiming to strengthen economic resilience, sustainable finance acknowledges the interconnections of the environment and the economy. Through the allocation of resources towards sustainable infrastructure, clean technology, and renewable energy, the aim is to establish an environmentally sustainable economy that is resilient to the effects of climate change and resource scarcity.

Environmental Imperatives: There has never been more urgency to combat climate change and reduce environmental hazards. Extreme weather, rising global temperatures, and ecological impacts emphasise the urgency of taking quick action. By offering a framework for coordinating financial decisions with environmental goals, sustainable finance makes sure that economic activity is carried out in a way that respects the planet's natural systems.

SUSTAINABLE FINANCE AND ESG

Sustainable finance refers to financial activities that consider not only economic factors but also "the environmental, social, and governance (ESG)" aspects to promote long-run sustainability and responsible investment. It involves channelling capital to projects and companies that align with "sustainable development goals", such as "combating climate change, promoting social equity, and enhancing governance transparency". Sustainable finance seeks to foster a more inclusive, resilient, and green financial system by encouraging investments in "renewable energy, energy efficiency, and low-carbon technologies". It promotes social impact initiatives, such as affordable housing, education, and healthcare. It supports companies that adhere to ethical governance standards and responsible business practices. Sustainable finance aims to balance the pursuit of financial returns with broader societal and environmental objectives, ensuring long-run value creation for all stakeholders.

ESG framework provides a structured approach to assessing the sustainability and ethical impact of investments in three key areas: -

Environmental (E) focuses on how a company or project impacts the natural environment. Investors assess factors like **Climate change mitigation, Carbon footprint, Resource efficiency** in water, energy, and raw materials, **Waste management**, and Biodiversity and the impact on ecosystems. Examples of environmentally sustainable investments include financing renewable energy projects, for instance, wind and solar power, and supporting companies that reduce carbon emissions or engage in sustainable farming.

The Social (S) aspect evaluates in what way a company manages dealings with its stakeholders, including workers, dealers, clients, and societies. Key considerations include "**Human rights** and labour standards, **Diversity, equity, and inclusion** in the workplace, **Health and safety"** policies for employees and consumers, **Community engagement**, and social impact. Investments that focus on the social component of ESG could involve microfinance initiatives for underserved populations and companies that prioritise fair wages, employee well-being, or ethical supply chains.

Governance (G) evaluates the internal practices and policies a company uses to govern itself, ensuring transparency, accountability, and compliance with laws. Governance factors include **Board diversity and independence, Executive compensation** aligned with long-term performance, **Ethical business practices**, anti-corruption measures, **Transparency** in financial reporting, and shareholder relations. Examples of governance-focused investments include supporting companies with diverse and independent boards and investing in firms with a strong record of corporate governance and ethical leadership.

PRINCIPLES FOR RESPONSIBLE INVESTMENTS

The **Principles for Responsible Investments (PRI)** is a set of voluntary rules propelled by the United Nations in 2006 to encourage depositors to incorporate ESG factors into their investment decisions. The goal is to promote sustainable and ethical investments that contribute to long-term value creation. PRI aims to create a worldwide network of investors devoted to assimilating ESG elements into investment decisions to promote sustainable markets. By following the PRI principles, investors can help align capital with broader social goals, for instance, combating "climate change, reducing inequality, and fostering responsible business practices". PRI encourages long-term thinking in investment strategies, helping to mitigate risks and capitalise on opportunities associated with sustainability.

PRI principles are as follows:

"Incorporating ESG Issues into Investment Analysis and Decision-Making": Investors should systematically integrate ESG factors into their investment processes, considering how environmental, social, and governance risks and opportunities may affect the financial performance of their portfolios.

"Being Active Owners and Incorporating ESG into Ownership Policies": Responsible investors should actively engage with the companies they invest in, using shareholder rights to influence corporate behaviour and improve ESG performance.

"Seeking Appropriate Disclosure on ESG Issues by Investee Companies": Investors should encourage the companies they invest in to provide transparent, regular, and accurate reporting on ESG issues, ensuring that they have sufficient information to assess risks and opportunities.

"Promoting Acceptance and Implementation of the Principles within the Investment Industry": Investors should work to raise awareness about responsible investing practices and encourage other investors, asset managers, and service providers to adopt the PRI principles.

"Working Together to Enhance Effectiveness in Implementing the Principles": Collaboration among investors is encouraged to increase the impact of ESG efforts. Working together allows investors to pool resources, share best practices, and engage more effectively with companies.

"Reporting on Activities and Progress Toward Implementing the Principles": Investors should regularly report on their progress in implementing the PRI principles, ensuring transparency and accountability in their approach to responsible investment.

FINTECH'S ROLE IN ENHANCING SUSTAINABILITY

Fintech has completely transformed the approach to financial transactions by utilising digital breakthroughs like "blockchain, artificial intelligence, and big data analytics". Green financial services are creating new opportunities for sustainable and inclusive finance. Financial technology can expedite the shift to a "low-carbon economy", improve environmental hazard management, and inspire responsible investing from the perspective of sustainability and green finance. There is a rare chance to address urgent social and environmental issues at the nexus of fintech and sustainable finance. Fintech businesses are in a unique position to use their technology know-how to advance sustainable business practices and positive change in the financial sector. The creation of novel financing structures is one of the main ways fintech is advancing sustainable finance. "Green bonds" are financial instruments that are used to raise money for initiatives that are environmentally sustainable. By facilitating communication between investors and issuers and offering clear details about the underlying projects, fintech platforms have simplified investor involvement in the green bond market. Impact investing is another sector in which fintech is having a big influence. Investments made to produce measurable social and environmental welfare in addition to financial returns are referred to as impact investments. Fintech platforms enable individuals and institutions to support initiatives that are consistent with their beliefs by facilitating the pairing of impact investors with social entrepreneurs and sustainable projects. Because they offer cutting-edge instruments for monitoring and lowering carbon footprints, fintech solutions are significantly contributing to the progression of environmental goals. To quantify and verify the environmental effect of investments and businesses, for example, blockchain technology can be used to produce transparent and immutable records of carbon emissions. Fintech platforms are also making it possible for people and companies to quantify their carbon footprints and make investments in renewable energy projects to offset those footprints. With the help of these platforms' intuitive interfaces and automated procedures, people are finding it simpler to take proactive steps to lessen their environmental impact. According to Elsaid (2023), fintech companies have the potential to shift banks in some markets, hence forcing banks to adopt cutting-edge innovations and technology. The strategic alliances and collaborations can be valuable for banks and fintech companies alike. According to Cen and He (2018), fintech has a positive effect on sustainable finance by lowering transaction costs, increasing capital productivity, refining risk management, lowering information irregularities, and expanding the scope of green finance. According to Mejia-Escobar et al., (2020), sustainable financial resolutions thrive in the rapidly developing fintech ecosystem, mainly when viewed through the lens of societal and financial inclusiveness in the Latin American context. In a similar way, Yang (2020) described how fintech contributes to the progress of green finance by lowering bank credit risk, raising the bar for regulation, encouraging product innovation, and refining the information-sharing system. According to Moro-Visconti et al., (2020), fintech will increase access to capital and investment by enhancing financial inclusion, which further supports these ideas. One of the key benefits is financial inclusion, which is particularly important for developing nations because, in addition to individuals, many SMEs that contribute to production need access to financial services because they lack investment. It is important to incorporate and address the economic and social demands of as many businesses as feasible in the financial system for green finance to successfully adhere to the core principles of distributing funding to practices in line with the SDGs. According to Tseng et al., (2018), the environmental aspects of sustainable supply chain finance are influenced by the economic and social components. Anshari et al., (2019) offer a concept of a fintech-enabled digital marketplace that empowers farmers with payment and crowdfunding methods to include those who are economically disadvantaged in production. Other authors focused on the combined effects of sustainability and fintech on the financial services sector, contending that they are simultaneously bringing about a noteworthy change in the financial sector. For instance, Hommel and Bican (2020) studied how fintech and traditional institutions might work together through outsourcing, partnership, or venture capitalist investment. Though this is a genuine argument, Puschmann et al., (2020) examined this alliance from a different angle, contending that sustainability and digitisation are indisputably the key forces behind a shift in the financial services sector and that "green FinTech" is still understudied. The authors precisely addressed how green fintech affects "customer-to-customer, business-to-business, and business-to-customer service" sectors along the entire financial services value chain. According to Chueca Vergara and Ferruz Agudo (2021), fintech and sustainable finance have many features, and by encouraging green financing, fintech can aid financial firms in becoming more sustainable overall.

Fintech increases total business sustainability and advances green financing (Cristina Chueca Vergara & Luis Ferruz Agudo, 2021). Through digital platforms for sustainable investment management, data visualisation tools, and advanced analytics, ESG integration is made easier (Varsha, V. R., 2024). By encouraging green finance, boosting ESG performance, expanding financial inclusion, and assisting with investments in renewable energy, fintech catalyses sustainable development (Huang, 2025). Fintech supports sustainable practices in the financial industry, and scholars are becoming more interested in comprehending this connection (Rahman et al., 2024). While maintaining financial stability and inclusion, the combination of fintech with sustainable finance has exciting prospects for promoting favourable social and environmental results. Fintech can maximise social impact in areas such as Sub-Saharan Africa by including environmental, social, and governance variables into investment decisions (Simo et al., 2025). By encouraging inclusiveness, particularly among excluded populations, and having a beneficial impact on corporate financial performance, it has changed the financial landscape (Ghose et al., 2025). Innovation is being fueled by cutting-edge technology like blockchain, AI, and big data analysis in several financial industries (Kumar, 2024). Financial sectors are changing as a result of fintech advancements, including blockchain, artificial intelligence, and big data analysis (Kumar, 2024). Particularly during the COVID-19 pandemic, when digital platforms became indispensable, these technologies are vital to the implementation of the Sustainable Development Goals (SDGs) (Zahid & Jillani, 2023). Four major clusters have emerged as a result of the integration of fintech with Environmental, Social, and Governance (ESG) principles: big data, AI, cryptocurrency, and sustainable fintech (Alqudah et al., 2024). Only one article published between 2019 and 2022 explicitly addresses the intersection of fintech and sustainable finance, despite the growing significance of fintech in this field (Pratiwi & Simorangkir, 2025).

SUSTAINABLE FINTECH IN INDIA AND GLOBAL COMPARISONS

The evolution of fintech as a transformative force in financial markets has coincided with the global imperative to address climate change and social inequalities, giving rise to the domain of sustainable fintech. The historical trajectory of this convergence shows how technology-first solutions in payments, lending, and asset management gradually integrated sustainability through the demand for transparency, responsible investing, and climate-risk mitigation. In India, this evolution has been shaped by its longstanding struggle with financial exclusion and underdeveloped capital markets. Unlike advanced economies where fintech initially focused on efficiency and customer experience, Indian fintech has been closely tied to developmental goals, often aiming to provide access to unbanked and underbanked populations (Jena, 2025). This orientation created fertile ground for the embedding of sustainability objectives. Rooftop solar financing, for example, demonstrates how India applies fintech beyond traditional finance, using public credit guarantees and digital risk modelling to make renewable energy more affordable for households and small businesses (Jena, 2022). At the same time, India's regulatory innovations such as the Unified Payments Interface (UPI) and Aadhaar-based authentication have lowered transaction costs, allowing sustainable financial products like green loans and ESG-linked investment instruments to reach millions at scale. Yet, the very speed of this growth raises questions about oversight. Sreenu & Verma (2024) emphasises that the green bond market in India, while expanding, faces challenges in verification and risk assessment, which can undermine investor confidence if not addressed. Moreover, India's pilot programs in central bank digital currencies (CBDCs) point toward new possibilities in programmable finance, with sustainability-linked disbursements for agricultural subsidies or renewable energy adoption, though their success will depend on trust, usability, and public acceptance (Sandhu, Dayanandan, & Kuntluru, 2023). Globally, sustainable fintech adoption reflects different trajectories: Europe leads through regulatory enforcement and carbon accounting platforms; the United States leverages advanced analytics for institutional ESG products; and China pushes digital green lending despite opacity in disclosures (Sreenu & Verma, 2024). The diversity of these approaches highlights that sustainable fintech is not a monolithic phenomenon but rather a mosaic shaped by unique institutional contexts.

India's sustainable fintech landscape is further distinguished by its ability to integrate public digital infrastructure with private innovation, creating a model distinct from both advanced and other emerging economies. Research shows that financial inclusion in rural India depends on digital literacy, trust, and local infrastructure (Jena, 2025), factors that remain barriers but are being systematically addressed through government-backed digital frameworks. This contrasts with regions such as Latin America and sub-Saharan Africa, where digital finance has grown rapidly but without the same depth of public infrastructure, leading to fragmentation. For example, while Brazil channels fintech innovation toward biodiversity and forest conservation finance, and African economies deploy green microfinance models, their scalability remains constrained by limited interoperability and uneven regulatory support (Jena, 2025). Europe, in comparison, benefits from a harmonised sustainable finance taxonomy, which enhances investor trust and fosters fintech adoption in ESG compliance and reporting (Kishor, Bansal, & Kumar, 2025). The US market emphasises institutional sophistication, applying AI and blockchain to model climate risks for asset managers, yet struggles with fragmented regulations across states (Sandhu et al., 2023). The UK's innovation sandboxes provide a middle ground, balancing regulation with experimentation in green products. Meanwhile, China's strong digital lending ecosystem integrates sustainability through large-scale financing of renewable energy projects but lacks standardised ESG verification mechanisms (Sreenu & Verma, 2024). India, by contrast, has scaled its green debt markets while simultaneously leveraging fintech to democratize access, resulting in a dual orientation: achieving inclusion and sustainability in tandem. This positions India uniquely, with lessons that could inform other emerging economies seeking to align digital finance with sustainability goals. However, these achievements remain tempered by gaps in ESG verification, risks of greenwashing, and a persistent rural-urban digital divide. Kishor et al., (2025) argue that fintech holds significant potential to accelerate the Sustainable Development Goals (SDGs) by embedding ESG factors into financial systems, but they also highlight the necessity of standardised metrics and governance frameworks—areas where India must continue to evolve.

Table 1.

Dimension	India	Global (Europe, US, China, Emerging Markets)	Source(s)
Primary Drivers	Financial inclusion, developmental priorities, public digital infrastructure (UPI, Aadhaar), rooftop solar finance	Europe: compliance & ESG reporting; US: advanced analytics & institutional ESG products; China: large-scale green lending; LATAM/ Africa: biodiversity & microfinance	Jena (2022, 2025); Kishor et al., (2025); Sreenu & Verma (2024)
Digital Infrastructure	UPI, Aadhaar, Digital Public Infrastructure (DPI), CBDC pilots enabling scalable, sustainable finance	Europe: open banking + taxonomy frameworks; US: fragmented regulation but advanced platforms; Africa/Latin America: fragmented infrastructure, limited interoperability	Jena (2025); Sandhu et al., (2023)
Sustainable Finance Instruments	Green bonds, ESG-linked loans, rooftop solar financing, digital credit guarantees	Europe: standardised green bonds & carbon accounting; US: AI-driven climate risk models; China: opaque but large renewable energy lending	Jena (2022); Sreenu & Verma (2024)
Regulatory Orientation	Proactive but evolving – focus on financial inclusion first, sustainability second; limited ESG verification frameworks.	Europe: strong, standardised taxonomy; US: fragmented, innovation-led; China: policy-driven but weak ESG transparency	Kishor et al., (2025); Sreenu & Verma (2024)
Inclusion & Accessibility	High priority – fintech used to bring sustainability-linked products to rural & underserved populations	Global North: focused on institutional investors; LATAM & Africa: inclusion is present but limited by infrastructure gaps	Jena (2025); Kishor et al., (2025)
Innovation Examples	Rooftop solar financing (credit guarantees), CBDC-linked subsidies for agriculture & renewables (pilot stage)	Europe: ESG compliance platforms; US: blockchain-based carbon markets; China: green digital lending platforms	Jena (2022); Sandhu et al., (2023); Sreenu & Verma (2024)
Key Challenges	Digital divide, weak ESG verification, risk of greenwashing, regulatory uncertainty	Europe: costly compliance; US: fragmented regulation; China: opacity & credibility issues; Emerging economies: scale & governance	Kishor et al., (2025); Sreenu & Verma (2024)
Strategic Position	Unique hybrid: combines inclusion (scale) + sustainability (green finance instruments)	Advanced economies: institutional ESG sophistication; Emerging markets: fragmented but innovative	Jena (2025); Kishor et al., (2025)

The challenges and opportunities facing India's sustainable fintech ecosystem illustrate the broader dynamics of the global transition to sustainable finance. A comparative perspective underscores that while Europe's strength lies in compliance and verification, and the US in technological sophistication, India's advantage lies in its ability to reach vast underserved populations through scalable digital platforms (Jena, 2025). Yet, this inclusivity-driven model faces risks: without robust taxonomies, India's green bond and ESG-linked products risk credibility erosion, echoing challenges seen in China's opaque green lending practices (Sreenu & Verma, 2024).

Similarly, while programmable CBDCs offer a transformative opportunity to link subsidies or credit to sustainability outcomes, their adoption is uncertain, as user trust and institutional readiness remain critical (Sandhu et al., 2023). At the same time, the digital divide poses both a social and environmental risk, as expanding digital finance infrastructure requires significant energy inputs, raising questions about net sustainability impacts (Kishor et al., 2025). Nevertheless, India's progress highlights the possibility of crafting sustainable fintech models that are both inclusive and scalable, a path that contrasts with advanced economies' focus on institutional ESG integration. For India to consolidate its leadership role, it must address regulatory uncertainty, build robust ESG verification systems, and invest in digital literacy to ensure equitable access. If successful, India could emerge as a blueprint for other emerging economies, demonstrating that sustainable fintech can simultaneously drive financial inclusion and climate action. By balancing rapid innovation with careful governance, India has the potential to transform sustainable fintech from a niche to a mainstream mechanism for achieving the twin goals of equitable development and environmental resilience (Jena, 2022; Jena, 2025; Kishor et al., 2025; Sandhu et al., 2023; Sreenu & Verma, 2024).

TRENDS IN SUSTAINABLE FINTECH

Green loans and sustainable finance: Banks through green financial programs include "HSBC's Green Hub, Lloyds' Clean Growth Financing Initiative, and Barclays' Green Loan". Financial facilities providers can develop mortgage products that encourage businesses to prioritise sustainability. The advantages of these mortgages can include lower interest rates or other financial inducements for industries investing in energy-efficient technologies.

Digital payments and signatures: Electronic signatures and mobile banking choices are significantly assisting in lowering the environmental effect of traditional banking techniques and resulting in a decrease in cash use as digital payments proliferate across markets and industries. The use of paper in banking branches and offices has significantly decreased as a result of back-end digitalisation. In fact, the move to digital banking has resulted in more sustainable financial practices as well as greater accessibility for customers.

Green Investments: The amount of money invested globally in green projects has increased dramatically recently. Bank investment arms continue to support green investment portfolios, while investment firms that specialise in providing green money to environmentally friendly initiatives, such as Green Investment Group and Green Investment Partners, are growing in popularity.

Carbon tracking: Technology that tracks carbon emissions has been introduced to satisfy consumer demands to understand the carbon footprint of the products they buy. Fintech companies, such as Ecolytiq, recognise the importance of providing carbon tracking technology to assist in monitoring emissions, given their growing popularity and commercial scale as financial institutions. Additional digital technologies, such as blockchain, allow for the real-time tracking of CO2 emissions, which helps businesses reduce their environmental impact and better manage their carbon footprints.

Mobile payment solutions for carbon offsetting: The use of mobile payment methods to offset carbon emissions has increased. With the help of these services, consumers can reforest areas or support renewable energy initiatives to offset the carbon emissions caused by financial transactions. By offsetting their environmental impact, mobile applications like "TreeCard and Doconomy" help consumers track their carbon footprint and make eco-friendly decisions, supporting efforts to combat climate change.

Carbon-neutral payment processing methods: Through renewable energy projects, carbon emissions are offset by carbon-neutral payment processing techniques. These initiatives, which are specifically designed with payment processors in mind, support the adoption of energy-efficient technologies and the choice of renewable energy sources to lessen the negative environmental effects of payment processors and contribute to the goal of a net-zero carbon footprint. "Pay-As-You-Go" solutions, such as those provided by Switch2Zero, allow businesses to balance their impact on a range of environmentally beneficial projects.

Contactless payments for sustainable transportation: Because contactless payments make card payments easier to complete, they have eliminated the need for cash and paper tickets on public transit, reducing the amount of paper used and eliminating the need for currency. These days, contactless payments have made it easier to use bike and scooter rental services like Lime, encouraging the use of non-automotive transportation in large cities and lessening the effect of automobile emissions.

Digital wallets to reduce waste and emissions: Smartphone digital wallets make it easier to finish payments made with a mobile device. This lessens the requirement for paper documents as well as the amount of plastic trash produced by credit and debit card wear and tear. Customers are using mobile wallets more frequently as a more suitable method of payment, encouraging the use of sustainable infrastructure and renewable energy sources.

PROJECTED SUSTAINABLE FINTECH TRENDS (2025–2030) IN INDIA AND GLOBALLY

India's sustainable fintech ecosystem is poised for transformative growth between 2025 and 2030, largely due to the convergence of digital public infrastructure, government initiatives, and private innovation. The domestic green bond market, which reached USD 10.3 billion in 2023, is projected to expand at an annual growth rate of around 35 per cent, with volumes potentially surpassing USD 50–60 billion by 2030 (Sreenu & Verma, 2024). Fintech-enabled mechanisms such as digital lending and public credit guarantees are expected to accelerate renewable energy adoption, particularly in rooftop solar and electric vehicles, with SME participation projected to rise by 30–40 per cent (Jena, 2022). India's digital backbone, built through the Unified Payments Interface (UPI) and Aadhaar, creates a unique advantage by combining efficiency with scale. UPI already processed more than 12.2 billion monthly transactions in 2023, while Aadhaar authentication covers over 1.3 billion citizens, allowing sustainability-linked products to reach even the most underserved segments (Jena, 2025). Complementing this, the Reserve Bank of India's central bank digital currency (CBDC) pilot—the Digital Rupee—could reduce subsidy transaction costs by up to 25 per cent, while enabling programmable payments tied to environmental outcomes (Sandhu, Dayanandan, & Kuntluru, 2023). Despite these gains, challenges remain. Weak ESG verification systems, the risk of greenwashing, and limited rural financial literacy pose barriers. However, the introduction of a national ESG taxonomy by 2027 is expected to strengthen disclosure practices and align India more closely with global standards (Kishor, Bansal, & Kumar, 2025). Collectively, these developments indicate that India's trajectory is not just about financial growth but about embedding sustainability into its inclusive digital finance architecture—an approach that could serve as a blueprint for other emerging economies.

Globally, the sustainable fintech landscape is also projected to evolve rapidly, but in different ways across regions. Europe is expected to remain the global leader, accounting for more than half of global green bond issuance by 2030, largely because of its harmonised EU taxonomy and strong regulatory alignment. The rollout of the Digital Euro is likely to further integrate sustainability into mainstream financial infrastructure (Sreenu, 2024). The United States, by contrast, is expected to deepen its reliance on blockchain, AI, and advanced data analytics for climate-risk modelling, though fragmented state-level regulation could constrain uniform adoption (Sandhu et al., 2023). China's strategy is centred on scaling the digital yuan (e-CNY) for green lending and renewable project financing, but persistent weaknesses in ESG transparency may limit its global credibility (Sreenu & Verma, 2024). Meanwhile, Latin America and sub-Saharan Africa are projected to expand financial inclusion significantly through mobile platforms, though ESG integration will likely progress more slowly due to infrastructure gaps and weaker regulatory capacity (Jena, 2025). Kishor et al., (2025) emphasise that fintech's contribution to achieving the Sustainable Development Goals (SDGs) will ultimately depend on the adoption of standard taxonomies, stronger governance, and cross-border collaboration. This creates a clear bifurcation: advanced economies will focus on compliance-driven ESG sophistication, while emerging economies such as India will experiment with scalable, technology-driven models of inclusion and sustainability. If India successfully addresses credibility and literacy challenges, it could not only narrow the regulatory gap with advanced economies but also define a new global paradigm for how fintech can democratize access to sustainable finance.

CHALLENGES AND POTENTIAL RISKS OF FINTECH IN SUSTAINABLE FINANCE

Data Privacy and Security: Fintech has a lot of potential to advance sustainable finance, but it also has risks and limitations. The requirement for strong data privacy and security procedures is one of the main obstacles. It is essential to make sure that the vast volumes of personal and financial data that fintech platforms gather and handle are shielded from abuse and illegal access.

Potential for Algorithmic Bias: Potential algorithmic bias is another problem. Algorithms are frequently used by fintech services to automate choices like investment advice or loan approvals. These algorithms have the potential to maintain discrimination and inequality if they are trained on skewed or inadequate data. To guarantee just and equitable results, fintech companies must aggressively address and minimise these prejudices. It is a valid argument in favour of keeping people informed, which is something we definitely do.

FUTURE TRENDS AND OPPORTUNITIES IN THE FIELD OF FINTECH

Fintech in sustainable finance is not without dangers and problems, but these may be managed with strong regulatory frameworks and ethical business practices. Fintech's future in sustainable finance looks bright, with new developments and opportunities in store. We should anticipate more environmental and social considerations being incorporated into financial decision-making processes as technology develops. Sustainable finance activities will continue to be streamlined and automated by fintech platforms, increasing their use and accessibility. Furthermore, new prospects for sustainable finance are brought about by the development of blockchain technology and decentralised finance (DeFi). DeFi systems increase accessibility by doing away with the need for middlemen and providing decentralised, transparent financial services. This has the potential to democratise sustainable finance by enabling people to actively engage in initiatives and projects that are consistent with their values. Fintech has become a potent instrument for encouraging sustainability and igniting constructive social change. Fintech companies are transforming sustainable finance by incorporating social and environmental considerations into investment decision-making processes through the use of cutting-edge technologies. We can expedite the shift towards a more sustainable and equitable global economy, where environmental and social objectives are prioritised in financial decision-making, by utilising the revolutionary potential of fintech.

IMPLICATIONS AND CONCLUSION

The growing convergence of fintech and sustainable finance has significant implications for policymakers, financial institutions, investors, fintech firms, and researchers. For policymakers and regulators, the findings highlight the need to establish robust regulatory frameworks that encourage responsible fintech innovation while ensuring data privacy, cybersecurity, algorithmic transparency, and standardised ESG disclosures. Financial institutions should leverage emerging technologies such as artificial intelligence, blockchain, big data analytics, and digital platforms to enhance sustainable investment practices, improve ESG risk assessment, expand green financing, and promote financial inclusion, particularly for underserved individuals and MSMEs. Fintech firms can capitalise on these opportunities by developing innovative financial products such as green lending, carbon-tracking solutions, impact investing platforms, and sustainable digital payment systems that support the achievement of the Sustainable Development Goals (SDGs). For investors, fintech-enabled ESG analytics can facilitate more transparent, data-driven, and responsible investment decisions while improving the measurement and monitoring of environmental and social impacts. From an academic perspective, the review identifies substantial research gaps, particularly concerning empirical evidence on the effectiveness of green fintech, the long-term impact of AI-driven financial services on sustainability outcomes, and cross-country comparative analyses in emerging economies. Future research should therefore focus on developing integrated theoretical and empirical frameworks that examine the dynamic relationship between fintech innovation, ESG performance, financial inclusion, and sustainable economic development across diverse institutional contexts.

Investors are becoming more willing to consider non-financial factors in addition to financial ones when making investment decisions, which has resulted in the emergence of various financial tools and trends. These include concerns about environmental issues and global warming, the importance of corporate social responsibility, and environmental, social, and governance factors. As it is responsible for funding the investments required to turn our economy into one that is more sustainable, the financial sector is crucial to the battle against climate change in the current context. Traditional providers as well as Fintech companies—which strive to innovate, improve, and automate financial services—offer new financial services related to sustainability. Fintech companies, which employ specialised apps and software to help businesses, investors, and consumers manage their financial activities, are growing in popularity and are expected to continue expanding. In addition, the Fintech sector contributes to sustainable economic growth in several ways that help society and the environment itself. Fintech can encourage the use of finances for energy and environmental projects, as well as the building of renewable energy and environmental infrastructure, in order to contribute to ecological and environmental development. Fintech uses techniques like crowdfunding, big data analytics, blockchain technology, and artificial intelligence to demonstrate stability and consistency with ESG requirements. Fintech may raise the sustainability of the financial industry as a whole by promoting green money.

REFERENCES

Al Hammadi, T., & Nobanee, H. (2019). *FinTech and sustainability: A mini-review. SSRN*. DOI: 10.2139/ssrn.3500873

Alqudah, H., Akour, I., Al-Debei, M. M., & Al-Lozi, E. (2024). Integration of fintech with ESG principles: Emerging clusters and implications. *Journal of Sustainable Finance & Investment, 14*(2), 215–232.

Anshari, M., Almunawar, M. N., Masri, M., & Hamdan, M. (2019). Digital marketplace and FinTech to support agricultural sustainability. *Energy Procedia, 156*, 234–238. DOI: 10.1016/j.egypro.2018.11.134

Arner, D. W., Barberis, J., & Buckley, R. P. (2016). The evolution of FinTech: A new post-crisis paradigm? *Georgetown Journal of International Law, 47*, 1271–1319.

Belleflamme, P., Lambert, T., & Schwienbacher, A. (2014). Crowdfunding: Tapping the right crowd. *Journal of Business Venturing, 29*(5), 585–609. DOI: 10.1016/j.jbusvent.2013.07.003

Cen, T., & He, R. (2018). FinTech, green finance and sustainable development. In *Proceedings of the International Conference on Management, Economics, Education, Arts and Humanities* (pp. 222–225). Atlantis Press.

Chueca Vergara, C., & Ferruz Agudo, L. (2021). FinTech, business sustainability, and green finance: A systematic literature review. *Sustainability, 13*(15), 8451.

De Filippi, P., & Hassan, S. (2016). Blockchain technology as a regulatory technology: From code is law to law is code. *First Monday, 21*(12). Advance online publication. DOI: 10.5210/fm.v21i12.7113

De Filippi, P., & Wright, A. (2018). *Blockchain and the law: The rule of code*. Harvard University Press.

Delmas, M. A., & Burbano, V. C. (2011). The drivers of greenwashing. *California Management Review, 54*(1), 64–87. DOI: 10.1525/cmr.2011.54.1.64

Demirgüç-Kunt, A., Klapper, L., Singer, D., Ansar, S., & Hess, J. (2018). *The global fintech revolution: Financial inclusion and beyond* (Policy Research Working Paper No. 9355). World Bank.

Deng, X., Huang, Z., & Cheng, X. (2019). FinTech and sustainable development: Evidence from China based on P2P data. *Sustainability (Basel), 11*(22), 6434. DOI: 10.3390/su11226434

Elsaid, H. M. (2023). A review of the literature on the impact of fintech firms on the banking industry. *Qualitative Research in Financial Markets, 15*(5), 693–711. DOI: 10.1108/QRFM-10-2020-0197

Fuerst, F. (2019). The role of machine learning in ESG analytics. *Journal of Sustainable Finance & Investment, 9*(4), 255–272.

Ghose, A., Sahoo, S., & Kumar, V. (2025). FinTech and financial inclusion: Impacts on corporate performance and excluded populations. *Journal of Financial Innovation, 11*(1), 77–95.

Gomber, P., Kauffman, R. J., Parker, C., & Weber, B. W. (2018). On the FinTech revolution. *Journal of Management Information Systems, 35*(1), 220–265. DOI: 10.1080/07421222.2018.1440766

Haddad, C., & Hornuf, L. (2019). The emergence of the global FinTech market. *Small Business Economics, 53*(1), 81–105. DOI: 10.1007/s11187-018-9991-x

Hommel, K., & Bican, P. M. (2020). Digital entrepreneurship in finance. *Sustainability (Basel), 12*(19), 8035. DOI: 10.3390/su12198035

Huang, Y. (2025). FinTech as a catalyst for sustainable development. *International Journal of Sustainable Development and World Ecology, 32*(3), 145–161.

IPCC. (2022). *Climate change 2022: Mitigation of climate change*. Cambridge University Press.

Jena, R. K. (2022). Examining the factors affecting the adoption of blockchain technology in the banking sector: An extended UTAUT model. *International Journal of Financial Studies, 10*(4), 90.

Jena, R. K. (2025). Factors influencing the adoption of fintech for the enhancement of financial inclusion in rural India using a mixed-methods approach. *Journal of Risk and Financial Management, 18*(3), 150.

Kabulova, J., & Stankevičienė, J. (2020). Valuation of FinTech innovation based on patent applications. *Sustainability (Basel), 12*(23), 10158. DOI: 10.3390/su122310158

Kishor, K., Bansal, S. K., & Kumar, R. (2025). The role of fintech in promoting financial inclusion to achieve sustainable development: An integrated bibliometric analysis and systematic literature review. *Journal of the Knowledge Economy, 16*(1), 5664–5692. DOI: 10.1007/s13132-024-02168-5

Kotsantonis, S., & Serafeim, G. (2019). Four things no one will tell you about ESG data. *The Bank of America Journal of Applied Corporate Finance, 31*(2), 50–58. DOI: 10.1111/jacf.12346

Kouhizadeh, M., Saberi, S., & Sarkis, J. (2021). Blockchain technology and the sustainable supply chain. *International Journal of Production Research, 59*(7), 2142–2162.

Kumar, R. (2024). Emerging technologies in FinTech: Blockchain, AI, and big data analytics. *Financial Innovation, 10*(4), 302–318.

Latour, B. (1992). Where are the missing masses? In Bijker, W., & Law, J. (Eds.), *Shaping technology/building society* (pp. 225–258). MIT Press.

Lee, I., & Shin, Y. J. (2018). Fintech: Ecosystem, business models, investment decisions, and challenges. *Business Horizons, 61*(1), 35–46.

Mejía-Escobar, J. C., González-Ruiz, J. D., & Duque-Grisales, E. (2020). Sustainable financial products in the Latin American banking industry. *Sustainability, 12*(14), 5648. DOI: 10.3390/su12145648

Moro-Visconti, R., Cruz Rambaud, S., & López Pascual, J. (2020). Sustainability in FinTechs. *Sustainability (Basel), 12*(24), 10316. DOI: 10.3390/su122410316

Narayanan, A., Bonneau, J., Felten, E., Miller, A., & Goldfeder, S. (2016). *Bitcoin and cryptocurrency technologies*. Princeton University Press.

Ozili, P. K. (2018). Impact of digital finance on financial inclusion and stability. *Borsa Istanbul Review, 18*(4), 329–340. DOI: 10.1016/j.bir.2017.12.003

Philippon, T. (2016). *The FinTech opportunity* (NBER Working Paper No. 22476).

Puschmann, T., Hoffmann, C. H., & Khmarskyi, V. (2020). How green FinTech can alleviate climate change. *Sustainability, 12*(24), 10691. DOI: 10.3390/su122410691

Rahman, M., Hossain, M., & Uddin, M. (2024). Understanding the role of FinTech in sustainable finance. *Environmental Science and Pollution Research International, 31*(12), 15689–15705.

Ryu, H. S., & Ko, K. S. (2020). Sustainable development of FinTech. *Sustainability (Basel), 12*(18), 7669. DOI: 10.3390/su12187669

Sandhu, K., Dayanandan, A., & Kuntluru, S. (2023). India's CBDC for digital public infrastructure. *Economics Letters, 231*, 111302.

Simo, A. A., Nkamleu, G. B., & Tchamyou, V. S. (2025). FinTech, social impact, and financial inclusion. *African Development Review, 37*(2), 249–267.

Sreenu, N., & Verma, S. S. (2024). Enhancing economic growth through digital financial inclusion: An examination of India. *Transnational Corporations Review, 16*(4), 200091.

Thakor, A. V. (2020). FinTech and banking: What do we know? *Journal of Financial Intermediation, 41*, 100833. DOI: 10.1016/j.jfi.2019.100833

Tseng, M. L., Wu, K. J., Hu, J., & Wang, C. H. (2018). Decision-making model for sustainable supply chain finance. *International Journal of Production Economics, 205*, 30–36. DOI: 10.1016/j.ijpe.2018.08.024

United Nations. (2015). *Transforming our world: The 2030 Agenda for Sustainable Development.*

Varsha, V. R. (2024). Digital platforms and ESG integration in sustainable finance. *International Journal of Finance & Economics, 29*(1), 115–132.

Winner, L. (1980). Do artefacts have politics? *Daedalus, 109*(1), 121–136.

Yang, X. (2020). FinTech is promoting the development of green finance in China. In *Proceedings of the 4th International Seminar on Education Innovation and Economic Management.*

Zhang-Zhang, Y., Rohlfer, S., & Rajasekera, J. (2020). An eco-systematic view of cross-sector FinTech. *Sustainability (Basel), 12*(21), 8907. DOI: 10.3390/su12218907

Chapter 6
Green FinTech Revolution:
Aligning Digital Payment Systems With ESG Goals for a Sustainable Financial Future

Amandeep Kaur
http://orcid.org/0009-0004-5716-7298
Advance Centre of Research & Innovation, CGC University, Mohali, India

Gaganpreet Kaur
http://orcid.org/0009-0006-2957-5352
School of Management Studies, CGC University, Mohali, India

Ramandeep Sandhu
http://orcid.org/0000-0003-2595-4030
Lovely Professional University, India

ABSTRACT

As the world accelerates toward sustainable development, the financial sector plays a pivotal role in driving environmental and social responsibility. Green Digital Payment Systems (GDPS) a new frontier in financial technology are redefining how transactions can align with Environmental, Social, and Governance (ESG) compliance standards. This chapter explores the emergence, evolution, and impact of green digital payment systems that not only facilitate cashless economies but also embed sustainability into their core design and functionality. These innovative platforms leverage technologies such as blockchain, carbon footprint tracking, AI-driven ESG analytics, and eco-friendly payment infrastructures to promote green

DOI: 10.4018/979-8-3373-5437-8.ch006

consumer behavior, ethical investing, and climate-conscious financial decisions. From biodegradable payment cards to platforms that reward low-emission purchases, GDPS are reshaping the landscape of responsible finance.

1. INTRODUCTION

The financial sector is experiencing a paradigm shift as sustainability becomes a fundamental driver of decision-making across industries. Unlike traditional finance, which has historically prioritized efficiency and profitability, modern finance increasingly incorporates environmental and social considerations into its operational framework. This transformation is motivated by the pressing need to combat climate change, reduce ecological footprints, and foster inclusive growth. Within this evolving context, *Green Fintech* has emerged as an innovative frontier, combining the power of digital technologies with the principles of Environmental, Social, and Governance (ESG) accountability (PwC India, 2022).

Among its many domains, Green Digital Payment Systems (GDPS) represent one of the most impactful applications. These systems go beyond facilitating seamless transactions by embedding sustainability directly into their infrastructure. For instance, digital wallets, contactless cards, and blockchain-based payment networks are increasingly being designed to minimize resource consumption, provide carbon tracking functionalities, and enhance transparency in financial flows. In this sense, GDPS are not only transactional tools but also catalysts for promoting responsible consumer behavior and sustainable investment practices (Redbridge, 2024).

1.1 From Traditional to Green Digital Payments

Historically, payment systems have relied heavily on physical infrastructure such as plastic cards, cash handling, and paper receipts, all of which contribute to environmental degradation. With the rise of Green Fintech, these legacy practices are being reimagined. Modern payment systems are now supported by AI-driven ESG analytics, energy-efficient cloud computing, and biodegradable payment cards, reflecting an intentional shift towards climate-conscious finance (The Payments Association, 2024).

The move toward green digital payments aligns strongly with global sustainability agendas such as the Paris Climate Agreement and the UN Sustainable Development Goals (SDGs). Specifically, GDPS support SDG 12 (responsible consumption and production) and SDG 13 (climate action) by encouraging consumers to make environmentally friendly financial choices (Nature, 2025).

1.2 ESG as a Core Pillar of Digital Payments

The integration of ESG principles into payment systems ensures that environmental and social concerns are not treated as afterthoughts but as integral to financial operations. This involves three dimensions:

- Environmental: Adoption of carbon footprint calculators, renewable-powered data centers, and platforms rewarding eco-friendly purchases.
- Social: Strengthening financial inclusion by reaching underbanked populations, promoting ethical consumerism, and ensuring digital literacy.
- Governance: Enhancing trust through blockchain-enabled transparency and adherence to ESG reporting standards (OpenWay, 2024).

Together, these dimensions allow GDPS to redefine finance as a system that not only facilitates economic growth but also advances sustainability.

1.3 Comparative Perspective

To highlight the distinctiveness of GDPS, Table 1 contrasts the characteristics of traditional and ESG-aligned digital payment systems.

Table 1. Traditional vs. ESG-Aligned Digital Payment Systems

Feature	Traditional Payment Systems	ESG-Aligned Digital Payment Systems (GDPS)
Core Objective	Transaction efficiency & profitability	Transaction efficiency + ESG integration
Technology Backbone	Legacy IT systems, card networks	Blockchain, AI, carbon tracking analytics
Environmental Impact	High (plastic cards, paper receipts)	Low (biodegradable cards, carbon-neutral digital wallets)
Social Responsibility	Limited inclusion, profit-driven	Financial inclusion, fair trade, ethical consumption
Governance	Minimal transparency	Strong transparency, compliance with ESG reporting

1.4 Conceptual Framework

The relationship between GDPS and ESG integration can be visualized in Figure 1.

Figure 1. ESG-Aligned Digital Payment Ecosystem

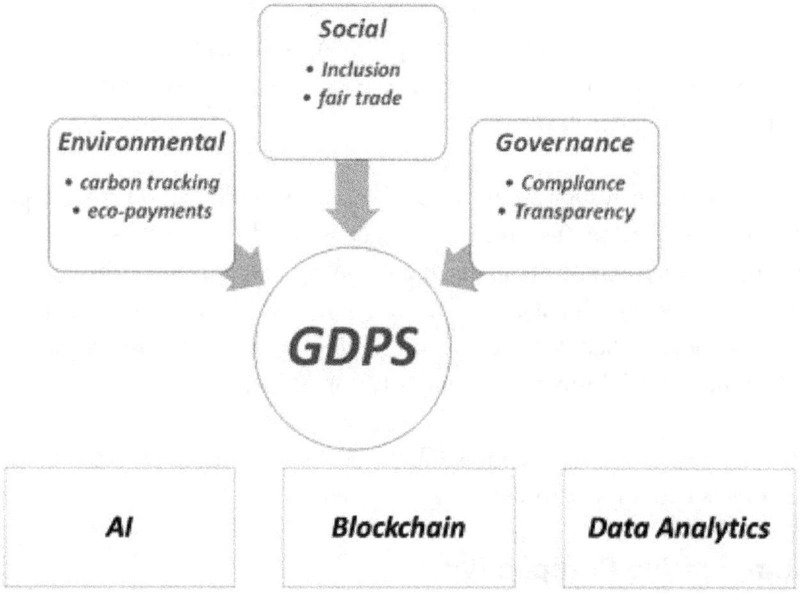

Illustration: GDPS at the center, linked to Environmental (carbon tracking, eco-payments), Social (inclusion, fair trade), Governance (compliance, transparency), and supported by technologies such as AI, blockchain, and data analytics.

1.5 Chapter Objectives

This chapter aims to:

1. Explore the evolution and emergence of GDPS.
2. Analyze the integration of ESG principles into payment ecosystems.
3. Evaluate case studies of green fintech solutions globally.
4. Identify challenges and opportunities in scaling GDPS.
5. Present a roadmap for mainstreaming sustainable digital payments.

By addressing these objectives, the chapter emphasizes how financial technology and sustainability converge to reshape the global economy, ensuring finance becomes a catalyst for climate action and social equity (PwC India, 2022; Nature, 2025).

2. CONCEPTUALIZING GREEN DIGITAL PAYMENT SYSTEMS

The integration of sustainability within financial technology is no longer an abstract ideal but a concrete requirement in the age of climate change and corporate accountability. Green Digital Payment Systems (GDPS) embody this transformation by combining technological innovation with Environmental, Social, and Governance (ESG) objectives. They are designed not merely as tools for conducting transactions but as instruments that actively shape consumer behavior, corporate strategies, and governance structures. In this way, GDPS transcend traditional payment infrastructures, evolving into catalysts for systemic sustainability in finance (PwC India, 2022).

ESG Integration in Digital Payments

Financial institutions are increasingly incorporating ESG principles into their operations, recognizing the benefits of reduced costs, enhanced financial inclusion, positive stakeholder impact, and sustainable value creation. Regulatory bodies such as the Reserve Bank of India (RBI) and the Securities and Exchange Board of India (SEBI) are also focusing on ESG parameters, prompting operators in the banking industry to act sustainably. This shift from ESG being just a buzzword to its actual application in global organizations is evident (PwC India, 2022a).

Impact of Digital Payments on Greenhouse Gas Emissions

The rapid adoption of digital payments in India, particularly through platforms like Unified Payments Interface (UPI), has led to a significant reduction in greenhouse gas (GHG) emissions. Traditional payment methods such as cash and cheques have higher carbon footprints due to factors like fuel consumption, energy use in devices, and paper usage. In contrast, digital payments, while requiring energy for devices and data centers, have resulted in overall GHG emission savings. For instance, the introduction of digital Know Your Customer (KYC) processes and the reduction in bank branches have contributed to a decrease in carbon emissions (PwC India, 2022b).

Role of FinTech in Sustainable Finance

Financial technology (FinTech) is playing a pivotal role in promoting sustainable finance. Innovations such as open banking, digital payments, and mobile-based financial services are facilitating financial inclusion, especially in rural areas. Initiatives like digital banking correspondents and mobile-based agricultural finance are expanding access to financial services, thereby contributing to the transformation of the financial landscape in India (PwC India, 2022c).

Regulatory Support for ESG Initiatives

India's GIFT International Financial Services Centre (IFSC) is fostering the growth of ESG and sustainable finance. As of December 2023, there was a cumulative debt listing of USD 10.43 billion in green, ESG, and sustainable debt instruments, reflecting the country's commitment to sustainable financial practices (PwC India, 2022d).

The evolution of Green Digital Payment Systems signifies a paradigm shift in the financial sector, where sustainability is seamlessly integrated into the core of financial operations. Through the adoption of ESG principles, reduction in GHG emissions, and promotion of financial inclusion, GDPS are not merely facilitating transactions but are actively contributing to a sustainable financial ecosystem. This transformation underscores the critical role of technology in achieving environmental and social objectives within the financial sector (PwC India, 2022).

2.1 Definition and Scope

Green Digital Payment Systems (GDPS) represent a transformative shift in the financial sector, integrating Environmental, Social, and Governance (ESG) principles directly into their operational frameworks. Unlike traditional payment systems, which primarily focus on efficiency and transaction speed, GDPS emphasize sustainability, ethical practices, and transparency. Their scope encompasses various financial transactions, including retail payments, corporate transactions, cross-border remittances, and government disbursements aimed at supporting inclusive growth initiatives.

Environmental Impact and Consumer Education

GDPS platforms are increasingly incorporating features that educate consumers about the environmental consequences of their purchases. For instance, retail platforms can embed carbon footprint calculators that provide real-time data on the environmental impact of individual transactions. These tools empower consumers to make informed decisions, promoting sustainable consumption patterns. Such initiatives align with the growing demand for transparency and accountability in consumer behavior.

Corporate ESG Compliance and Reporting

At the corporate level, GDPS facilitate adherence to global ESG reporting standards such as the Global Reporting Initiative (GRI) and the Sustainability Accounting Standards Board (SASB). These frameworks guide companies in disclosing their sustainability practices, ensuring that their operations align with international benchmarks for environmental stewardship, social responsibility, and governance. By integrating these standards into payment systems, GDPS enable seamless reporting and compliance, reducing the administrative burden on businesses and enhancing their credibility in the eyes of stakeholders.

Inclusivity and Social Responsibility

Beyond environmental considerations, GDPS also promote social inclusivity. Digital payment platforms can be designed to ensure accessibility for underserved populations, including those in rural areas and individuals with disabilities. By providing equitable access to financial services, GDPS contribute to social inclusion and economic empowerment, aligning with the social aspect of ESG principles.

Governance and Transparency

GDPS enhance governance by ensuring transparency in financial transactions. Blockchain technology, for example, can be utilized to create immutable records of transactions, reducing the risk of fraud and increasing trust among users. Moreover, these systems can be designed to comply with data protection regulations, safeguarding user information and reinforcing the governance aspect of ESG.

In conclusion, Green Digital Payment Systems are not merely tools for facilitating financial transactions; they are instruments of change that integrate sustainability into the core of financial operations. By embedding ESG principles into their frameworks, GDPS contribute to a more sustainable, inclusive, and transparent financial ecosystem. As the financial sector continues to evolve, the adoption of GDPS will play a crucial role in shaping a future where economic growth aligns with environmental and social well-being.

2.2 Technological Foundations

The foundation of GDPS rests on advanced digital technologies that enable both functionality and sustainability. Blockchain technology, for instance, provides transparency, immutability, and traceability of transactions, making it particularly effective for green bonds, carbon credits, and ESG-compliant remittances. Artificial Intelligence (AI) complements this by offering data-driven insights into energy consumption, carbon intensity, and fraud detection, allowing institutions to make informed sustainable financial decisions. Another technological component, carbon footprint tracking, is increasingly popular among payment providers such as Mastercard, whose Carbon Calculator enables customers to assess the emissions linked to their spending activities (The Payments Association, 2024). Finally, eco-infrastructure innovations—such as biodegradable payment cards, cloud systems powered by renewable energy, and the replacement of paper receipts with digital confirmations—demonstrate how digital payments can minimize ecological footprints while enhancing efficiency (OpenWay, 2024).

Table 2. Core Technologies Supporting GDPS

Technology	Function in GDPS	ESG Contribution
Blockchain	Transparency, traceability of funds	Fraud reduction, carbon credit validation
Artificial Intelligence	ESG data analytics, fraud detection	Informed sustainable decision-making
Carbon Footprint Tracking	Consumer awareness of environmental impact	Encourages climate-conscious spending
Eco-Infrastructure	Biodegradable cards, renewable-powered data centers	Reduction of environmental footprint

2.3 ESG Integration Mechanisms

The integration of ESG principles within Green Digital Payment Systems (GDPS) operates simultaneously at both consumer and institutional levels, creating a comprehensive framework that promotes sustainable financial practices.

At the consumer level, GDPS are designed to empower individuals to make environmentally and socially responsible choices. Digital payment platforms now incorporate features such as carbon footprint tracking, which calculates the estimated environmental impact of each transaction based on the type of product or service purchased, the supply chain emissions, and the energy consumption associated with the transaction (PwC India, 2022). In addition, GDPS can provide rewards or incentives for low-emission purchases, such as discounts, loyalty points, or cashback for buying sustainable products. These mechanisms serve a dual purpose: they educate consumers about the consequences of their consumption patterns and actively encourage behavior that aligns with global sustainability goals. Moreover, some advanced GDPS integrate gamification elements, sustainability scoreboards, or personalized recommendations to further engage users in ethical spending practices, thereby fostering long-term behavioral change and creating a culture of conscious consumption (Redbridge, 2024).

At the institutional level, GDPS support organizations in embedding sustainability into their operational and strategic decision-making. Companies can utilize GDPS to streamline ESG reporting by automatically aggregating transaction-level data and linking it to international frameworks such as the Global Reporting Initiative (GRI) or the Sustainability Accounting Standards Board (SASB). This reduces the administrative burden of manual reporting and ensures compliance with regulatory requirements for ESG disclosures. Furthermore, GDPS enable institutions to generate analytics on sustainable spending patterns, carbon emission reductions, and social impact, which can inform strategic initiatives such as supplier selection, investment in green projects, or alignment with corporate social responsibility (CSR) goals. Financial institutions can also leverage GDPS to ensure transparency and accountability in governance by integrating audit trails, fraud detection mechanisms, and blockchain-based transaction verification, which enhance the credibility of ESG claims (PwC India, 2022; Redbridge, 2024).

The dual-level integration of ESG principles ensures that the financial ecosystem facilitated by GDPS is both economically efficient and socially responsible. At the consumer end, it creates awareness and incentivizes sustainable behavior, while at the institutional end, it provides tools for accountability, performance measurement, and strategic sustainability management. Collectively, these efforts contribute to broader global objectives such as the United Nations Sustainable Development Goals (SDGs), particularly those related to responsible consumption and production (SDG 12), climate action (SDG 13), and reduced inequalities (SDG 10). By bridging individual behavior with organizational governance, GDPS exemplify how fintech can become a transformative force in achieving systemic sustainability in the financial sector.

Moreover, GDPS facilitate inclusive growth, particularly in emerging economies. By integrating features that promote financial inclusion—such as low-cost digital wallets, microloan disbursement, and accessible digital banking interfaces—GDPS extend the benefits of sustainable finance to underserved populations. This aligns with the social dimension of ESG, ensuring that the adoption of sustainable financial technologies does not exacerbate existing inequalities but rather fosters economic empowerment and participation across different demographic segments (Redbridge, 2024).

In conclusion, Green Digital Payment Systems demonstrate that digital finance can go beyond transactional efficiency to actively embed sustainability into financial behavior and organizational governance. Through consumer-oriented tools, institutional reporting mechanisms, and features that enhance social inclusion and transparency, GDPS represent a holistic approach to ESG integration. Their adoption is instrumental in creating a financial ecosystem where economic growth, environmental stewardship, and social responsibility coexist, paving the way for a sustainable and equitable global financial system.

2.4 Comparative Advantage

Green Digital Payment Systems provide distinct advantages when compared to traditional payment infrastructures. While conventional systems have historically been transaction-centric, focusing solely on efficiency and profitability, GDPS adopt an impact-centric approach that evaluates the long-term sustainability of financial flows. Their emphasis on accountability, inclusivity, and climate responsibility positions them as superior models in a world where financial services are expected to contribute to the common good. Moreover, GDPS enhance consumer trust by ensuring transparency through blockchain-enabled traceability, which is becoming a critical factor in attracting environmentally conscious customers and ESG-focused investors (Nature, 2025).

2.5 Conceptual Challenges

Despite their advantages, the conceptualization of GDPS is not without challenges. The absence of standardized ESG metrics across jurisdictions creates inconsistencies that hinder global scalability. Additionally, the integration of blockchain, AI, and other advanced technologies involves high capital costs, posing barriers for smaller fintech firms. Another major challenge is the risk of greenwashing, where institutions may market themselves as sustainable without verifiable ESG performance. Cyber-security threats also persist, given the reliance of GDPS on digital infrastructures that are vulnerable to attacks (The Payments Association, 2024). Overcoming these challenges requires regulatory harmonization, stronger verification frameworks, and collaborative innovation across stakeholders.

3. ESG INTEGRATION IN DIGITAL PAYMENT ECOSYSTEMS

The integration of Environmental, Social, and Governance (ESG) principles into digital payment ecosystems represents a transformative shift in how financial systems are designed and managed. Traditionally, payment infrastructures were valued primarily for their efficiency, reliability, and profitability. However, as global economies increasingly align with sustainable development frameworks, payment systems are expected to go beyond technical efficiency and actively contribute to environmental sustainability, social equity, and transparent governance. This repositioning underscores the need for payment platforms to function not only as transactional hubs but also as mechanisms of climate responsibility and ethical finance (PwC India, 2022).

3.1 Environmental Integration

The environmental dimension of ESG integration in payment systems focuses on reducing the carbon footprint of financial transactions. Modern digital platforms are beginning to adopt biodegradable cards, cloud-based infrastructures powered by renewable energy, and paperless digital receipts. For example, Mastercard's Carbon Calculator is an application embedded in payment systems that allows users to assess the carbon impact of their transactions, thereby encouraging sustainable consumer behavior (The Payments Association, 2024). Similarly, blockchain-based solutions ensure the integrity of carbon credit markets, reducing double counting and enabling transparent green financing. These measures highlight how digital payment ecosystems can play an instrumental role in mitigating environmental degradation (Redbridge, 2024).

3.2 Social Integration

The social dimension emphasizes financial inclusion, ethical consumerism, and equitable access to financial services. Green digital payment platforms are uniquely positioned to serve underserved populations by providing low-cost, mobile-first financial tools. This inclusion addresses global challenges of inequality and ensures that marginalized communities have access to banking, remittance services, and digital commerce opportunities (Nature, 2025). Beyond inclusion, social integration in GDPS also supports fair-trade practices and rewards ethical consumption. For instance, some payment applications now allow users to direct a percentage of transaction fees toward social development projects, thereby linking individual consumer behavior with broader societal goals (OpenWay, 2024).

3.3 Governance Integration

Governance integration ensures that digital payment systems operate with transparency, accountability, and compliance. Blockchain-based infrastructures enhance auditability by recording immutable transaction histories, reducing the likelihood of fraud and ensuring trust among users. Moreover, ESG reporting frameworks such as the Sustainability Accounting Standards Board (SASB) and the Global Reporting Initiative (GRI) are increasingly being adopted by fintech firms to align payment processes with global sustainability standards (PwC India, 2022). Such integration improves not only operational governance but also reputational capital, as organizations that demonstrate transparency and compliance are more likely to attract ethically conscious consumers and investors.

3.4 Comparative Analysis of ESG Dimensions in GDPS

A comparative view of the three ESG dimensions within digital payment systems reveals how environmental, social, and governance elements complement each other to create holistic sustainability outcomes.

Table 3. ESG Dimensions in Digital Payment Systems

ESG Dimension	Key Mechanisms in GDPS	Outcomes Achieved
Environmental	Carbon calculators, renewable-powered infrastructure	Reduction in ecological footprint, sustainable choices
Social	Financial inclusion tools, ethical payment incentives	Greater equity, responsible consumerism
Governance	Blockchain transparency, ESG reporting standards	Trust, accountability, reduced greenwashing risks

3.5 Conceptual Model of ESG Integration

The integration of ESG into GDPS can be represented through a conceptual model in which payment systems act as the central node connecting environmental sustainability, social inclusivity, and governance transparency. Technologies such as AI, blockchain, and carbon tracking tools act as enablers, while global frameworks like the SDGs and ESG reporting standards provide direction.

3.6 Challenges and Opportunities

Despite progress, the integration of ESG into digital payments faces hurdles. Regulatory fragmentation across countries makes it difficult to standardize ESG criteria, while high technological investment costs create barriers for smaller fintech firms. Additionally, there is a persistent risk of "greenwashing," where companies exaggerate their sustainability claims without delivering measurable outcomes (Redbridge, 2024). On the other hand, opportunities abound, particularly in the development of green central bank digital currencies (CBDCs), AI-driven ESG credit scoring, and international collaborations to harmonize sustainability standards (Nature, 2025).

The integration of ESG dimensions into digital payment ecosystems is essential for the long-term sustainability of the global financial system. By embedding environmental responsibility, social equity, and governance transparency into their operational core, GDPS redefine the role of finance from being purely transactional to becoming a key enabler of sustainable development. With proper regulatory support, technological innovation, and consumer engagement, ESG integration in payments can transform financial ecosystems into engines of inclusive and climate-resilient growth.

4. CASE STUDIES OF GREEN FINTECH SOLUTIONS

The practical implementation of Green Digital Payment Systems (GDPS) can be better understood through real-world case studies that demonstrate how financial technology firms, banks, and governments are embedding sustainability into digital payment ecosystems. These examples highlight the varied approaches taken to integrate Environmental, Social, and Governance (ESG) dimensions into financial transactions. From carbon footprint calculators embedded in payment apps to blockchain-based carbon credit markets, these case studies illustrate both the opportunities and challenges of aligning digital finance with sustainability objectives.

4.1 Mastercard's Carbon Calculator

One of the most widely recognized initiatives in the green payments domain is Mastercard's Carbon Calculator, developed in partnership with the Swedish fintech company Doconomy. Integrated into banks' and payment providers' apps, this tool calculates the carbon impact of consumer purchases and provides insights into how individual spending contributes to climate change. Beyond measurement, the system also enables users to contribute to reforestation or renewable energy projects directly from the app (The Payments Association, 2024). This model demonstrates how consumer-facing payment solutions can raise awareness and promote behavioral shifts toward sustainable consumption.

4.2 RevFin India: Financing Electric Mobility

RevFin, a fintech startup based in India, focuses on expanding access to green mobility by providing digital lending solutions for electric vehicles (EVs). Through its platform, RevFin uses alternative credit scoring methods that integrate behavioral and digital transaction data, thereby including customers who are excluded from traditional credit systems. By financing EV purchases and integrating repayment through digital wallets, RevFin directly contributes to the reduction of carbon emissions while enhancing financial inclusion (PwC India, 2022). This case illustrates how GDPS can advance both environmental and social dimensions of ESG simultaneously.

4.3 DCarbonX: Blockchain for Carbon Markets

DCarbonX represents a blockchain-based platform that specializes in carbon credit trading. Using distributed ledger technology, it ensures transparency, traceability, and verification of carbon offsets, mitigating the risks of double counting and greenwashing. The platform employs smart contracts to automate transactions, ensuring efficiency and compliance with ESG frameworks. Its adoption across corporate sectors underscores the role of blockchain-based GDPS in promoting credible and scalable green finance solutions (Redbridge, 2024).

4.4 Ant Group's Green Digital Finance Initiatives

In China, Ant Group's Ant Forest program has become a globally recognized example of gamifying sustainability in digital finance. Through Alipay, users are rewarded with virtual "green energy points" for making low-carbon lifestyle choices such as using public transportation or paying utility bills digitally. These points are then converted into real trees planted in arid regions of China, linking digital payments with large-scale environmental restoration. The program has planted over 220 million trees since its inception, highlighting the potential of GDPS in engaging consumers at scale (Nature, 2025).

4.5 Comparative Analysis of Case Studies

The reviewed case studies reflect the diversity of strategies employed across different geographies and contexts. Mastercard focuses on consumer awareness through carbon tracking; RevFin demonstrates the potential of digital lending for environmental and social outcomes; DCarbonX highlights the role of blockchain in governance and transparency, while Ant Group's Ant Forest program illustrates the use of behavioral incentives to encourage sustainable practices.

Table 4. Comparative Overview of Green Fintech Case Studies

Case Study	Core Focus	ESG Dimension Highlighted	Key Contribution
Mastercard Carbon Calculator	Carbon tracking in payments	Environmental	Promotes climate-conscious consumption
RevFin India	Financing electric mobility	Environmental + Social	Reduces emissions and expands financial inclusion
DCarbonX	Blockchain for carbon credits	Governance	Ensures transparency and prevents greenwashing
Ant Group (Ant Forest)	Gamified digital payments	Environmental + Social	Mass consumer engagement in reforestation

4.6 Conceptual Visualization

The interaction between different ESG dimensions across these case studies can be visualized as a framework where each solution emphasizes one or more dimensions but collectively contributes to holistic sustainability.

4.7 Insights and Lessons

The lessons from these case studies underscore three important insights. First, consumer engagement tools such as gamification and carbon tracking are effective in driving behavioral change. Second, financing models for green technologies such as EVs are vital for scaling adoption, especially in emerging markets. Third, technology-enabled transparency is crucial to maintaining credibility and preventing reputational risks. Together, these insights provide a roadmap for how GDPS can evolve into mainstream instruments for achieving sustainability.

5. CHALLENGES AND OPPORTUNITIES IN GREEN DIGITAL PAYMENT SYSTEMS

While Green Digital Payment Systems (GDPS) hold immense promises for reshaping the financial sector around sustainability principles, their implementation is fraught with challenges. These challenges arise from regulatory gaps, technological barriers, high costs, and risks of greenwashing. At the same time, the sector presents significant opportunities, ranging from new business models and consumer engagement mechanisms to technological innovations and global collaborations. Understanding both sides of the spectrum is essential to designing robust strategies for the future of sustainable finance (PwC India, 2022).

5.1 Regulatory and Standardization Challenges

One of the foremost challenges lies in the lack of standardized ESG metrics across jurisdictions. While some economies, particularly in Europe, have advanced in developing frameworks such as the EU Taxonomy for sustainable finance, others lack clear policies. This regulatory fragmentation makes it difficult for global payment providers to ensure consistency in ESG reporting and implementation. Furthermore, the absence of universally accepted benchmarks for measuring the sustainability of financial transactions creates ambiguities, opening space for manipulation and inconsistencies (Redbridge, 2024).

5.2 Technological and Infrastructural Challenges

The integration of advanced technologies such as blockchain, AI, and carbon tracking tools requires substantial investment in infrastructure. Smaller fintech firms often lack the resources to adopt these technologies, leading to disparities in implementation. Additionally, renewable-powered data centers, biodegradable card production, and carbon monitoring platforms involve high upfront costs. Technological scalability is also a concern, as carbon footprint calculators or blockchain-based systems require real-time processing of vast transaction data, which is energy-intensive (The Payments Association, 2024).

5.3 Risk of Greenwashing

A critical governance-related challenge is the risk of greenwashing, where companies claim ESG compliance without verifiable outcomes. This not only undermines consumer trust but also threatens the credibility of the broader sustainable finance ecosystem. For instance, some platforms market eco-friendly digital cards without ensuring that the materials or processes involved truly minimize environmental impact. Strengthening transparency through blockchain verification and mandatory ESG reporting is essential to counter these risks (OpenWay, 2024).

5.4 Cybersecurity and Data Privacy Concerns

The reliance of GDPS on digital infrastructures heightens risks related to cybersecurity and data privacy. Payment systems are frequent targets of cyberattacks, and the integration of additional ESG-related data such as carbon consumption or consumer behavior patterns increases vulnerability. Ensuring robust cybersecurity frameworks while maintaining compliance with global data privacy regulations, such as the EU's GDPR, is critical for safeguarding trust in GDPS (Nature, 2025).

5.5 Opportunities for Innovation and Growth

Despite these challenges, GDPS also offer numerous opportunities. One promising area is the development of Green Central Bank Digital Currencies (CBDCs), which can embed ESG compliance into monetary policy by incentivizing sustainable consumption and investment. Similarly, fintech startups are increasingly innovating with AI-driven ESG credit scoring, where individuals or businesses receive better financing terms based on their sustainability performance. Additionally, the gamification of consumer engagement, as demonstrated by Ant Group's Ant Forest program, shows how digital payments can link everyday behavior to broader environmental goals (PwC India, 2022).

5.6 Opportunities for Global Collaboration

The globalization of fintech ecosystems creates opportunities for cross-border collaboration in standardizing ESG frameworks and sharing best practices. Multilateral institutions such as the World Bank and IMF, along with regional organizations like the ASEAN and the European Union, are well-placed to harmonize ESG reporting criteria and provide funding support for developing economies. Collaborative efforts between governments, financial institutions, and technology providers can accelerate the mainstreaming of GDPS as default modes of sustainable finance (Redbridge, 2024).

5.7 Comparative View of Challenges and Opportunities

The dual nature of GDPS marked by challenges and opportunities can be understood through a comparative framework.

Table 5. Challenges and Opportunities in GDPS Implementation

Aspect	Challenges	Opportunities
Regulatory Framework	Lack of ESG standardization	Global harmonization of reporting standards
Technological Integration	High costs, scalability issues	Innovation in blockchain, AI, and carbon tracking
Governance	Risk of greenwashing	Blockchain-driven transparency and trust
Consumer Engagement	Limited awareness	Gamification and rewards for sustainable behavior
Security and Privacy	Cybersecurity vulnerabilities	Stronger data protection frameworks

5.8 Conceptual Visualization

The relationship between challenges and opportunities can be visualized as an ecosystem where barriers such as regulatory gaps and technological costs exist alongside innovations that can overcome them.

Figure 2. Challenges and Opportunities in GDPS

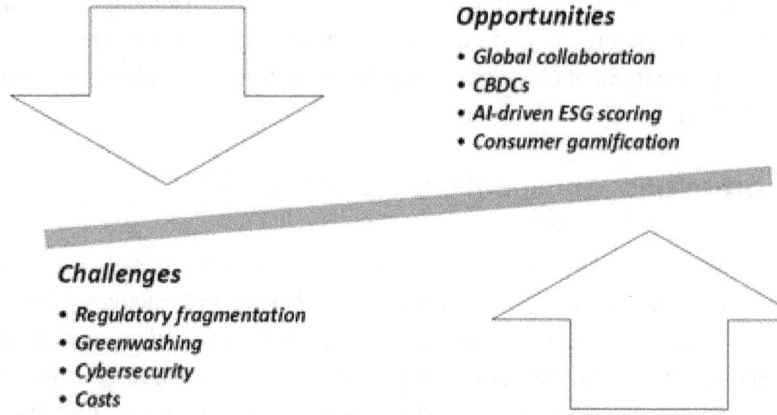

Figure: A two-column diagram, with "Challenges" on the left — regulatory fragmentation, greenwashing, cybersecurity, costs — and "Opportunities" on the right — global collaboration, CBDCs, AI-driven ESG scoring, consumer gamification. Arrows connect corresponding challenges to potential solutions.

The challenges associated with GDPS highlight the complexities of integrating ESG principles into digital payment ecosystems, but they also reveal fertile ground for innovation. By addressing regulatory inconsistencies, reducing technology costs, and enhancing governance transparency, fintech firms and policymakers can transform barriers into pathways for sustainable growth. The opportunities for innovation, collaboration, and consumer engagement position GDPS not as optional tools but as essential infrastructures for the transition toward a climate-conscious and inclusive financial future (OpenWay, 2024; Nature, 2025).

6. GREEN DIGITAL PAYMENT SYSTEMS AND THE UN SUSTAINABLE DEVELOPMENT GOALS

The United Nations Sustainable Development Goals (SDGs) provide a universal framework for addressing global challenges such as poverty, inequality, and climate change. Financial systems, as critical enablers of economic activity, play an essential role in advancing these goals. Green Digital Payment Systems (GDPS) are particularly aligned with the SDGs because they integrate Environmental, Social, and Governance (ESG) principles directly into their operations. By facilitating climate-conscious consumer behavior, expanding financial inclusion, and promoting transparency, GDPS provide concrete mechanisms for operationalizing the SDGs within the global financial ecosystem (PwC India, 2022).

6.1 Environmental Sustainability and Climate Action

GDPS directly support SDG 12 (Responsible Consumption and Production) and SDG 13 (Climate Action) by enabling individuals and institutions to monitor and reduce their environmental impact. Carbon calculators integrated into payment apps, such as those developed by Mastercard and Doconomy, allow consumers to visualize the carbon emissions associated with their purchases and make informed, eco-friendly decisions (The Payments Association, 2024). Additionally, the adoption of renewable-powered data centers, biodegradable payment cards, and digital receipts significantly reduces the ecological footprint of payment infrastructures (Redbridge, 2024). These features position GDPS as central tools for driving sustainable consumption patterns and mitigating climate change.

6.2 Promoting Financial Inclusion and Social Equity

Beyond environmental outcomes, GDPS contribute to SDG 1 (No Poverty), SDG 5 (Gender Equality), and SDG 10 (Reduced Inequalities) by broadening access to financial services. In developing economies, mobile-first payment platforms enable underserved populations to participate in digital commerce, access microcredit, and receive government subsidies in a transparent and efficient manner. For instance, fintech firms such as RevFin in India integrate digital lending with ESG principles to finance electric vehicles, simultaneously advancing clean energy adoption and improving economic opportunities for marginalized groups (Nature, 2025). This dual focus on inclusion and sustainability makes GDPS unique enablers of social equity in financial ecosystems.

6.3 Governance, Transparency, and Institutional Trust

The governance dimension of GDPS supports SDG 16 (Peace, Justice, and Strong Institutions) by embedding transparency and accountability into digital transactions. Blockchain-based payment infrastructures ensure immutable records, which enhance auditability and reduce opportunities for fraud and corruption (OpenWay, 2024). Moreover, by aligning with global ESG reporting frameworks such as the Global Reporting Initiative (GRI) and the Sustainability Accounting Standards Board (SASB), GDPS help build institutional trust. This strengthens not only financial governance but also citizen confidence in digital ecosystems, which is essential for fostering sustainable development on a broader scale.

6.4 Cross-SDG Synergies

The impact of GDPS is not limited to individual goals but extends to cross-SDG synergies. For example, by financing green mobility through digital lending platforms, GDPS simultaneously advance SDG 7 (Affordable and Clean Energy), SDG 11 (Sustainable Cities and Communities), and SDG 13 (Climate Action). Similarly, initiatives such as Ant Group's Ant Forest program link SDG 12 (Responsible Consumption) with SDG 15 (Life on Land) by incentivizing consumers to adopt low-carbon behaviors that result in large-scale tree planting (Redbridge, 2024). These synergies highlight the integrative potential of GDPS in promoting systemic sustainability.

6.5 Comparative Mapping of GDPS Contributions to SDGs

The alignment of GDPS with the SDGs can be summarized through a comparative mapping of their contributions across environmental, social, and governance dimensions.

Table 6. GDPS Contributions to the UN SDGs

SDG	GDPS Contribution	Example
SDG 12: Responsible Consumption	Carbon calculators, eco-friendly payment cards	Mastercard Carbon Calculator
SDG 13: Climate Action	Renewable-powered data centers, carbon tracking tools	Blockchain-enabled carbon credit platforms
SDG 1 & 10: Poverty & Inequality	Financial inclusion via mobile payments	RevFin digital lending for EVs

continued on following page

Table 6. Continued

SDG	GDPS Contribution	Example
SDG 5: Gender Equality	Access to inclusive financial products for women	Mobile-first wallets in emerging markets
SDG 16: Strong Institutions	Blockchain transparency, ESG reporting standards	DCarbonX carbon credit trading platform
SDG 15: Life on Land	Incentivized eco-behavior leading to reforestation	Ant Forest tree-planting initiative

6.6 Conceptual Model of GDPS-SDG Alignment

The conceptual alignment between GDPS and the SDGs can be represented through a systemic model that highlights their interdependence.

Green Digital Payment Systems play a pivotal role in operationalizing the UN Sustainable Development Goals by embedding environmental sustainability, social inclusion, and governance accountability into the financial ecosystem. They not only advance specific goals such as climate action and financial inclusion but also generate cross-goal synergies that accelerate systemic progress toward sustainable development. As global economies pursue the 2030 Agenda, the strategic deployment of GDPS will be indispensable in building inclusive, transparent, and climate-resilient financial systems (PwC India, 2022; Nature, 2025).

7. ROADMAP FOR FUTURE INNOVATION IN GREEN DIGITAL PAYMENT SYSTEMS

The evolution of Green Digital Payment Systems (GDPS) is still in its nascent stages, but the trajectory indicates vast potential for transforming finance into a sustainable and inclusive ecosystem. To realize this potential, it is necessary to establish a clear roadmap that outlines technological, regulatory, institutional, and consumer-focused strategies. Such a roadmap not only addresses the existing challenges but also leverages opportunities for innovation, ensuring that GDPS become integral to achieving global sustainability agendas such as the UN SDGs and the Paris Climate Agreement (PwC India, 2022).

7.1 Technological Innovations

Future innovation in GDPS will be driven by next-generation technologies that enhance transparency, efficiency, and sustainability. Blockchain is expected to become more energy-efficient with the adoption of proof-of-stake consensus mechanisms, thereby reducing the environmental impact of distributed ledger systems. Artificial Intelligence (AI) and Machine Learning (ML) will advance predictive ESG analytics, enabling both consumers and institutions to make informed, sustainability-driven financial decisions. Additionally, the integration of the Internet of Things (IoT) with GDPS could allow real-time monitoring of energy usage and carbon emissions linked to specific financial activities (Redbridge, 2024). These innovations will ensure that GDPS move beyond being transactional systems to becoming intelligent platforms for sustainability management.

7.2 Regulatory and Policy Frameworks

The success of GDPS depends heavily on supportive regulatory ecosystems. Policymakers must work toward standardized ESG reporting frameworks that ensure consistency across borders. The development of Green Central Bank Digital Currencies (CBDCs) represents another transformative avenue, embedding ESG compliance directly into national monetary systems. Furthermore, public-private partnerships should be strengthened to fund innovations in eco-infrastructure, ensuring that smaller fintech firms can participate in the green payments revolution without being disadvantaged by high entry costs (The Payments Association, 2024).

7.3 Institutional and Organizational Strategies

Financial institutions, including banks and fintech firms, must embed ESG objectives into their corporate strategies and business models. This involves establishing sustainability-linked performance metrics, publishing transparent ESG reports, and aligning with global frameworks such as the Global Reporting Initiative (GRI) and Task Force on Climate-Related Financial Disclosures (TCFD). Institutions must also build collaborative platforms to share best practices, thereby creating industry-wide synergies that accelerate innovation in GDPS (OpenWay, 2024).

7.4 Consumer-Centric Innovations

Consumers are central to the success of GDPS, and future innovations must prioritize user engagement and awareness. Gamification strategies, similar to Ant Group's Ant Forest, can incentivize sustainable behaviors by linking eco-friendly actions with tangible rewards. Educational tools embedded in payment apps can further empower users by providing real-time insights into the ESG impact of their purchases. As digital literacy grows globally, consumer-driven demand for sustainable payments is likely to push institutions toward adopting greener infrastructures (Nature, 2025).

7.5 Global Collaboration and Partnerships

International collaboration will be crucial in mainstreaming GDPS. Multilateral institutions such as the IMF, World Bank, and United Nations should provide funding, policy guidance, and technological support for developing economies to adopt GDPS. Cross-border collaboration among fintech firms can also harmonize ESG standards, enabling seamless green transactions across jurisdictions. Such partnerships will accelerate the diffusion of sustainable practices in the global financial ecosystem, making GDPS a cornerstone of international finance (PwC India, 2022).

7.6 Roadmap Framework

The roadmap for GDPS innovation can be summarized across five domains: technological, regulatory, institutional, consumer-focused, and global collaboration.

Table 7. Roadmap for Future Innovation in GDPS

Domain	Key Innovations/Strategies	Expected Outcomes
Technological	AI-driven ESG analytics, IoT integration, efficient blockchain	Smarter, greener financial ecosystems
Regulatory	ESG reporting standards, Green CBDCs, public-private partnerships	Transparent, harmonized global frameworks
Institutional	Sustainability-linked business models, ESG reporting	Stronger accountability and industry synergies
Consumer-Centric	Gamification, carbon calculators, digital ESG education	Informed and engaged sustainable consumption
Global Collaboration	Multilateral support, cross-border ESG harmonization	Mainstream adoption of GDPS across global markets

7.7 Conceptual Visualization

The roadmap can be visualized as a layered ecosystem where technological innovation forms the foundation, regulatory and institutional strategies provide the structural framework, consumer engagement drives adoption, and global collaboration ensures long-term scalability.

The roadmap for future innovation in GDPS highlights that the transition toward sustainable digital payments requires multi-level interventions. Technological advancements, harmonized regulations, institutional accountability, consumer empowerment, and global collaboration must converge to ensure the long-term success of GDPS. If strategically pursued, these systems have the potential to become default infrastructures for sustainable finance, aligning financial ecosystems with the pressing demands of climate responsibility, social equity, and transparent governance (OpenWay, 2024; Nature, 2025).

8. CONCLUSION AND POLICY IMPLICATIONS

The rise of Green Digital Payment Systems (GDPS) marks a pivotal moment in the transformation of global finance. As the financial sector confronts the urgent imperatives of climate change, social inequality, and governance accountability, GDPS offer a pathway to embed Environmental, Social, and Governance (ESG) principles into everyday financial interactions. Unlike traditional payment infrastructures, which prioritize efficiency and profitability, GDPS integrate sustainability at the structural level, making them not just instruments of commerce but also levers for systemic change (PwC India, 2022).

This chapter has demonstrated that GDPS play a multi-dimensional role in advancing sustainability. On the environmental front, they contribute to reducing carbon footprints through eco-friendly payment infrastructures, renewable-powered data centers, and consumer-facing carbon calculators. Socially, they foster inclusion by extending financial services to underserved populations and incentivizing ethical consumption. From a governance perspective, GDPS enhance transparency, accountability, and compliance by leveraging blockchain technologies and aligning with global reporting frameworks (Redbridge, 2024; OpenWay, 2024).

8.1 Key Insights

The analysis across sections highlights three critical insights. First, technological innovation particularly blockchain, AI, and IoT is central to embedding ESG compliance in payment ecosystems. Second, consumer engagement, through gamification and awareness tools, remains essential for driving behavioral change at scale. Third, global collaboration and regulatory harmonization are indispensable for ensuring scalability, credibility, and resilience of GDPS (The Payments Association, 2024).

8.2 Policy Implications

For policymakers, GDPS present both opportunities and responsibilities. Governments must establish clear ESG reporting standards that prevent greenwashing and ensure comparability across markets. Investment in digital infrastructure powered by renewable energy should be prioritized to reduce the ecological impact of expanding payment ecosystems. Furthermore, the development of Green Central

Bank Digital Currencies (CBDCs) could institutionalize sustainability at the core of national financial systems, embedding climate-conscious incentives into monetary policy (Nature, 2025).

Financial regulators should encourage public–private partnerships to accelerate the diffusion of GDPS, while also safeguarding data privacy and cybersecurity. Importantly, policies should promote financial literacy and digital inclusion, ensuring that vulnerable populations are not excluded from the benefits of sustainable finance. By aligning national financial regulations with international ESG frameworks, countries can ensure consistency, transparency, and accountability in the global adoption of GDPS (PwC India, 2022).

8.3 Strategic Directions for Stakeholders

The transition to GDPS requires the active participation of multiple stakeholders.

- Governments and Regulators must establish standardized frameworks and incentivize green payment infrastructures.
- Financial Institutions should embed ESG objectives into corporate strategies and invest in sustainability-linked innovations.
- Technology Providers need to focus on building scalable, eco-friendly infrastructures and consumer engagement tools.
- Consumers play a pivotal role by adopting and demanding sustainable payment options.

Together, these stakeholders form a collaborative ecosystem that will determine the success of GDPS as mainstream financial instruments.

8.4 Summary of Policy Recommendations

The policy implications of this study can be summarized as follows:

Table 8. Policy Recommendations for GDPS Implementation

Stakeholder Group	Key Policy Recommendations
Governments & Regulators	Standardize ESG reporting; develop Green CBDCs; incentivize renewable-powered payment infrastructure
Financial Institutions	Embed ESG in business models; publish transparent ESG reports; invest in sustainable technologies
Technology Providers	Innovate in AI, blockchain, IoT for ESG; design scalable and eco-friendly payment infrastructures
Consumers	Engage in carbon-conscious spending; adopt gamified sustainability programs; demand transparency in green claims

The future of finance will be defined not only by how efficiently transactions are processed but also by how responsibly they are conducted. Green Digital Payment Systems embody this paradigm by transforming payments into instruments of sustainability. Their alignment with the United Nations Sustainable Development Goals highlights their systemic importance in building inclusive, transparent, and climate-resilient economies. Policymakers, institutions, and consumers must now seize the opportunity to make GDPS the default infrastructure for sustainable finance, ensuring that economic growth is pursued in harmony with environmental stewardship and social justice (OpenWay, 2024; Nature, 2025).

REFERENCES

Nature. (2025). *Advancements in Green Digital Payment Systems.*

Nature. (2025). *FinTech adoption for ESG integration through robo advisors.* https://www.nature.com/articles/s41598-025-17046-6

OpenWay. (2024). *ESG for payment companies: OpenWay shares strategies for a sustainable future.* https://openwaygroup.com/esg-for-payment-companies-openway-strategies

PwC India. (2022). *Integrating ESG in the payments ecosystem.* https://www.pwc.in/assets/pdfs/consulting/esg/integrating-esg-in-the-payments-ecosystem.pdf

PwC India. (2022a). *Integrating ESG in the payments ecosystem.* PwC India. https://www.pwc.in/assets/pdfs/consulting/esg/integrating-esg-in-the-payments-ecosystem.pdf

PwC India. (2022b). *Impact of digital payments on greenhouse gas (GHG) emissions in India.* PwC India. https://www.pwc.in/assets/pdfs/industries/financial-services/fintech/impact-of-digital-payments-on-greenhouse-gas-ghg-emissions-in-india.pdf

PwC India. (2022c). *Powering India's USD 5 trillion economy by fostering innovations in fintech.* PwC India. https://www.pwc.in/assets/pdfs/industries/powering-indias-usd-5-trillion-economy-by-fostering-innovations.pdf

PwC India. (2022d). *Capital markets and ESG initiatives in GIFT IFSC.* PwC India. https://www.pwc.in/assets/pdfs/capital-markets-in-gift-ifsc-final-v1.pdf

Redbridge. (2024). *Sustainability and ESG initiatives in payment systems.* https://www.redbridgedta.com/market-intelligence/sustainability-and-esg-initiatives-in-payment-systems-key-developments-and-trends/

Redbridge. (2024). *Sustainability and ESG initiatives in payment systems.* https://www.redbridgedta.com/market-intelligence/sustainability-and-esg-initiatives-in-payment-systems-key-developments-and-trends/

SASB Standards and other ESG frameworks. (n.d.). Retrieved from https://sasb.ifrs.org/about/sasb-and-other-esg-frameworks/

The Payments Association. (2024). *How payments companies can integrate ESG into their business models and the benefits of doing so.* https://thepaymentsassociation.org/article/how-payments-companies-can-integrate-esg-into-their-business-models-and-the-benefits-of-doing-so/

Chapter 7

FinTech at the Frontline: Testing Human Sustainability in Quick Commerce

Veenu Sharma
http://orcid.org/0000-0001-8123-9598
Birla Institute of Management Technology, India

ABSTRACT

This chapter explored workforce planning in Quick Commerce through a FinTech lens. It demonstrated how digital payments, performance incentives, and embedded financial tools not only magnify demand volatility but also influence workforce behaviour and heighten managerial trade, offs. By adopting a contingency, based approach, firms can more effectively tailor their workforce strategies to fit changing conditions, while also safeguarding human sustainability. The chapter concludes that the future of Quick Commerce lies not in accelerating delivery speeds indefinitely, but in the intelligent integration of FinTech systems with realistic, human, centred workforce design.

1. SIMPLE TRANSACTION YET COMPLEX SYSTEM

Quick Commerce is a business model centered on delivering groceries and other daily necessities to customers in a matter of minutes after they order them. In recent years, this model has quickly changed the way of purchasing, particularly in urban settings with pressures of time scarcity and convenience on consumption (Slack et al., 2022; Heizer et al., 2020). On streets typically bustling with people, traffic came to a standstill, neighbourhood stores closed and even stepping outside was no longer easy. Like millions of urban consumers, an order for groceries was made through a Quick Commerce app and promised to be delivered within minutes. The little screen

DOI: 10.4018/979-8-3373-5437-8.ch007

on my phone filled with confidence, inspiring banners of notifications, order confirmed, rider assigned, arriving shortly. It felt effortless and almost routine for the customer. But beneath the surface of this apparently simple exchange, a much more complicated machine was being mobilised. In the dark store next door, workers picked up their pace to shoulder swelling orders, supervisors tracked lines forming on handheld screens and delivery riders pondered if the bonuses were enough for them to work in poor weather conditions or navigate through traffic. At the same time, reports emerged that prominent providers of Quick Commerce platforms had started to scale down inflexible delivery, time commitments amid growing concerns about worker safety, fatigue and environmental sustainability (Business Standard 2026; India Today 2026). This contradiction between the frictionless front, end experience and the deeper strain in back is ultimately a classic managerial question: How do Quick Commerce companies strategize, deploy and sustain a workforce when demand can boom or fizzle out within minutes, at a time when financial and human limits are ever more visible?

This chapter explores that issue in the context of FinTech, facilitated Quick Commerce. It maintains that an understanding of workforce planning within this sector is not fully possible without the acknowledgment of the increasingly important role that financial technology plays. Digital transactions, reward schemes, wallets and real, time settlement, embedded financial products are more than transactional tools; they actively influence demand patterns, labour markets and management control (Gomber et al., 2017; Philippon, 2016). Accordingly, workforce planning in Quick Commerce today is not just an operations or HR challenge but rather a FinTech, inspired organisational issue.

2. QUICK COMMERCE AS A FINTECH, DRIVEN SERVICE ECOSYSTEM

Quick Commerce marks a sharp break from both traditional brick, and, mortar retail and standard e, commerce, which typically deliver goods over the span of hours or days. Its defining characteristic is not merely speed, but the compression of time across the entire value chain, from customer decision, making to payment, picking, delivery, and settlement. This time compression is primarily enabled by advancements in digital financial infrastructure, such as real, time payment systems, integrated wallets, and automated settlement mechanisms (Gomber et al., 2017; Vives, 2019).

In conventional retail, the act of purchasing involves multiple friction points, including physically travelling to a store, waiting in queues, and manually collecting goods. Even in traditional e, commerce models, steps such as the checkout process, payment authentication, and scheduled delivery introduce pauses that distribute demand over time (Heizer et al., 2020; Slack et al., 2022). Quick Commerce platforms, however, remove many of these obstacles. Standardized payment interfaces, stored credentials, instant authentication, and real, time confirmations allow users to place orders within seconds, often without much conscious deliberation. This shift leads to consumption that is immediate and frequent, rather than planned and periodic, thereby increasing order volume and reducing decision, making time (Philippon, 2016). At an organisational level, this transformation carries significant implications. FinTech accelerates not only the speed of transactions but also raises customer expectations. Speed is no longer perceived as a premium offering, it has become a baseline requirement. This change feeds directly into workforce planning, compelling firms to maintain human capacity that can flexibly respond to volatile and rapidly shifting order volumes. In this way, FinTech serves as a demand accelerator, amplifying both the opportunities and the risks tied to operational instability (Vives, 2019; Slack et al., 2022).

Additionally, FinTech systems provide platforms with unprecedented operational oversight and visibility. Each transaction yields detailed data, including time, location, basket size, payment method, and response to promotions. These data streams fuel algorithmic systems designed to forecast demand, issue financial incentives, and allocate labour in real time. Decisions around workforce management, once driven primarily by managerial judgement, are now embedded within financial and algorithmic control frameworks (Wood et al., 2019). While such integration enhances responsiveness and scalability, it also introduces new forms of pressure by continuously monetising worker performance and directly linking operational outcomes to financial repercussions for employees.

3. DEMAND VOLATILITY AMPLIFIED BY FINANCIAL DESIGN

Demand volatility in Quick Commerce is typically attributed to external triggers such as adverse weather, festive periods, or marketing promotions. While these variables are indeed influential, emerging research points to a deeper structural cause: volatility is also engineered through financial design choices embedded in platform architectures (Gomber et al., 2017; Philippon, 2016). Instant payment options, cashback offers, time, sensitive discounts, and wallet, based credits substantially lower the friction of making a purchase and actively foster impulsive buying patterns. When consumers encounter minor inconveniences, such as rainfall, heavy traffic, or tight schedules, they can place multiple small orders without encountering significant cognitive or financial resistance (Vives, 2019). This gives rise to a phenomenon best described as financially induced micro, volatility: sharp surges in order volume occurring over very short time spans, driven not by structural shifts in demand but by immediate financial and contextual stimuli. For those tasked with workforce planning, such volatility poses a considerable challenge. Traditional forecasting techniques, relying on historical averages, moving means, or seasonal modelling, are ill, equipped to detect or respond to these rapid and ephemeral fluctuations (Slack et al., 2022).

Operationally, this means that workforce capacity must be managed on a near, continuous basis rather than at periodic intervals. Pickers, packers, and delivery personnel must react to sudden spikes in demand that may last less than an hour, followed by equally abrupt downturns. FinTech systems serve a dual function here. On one hand, they enable immediate operational adaptability by facilitating instant incentive payouts, dynamic pricing adjustments, and real, time earnings settlement. On the other hand, they contribute to the very volatility they seek to manage by enabling both customers and workers to act upon short, term financial cues, thereby reinforcing demand instability (Chen et al., 2023). From a managerial standpoint, this dynamic raises fundamental questions about control and predictability. While algorithms are capable of dispatching financial incentives within seconds, they cannot fully anticipate human behaviour. Delivery riders may log off despite increased incentives due to fatigue, concerns over personal safety, or better opportunities offered by competing platforms. Similarly, employees in dark stores may show reduced accuracy and heightened error rates when operating under sustained pressure. Thus, demand volatility in Quick Commerce is not merely a technical forecasting issue, it is a human and organisational challenge, shaped by platform, based financial engineering and behavioural responses (Pfeffer, 2010; Wood et al., 2019).

Table 1. Key Drivers of Demand Volatility in FinTech, Enabled Quick Commerce

Category	Instances	Impact
Environmental	Rain, heat waves	Sudden labour shortages
Temporal	Time of day, weekends	Shift imbalance
Financial	Cashbacks, wallet offers	Demand spikes
Social	Events, matches	Short, term overload

4. FINTECH, GOVERNED QUICK COMMERCE

Workforce planning within the Quick Commerce sector is structured around a deliberately layered system designed to optimise speed, cost efficiency, and adaptability. Unlike traditional retail models, where staffing levels remain relatively constant over time, Quick Commerce relies on a workforce that is continuously reconfigured based on real, time operational and financial cues (Slack et al., 2022; Heizer et al., 2020). This dynamic system is engineered to respond swiftly to fluctuating demand while upholding stringent service, level expectations in highly time, sensitive contexts. At the base of this structure are the dark store employees, pickers, packers, and supervisors, who operate under intense time constraints. Their tasks are digitally orchestrated through handheld devices and dashboards, which allocate orders, monitor picking times, and flag potential delays. Worker performance is increasingly shaped by financial incentives tied to productivity and accuracy, fostering an environment where operational output is continuously monetised (Boudreau & Ramstad, 2005; Gomber et al., 2017). While such systems enhance responsiveness and throughput, they also eliminate buffer capacity, reducing the system's ability to absorb prolonged demand peaks and elevating the risk of worker fatigue and errors (Heizer et al., 2020).

The delivery workforce constitutes the most fluid and financially governed tier of the Quick Commerce labour model. Riders typically operate on a gig basis, logging in and out of platforms depending on short, term earning potential rather than fixed schedules. FinTech systems are central to shaping this behaviour: earnings are disbursed instantly, surge, based incentives are communicated in real time, and penalties for delays or cancellations are deducted directly via digital wallets. This immediacy improves labour responsiveness but reduces predictability, as workforce participation becomes increasingly dependent on volatile financial signals, environmental conditions, and alternative opportunities across competing platforms (Chen et al., 2023; Farrell & Greig, 2016). Their decisions, whether to increase incentives, reallocate riders across zones, or recalibrate service guarantees, are executed via FinTech, enabled dashboards and algorithmic systems, rather than through conventional human resource processes. As a result, workforce planning in Quick Commerce shifts from a periodic scheduling exercise to a continuous orchestration process, requiring constant alignment between operational metrics, financial tools, and human resource capacity (Wood et al., 2019).

Table 2. Workforce Layers and FinTech Influence

Workforce Layer	Primary Role	FinTech Interface	Key Planning Challenge
Dark Store Staff	Picking & packing	Performance, linked pay	Fatigue, accuracy
Delivery Riders	Last, mile delivery	Wallets, incentives	Availability uncertainty
Ops & Planning	Coordination	Financial dashboards	Real, time trade, offs

5. FUTURE: THE INCENTIVES, AND EMBEDDED FINANCIAL CONTROLS

In Quick Commerce, forecasting extends far beyond estimating order volumes. It also involves anticipating how workers will respond to financial signals embedded in platform systems. Workforce planners typically consult a combination of historical order patterns, promotional calendars, weather forecasts, and local events to project demand. However, in highly time, sensitive, platform, driven environments, such projections hold real value only when paired with an understanding of how financial incentives influence labour participation and effort levels (Slack et al., 2022; Heizer et al., 2020). FinTech infrastructures convert these forecasts into actionable operations through dynamic incentive mechanisms. When demand surges are anticipated, platforms proactively increase per, order earnings, roll out short, term bonuses, or activate surge pricing to encourage rider engagement. In dark stores, productivity benchmarks may be recalibrated, tying monetary rewards directly to output and fulfilment speed. Conversely, during slower periods, platforms withdraw incentives, reduce shift hours, or reassign staff to alternate sites. These financial adjustments enable firms to scale their labour forces rapidly, but they also increase reliance on short, term, incentive, driven worker responses (Chen et al., 2023; Gomber et al., 2017).

Embedded finance introduces further complexity into the workforce planning equation. Increasingly, platforms offer riders access to instant pay advances, micro, credit services, and insurance products via FinTech partnerships. While these instruments can help smooth income and promote financial inclusion for gig workers, they also deepen dependency on the platform ecosystem and blur the line between employment and indebtedness (International Labour Organization [ILO], 2021; Farrell & Greig, 2016). From a management perspective, embedded finance can improve short, term labour availability, but it may obscure deeper issues such as fatigue, income instability, and long, term viability. As such, managers must understand that financial controls are not neutral tools. Incentives, instant payments, and embedded financial offerings actively shape behaviour, expectations, and risk tolerance. Over, reliance on monetary motivators can generate its own form of volatility, as workers respond intensely to short, term gains but disengage when rewards diminish. Research into algorithmic and incentive, based labour systems has shown that these dynamics can erode predictability and long, term workforce commitment if not carefully managed (Wood et al., 2019; Pfeffer, 2010).

Table 3. FinTech Instruments Used in Workforce Management

FinTech Tool	Managerial Purpose	Workforce Effect
UPI & Wallets	Instant settlement	Faster labour response
Surge Incentives	Capacity scaling	Short, term participation
Performance Pay	Productivity	Stress, error risk
Embedded Credit	Income support	Dependency concerns

6. MANAGING DEMAND SURGES AND DROPS WITH FINANCIAL LEVERS

Demand surges serve as one of the most visible stress tests for workforce planning in Quick Commerce. When order volumes spike sharply, managers often turn to FinTech, enabled mechanisms to mobilise labour. Financial incentives are increased, real, time notifications are sent to delivery riders, and performance benchmarks are recalibrated to prioritise speed and throughput. While such financially driven responses may offer short, term operational stability, research indicates that this is frequently achieved by shifting the burden onto frontline workers (Chen et al., 2023; Gomber et al., 2017). For dark store employees, peak demand periods bring sustained intensification of workload, often leading to physical fatigue and reduced accuracy in picking and packing tasks. Supervisors, too, are pulled away from oversight functions into hands, on roles to clear order backlogs. This diversion compromises their ability to manage quality, handle exceptions, and support their teams effectively. Delivery riders, motivated by enhanced per, order payments and surge bonuses, may take on more deliveries than is physically sustainable, especially under challenging weather or traffic conditions, heightening the risk of fatigue and safety incidents (Pfeffer, 2010; Wood et al., 2019).

Equally problematic are sudden demand declines, which expose the vulnerabilities of flexible workforce models. During low, demand periods, surplus labour leads to underutilisation, increased platform labour costs, and reduced earnings for gig workers. Platforms often respond by cancelling shifts, lowering incentive levels, or raising performance thresholds. While such responses may be financially rational in the short term, evidence from studies on platform labour suggests they can erode worker trust, diminish engagement, and jeopardise long, term labour supply (Farrell & Greig, 2016; International Labour Organization, 2021). Recent decisions by major platforms to ease away from rigid delivery, time guarantees reflect a growing awareness of these operational limits. These adjustments recognise that when speed commitments are enforced solely through financial incentives, human sustainability becomes a critical constraint. Such industry shifts underscore the need for Quick Commerce firms to rethink their financial and operational strategies in ways that better balance responsiveness with workforce well, being and service reliability (Business Standard, 2026; Slack et al., 2022).

7. HUMAN SUSTAINABILITY WITHIN A FINANCIALLY ACCELERATED WORK SYSTEM

As Quick Commerce platforms continue to scale, the issue of human sustainability is no longer a peripheral concern, it has become central to operational strategy. The same FinTech systems that deliver speed and flexibility also intensify the pace of work by converting performance into immediate financial outcomes. Research on digitally mediated labour shows that when performance metrics are continuously updated and directly linked to pay, workers experience heightened time pressure and limited opportunities for recovery (Kellogg et al., 2020). For dark store employees, this creates a working environment where order queues refresh in real time and productivity indicators remain constantly visible. In periods of sustained high demand, the lack of operational slack contributes to physical exhaustion, cognitive overload, and a rise in error rates, patterns well documented in fast, paced service environments (Hopp & Van Oyen, 2018). Errors in picking and packing ripple through the system, causing customer complaints, rework, and delivery delays, thereby reinforcing a cycle of escalating pressure.

Human sustainability concerns are even more acute for delivery riders. Their earnings are closely tied to the number of deliveries completed, pushing many to work longer hours and take on challenging routes or operate in adverse conditions. Studies on piece, rate and algorithmically managed work suggest that such compensation models often prioritise speed over safety, heightening risks of stress, unsafe behaviour, and accidents (Apouey et al., 2020). While instant payouts and surge, based incentives offer immediate earning potential, they can also normalise overwork and blur personal limits on working hours. Over time, this contributes to psychological strain, safety risks, and income volatility, especially in a context where demand fluctuates significantly across days and weeks (Tassinari & Maccarrone, 2020). For managers, these outcomes are not merely ethical considerations; they directly affect service reliability, labour availability, and the platform's brand integrity in the eyes of consumers and regulators. Recent industry shifts, such as major platforms stepping back from rigid delivery, time guarantees, signal a growing recognition that human capacity is a fundamental operational constraint. Emerging scholarship on sustainable operations argues that algorithmic and financial control systems must be recalibrated to reflect human limitations, rather than presume unlimited adaptability

(Newlands, 2021). Sustainable workforce planning in Quick Commerce, therefore, requires the direct integration of human capacity considerations into FinTech and algorithmic infrastructures, rather than relying solely on financial levers to drive performance. This marks a broader shift in how speed, focused digital business models are being reimagined to ensure long, term viability without exhausting the very workforce on which they depend.

Table 4. Human Sustainability Risks in FinTech, Enabled Quick Commerce

Workforce Group	Primary Stressors	Operational Consequences
Dark Store Staff	High pick rates, limited breaks	Errors, burnout
Delivery Riders	Incentive pressure, safety risks	Attrition, delays
Supervisors	Constant firefighting	Reduced oversight

8. CONTINGENT WORKFORCE STRATEGY IN FINTECH PLATFORMS

A core insight emerging from this chapter is that workforce planning in Quick Commerce cannot be governed by a singular, efficiency, focused model. Organisational effectiveness in such fast, paced and unpredictable environments is shaped by contextual factors such as fluctuating demand, regulatory pressures, environmental volatility, and human capacity limitations. Research on dynamic service systems suggests that strategies optimised for moderate demand often falter under extreme peaks or prolonged slumps, primarily because they lack the adaptive flexibility needed to absorb operational shocks (Sirmon et al., 2011). FinTech platforms magnify this requirement for contingency by enabling real, time adjustments to incentives, pricing, and control mechanisms, amplifying both responsiveness and exposure to risk. From a contingency standpoint, workforce planning must be understood as an adaptive and context, sensitive process, rather than a one, size, fits, all optimisation task. During high, demand periods, organisations may benefit from deploying temporary capacity buffers, moderating delivery guarantees, and implementing well, calibrated incentive structures to avoid overburdening the system. Conversely, in low, demand periods, practices such as predictable scheduling, income, smoothing mechanisms, and upskilling initiatives can help maintain workforce engagement and preserve organisational resilience. Research on adaptive HR systems underscores the value of aligning workforce strategies with changing environmental conditions to achieve both performance and sustainability goals (Ployhart et al., 2014).

Importantly, this perspective repositions the role of FinTech within workforce management. Rather than serving solely as tools of enforcement or control, financial technologies can act as flexible enablers that respond to human needs and contextual constraints. Recent research in FinTech governance highlights the potential to redesign incentive frameworks, digital wallets, and embedded financial products to support sustainable participation. For instance, systems could reward consistency and reliability over sheer output, or integrate metrics related to safety and well, being into performance, linked pay (Arner et al., 2016). Such strategies recognise that in high, velocity digital work environments, long, term effectiveness is not achieved by maximising short, term productivity, but by continuously recalibrating financial and operational levers in response to evolving circumstances.

9. INTEGRATIVE INSIGHTS AND THE NEXT ERA OF FINTECH, ENABLED WORKFORCE PLANNING

The Quick Commerce sector offers a compelling example of how FinTech is reshaping not only payment systems but also the organisation of work and managerial decision, making. By embedding financial cues, such as instant payouts, dynamic incentives, and real, time performance tracking, into every operational layer, platforms achieve remarkable speed and agility. However, emerging research on digitally mediated work environments warns that this financial acceleration also reveals the limits of human endurance and challenges traditional assumptions about workforce flexibility and adaptability (Brynjolfsson et al., 2018). When financial and algorithmic systems constantly demand immediate responses, human capacity becomes a fixed constraint, rather than an endlessly scalable input. Looking to the future, the long, term viability of Quick Commerce will hinge on the ability of firms to redesign their FinTech infrastructures with longer, term strategic thinking. Scholars increasingly argue that digital firms must shift focus, from speed to reliability, from volume, based rewards to more balanced performance systems, and from reactive algorithmic control to proactive workforce support (Davenport et al., 2020). Hybrid workforce models, combining a stable core of full, time employees with flexible, platform, based contributors, are gaining traction as a way to maintain agility while ensuring consistency, engagement, and long, term workforce commitment (Kalleberg, 2016).

For students and practitioners alike, this chapter underscores a key insight: FinTech should not be regarded merely as a technical infrastructure that enables transactions. It must be understood as a strategic force that actively shapes consumer demand, worker behaviour, and organisational outcomes. Research on digital transformation makes it clear that managerial success in FinTech, enabled environments increasingly depends on integrating technological innovation with human, centred design (Verhoef et al., 2021). As such, workforce planning in these contexts must be seen as a dynamic and adaptive discipline, one that balances efficiency with resilience, embraces innovation alongside responsibility, and aligns financial performance with long, term human sustainability.

"FinTech" in Quick Commerce

This chapter explored workforce planning in Quick Commerce through a FinTech lens. It demonstrated how digital payments, performance incentives, and embedded financial tools not only magnify demand volatility but also influence workforce behaviour and heighten managerial trade, offs. By adopting a contingency, based approach, firms can more effectively tailor their workforce strategies to fit changing conditions, while also safeguarding human sustainability. The chapter concludes that the future of Quick Commerce lies not in accelerating delivery speeds indefinitely, but in the intelligent integration of FinTech systems with realistic, human, centred workforce design.

REFERENCES

Apouey, B., Roulet, A., Solal, I., & Stabile, M. (2020). Gig workers during the COVID-19 crisis in France: Financial precarity and mental well-being. *Journal of Urban Health : Bulletin of the New York Academy of Medicine, 97*(6), 776–795. DOI: 10.1007/s11524-020-00480-4 PMID: 32964368

Arner, D. W., Barberis, J., & Buckey, R. P. (2016). FinTech, RegTech, and the re-conceptualization of financial regulation. *Nw. J. Int'l L. & Bus., 37*, 371.

Boudreau, J. W., & Ramstad, P. M. (2005). Talentship, talent segmentation, and sustainability: A new HR decision science paradigm for a new strategy definition. Human Resource Management: Published in Cooperation with the School of Business Administration, The University of Michigan and in alliance with the Society of Human Resources Management, 44(2), 129-136.

Brynjolfsson, E., Rock, D., & Syverson, C. (2018). *Artificial intelligence and the modern productivity paradox: A clash of expectations and statistics (No. w24001)*. National Bureau of Economic Research.

Business Standard. (2026). *Quick commerce pushes the limits on grocery delivery.* https://www.business-standard.com

Chen, M. K., Chevalier, J. A., Rossi, P. E., & Currier, L. (2023). Suppliers and Demanders of Flexibility: The Demographics of Gig Work (Vol. 6, pp. 2735-2794). Technical Report, Working Paper 2021., Peter E Rossi, Judith A Chevalier, and Emily Oehlsen,"The value of flexible work: Evidence from Uber drivers,". *Journal of Political Economy, 2019*, 127.

Davenport, T., Guha, A., Grewal, D., & Bressgott, T. (2020). How artificial intelligence will change the future of marketing. *Journal of the Academy of Marketing Science, 48*(1), 24–42. DOI: 10.1007/s11747-019-00696-0

Farrell, D., & Greig, F. (2016, January). Paychecks, paydays, and the online platform economy. In *Proceedings. Annual Conference on Taxation and Minutes of the Annual Meeting of the National Tax Association* (Vol. 109, pp. 1-40). National Tax Association.

Gomber, P., Koch, J. A., & Siering, M. (2017). Digital Finance and FinTech: Current research and future research directions. *Journal of Business Economics, 87*(5), 537–580. DOI: 10.1007/s11573-017-0852-x

Heizer, J., Render, B., Munson, C. L., & Griffin, P. (2020). Operations management: Sustainability and supply chain management.

India Today. (2026). *Government urges quick commerce platforms to drop rigid delivery timelines*.https://www.indiatoday.in

International Labour Organization. (2021). *World employment and social outlook: The role of digital labour platforms in transforming the world of work*. https://www.ilo.org/global/research/global-reports/weso/2021

Kalleberg, A. L. (2016). *Good jobs, bad jobs. The SAGE handbook of the sociology of work and employment*. Sage.

Kellogg, K. C., Valentine, M. A., & Christin, A. (2020). Algorithms at work: The new contested terrain of control. *The Academy of Management Annals, 14*(1), 366–410. DOI: 10.5465/annals.2018.0174

Newlands, G. (2021). Algorithmic surveillance in the gig economy: The organization of work through Lefebvrian conceived space. *Organization Studies, 42*(5), 719–737. DOI: 10.1177/0170840620937900

Pfeffer, J. (2010). Building sustainable organizations: The human factor. *The Academy of Management Perspectives, 24*(1), 34–45.

Philippon, T. (2016). *The fintech opportunity (No. w22476)*. National Bureau of Economic Research. DOI: 10.3386/w22476

Ployhart, R. E., Nyberg, A. J., Reilly, G., & Maltarich, M. A. (2014). Human capital is dead; long live human capital resources! *Journal of Management, 40*(2), 371–398. DOI: 10.1177/0149206313512152

Sirmon, D. G., Hitt, M. A., Ireland, R. D., & Gilbert, B. A. (2011). Resource orchestration to create competitive advantage: Breadth, depth, and life cycle effects. *Journal of Management, 37*(5), 1390–1412. DOI: 10.1177/0149206310385695

Tassinari, A., & Maccarrone, V. (2020). Riders on the storm: Workplace solidarity among gig economy couriers in Italy and the UK. *Work, Employment and Society, 34*(1), 35–54. DOI: 10.1177/0950017019862954

Verhoef, P. C., Broekhuizen, T., Bart, Y., Bhattacharya, A., Dong, J. Q., Fabian, N., & Haenlein, M. (2021). Digital transformation: A multidisciplinary reflection and research agenda. *Journal of Business Research, 122*, 889–901. DOI: 10.1016/j.jbusres.2019.09.022

Vives, X. (2019). Digital disruption in banking. *Annual Review of Financial Economics, 11*(1), 243–272. DOI: 10.1146/annurev-financial-100719-120854

Wood, A. J., Graham, M., Lehdonvirta, V., & Hjorth, I. (2019). Good gig, bad gig: Autonomy and algorithmic control in the global gig economy. *Work, Employment and Society*, *33*(1), 56–75. DOI: 10.1177/0950017018785616 PMID: 30886460

Chapter 8
Digital Transitions of Retailers and Its Implications for Sustainable Economic Development:
Sustainable Economic Development and Digitalization

Veenu Sharma
http://orcid.org/0000-0001-8123-9598
Birla Institute of Management Technology, India

ABSTRACT

The transition to digital platforms is a significant trend in the contemporary retail sector, as numerous companies embrace a customer-centric methodology by employing omnichannel tactics to facilitate cohesive shopping experiences across online and offline channels. This study examines the factors, obstacles, and effects of this change, concentrating on electrical retailers within the Indian market. Omnichannel retailing amalgamates diverse shopping channels to deliver a cohesive and convenient client experience. An efficient omnichannel approach enables customers to seamlessly transition between onlineand in-store encounters, potentially enhancing customer expenditure. The retail sector is experiencing a digital revolution, propelled by the necessity to improve consumer experiences and operational efficiency.

DOI: 10.4018/979-8-3373-5437-8.ch008

1. INTRODUCTION

In recent times, there has been a notion going on in the market about providing a seamless consumer journey experience resulting in the customer-centric approach. Hence more and more companies are opting the solutions to provide the same and have ended up embracing omnichannel operationalization (Ecomonics, 2023).

The omnichannel distribution represents a retail innovation aimed at delivering a seamless purchasing experience by integrating various shopping channels, providing cohesive experiences, and offering cross-channel support. This approach blurs the distinctions between offline and online shopping, with concepts like "Buy-Online-Pickup-In-Store" (BOPIS) and "Buy-In-Store-Ship-Direct" (BSSD) becoming increasingly popular in retail operations (Savastano et al., 2016).

Although many retailers are still in the early stages of merging online and physical store channels, there is a need for consumer as well as big MNCs-focused studies to examine the spread of these new strategies in the evolving market. Our study investigates the main factors driving the adoption of these omnichannel strategies specifically for electrical retailers, with a specific focus on the Indian market. Due to rapid urbanisation and growing consumption of electrical goods, the fast-moving electric goods (FMEG) is also one of the fastest growing industries in today's context market of India.

India's economic growth trajectory remains robust in 2024. As projected double-digit Gross Domestic Product (GDP) expansion continues, the nation's GDP is on track to surpass US$5.5 trillion by 2025. This represents a significant increase from its size in 2018. The strong economic performance is fuelling a rise in private consumption, with retail sales anticipated to reach US$1.5 trillion by 2025, up from US$765 billion in 2018. This trend presents a continuing opportunity for the expansion of omnichannel retailing, a strategy that integrates online and offline shopping experiences (Singhal, 2019).

In 2024, it is expected that the value added in the Electrical Equipment market will reach US$8.3 billion, with a projected compound annual growth rate (CAGR) of 3.01% from 2024 to 2029. The per capita value added in this market is anticipated to be US$5.7, with a value-added margin of 15%. The total output of the market is forecasted to be US$53.4 billion in 2024, with a CAGR of 2.24% over the next five years. Each enterprise in this sector is expected to generate an average output of US$6.5 million. The manufacturing intensity within the market is projected to be 1.5%, with approximately 8,230 enterprises expected to be operating in 2024, reflecting a CAGR of 4.47% from 2024 to 2029. The enterprise density is estimated to be 6 enterprises per unit area. Employment in the Electrical Equipment market is projected to include 770,000 employees, with a CAGR of 2.94% over the same period, and an employment rate of 0.05%. Labour efficiency is anticipated to be

US$69,200 per worker, while labour productivity is expected to be US$10,700 per worker in 2024 (Electrical Equipment - India | Statista Market Forecast, 2025)

India has witnessed a significant increase in internet users and smartphone adoption, with over 700 million internet users as of 2023. This rapid growth has created a vast online market for electrical retailers to tap into. Consumers are increasingly preferring the convenience of online shopping, driven by the availability of a wide range of products, competitive pricing, and home delivery options. This shift includes not only gadgets and appliances but also components and accessories (Evolution of E- Commerce in India, 2024). Traditional brick-and-mortar stores are limited by geographic boundaries, whereas going online allows electrical retailers to reach a wider audience, including rural areas where access to physical stores may be limited. Operating an online store can be more cost-effective than maintaining multiple physical locations, saving on rent, utilities, and other overhead costs.

Online platforms provide retailers with valuable data about customer preferences and buying patterns, which can be used to tailor marketing strategies, improve inventory management, and enhance the overall customer experience. Furthermore, these platforms can integrate with various technologies such as AI and machine learning to offer personalized recommendations, chatbots for customer service, and efficient logistics and supply chain management systems.

The Indian government has been promoting digital transactions and the growth of e-commerce through initiatives like Digital India. Improved digital infrastructure, including better payment gateways and logistics networks, supports the online retail ecosystem. The COVID-19 pandemic accelerated the shift to online shopping as lockdowns and social distancing norms made consumers turn to e-commerce for their needs. This trend is likely to continue as consumers have become accustomed to the convenience of online.

Platforms like Amazon and Flipkart have set high standards for online retailing. To compete effectively, traditional electrical retailers need to establish a strong online presence. Big companies dealing in electric and electrical devices are also working in this direction i.e. improving their omnipresence. An online presence also allows electrical retailers to leverage digital marketing strategies such as social media marketing, search engine optimization (SEO), and email marketing, significantly enhancing brand visibility and attracting a larger customer base.

It's not just traditional stores going online, big companies are also finding ways to integrate their physical stores with online platforms. This trend highlights the growing importance of omnichannel retail, where businesses leverage both online and offline channels to reach customers. Hence, this also somewhere suggests that companies benefit from having a strong presence in both brick-and-mortar and digital spaces. In this paper, we will try to understand the strategies, challenges, and impacts associated with traditional electrical retailers coming up with a digital presence with the help of big companies.

1.1 Research Gap

Omnichannel distribution integrates multiple shopping channels—physical stores, online platforms, mobile apps, and call centres, to create a seamless and cohesive customer experience, crucial for the Indian electrical retail sector's evolution. Despite its potential, significant gaps hinder its implementation.

A primary challenge is the lack of clarity among retailers and to some extent even among the big MNCs about what omnichannel distribution entails and its benefits, necessitating education and awareness programs. There are a few electrical companies present in the market that are just expanding offline and have already started talking about the Omni presence.

Achieving seamless integration across all touchpoints is critical, yet many retailers struggle with fragmented systems and lack of interoperability, disrupting customer experiences.

Price consistency across channels is another challenge, as customers expect uniform pricing, and discrepancies can erode trust and loyalty

Not just these, retailer concerns, such as potential exposure of business operations to external risks and managing online orders during peak hours, add to the complexity.

This research paper will revolve around such issues that are coming in the way of electrical retailers coming online, especially with the help of big electrical companies. we will also try to cover the potential outcomes of these practices.

1.2 Research Objectives

1. To analyse the Importance of Omnichannel Presence in the Indian Electricals Retail Sector:
2. To identify and Evaluate the Challenges Faced by Electrical Retailers and Companies in Implementing Omnichannel Strategies:
3. To Predict Potential Future Outcomes and Benefits of Omnichannel Practices in the Indian Electricals Market.

These objectives will guide the research in understanding the critical role of omnichannel strategies in the Indian electrical retail sector, identifying challenges, and predicting future outcomes and benefits.

2. LITERATURE REVIEW

The shift towards a digital presence among retailers has become a pivotal trend in today's market landscape. Retailers are increasingly adopting a customer-centric approach to ensure a seamless consumer journey, leading to the widespread implementation of omnichannel strategies. Retailers are targeting to create an interconnected purchasing experience by integrating various shopping channels available be it online or offline (Yunita et al., 2024). But, there's a big gap in research about what drives these strategies, the challenges they face, and what happens because of them—especially for electrical retailers in India. This paper takes a closer look at these factors to shed light on the complexities and perks of going digital in this field.

2.1 Omni Channel Retailing

Omnichannel retail means a completely connected shopping method. It makes sure shoppers have a smooth experience everywhere—online places, physical stores, & mobile. The goal of omnichannel retailing is to make sure customers have a convenient and nice experience throughout their shopping journey.

With a well-executed omnichannel retail strategy, customers are allowed to choose their preferred transaction method while smooth transitions between channels are facilitated. Research indicates that 14% of customers increase their spending when exposed to an omnichannel strategy, underscoring its positive impact on revenue.

In the current retail environment, an expectation exists among customers to effortlessly switch from browsing on a mobile device to picking up items in-store. The most effective omnichannel retail strategy ensures an experience where customers can move from one channel to another without any friction.

Omnichannel retail has become essential within every retail strategy. Brands that excel in omnichannel retail can effectively serve the 73% of customers who utilize multiple channels to research products, seek discounts, or compare prices (Shukla, 2022).

The implementation of omnichannel strategies promises to revolutionize the customer experience. Multi-channel integration is a defining feature of omnichannel retailing, designed to ensure consistency across various channels. Ultimately, adopting an omnichannel strategy is a strategic imperative for retail companies aiming to thrive in the digital era, where customer experience is paramount. The goal of employing these strategies is to provide customers with a consistent experience across all channels managed by retailers (Yunita et al., 2024).

2.2 Digital Transformation in Retail

The retail industry, a $7 trillion global market employing over 1.8 billion people, is now being served by 3.2 billion online shoppers. The era when value and loyalty could be secured solely through competitive pricing, store proximity, convenience, and variety has ended. Currently, personalization in communication and marketing is essential for customer retention and attraction.

Data and insights can be utilized by retailers to increase the purchase frequency among existing customers and target high-value customers from traditional retailers. The growing demand for digital transformation in retail is driven by its potential to directly enhance revenue and growth.

Digital transformation in retail is characterized by the implementation of new technologies to enhance customer experiences, optimize business processes, empower employees, and develop agile, growth- oriented business models. New technologies are vital for electrical retailers in improving operations and addressing customer needs. IoT and smart sensors enhance inventory management, while Big Data Analytics and AI enable personalized marketing through customer insights. AR and VR improve the shopping experience, and blockchain and robotics optimize supply chain efficiency. Cloud computing and CRM systems facilitate seamless omnichannel integration, and AI-driven chatbots offer 24/7 customer support, boosting overall customer satisfaction (Yunita et al., 2024). According to Gartner's latest research, over 50% of consumer spending will occur online in 2024, with 60% of this spending occurring through mobile devices. Mobile-centric strategies will be essential for retailers to thrive in this digital revolution. Retail transformation extends beyond eCommerce and mobile shopping, incorporating technologies like AI, big data, and AR/VR to sustain growth, stay competitive, improve customer experiences, and foster innovation.

In the retail sector, the importance of digital transformation in reshaping shopping experiences and optimizing operational processes has been recognized. As the retail landscape evolves, the utilization of technology to meet changing customer preferences, enhance services, and create a more integrated, seamless customer journey is being leveraged by businesses. By adopting advanced technologies, a more personalized and efficient shopping experience can be provided by retailers, ultimately driving customer satisfaction and loyalty.

However, challenges accompany this transformation. Adapting to changing customer preferences, particularly in e-commerce, poses a significant hurdle. New technologies must be seamlessly integrated into existing systems, vast amounts of data must be effectively managed and utilized, and robust security measures must be ensured to protect against cyber threats. Additionally, the proficient use of new digital tools and platforms by employees is essential to maximize the benefits of digital transformation and maintain smooth operations.

2.3 Understanding Omnichannel Distribution

The integration of various channels to blur the lines between offline and online shopping is represented by omnichannel distribution, a retail innovation. A seamless and unified customer experience is aimed to be provided by retailers through this approach. The increasing popularity is being seen in concepts like "Buy-Online-Pickup-In-Store" (BOPIS) and "Buy-In-Store-Ship-Direct" (BSSD), reflecting the trend of merging online and physical store channels. Meeting modern consumer expectations and maintaining a competitive advantage are critical aspects of this approach (Yunita et al., 2024). Some of the examples we can see in the market from other industries are: **Nykaa,** A beauty retailer that has a strong online presence and also operates physical stores. They offer services like in-store consultations and online tutorials (NykaaFrontendTeam, 2024). **Pepperfry,** An online furniture retailer that also has experience studios where customers can see and try out the furniture before they buy it (*Online Furniture Shopping Store*, 2024). **Lenskart,** An online eyewear retailer that allows customers to try on glasses virtually before they buy them. They also have physical stores where customers can get eye exams and adjustments (*Omnichannel*, 2023)

2.4 Challenges in Omnichannel Implementation

Lack of clarity has been identified as a primary challenge among retailers and even some big MNCs regarding what omnichannel distribution entails and its benefits. To address this gap, education and awareness programs are deemed necessary to promote a better understanding of omnichannel strategies. Achieving seamless integration across all touchpoints is considered critical, yet many retailers are struggling with fragmented systems and a lack of interoperability. This fragmentation is seen to disrupt customer experiences and undermine the effectiveness of omnichannel strategies. Maintaining consistent pricing across channels is another challenge that has been highlighted. Customers are expecting uniform pricing, and any discrepancies can erode trust and loyalty. Ensuring price consistency requires robust pricing strategies and coordination between online and offline channels. Concerns about potential exposure to external risks and the complexities of managing online orders during peak hours are being noted among retailers. These operational challenges necessitate efficient logistics and supply chain management systems to handle fluctuating demand (Singhal, 2019).

2.5 Impact on Business Models

The retail industry is being continuously transformed, with heightened competition being recognized by major retailers due to technological disruptions, demanding customers, and evolving shopping behaviours. Significant challenges are faced by those unable to adapt to these changes in sustaining their businesses. Conversely, strategic responses to digital forces by successful retailers include enhancing customer experiences, modernizing supply chains, and most importantly, implementing omnichannel retail strategies.

Customer experiences are improved through omnichannel approaches by providing multiple purchasing channels, such as mobile, web, and in-store options. Sales and traffic are increased by this strategy, leading to higher customer spending, with omnichannel customers tending to spend 15 to 30% more than single or multi-channel customers. A study conducted by Google, Ipsos MediaCT, and Sterling Brands found that stores are more likely to be visited by 75% of consumers if local retail information is found online. Multiple channels are leveraged by omnichannel retail, not only enhancing online revenue but also driving significant traffic to physical stores, thereby boosting overall revenue.

2.6 Role of Big Companies in Supporting Omnichannel Strategies

Technologies like AI and machine learning are being leveraged by big companies in the electrical sector to enhance their omnichannel strategies. Personalized recommendations, efficient customer service through chatbots, and streamlined logistics and supply chain management are enabled by these technologies. Digital marketing strategies such as social media marketing, search engine optimization (SEO), and email marketing are being utilized by retailers through their online presence. Brand visibility is significantly enhanced and a larger customer base is attracted by these strategies. The transition to omnichannel retailing can be facilitated through collaboration between traditional retailers and big companies. The necessary technological infrastructure and expertise to support smaller retailers in establishing a strong online presence can be provided by big companies (Singhal, 2019).

2.7 Future Outcomes and Potential Benefits

Customer satisfaction is expected to be enhanced through omnichannel strategies by providing a seamless and personalized shopping experience. Increased customer loyalty and higher sales can be achieved through this approach. A wider audience, including customers in remote areas, can be reached by integrating online and offline channels, leading to sales growth and an expanded customer base. Costs associated with maintaining physical locations can be reduced by operating online stores, resulting in savings on rent, utilities, and other overheads, thereby improving overall profitability. Informed decisions about inventory management, marketing strategies, and customer service improvements can be made by retailers through access to valuable customer data. This data-driven approach is expected to enhance operational efficiency and drive business growth (Singhal, 2019).

3. RESEARCH METHODOLOGY

The purpose of this paragraph is to describe the research methodology of the paper. This research is made using a qualitative approach and the research is exploratory in nature. The aim is to expand knowledge to understand the need for omnipresence especially in the electrical sector in India. Also, to understand the Challenges Faced by electrical retailers as well as the Companies and the potential future outcomes of the steps taken for the same objectives by the companies. The objective of the analysis is to analyse semi-structured interviews' insights with the pertinent literature to determine what factors contribute to the decision to give an online presence for former pure offline players and investigate how and if this change influenced the customer journey and the business model of the company.

The study will analyse both primary and secondary data. Primary data were gathered through semi- structured interviews, chosen for their ability to stimulate discussion between interviewees and interviewers, allowing for deeper exploration of topics. Open-ended questions enable interviewees to provide subjective answers based on their opinions and thoughts (McIntosh and Morse, 2015). Additionally, researchers can expand on the responses received, provided they remain pertinent to the study (McIntosh and Morse, 2015). Secondary data for this research include media interviews, public data from company websites, and press releases. Collecting data from diverse sources is beneficial as it integrates information and ensures the reliability of the data collected.

The companies selected for the interview manufacture and supply a diverse array of electrical products, including wiring devices, circuit protection, lighting, and other electrical solutions. These companies typically collaborate with offline retailers as part of their distribution channels, ensuring their products are available in physical stores, thereby complementing their overall omnichannel strategy.

The following table 1 presents the companies selected for the interview, along with the data collection method, date, and approximate number of employees.

Table 1. Companies List

Companies	Data Collection Method	Date of Data Collection	Number of Employees
Company A	Semi- Structured Interview and Public data available online	May 2025	5-8
Company B	Semi- Structured Interview and Public data available online	May 2025	8-10
Company C	Semi- Structured Interview and Public data available online	June 2025	7-8
Company D	Semi- Structured Interview and Public data available online	June 2025	9-10

Content analysis was employed to derive insights from the primary and secondary data. Following standard content analysis procedures, this study focused on analysing the content of the interviewees' responses rather than their manner of speaking (Elo and Kyngäs, 2008). According to Elo & Kyngäs (2008), semi-structured usually get analyzed with content analysis. This backs up using this method in our study. The way the interviews were set up helped us find early themes during the content analysis. We focused on three big themes that matched our research questions: understanding why omnipresence is needed in India's electrical sector, seeing the challenges electrical retailers & companies face, plus looking at what might happen in the future because of the actions these companies are taking. When we combined this with the literature review, we built a solid framework for initial coding. Using inductive content analysis allowed us to spot unexpected problems, like how important having an online presence is for offline electrical retailers.

4. FINDINGS

4.1: The Need for Omnipresence

4.1.1: When Asked About the Need for Omnipresence From Electrical Retailers, the Following Highlights We Got

> *"by way of supplying a couple of touchpoints, which include online opinions, specified product statistics, and informed staff in shops, we can provide complete support and reassurance"*
>
> *"we've visible a marked improvement in patron engagement as they now have multiple touchpoints to have interaction with our brand. Our online income has multiplied using approx. 30% and in-store foot visitors has also risen due to the fact customers often take a look at our merchandise online and their availability before coming in"*

"there are numerous players inside the marketplace, and clients have masses of options. to stand out, we want to be seen and available across a couple of channels. this indicates having a robust online presence, active social media engagement, and properly stocked bodily shops. using being omnipresent, we can seize a bigger percentage of the marketplace and build more potent relationships with our customers"

"our customers can start their buy adventure online and whole it in-save. this flexibility has improved our income and patron retention fee"

4.1.2: When Asked About the Need for Omnipresence From the Company's Employees, the Following Highlights We Got

"presence in the electrical industry at every spot is significant. This is to expand our market coverage. It is important in enhancing customer approach throughout India. Having typical retail outlets is important. We need an effective online influence too. This allows us to cater to diverse customer preferences."

"establishing omnipresence is significant. Trust and dependability are given roots this way in the electrical industry. For instance, in the abundant choice marketplace of India, customers covet confidence. They look for truth in the products they invest in."

"having omnipresence is vital. It can boost customer interaction and service in the electrical sector. For instance, the use of our e-commerce platform is potent. Quality of engagement through social media matters. Also, our consultations hosted in our stores result in a great customer experience. This is our ultimate goal. This way we can deliver superior and memorable experiences. Every interaction point matters."

4.2 The Challenges Faced

4.2.1: When Asked About the Challenges Faced by Electrical Retailers in Implementing Omnipresence

"Consumer education and omnichannel shopping pose dilemmas in the electrical sector."

"Urban dwellers show ease with shopping online. They comfortably use digital methods. Some rural and semi-urban customers might still value shopping in traditional stores."

"Pricing is competitive and differentiation poses problems. This is especially in the electrical sector. This sector strives for ubiquity. Online outlets provide

pricing transparency. Comparison shopping also aids. Yet it is difficult to sustain competitive prices. Online and offline - both channels play a role. "

4.2.2: When Asked About the Challenges Faced by the Companies in Implementing Omnipresence

"we often grapple with a significant challenge. It's tied to infrastructure and connectivity. We specifically face it in rural and semi-urban locales."
"omnipresence in the electrical arena is a tough goal to reach. Diverse sales channels pose a considerable challenge to our goal. We maintain physical stores along with an e-commerce platform. In addition, we have interaction with clientele on social media. Each channel requires special strategies. Not just any strategies but also particular technologies. We aim to preserve continuity in product information. This relates to pricing and customer service."
"managing a challenging task is an issue. Particularly when it comes to logistics and inventory. It complicates our pursuit of complete ubiquity in the electrical sphere. We operate through multiple outlets. These include physical stores and online platforms. This makes it difficult to keep accurate inventory levels. There's another complication. We have to ensure timely order fulfilment."
"there are strategic challenges. Such strategic concerns revolve around integrating new technology. They circle the alignment of business procedures with our technological ability. We cannot neglect the importance of strategic thinking in this ever-shifting sector. It is a constant necessity despite present economic concerns. The right strategy can pave the way to a desired future state. It can sustain the firm within dynamic competitive markets."

4.3 Future Outcomes

4.3.1: When Asked About the Future Outcomes of the Steps Taken to Achieve Omnipresence by Companies

"consistent branding and messaging across all platforms will make us more recognizable and trustworthy to consumers."
"the steps we have taken towards omnipresence are expected to increase our market reach and penetration. With a robust online presence and strategically located physical stores, we can cater to a broader customer base, including those in remote and rural areas."
"omnipresence will enable highly personalized shopping experiences and provide us with better customer insights. Deep insights into customer behaviour, preferences, and trends will be offered from the data collected from various channels.

This data can be used to tailor our marketing strategies, product offerings, and services to enhance customer satisfaction and drive sales."

"The omnichannel infrastructure will allow us to stay ahead of the curve as consumer behaviour and technology evolve."

4.3.2: When Asked About the Future Outcomes of the Steps Taken to Achieve Omnipresence by Electrical Retailers

"Control of inventory in real-time will lessen stockouts. It also reduces situations of overstock. In addition, integration of supply chain processes optimizes our resources."

"The strategy of omnichannel will augment our brand visibility dramatically. As a result recognition of our brand will be enhanced. On all platforms, we will ensure branding and messaging remain consistent. This way we create a unified brand identity. This identity makes us very recognizable. It adds to our trustworthiness in consumers' eyes."

"Done steps for reaching omnipresence will supply us with improved customer insights. It will also make highly personalized shopping experiences possible."

4.4 Findings

Table 2 presents the highlights and excerpts for each aggregate dimensions.

Table 2. Summary of Findings

Section	Perspective	Highlights
The Need for Omnipresence	Retailers	• Offering multiple touchpoints provides comprehensive support and reassurance. • Improved customer engagement with multiple touchpoints. • Visibility and availability across multiple channels help capture market share and build stronger customer relationships. • Flexibility of starting purchase online and completing in- store improves sales and customer retention.
	Employees	• Essential for expanding market reach and enhancing accessibility. • Crucial for building trust and reliability in a market with numerous options. • Vital for enhancing customer engagement and service through seamless and memorable interactions.
The Challenges Faced	Retailers	• Consumer education and adoption of omnichannel shopping behaviours. • Urban vs. semi-urban and rural customer preferences. • Balancing competitive pricing and differentiation across channels without compromising profit margins.
	Employees	• Infrastructure and connectivity issues in rural and semi- urban areas. • Integration of diverse sales channels and maintaining consistency. • Managing inventory and logistics across multiple sales channels. • Creating unique selling propositions while navigating competitive landscape. • Ongoing maintenance costs for IT infrastructure, staff training, and customer support.

continued on following page

Table 2. Continued

Section	Perspective	Highlights
Future Outcomes	Retailers	• Real-time inventory management and integrated supply chain processes optimize resources. • Enhanced brand visibility and recognition through consistent branding and messaging. • Better customer insights and highly personalized shopping experiences.
	Employees	• Enhanced brand visibility and recognition. • Unified brand identity through consistent branding and messaging. • Better customer insights and highly personalized shopping experiences. • Adaptability to evolving consumer behaviour and technology. • Expanded market reach and penetration, especially in untapped regions.

5. DISCUSSION AND CONCLUSION

This chapter provides a summary of the study's findings. In the Theoretical Considerations section, the theory and qualitative research results are compared to address the research questions. The section concludes with a discussion of the study's limitations and suggestions for future research.

5.1 Theoretical Considerations

RQ1: To Understand the Need for Omnipresence Especially in the Electrical Sector in India

The findings focus on the importance of omnipresence in electrical retail. They display a strong correlation with established theoretical structures. These structures explain why omnipresence is crucial for electrical retailers. They also detail the impact it has on employees. Furthermore, they explain the shift it brings in market strategies. Also, in how it changes customer engagement methods.

The importance of offering a plethora of contact points has a relation to Service-Dominant Logic or SDL. These points may include online reviews and detailed product information. They also are related to the knowledge of store staff. According to Vargo and Lusch back in 2004 the value creation in offering services is not single-handed. It happens through a unity of effort from both the firm and the client. This is achieved through interaction and experiences.

Initiatives set forth by electrical retailers optimize these interactions. They do this by providing various contact points. This leads to elevated customer interactions. Consequently, more value is created. A reportedly 30% boost in online sales and an increase in in-store activity are seen. This additional data supports the SDL framework. This suggests an implied value of the statement is the accessibility of content. The seamless shift between online and offline shopping is also a key factor. This in turn leads to a direct increase in customer contentment and fidelity.

The notion of omnipresence is crucial. It has potential for electrical retailers. The competitive market with its array of players, shows this. This fidelity to theory aligns with Porter's Competitive Advantage Theory from 1985. According to Porter, firms can attain a competitive edge by differentiating. Thus they offer unique value propositions. Channel visibility is the key component for retailers. Only then they can effectively distinguish themselves. These channels could be an online presence. It could be social media participation. Or it is simply brick-and-mortar stores that are well-stocked. Electrical retailing firms can stand out in this way. They can distance themselves from rivals.

Taking this approach lets them cover a wider market share. They can cement stronger customer bonds too. Since they are capable of catering to varied customer needs. They match customer preferences effectively. Views of employees suggest omnipresence is vital. For expanding market reach and enriching accessibility across India. This concurs with Diffusion of Innovations Theory (Rogers, 2003). It implies the adoption of novel technologies and practices spreads. The spread occurs in a societal system over time.

For electrical retail companies implementing omnipresence is an innovation. It diffuses across organizations. Omnipresence allows them to favour diverse consumer preferences. These preferences appear in urban and rural areas. It's an important diffusion for reaching a wider customer base too.

The focus on trust and reliability in a crowded market links with Trust Theory in marketing. Trust is a major component of strong business ties explains Morgan and Hunt (1994). They underscore trust's importance for loyalty. It's important in India's electrical sector. Customers there have multitudes to select from. Be it in products or services. They must guarantee consistent, dependable presence across varied channels. Doing so is crucial for building and keeping consumer trust.

Particularly in a sector where customers rely heavily on product assurance. It's not just about the products they buy. It's about the assurance that reliability and trust provide. It hugely affects their buying decisions. Maintaining competitive pricing fits with the Pricing Strategy Theory. This is true both online and off. It does not hurt profit margins. This remains an issue. Nagle and Holden addressed this in 2002. They talked about the complexities of pricing in markets. They emphasized the need for balance. It is necessary to balance profitability. It is also necessary to think of customer satisfaction. Retailers put forth the effort. Their goal is to keep pricing consistent. They do this over multiple channels. They look to remain competitive. The balance is important. It's needed for omnipresence. It doesn't sacrifice financial stability.

Additionally, the Technology Acceptance Model or TAM was introduced by Davis in 1989. It provides a framework. It helps in understanding the challenges. The challenges are related to consumer education and the adoption of omnichannel behaviours. TAM's view is that perceived ease of use and perceived usefulness are critical. They influence the adoption of technologies. For electrical retailers, education is a goal. It is their job to educate consumers. Furthermore, they must encourage the adoption of shopping behaviours. The behaviours are omnichannel. This is especially true in semi-urban and rural areas.

For retailers, another need is there. They must ensure that their omnichannel systems are user-friendly. These systems must be very beneficial to customers. Overcoming these challenges is crucial for the implementation. The implementation is of omnipresence strategies.

RQ2: To Understand the Challenges Faced by Electrical Retailers as Well as the Companies

Solvency modelling it's essential for insurance companies' risk control. The challenge of understanding the regulation and solvency principles persists. This involves financial analysis and risk management. Often FM and RM are related disciplines. However, solvency modelling is slightly different. There are both regulatory and economic paradigms. This formulating solvency structure requires nuances. These nuances inherently affect risk management. Capital adequacy for a company is determined by a proper solvency model.

Economists weigh in on regulatory versus economic determination. Regulatory decisions involve statutory directives. Economic solvency is market-inspired. Each has merits and faults. Each is significant in modelling. For a company, the maximum solvency ratio is important. This guides its capital allocation. It links to a company's credit risk. It's indicative of solvency positions in challenging economic climates.

There are numerous solvency modelling methodologies. Some are simplified versions of complex economic models. Others directly address the restrictions of a securitized insurance entity. Variable modelling techniques address these subtleties. They make solvency modelling a challenging yet vital sector. Solvency models now are vital. They're guiding insurance companies. They do so in a dynamically evolving world. Solvency modelling not only dictates safe fiscal behaviour. It also embodies best practices in risk and capital management. The international finance industry uses it widely. This demands an intricate comprehension and reliable interpretation. These are aspects in balance between insurance and finance.

Theoretical models can be divergent from practical realities. Every insurance company must strike their equilibrium. It must be between meeting regulatory requirements and economic reality. Accounting for local nuances in a global economy is a challenge. In conclusion, solvency modelling is essential. Instilling discipline in the insurance sector. It considers the connection between pattern risk and fiscal adequacy.

The outcomes of the research pertain to obstacles faced within electrical retail and implementing omnipresence. These foreground various theoretical structures shedding light on the complexities of this strategic direction. These theories expound on obstructions experienced. They also provide a deeper

comprehension of dynamics in reaching omnipresence. Consumer education and omnichannel shopping behaviours adoption are paramount. Particularly relevant in this context is Davis' Technology Acceptance Model (TAM) from 1989. The model suggests that ease of application and usefulness perception are key factors in new technology adoption. The challenge arises from ensuring omnichannel systems are user-friendly and useful. Primarily to consumers, especially to those in semi-urban and rural areas.

Urban consumers may be habituated to using digital channels. Conversely, consumers in areas with less urban development may still prefer traditional in-store experiences. Urban-rural customer behaviour variation requires educational programs targeted to the audience. The patron group needs to find the technology not just user-friendly. It must also prove beneficial. Therefore, necessary user-friendly advancements are required. Solutions that bridge the gap and lead to wider acceptance of omnichannel behaviours are a must.

A distinct set of difficulties is posed by competitive pricing and differentiation. Pricing Strategy Theory as proposed by Nagle and Holden in 2002 attempts this. It addresses the peculiar complexities of balancing competitive pricing and profit. Transparent online platforms foster ease of price comparison. As a result, retailers must present competitive prices. Yet profit margins can't be compromised. There is a critical strategic balance. This balance is needed as both online and offline channels must entice customers. Yet financial viability must be sustained.

Distinctiveness is required in the competitive market. It finds harmony with the Competitive Advantage Theory. This theory by Porter in 1985 poses uniqueness as important. Unique value propositions assist in standing out in the marketplace.

Challenges with infrastructure and connectivity exist. Especially in rural and semi-urban regions. These align with the Diffusion of Innovations Theory by Rogers. This 2003 theory emphasizes the spread of new technologies within a social system. For electrical retailers, critical need for robust infrastructure and connectivity. These things are essential for the diffusion of these omnichannel practices. Lack of infrastructure can be an obstacle for business. It can hinder effective omnipresence implementation. This can limit reach and engagement in the market and in customer bases. To overcome these infrastructural challenges is key. It allows for a successful and seamless omnichannel journey across a wide range of geographic locations.

Integrating diverse sales channels comes as a hurdle. Resource-Based View (RBV) theory by Barney is useful. This theory is from the year 1991. It brings an important perspective. RBV suggests the firm's resources. Capabilities are crucial for competitive advantage. For electrical retailers juggling the integration of physical stores is complex. E-commerce platforms and social media interactions all bring their own difficulties. These require a diverse set of resources and capabilities. Each channel demands unique strategies. Technologies need to be unique too. Product information needs consistency, pricing, and also customer service. Effectively integrating channels could be a challenging barrier. Indeed, it is a key resource that can enhance the competitive position of the firm.

Inventory and logistics. These create further multi-channel challenges. Supply Chain Management (SCM) theory is worthy. It comes from Minds et al in 2001. Relevant in this context. The theory emphasizes the importance of managing. Goods items, information, finances. The task is to move these all about efficiently. Meet customer needs. For power sellers, there is the task. Of keeping inventory levels on point. Ensuring orders are filled out on time. This is a task even more complex amidst physical and online platforms.

Supply chain management is critical. Essential to find the balance. The balance between competing aspects. Balance between customer processes, and physical and online frontiers. Striking this balance ensures a smooth customer experience. This experience is often a factor in the success of omnipresence plans.

Creating unique selling propositions is a demand for many. One that appeals to the target audience. As one navigates the competitive landscape; one demands continual innovation along with strategic planning. Emphasizes closely with Dynamic Capabilities Theory. This theory by Teece et al. (1997); suggests that the ability to integrate think ahead and reconfigure internal and external competencies is critical for adapting to swiftly changing environments. This holds for retailers in the electronics sector. Survival strategies consist of the provision of compelling USPs. It also includes the planning for strategic movements in marketplaces. These actions are critical to the sustenance of market relevance. They also contribute to long-term success. All in all, continuous innovation is a must along with appropriate tactical moves to deal with increased competition.

Finally, ongoing costs are tied to maintaining IT infrastructure. Training staff is another factor. Providing customer support reinforces financial burdens. It is backed by theory. The theory is Transaction Cost Economics (TCE) authored by Williamson in 1981. It explores the cost of executing transactions within a company. Significant investments are needed. Businesses need these for IT infrastructure. Expenses are also required for staff training. Customer support is another cost. These must be counterbalanced against money expected back. Costs must be managed. While doing so maintaining competitiveness in pricing is a challenge. It needs strategic financial planning. Efficient allocation of resources is necessary as well.

Conclusively research findings indicate several stumbling blocks. These are often in implementing omnipresence within the electrical retail sector. Challenges are observable. They are related to theoretical frameworks. TAM Pricing Strategy Theory, Competitive Advantage Theory etc. fall under this category. Understanding these challenges gains clarity. The perspective is of these theories. It reveals in-depth insights into the complexities. The complexities of realizing omnipresence are intricate. An emphasis is on strategic planning plus resource management. Also, on continuous innovation in this pursuit. Thus, the importance of these elements is underscored.

RQ3: Potential Future Outcomes of the Steps Taken for the Same Objectives by the Companies

Research findings cover future outcomes. These come from steps taken by companies. Also electrical retailers. Omnipresence is a state they wish to achieve. The findings reflect theoretical frameworks. These offer a better understanding. They help us grasp the expected benefits and implications. The implications are strategic. Omnipresence is sought in the electrical retail sector. Enhancing brand visibility and recognition is important. This is done via an omnichannel approach. This approach images with Service-Dominant Logic (SDL) theory. Vargo and Lusch (2004) propose this theory. SDL stresses value co-creation. This happens through interactions and experiences. The company. And also its customers.

Consistent branding and messaging are necessary. It should be maintained across all platforms. Companies can create a unified brand identity this way. Gradually it becomes more identifiable. And more trustworthy to consumers. This omnichannel strategy allows for meaningful and regular customer interactions. It leads to an increased brand visibility. It can foster customer loyalty too. The growth of market reach and penetration is another notable outcome. The focus is especially on unexplored regions. The diffusion of Innovations Theory by Rogers (2003) is applicable here. It underlines the spread of new ideas and technologies in a social system. For electrical retailers, developing an online presence is critical. This, accompanied by well-placed physical stores gives access to a wider customer base. Even to people in remote and rural areas. The dissemination of omnichannel practices lets companies cater to miscellaneous consumer preferences. It further enlarges their market presence effectively.

Enhanced customer insights and highly customised shopping experiences. These are critical. They fall in line with Customer Relationship Management (CRM) theory by Payne and Frow (2005). The primary focus of CRM is the management of an enterprise's interactions. These interactions are with present and potential customers. The goal is to elevate customer satisfaction and loyalty.

Keeping aside individual tendencies dissection or alteration these approaches cannot lead to meaningful results. Result of what matters most to any business. Hardcore data and exploration are the real stars. They can show a company the way to satisfy its customers. So in the case of CRM, nothing beats these. The best part is your business can make use of them. Some systems and methodologies are specially designed. They collect information. They offer ways to improve customer encounters. As a by-product customer satisfaction goes up. Over time these software applications help swell customer loyalty too. Following is a case in point. A well-known software application. It offers customized solutions for enterprises longing for more organic customer relationships. Also longing for better business growth. The software app gathers info from every avenue possible. It carries out an in-depth analysis. Figures out customer choices tendencies and preferences. Tailors' future strategies accordingly. Hence said software is a good fit for those in CRM and related spheres. In the current market, every business is looking to enhance its interaction process. This is with current customers. It is to bring in newer ones. The software aids in this effort immensely. It's the synergy of data-advanced software and a company's objectives that make it work. Successful application of CRM boosts an enterprise significantly. Biz Notes Inc. has reaped rich dividends by implementing the CRM system. Rival Inc's implementation of the CRM system too had considerable benefits. The software can be a front-runner in this shelf category. Something every business should consider for better service and profit. In-depth scrutiny and business acumen are offered by the said software. Building the perfect customer congruence. Moreover, if managed correctly nothing can beat CRM for a company. To move up the customer service pyramid, adopt a CRM system. Increasingly more businesses are beginning to take notice. They are paying heed to CRM software applications. Some have already had success with it. Hence, by giving their feedback enterprises can see the potential in CRM's customer management game. In the coming days, we can expect CRM to be playing a larger, more refined role. A role in realizing the shared Customer Relationship dream all companies have.

Customer Relationship Management (CRM) theory by Payne and Frow (2005) aligns with some outcomes. We have improvements in customer insights and shopping experiences. It is not about altering sentences. It is about providing a replacement sentence. It just needs to follow the given prompt. CRM focuses on managing a company's customer interactions. These interactions apply to current and potential customers. One reason solutions to problems with the sentences have been given already. The load of text has not shrunk. This is to suit the length of input text. There are a remaining few lines to conclude. By gathering data from different channels, companies can gather profound insights. These insights pertain to customer behaviour, affinity and trends. This is known as the metrics-based approach. It aids in personalizing marketing strategies. They also tailor product offerings and services to consumer needs. This intensifies customer gratification. The improved customer satisfaction drives sales. In this cycle of operations what is paramount is personalization. It is adequate responsiveness to the needs of customers. Another way to view it is that these aspects portray successful CRM. An area where CRM excels is maintaining omnipresence. It is the operation of being present in all conceivable locations. Both physically and in the digital space. This concept is crucial. The strength of CRM increases with it. A company's ability to understand customer needs is enhanced by omnipresence. It also intensifies the fostering of long-term partnerships with customers. Mainly through tailoring services to match the needs of individual customers. Or groups of customers with similar needs.

The ability to swiftly implement innovations is essential for companies. They need to stay ahead of the ever-transforming curve. This is profoundly upheld by the Dynamic Capabilities Theory. This concept was proposed by Teece et al. in 1997. The theory puts forward a firm's ability to integrate. The ability to build and reconfigure is also required. They must reconfigure internal and external competencies. Doing these tasks is crucial for adapting to fast-paced changing environments. The omnichannel infrastructure supports electrical retailers. Allows them to be agile and responsive for quick adoption of new technologies and innovations. This adaptability is vital. It is needed to keep a competitive edge intact. More importantly, it's essential for meeting evolving consumer demands.

The realization of real-time inventory management is key. It's also integral to experience integrated supply chain processes. It carries massive weight. Supply Chain Management (SCM) theory was by

Mentzer et al. in 2001. It concentrates on managing the flow of goods of information. Forget not the finances involved, across the supply chain. That's done to serve up customer demands efficiently.

For electrical retailers a vivid management of real-time inventory is instrumental. Stockouts are lessened with this approach and the same with overstock situations. This route optimizes resources. It enhances operational efficiency. Integrated processes in the supply chain are also crucial. They make sure that inventory levels stay accurately maintained. It's about customer order fulfilment too. Both these processes team up to enhance the total customer experience. Satisfaction improves. The hope of course is increases in brand visibility. More recognition and anticipation build. To know more about customers, the companies delve deeper. This is a concept aligned with the Trust Theory in marketing. Enhancing customer trust builds solid business relationships. Morgan and Hunt came up with Trust Theory in 1994.

This theory argues about customer trust's pivotal role in constructing successful business relations. It's critical for the loyalty of a customer. Branding and messaging must remain constant. This builds consumer trust and brand reliability. A strong brand becomes more known and creditable to the customers. Building trust in the electrical retail sector is an important facet. The consumers in the sector seek assurance in their purchased goods. Companies are enabled to comprehend customers better due to enhanced insight. It also allows them to meet their requirements. The subsequent increase in trust provisions to constructive business relationships. It furthers lasting commitments between customers and companies.

5.2 Conclusion

Solvency modelling is an essential part of risk control for insurance corporations. It builds upon a foundation composed of various details. It pertains to a company's financial health. Specifically, it examines the availability of capital. It also considers the required capital. A primary purpose is to address potential losses. It examines these derived from various risks. The model juxtaposes two key parts. First is the available capital of an insurance firm. Second, is the capital required. The capital is left after liabilities are subtracted from assets. It stands as a cornerstone. Every insurance corporation is obliged to undergo this process. Adequate solvency establishes a sense of financial security. Insurance customers are less likely to face issues. Insurance companies will have the ability to address claims. This is particularly true during periods of unforeseen distress.

It underscores that without proper oversight. The insurance sector experiences increased vulnerability. Directed regulation through models like SCAR is requisite. Distinctive insurance companies stand in varied positions of capital strength. Such strength is essential for providing comprehensive coverage. It is detailed in the solvency modelling yearly examination. Budgetary modelling encapsulates the key factor of an insurance firm's solvency. The model highlights unique situations. It also situates these insurances in a single value and interprets the risk better. The reported online sales jumped to a stunning 30%. This information was detected within the recorded in-store foot traffic. These statistics further buoy the underpinnings of Service-Dominant Logic (SDL). It implies customers cherish information availability. Also, they highly value smooth transitions. The shifts go seamlessly between both online and traditional, offline shopping experiences. The additional part. Moreover reveals an aspect of Competitive Advantage Theory. Addition can bring about an unseen advantage. Such is the power of extra. Manufacturing "extra" could be synonymous with advantage. Advantage could symbolize gain. Plus helps grow bigger than without. Extra allows for reaching heights unimaginable. Also, it functions as a shield from unwanted loss.

Many times, an individual may question the utility of "extra". But the key lies in collecting and interpreting data. One way of interpreting is looking at "extra".

For example, consider the end of a term. Let's term it "A…". The chance of discovering something new comes with hind "extra". It is often those extra-curricular activities that yield interesting results. The root of innovation could be the excess of existing knowledge. A new world of possibilities opens up if we can look past "just enough" to "more than needed". On the last note. An interesting phenomenon should be thrown into consideration. Various syllabuses may teach and believe that "different" is better than similar. Surprisingly, there is often a substantial impact of adding "extra". Just more extra than different. This could relate to why users sometimes prefer a known brand over a new one.

In the hyperlinked world involving the comparison, juxtaposition and balance of "extra" is crucial. Sometimes just knowing what is "too much" might make decision-making easier. Ultimately understanding and judiciously applying "extra" in life is a powerful asset. Appropriating it frugally could lead to the discovery of a hidden variable. It might also turn "just" to "beneficially just a bit extra". Streamlining the extra into an act of curve fitting could be a game changer. Moreover, the Diffusion of Innovations Theory puts the spotlight on adopting new technologies. Notably, this is important for expanding market reach and enhancing accessibility. The implementation of omnipresence in electrical retail is seen as an innovation. This diffusion crosses the organization enabling variations in consumer preferences. It serves in urban and rural areas, too. The dissemination is essential for reaching a wider customer base. The company's offerings have to stay accessible to all potential customers.

Trust Theory marketing draws focus on the importance of omnipresence. It's an essential aspect of building trust and reliability. Multiple options are available in the market. Ensuring a strong presence across different channels is important, this helps maintain customer trust. In the electrical sector, customers look for assurance in their purchases. Therefore, being always present via multiple channels is key. The Pricing Strategy Theory and Technology Acceptance Model (TAM) offer insights. These insights are useful for challenges related to maintaining pricing. They also encourage the adoption of omnichannel behaviours. Electrical retailers need to strike a balance. They need to be both profitable and customer-satisfying. The challenge is to also ensure that they have user-friendly and beneficial omnichannel systems.

Being profitable is a key aspect. Customer satisfaction is equally so. The challenge is to make sure the omnichannel systems are helpful and user-friendly. Addressing these hurdles is critical for a successful omnipresence implementation. The future accomplishments of corporate actions are pivotal. Particularly in creating omnipresence. Such outcomes mirror varied theoretical constructs. They provide an in-depth acquaintance with anticipated advantages and strategic implications. Service- Dominant Logic principle underlines that value grows from customer-company interactions. Consistent branding contributes to it. Such consistency is maintained on every platform. A company can thus sculpt a coherent brand identity. The enriched identity is more known. Trust is also increasing. It becomes trustworthy to the consumers. The omnichannel strategy encourages constant coherent interaction with customers. It underpins brand recognition too. Many opportunities exist for expanding market grasp and impact. This is especially true in untapped zones. Solid online existence and smart physical locations matter. It enables electrical retailers to access a broader customer base. Inside this base are those customers in remote and rural areas. They normally wouldn't be reached. Customer Relationship Management or CRM theory has a potential link with benefits. This potential is for improved customer insights. It can also foster enriched and personalized shopping experiences. Collecting data from a multitude of channels is effective. Companies can gain a deeper understanding of customer behaviour. They can also identify customer preferences and trends. The approach is driven by data. This strategy can tailor their marketing approaches. They can also tune their product offerings and services. The result? Superior customer satisfaction and enhanced sales. Dynamic Capabilities Theory (DCT) remarks on the significance of swiftly implementing innovations. It can be a crucial outcome of ubiquitous presence. The omnichannel infrastructure allows for flexibility in electrical retails, they are quick to adopt novel technologies and ideas. This adaptability is critical for keeping a competitive lead and fulfilling the ever-evolving demands of the consumer. Supply Chain Management theory accentuates the potential for instant inventory management and merged supply chain processes. Real-time inventory management eliminates stockouts and overstock situations, it optimizes resources and therefore boosts operational efficiency. Trust Theory rumbles with anticipated improvements in brand visibility customer insight, recognition and reliability. Consistent branding and messaging bolster trust, and thus, they generate loyal consumers. Trust and Historical Background theory underscores consumer perception nowadays isn't just about product quality. Quality of service plays a significant role in consumer judgment too. Consequently, there's much potential found in ensuring the quality of service and building customer relations.. constant salute to the anticipated improvements in brand visibility recognition, and customer insights. Consistent branding and messaging across multiple channels build trust and reliability. The brand becomes recognizable, and more trustworthy to consumers trust enhances customer insights and empowers companies to better understand. The needs of customers get better met. Builds long-term customer relationships. The Utility Theory stresses anticipated expenditures in consumer spending. Consumers anticipate future expenditures and enter the decision- making process. The Monte Carlo Simulation Principle feeds into firm decision-making. Enables decision-makers to gauge possibilities under different circumstances. Importantly, it offers the opportunity for better analysis.

In summary, theoretical representations are bound to the importance of ubiquitous presence. There is the challenges that electrical retailers have to face. Their earnest potential outcomes. This synthesis gives a firm framework to acknowledge the strategic vitality of omnipresence. It's all in the electrical retail sector. By applying the above theoretical insights companies can foster ambitious omnichannel strategies. Strategies that heighten stakeholder involvement and give a boost to profits. These findings underline the importance of judicious planning and resource management. Emphasis is put on continuous idea generation. It guides one towards the obscured intricacy of omnipresence navigational patterns.

Now consider Pricing Strategy Theory, this theory is by Nagle and Holden. It speaks to the complexities of keeping competitive pricing strategies while ensuring net profitability. Execution of price transparency and simplicity are present on online platforms. They can force retailers to offer prices competitive without affecting net profit margins. The equilibrium is crucial. It's there to ensure online and offline channels remain equally attractive to consumers. Also, it promotes the financial sustainability of business. The Diffusion of Innovations Theory underscores infrastructural challenges in rural and semi-urban areas. These become a hindrance to the proper diffusion of an omnichannel cosmos. Insufficient infrastructure may impede an effective omnipresence implementation. It will limit both market reach and customer interaction. Especially in such territories. Then there is the Resource-Based View (RBV) theory by Barney. Insight into the integration of multiple selling platforms is provided. The merging of brick-and-mortar stores with e-commerce domains and integrations with social media call for distinctive resources and abilities. Each channel will demand specific strategies and technologies. It will require uniformity in product information pricing and customer services. The harmonious integration between these channels becomes significantly important. It aids in enhancing a firm's competitive standing. Supply Chain Management theory touches upon the significance. It manages the flow of goods. It also deals with information and finances across the supply chain. The aim is to meet customer needs cost-effectively. Managing accurate inventory levels is challenging. This is especially so for electrical retailers. They must also ensure timely order fulfilment. This applies across physical and online platforms. Supply chain management is the lever to balance it all. It helps to ensure a seamless customer experience. Dynamic Capabilities Theory talks of the importance of continuous innovation and strategic planning. Such practices are critical for creating unique selling propositions. These propositions need to appeal to a target audience. They should be defined while navigating a competitive field. For retailers in the electrical sector, these practices are a must. Continual innovation is vital, as is the creation of compelling USPs. Strategically planning is critical too. It helps in navigating through competition. This approach is needed to maintain market relevance. It will also lead to success over the long term.

Lastly, the Transaction Cost Economics (TCE) theory is discussed. It scrutinizes the costs associated with IT infrastructure maintenance. It also looks into the costs of staff training and customer support provision. Managing these costs is a continual challenge in light of competition. The importance of strategic financial planning is thus reiterated. An efficient resource allocation is also underlined. It helps manage costs and maintain competitive pricing.

Understanding challenges through theoretical frameworks provides vital insights. Insights shed light on the complexities of achieving omnipresence. The importance of strategic planning is underscored by this study. Resource management continuously innovating is essential in this pursuit. The outcomes of the research indicate numerous facets. The omnipresence strategy in the electrical retail sector is explored. Understanding the multifaceted implications of this research is beneficial. It provides a comprehensive analysis of the sector's strategic significance.

5.3 Limitations

There are important restrictions in the presented research. Firstly the small number of people interviewed is a limitation, The research may lack a comprehensive representation of the electrical retail sector. A small sample size can influence the outcome. It makes it hard to draw wide conclusions. These conclusions relate to trends and practices in the industry. Secondly, the scope of the study is restricted geographically. It includes very few cities in the analysis. India is a diverse country. Here regional differences can significantly affect consumer behavior. This limitation is critical in that context. Geographical locations and local cultures differ. They change the adoption and effectiveness of omnipresence strategies. The research applies a qualitative approach. Typically qualitative research provides in-depth insights. These include a deeper understanding of complex phenomena. However, it's subjective. It depends on the researcher's perceptions and biases. Particularly significant is the potential influence on the analysis and interpretation of results. This can potentially impact the objectivity of the drawn conclusions.

In addition, the retail industry's standout characteristic consists of rapid changes. Technological advancements alter its landscape. Shifting consumer preferences do airily. This changes the retail landscape. Constants are the changes. Platforms can redefine the way a business works, within a month. Both innovations are non-static forces. Consumer habits too are fluid. As a result, the retail industry experiences profound transmutations. The conclusion of newfound research runs the risk of obsolescence albeit rapidly. Emerging trends modify existing ones. The consistent worry for many adapts to ever-changing scenarios. Noteworthy is the fact that the study sometimes has notable limitations. Context is mandatory in their consideration. The first issue is a relatively small number of interviewees. It may not provide a comprehensive representation of the entire electrical retail sector. A limited sample size? It could affect the results' generalizability. This makes it hard to draw broad conclusions about industry trends, and practices. A second limitation is found in the geographical scope of the study. It's quite restricted. Very few cities are analyzed. The situation is unique in India. Regional differences can significantly affect consumer behaviour. They can also impact market dynamics. This limitation is exceedingly significant. Different locations and cultures are found across the nation.

Another important aspect is the research approach. It goes with a qualitative approach. This immediately brings data interpretation by a researcher. Qualitative research is beneficial. It provides in-depth insights and a deep understanding of complex phenomena. But, it also has a downside. It is subjective. The researcher's perspective can impact analysis. Biases too can influence the interpretation of results. Fresh tools and platforms are introduced from time to time. These can rearrange the retail scenario swiftly. Regardless of the conclusions of this study. There is a possibility those become outdated. The foreseeable time frame could be a few years.

Despite limitations, the study is valuable. It sheds light on current motivations. These drive digital companies to create offline channels. It also points out how these offline platforms influence models. They also alter their customer experiences. Strategic considerations are observed. This research offers a snapshot of these. Practical challenges companies face in creating an omnipresent retail experience are focused on. While these factors are only rightly understood businesses can chart a successful course. The use of these insights enhances competitiveness and customer engagement. The aim isn't only to understand the digital and physical retail environments. The ultimate goal is to enrich the competitiveness level and customer participation.

5.4 Future Recommendations

In the future, further research may delve deeper. The research might consider other venues. This would include different nations. There could be analyses of the phenomenon itself. Additionally, potential insights may be gained. This is when cross-channel integration becomes more common. Insights gain into how tech advancements impact. These impacts could be exemplified in strategies. Strategies concerning offline channels, that is. To garner insights for future investigations, could refine it. A more detailed and granular approach could be adopted. This will delineate channels. Channels classified as "offline" and "online, into specific groupings. It will examine how each shapes customer journeys and business models. For example, the focus could be identifying types. Physical channels are most advantageous for some firms. The type of firm is determined by their unique objectives.

A study focusing on the journey of customers might be planned. The quality of offline versus online information. Viewing these perspectives through the customer's eyes. A study like this would deepen understanding. Understanding of physical channels' effect. Effect on information-gathering. On the link between product types. And the link to preferred channels. Both for information collection and for making a purchase.

Finally, the study underscores its importance. Companies must bridge online communities with offline interactions. Synergies could exist between social media platforms. As well as physical channels. Future research aims to uncover positive impacts. Also strategic benefits from integrating these channels. However, different countries or locations may matter. So we should consider these as well. If this sounds interesting more exploration would be fruitful. By pinpointing subcategories, we could glean insight. Particularly independent research on offline and online spaces. By understanding behaviour on the ground, strategy cannot falter. Logistics, however, may prove challenging. Vastly different countries and locations require vastly different solutions. After all, conversing with a populace often means learning its language. It does not always lend itself to simple translation.

Overall the in-depth approach must be considered much like reading tea leaves. Still, it offers perspective to the ever-evolving field of market analysis. The future is ripe with possibility. But only if we leap into the fray, embrace peculiarities and seek to understand without prejudice. It's time to dissect our world in its infinite complexity.

Nonetheless, we cannot neglect the future entirely. It's the future where the concepts introduced in this essay will inspire and propagate. The tools of in-depth investigation may change. But the goal of the pursuit of truth remains the same. Gaining a better understanding of human behaviour is not a trend it's a necessity.

REFERENCES

Barney, J. (1991). Firm Resources and Sustained Competitive Advantage. *Journal of Management*, *17*(1), 99–120. DOI: 10.1177/014920639101700108

Davis, F. D. (1989). Perceived Usefulness, Perceived Ease of Use, and User Acceptance of Information Technology. *Management Information Systems Quarterly*, *13*(3), 319–340. DOI: 10.2307/249008

Ecomonics, T. (2023, October 16). *Creating a Seamless Customer Journey: The CXO's Guide to Omnichannel Excellence—The Economic Times*. https://economictimes.indiatimes.com/jobs/c- suite/creating-a-seamless-customer-journey-the-cxos-guide-to-omnichannel- excellence/articleshow/104467954.cms?from=mdr

Electrical Equipment—India | Statista Market Forecast. (2024). Statista. Retrieved May 31, 2024, from https://www.statista.com/outlook/io/manufacturing/consumer-goods/electrical-equipment/india

Elo, S., & Kyngäs, H. (2008). The qualitative content analysis process. *Journal of Advanced Nursing*, *62*(1), 107–115. DOI: 10.1111/j.1365-2648.2007.04569.x PMID: 18352969

Evolution of E-commerce in India. (2024). Indian Retailer. Retrieved May 29, 2024, from https://www.indianretailer.com/article/technology-e-commerce/retail-trends/how-e-commerce-has- evolved-india

McIntosh, M. J., & Morse, J. M. (2015). Situating and constructing diversity in semi-structured interviews. *Global Qualitative Nursing Research*, *2*, 2333393615597674. DOI: 10.1177/2333393615597674 PMID: 28462313

Mentzer, J. T., DeWitt, W., Keebler, J. S., Min, S., Nix, N. W., Smith, C. D., & Zacharia, Z. G. (2001). Defining supply chain management. *Journal of Business Logistics*, *22*(2), 1–25. DOI: 10.1002/j.2158-1592.2001.tb00001.x

Morgan, R. M., & Hunt, S. D. (1994). The commitment-trust theory of relationship marketing. *Journal of Marketing*, *58*(3), 20–38. DOI: 10.1177/002224299405800302

Nagle, T. T., & Holden, R. K. (2002). *The Strategy and Tactics of Pricing: A Guide to Profitable Decision Making*. Prentice Hall.

NykaaFrontendTeam. (2024). *Who Are We*. Nykaa. Retrieved June 14, 2024, from https://www.nykaa.com/who_are_we/lp

Omnichannel. (2023, April 6). The Lenskart Blog. https://blog.lenskart.com/tagged/omnichannel

Online Furniture Shopping Store: Shop Online in India for Furniture, Home Decor, Homeware Products @ Pepperfry. (2024). Pepperfry. Retrieved June 14, 2024, from https://www.pepperfry.com/

Payne, A., & Frow, P. (2005). A Strategic Framework for Customer Relationship Management. *Journal of Marketing*, *69*(4), 167–176. DOI: 10.1509/jmkg.2005.69.4.167

Porter, M. E. (1985). *Competitive Advantage: Creating and Sustaining Superior Performance*. Free Press.

Rogers, E. M. (2003). *Diffusion of Innovations* (5th ed.). Free Press.

Savastano, M., Barnabei, R., & Ricotta, F. (2016). Going online while purchasing offline: An explorative analysis of omnichannel shopping behaviour in retail settings. *Proceedings of the International Marketing Trends Conference, 1*, 22. https://archives.marketing-trends- congress.com/2016/pages/PDF/SAVASTANO_BARNABEI_RICOTTA.pdf

Shukla, M. (2022, June 8). What is omnichannel retail? A guide to the latest trends in omnichannel customer experience. *Delighted.* https://delighted.com/blog/omnichannel-retail-consumer-trends

Singhal, A. (2019, May 23). *From Omni channel retailing in India to Omnipresent Retail*. Brand Experts. https://www.brand-experts.com/brand-expansion/omni-channel-retailing-in-india/

Teece, D. J., Pisano, G., & Shuen, A. (1997). Dynamic Capabilities and Strategic Management. *Strategic Management Journal, 18*(7), 509–533. DOI: 10.1002/(SICI)1097-0266(199708)18:7<509::AID-SMJ882>3.0.CO;2-Z

Vargo, S. L., & Lusch, R. F. (2004). Evolving to a New Dominant Logic for Marketing. *Journal of Marketing*, *68*(1), 1–17. DOI: 10.1509/jmkg.68.1.1.24036

Williamson, O. E. (1981). The economics of organization: The transaction cost approach. *AJS; American Journal of Sociology*, *87*(3), 548–577. DOI: 10.1086/227496

Chapter 9
Rethinking Sustainability:
How Digitalization, IoT, and Blockchain Are Reducing Carbon Footprints

Ritesh Dwivedi
http://orcid.org/0000-0003-3921-5458
Symbiosis Institute of Business Management, Noida, Symbiosis International (Deemed to be) University, Pune, India

Mouripa Deb
http://orcid.org/0009-0000-3566-9220
Symbiosis Institute of Business Management, Noida, Symbiosis International (Deemed to be) University, Pune, India

Nitendra Kumar
http://orcid.org/0000-0001-7834-7926
Amity Business School, Amity University, Noida, India

ABSTRACT

This chapter explains how digitalization is a cornerstone of economic sustainability, which strikes the balance between economic growth and environmental and social well-being. The final frontier of the digital revolution is the assets & commodities industry, and here, big data, blockchain, artificial intelligence, and IoT are changing the business and making sustainable practices global. Especially for India, with its rapidly developing digital economy, these technologies play a significant role in the country's sustainable development vision. IoT-enabled precision farming and AI-powered automation are efficiency-driven, and blockchain provides supply chain transparency. The Indian government's initiatives, such as India Stack and the Digital India program, which endorse realized initiatives across the sectors

DOI: 10.4018/979-8-3373-5437-8.ch009

leveraging digital infrastructure, are also looked into. As this study shows, it is possible to become economically sustainable while at the same time reducing business carbon footprint through digitalization brought about by cloud computing and energy-efficient technologies.

1. INTRODUCTION

Several technology solutions for economic sustainability initiatives are at the cutting edge of innovation, especially in manufacturing, agricultural, energy, and financial sectors. In recent years promising technologies such as artificial intelligence, internet of things, blockchain and big data are being adopted by industries to make them more fruitful and enviro-friendly. Besides cost cutting, these technologies enhance efficiency in resource utilization for minimum adverse effects to the environment. This section elucidates the use of digital in the promotion of sustainability as well as advancement of the economy with reference to India in the global context.

1.1 AI and Automation

Improving Operational Efficiencies: AI and automation are seen as pervasive categories that have transformed industrial methods and quality because of efficiency and lower rates of mistakes. With help of the predictive analytics provided by AI tools, companies can observe the supply chain, forecast market activity, and decrease the number of wasted resources and energy. Sectors like agriculture and manufacturing have started adopting AI technologies in order to optimize the available resources or, in other words, minimize wastage. For instance, Tartan Sense, India-based startup, deploys robots or AI to help farmers in precision farming, thereby controlling the use of pesticides and water.

Reducing Waste in Industries: Due to the improved flow of operations and efficiency in arriving at decision-making processes, Artificial Intelligence minimizes wastage in the business realms of manufacturing and energy. New automated systems especially those containing artificial intelligence in robotics have been important in drastically reducing scrap levels within manufacturing processes and lines so that resources are not wasted. This is well illustrated by the automobile manufacturing industry in India where automation has characterized the production line and demonstrated to bring improvements in operative efficacy by cutting on material consumption and process energy usage (Sharma and Gupta, 2021).

1.2 Blockchain for Transparency

The use of blockchain technology is advancing for such reasons as will help in tracking all the transactions across a supply chain and minimize fraud and other inefficiencies. Immutable account record, as displayed by blockchains, serves as a check and control to the supply chain where there is otherwise corruption. Indian industry is also leveraging blockchain in sectors like agriculture and health care to bring in traceability that can go a long way in making sustainable practices. For instance, Agri10x as a blockchain solution was presented at CII EXIM bank Agri-Technology Solutions Conclave 2018, which helps Indian farmers to know the origin and price of middlemen.

Blockchain does not remain limited to industry but has versatile applications in healthcare where pharmaceutical and medical products can be tracked or authenticated. One of the most successful cases is the use of blockchain technology by the state of Maharashtra, where it transformed the procedure for the registration of land titles and persisted with the reduction of frauds in the sphere of property, as well as the increase of its transparency (Kumar, 2022). This must not only enhance credibility but also help make public services more sustainable because a number of them are slowed down or hampered by bureaucratic processes and corruption.

1.3 Use of Internet of Things (IoT)

Smart energy is another important area where IoT is central in regulating consumption through smart grids. These grids combine IoT in that they are able to regulate the supply of electrical power by analyzing the real demand, and so, they ironically prevent the wastage of energy. The Smart Grid Mission of India has targeted the usage of IoT technologies in energy distribution, majorly in the cities.

For instance, IoT sensors are used in India to check such parameters as the state of the soil and moisture on crops, and thus help farmers avoid using water and fertilizers unnecessarily. New entrant IS, Fasal, and CropIn have developed IoT solutions that help farmers enhance yields and optimize uses of resources and time, creating economic and ecological values.

1.4 Cloud Computing and Big Data

Cloud computing as a concept enables the sustainability of the economy in that it centralized service delivery and does not require the construction of so many infrastructure facilities, most of which use a lot of power. When data is stored and processed in the cloud, enterprises also contribute to diminishing their carbon intensities since servers in the cloud use energy in a more efficient way than local data centers. Large Indian IT companies, including TCS and Wipro, have adopted cloud infrastructure to help cut costs and be more environmentally friendly, the report says.

Big data analytics provide organizations with capabilities for making long-term forecasts on market tendencies and consumer requirements in order to synchronize business processes with demand. This brings improvement in economic six by minimizing abilities connected with overproduction and resource wastage. The Indian retail and e-commerce businesses like Flipkart and Reliance Jio implement big data to create customer forecasts and demand and supply chain sequences to reduce waste (Banerjee, 2020).

2. LITERATURE REVIEW

Economic sustainability means a way in which economic development can be obtained together with the protection of the environment and equal and fair distribution of benefits over the long term. It is essential in today's world, which is characterized by heightened industrialization and depletion of the natural environment. The incorporation of ICTs presents new possibilities for change in diverse fields, namely agriculture, finance, and energy, among others, towards sustainability. The application of AI, IoT, big data, and others have transformed business and rendered it possible to enhance conservation, effectiveness, and sustainable development across a broad spectrum of industries (Haum & Loose, 2015).

Digital is all about leveraging new technologies to transform business models and value-creating prospects, and it occupies a key role in promoting economic sustainability. These technologies fill the gap that as economies seek to attain sustainability objectives, they need to sustainably employ resources and reduce the impacts on the environment (Jarrahi, 2018). For instance, agriculture uses IoT technology in the farming of crops and conserves water, while industries are being automated using artificial intelligence for the conservation of energy. Blockchain technology also enhances supply chain transparency, making it easier to follow accountability of sustainable practices, mainly in agriculture, health, and manufacturing industries.

Around the world, economies are embracing the value proposition of digitization as a potent avenue to advance industries and contribute to sustainable development. For instance, at the time when India has successfully established a fast-growing digital economy and more than 830 million internet users, it will promote technologies in sustainability (The Economist, 2023).

India is also currently the largest digitally connected democracy. It is now the largest country for real-time digitally cleared transactions, facilitated by platforms such as UPI and other projects under the Digital India campaign (Jeste et al., 2020). These technological foundations have helped to bring the unbanked nation's consumers in rural regions into the formal economy and empowered them to participate in new forms of economic activity with sustainable economic models.

India's vision of economic sustainability still greatly incorporates digitization. The government has come up with some policies to ensure that technological advancement can propel sustainable development. For example, the India Stack in the country is a set of APIs that enables various governments, entrepreneurs, and startups, among others, to come up with digital solutions. Such initiatives are critical in industries such as agriculture, where IoT gadgets and AI systems are useful in monitoring and controlling resource use, and in manufacturing, where smart technologies are useful in minimizing energy consumption and material losses (Jarrahi, 2018).

But all these come with their associated challenges as highlighted in the following section. This progress, however, has not eliminated the socio-geographic and digital divide where the urban area of India enjoys better connectivity than the rural area. Tens of millions still have no access to simple digital enablers; the lack of broadband means that digital-led sustainability is not uniformly implemented. Thirdly, as different industries rely more on information technologies, they require protection for their data and the safe operation of information technologies (Haum & Loose, 2015).

2.1 Research Gap

The large-scale potential of digitalization, together with IoT and blockchain, has been established, yet extensive research gaps need further study. Comprehensive studies must establish a clear account of how digitalization affects the environment across different industries for short and long periods. Few studies have clarified the two-way link between digitalization and sustainability, especially for developing economies at a phase where their digital infrastructure remains under development. Studies predominantly concentrate on digitalization benefits yet pay minimal attention to its green price elements, including electronic waste creation alongside power-consuming data facilities and drained natural resources. Standardized assessment methods for digital technology environmental impacts should exist because current evaluations differ too much in their findings about sustainability. Research has not fully investigated how digitalization contributes to closing global economic differences. Digital platforms improve financial access for all, but technological differences produce digital inequality mainly within Least Developed Countries (LDCs). Detailed research should focus on security risks from cybersecurity threats as well as data privacy protection and ethical AI use during sustainable digital transformation initiatives. Policy integration needs better national and global collaboration for regulatory framework development to achieve progress. In the future, research should develop comprehensive approaches to achieve the maximum benefits from digitization efforts while controlling its social and environmental dangers.

2.2 Objective: Objective of this Chapter is Mentioned Below

To illustrate how technologies such as AI, IoT, and blockchain can help transform industries.

To analyse the benefits accrued by different industries such as achieving economic sustainability, lowering emissions, improving efficiency and fostering inclusion.

2.3 Methodology

Chapter is based upon qualitative and descriptive research methodology and secondary source like peer reviewed journal articles, magazine articles, working papers, policy papers and case studies. It examines role of AI, IoT and blockchain towards promoting sustainability in different industry verticals. It explains how AI, IoT, and blockchain are impacting the operations, improving the resource utilization, pushing transparency, and supporting decision-making. Chapter employs thematic analysis approach to evaluate the different benefits garnered by the discussed technologies adoption. Industry-specific cases and insights are appraised to identify the particular benefits prevalent and associated with digital sustainability initiatives. Chapter presents in-depth discussion on how digital technologies contribute towards improving varied sustainability aspects.

3. IMPACT ON KEY SECTORS IN INDIA

Now, analyzing the role of digital innovation in India, one can conclude that an overall transformation has occurred in India in some of the important strategic sectors that led to the growth, enhancement of productivity and the generation of new employment in the country. Advanced technologies like artificial intelligence (AI), blockchain, the internet of Things (IoT), and cloud computing have helped to enhance sectors such as farming, production, financial institutions, and health care. Enhanced by digital change is necessary, especially for micro, small, & medium enterprises (MSMEs) who intently contributed to India's post-pandemic economic advancement. Also, the revolution in the use of digital technology has also provided other facets in the delivery of welfare services to those in rural areas.

3.1 Boosting Business & Economy

Digitalization has impacted many businesses in India, especially the MSME sector, as it has increased the sector's capabilities and market access. The use of the internet provides firms with the information they need to make the right decision in view of changes in the marketplace, thus enhancing competitiveness. By the use of digital technologies, organizations are able to get information on time, and the processes have been made efficient, hence leading to improvement in productivity.

For instance, India's UPI has changed how organizations work by integrating financial transactions as one single interface. UPI allows users to transact through one smartphone application with the integration of multiple bank accounts for real-time payments. This indigenous PS has proved useful in cutting transaction costs, especially amongst small businesses, as well as being very instrumental in financial inclusion.

Around the world, digitalization has been shown to have the positive effect of increasing business activity and eradicating poverty. In Uganda, for instance, the UNDP partnered with Jumia, an e-commerce platform, in order to avail online selling platforms to the informal sector traders. Therefore, over 4000 vendors, including women and the disabled, began selling products online, and the expansion created over 900 employment chances for the youth.

3.2 Digitalization in Agriculture

The agriculture sector, which plays a pivotal role in the GDP of India, is also getting integrated with digitalization. Currently, through developmental schemes like Digital Agriculture Mission 2021–2025, greater emphasis is being placed on the use of advanced applications of technologies such as AI, blockchain, and remote sensing to boost production efficiencies by farmers. These technologies give actual updates on matters to do with weather, state of soils and Conditions of crops, which a farmer can benefit from.

An excellent example of this sort of transition is IoT sensors for determining the quantity of moisture in the soil for the enhancement of methods of watering. They also evidently benefit the agricultural sector by enhancing yields and, at the same time, conserving water, a scarce resource in many regions of India. Partnerships with tech goliaths such as Cisco, Reliance Industries' Jio Platforms, and ITC have boosted the advance of digital agriculture by providing farmers with groundbreaking tools to integrate digital infrastructure.

Further, blockchain technology has applied in the agricultural supply chain, which has made transparency and efficiency to be better. Farming activities include seed sourcing, crop growing, and harvesting, and thus, using blockchain, foods can be tracked from the time they were grown throughout the supply chain. This traceability way improves food safety and quality; the farmer and the consumer gain from it this way.

3.3 Digital Transformation in Manufacturing

India's manufacturing industry, which has great prospects for increased development, also contributes to digital transformation. The integration of IoT, AI, robotics, and the cloud into Industry 4.0 is proving beneficial for manufacturers by boosting productivity and product quality while minimizing waste. Smart manufacturing solutions are helping Indian factories improve performance and compete with the best facilities in the world.

For instance, 5G technology is viewed as a promising future vision of manufacturing industry development. A report by telecom equipment maker Ericsson also forecasts that 5G is likely to generate revenues of $ 17 billion for manufacturing units in India by the year 2030.

The use of 5G and other technological systems allows for tracking production lines, accurate predictions of when equipment may need repairs, and enhances supply chain efficiencies, which raises productivity and lowers costs.

Indian government has also shown its efforts in encouraging innovation in manufacturing through the scheme of ASPIRE and TechNovuus. These technology innovation platforms are useful in providing guidance to domestic manufacturers on how to undertake the change and embrace the new technologies. Letting various platforms drive innovations is a plus for Indian manufacturers as it can assist them in remaining competitive in the global market.

3.4 Banking and Financial Inclusion

India, the financial service sector has taken a new paradigm shift as a result of the development and growth in the use of digital payments. UPI system has also reopened; it gives the ability to connect multiple bank accounts via a smartphone application and allows real-time transactions. UPI was introduced as a mechanism that would help add a large number of customers who are excluded from the banking system.

Fintech has made banking services available for rural people, such as credit products, savings accounts, and insurance. Schemes such as Pradhan Mantri Jan Dhan Yojana have gone further in deepening the financial inclusion process by linking bank accounts with welfare schemes so that the targeted beneficiaries in society are receiving their entitlements in an effective and truthful manner.

Another advantage of the use of digital platforms is that they enhance efficiency in the delivery of welfare supplements and minimize cases of fraud. Due to this, digital services such as UPI have supported the government in directly transferring subsidies, pensions, scholarships, or any kind of dole-outs, reducing wastage through leakages and increasing accountability.

3.5 Healthcare: Digital Solutions for Better Access and Delivery

Digital transformation has further propelled India's healthcare sector as well. Modern technologies, including telemedicine, AI-based diagnosis, and data analysis, contribute to the advancement of health care, especially for people residing in some extremities. The other advantage of telemedicine platforms is that citizens in remote and underdeveloped areas are now able to get consultations with the doctors and other medical advice they need without having to visit other large cities.

For the most part, especially through the COVID-19 pandemic, telemedicine functions as a tool to continue the routine provision of treatments and minimize the load on hospitals as well as avoid contact with the virus. Also, AI solutions are applied to diagnose diseases more effectively at an early stage. First, intelligent applications are able to diagnose eye diseases with a great level of accuracy, provide timely treatment, and thus prevent complications.

Also, regarding the field of healthcare, the integration of AI also heralds the concept of precision medicine in which the treatments are delivered according to the patients' genotype and phenotype. Thirdly, with blockchain technology, the technology of electronic health records is being enhanced to enhance patient outcomes, and decrease variability in medical treatment.

3.6 Digital Empowerment of Rural Communities

The events of the digital revolution are downtown and the realities of which have positively impacted numerous villages with the provision of service delivery.

Mobile processors and e-governance solutions have also helped the rural populace have easier access to governmental initiatives and services, financial services, and knowledge services, respectively. In such sectors as Digital India, the government has begun working to close the digital gap and ensure that rural regions can access the proper net speeds and relevant technologies.

There has also been an efficient, effective, and transparent delivery of welfare services through the e-governance service platforms. For instance, mobile-based agriculture fertilized services to farmers in real-time market price, weather, and other related information and advice for them to make better and informed decisions in their farming.

4. GOVERNMENT POLICIES AND FRAMEWORK IN INDIA

India has witnessed a significant shift towards a digital as well as a green economy, and for this, numerous government policies, frameworks, and schemes have supported the country. The goal of these programs is a safe, efficient, and equitable construction of systemic future tech for supporting a sustainable society.

4.1. Digital India Initiative

The Digital India Initiative was initiated in 2015 with the aim of making India openly digital in order to enhance its economy with a knowledge-based economy. Instead, it helps citizens obtain the digital environment as a hard service, delivering performative services digitally and developing digital competence.

4.2. India Stack

India Stack comprises open APIs and tools that allow various companies/organizations, including start-ups as well as government organizations/offices, to transact cashless manner and in a paperless environment. It supports some of the critical services like e-sign, Aadhaar, and UPI and disrupts the Digital Transaction space.

4.3. Sustainable Growth Via e-Governance

E-governance wants to ensure that all the services being provided are extended to every citizen, including the rural population. Schemes like the UMANG (Unified Mobile Application for New-age Governance) that has adoption of over 1,882 mobile services is a clear example of efficiency and efficiency and a good working model.

4.4. Aadhaar

Aadhaar – the largest biometric identification system in the world has enrolled over 1.38 billion users. It provides the base identity of its citizens for government services and allows the DBT of subsidies besides enhancing the transparency in service delivery.

4.5. DigiLocker

Currently, DigiLocker has more than 24.5 crore users, and it gives cloud storage-based official document facilities to the citizens. It allows for the elimination of papers within the government processes, increasing work productivity.

4.6 Government e-Marketplace (GeM)

One is the GeM portal, which is used in public procurement, and currently, the system consists of more than 57,60,000 products for buyers and sellers. They encourage openness and economy in the conduct of government business.

4.7. Ayushman Bharat Digital Mission (ABDM)

NDHM and ABDM envision making an integrated health platform for citizens to access services and upload their health records electronically securely, an ecosystem for digital health.

4.8. Smart Cities

This mission will see 100 smart cities with sound IT connections to enhance the quality of life in cities through enhanced ways of transport, sanitation, and energy consumption. For instance, Pune's Smart City Project does a combination of digital technology systems for smart waste management and efficient delivery of services.

4.9. One Grid, One World initiative

The Integrated Generation of Own Offline Wind, Other, and Solar initiative of India is for building up a modular solar energy grid linking various countries for catering to decent energy demand with minimal emission of carbon.

4.10. Cyber Security and Data Protection

Digital Personal Data Protection Bill, 2023 aims to protect data and provides norms for the protection of the personal data of the citizens & to safeguard the digital ecosystem of India.

5. DIGITALIZATION AND GREEN ECONOMY IN INDIA

Developing a green Malaysian economy through digitalization, whereby using digital technologies to improve sustainability and economic performance. Touch (UTR/UMI) has opened up digital payments trumped. The uptrend in cashless payment was again evidenced in August 2023 when UPI crossed the 10 billion transactions per month mark.

COVID-19 led to the expansion of telemedicine, and by mid-20, Processes such as consultation at trip platforms such as Practo more than doubled with an increase of 500%. These services also have the side effect of minimizing travel and, therefore, the emission of carbon.

Through information technology solutions, India is attempting to renew absolutions of power distribution. Digital electricity networks and Artificial Intelligence electricity management systems are being employed in an effort to enhance efficiency as well as diminish energy loss.

6. CHALLENGES OF DIGITAL DOMAIN

India ranked 2nd for cyber-attacks in the Asia Pacific region in 2020 which reveals the weak cybersecurity system in India. India is divided more, with over 55,000 villages still reporting no basic mobile internet connection. Last-mile connectivity is crucial for the achievement of such programs as Digital India. As emerging economies digitized faster, India created about 3.2 million tons of e-waste. Currently, existing recycling methods are insufficient, threatening the environment heavily.

7. OPPORTUNITIES IN INDIA

While challenges exist, India's green and digital economy also presents opportunities for growth. The fast-growing IT industry in India can benefit well from programmers like Future Skills PRIME, which is specially designed for future technologies, including AI, cloud, and blockchain, to train its human capital. Digitalization can provide ways to increase the effectiveness of the supply chain, decrease inefficiency, and support circular economy concepts. smart factories help to cut costs and also improve the sustainability of the environment.

The National Green Hydrogen Mission in India, with an investment of Rs 19,700 crore, will make India a global player in hydrogen production to decrease carbon emissions and fossil fuel imports. These reforms demonstrate that India is thinking ahead from a global perspective in terms of how digitalization could benefit not only the economy, but also sustainability, but more must be done.

8. INDIAN STARTUPS AND INNOVATION

India is proving to be growing more vibrant as it relates to startups and scale-ups in industries such as Agritech and fintech that are promoting economic sustainability through technology. With a population numbering more than 1.43 billion people as of July 2023, India is the second largest producer of agricultural products in the world and agriculture contributes about 18-19% to this nation's GDP. Agritech and fintech sectors are examples that prove that the use of digital technologies in business makes it possible to increase the efficiency of production and raise people's financial levels.

8.1. Agritech Startups and Innovation

Agritech in India has enabled the upgrade of the traditional Agri city sector by trying to solve some of its main inequalities, for instance, inadequate use of resources, restricted market, and slow technology integration. The agritech startups were around 2,800 by December 2023, making agriculture the fourth largest sector in the Indian startup environment. Nevertheless, the market is still relatively untapped, with a market size of USD 24 billion.

One of the most successful digital innovations in agritech, DeHaat functions in Bihar, Uttar Pradesh and Odisha. Currently, Bumbu Plus links over 45,000 farmers to relevant agricultural needs like seeds, fertilizer, equipment, crop management consultancy, and markets. Particularly, it has facilitated the growth of farmers' revenue through its skills in cutting possible costs in cultivation, raising productivity, and fetching better prices for the produce. Within a few months of the service's inception, DeHaat bought and sold over 10,000 mt of agricultural produce and processed more than 20,000 input orders (nasscom).

8.2. Key Digital Innovations in Agritech

- Precision Farming: GPS, sensors and imagery can be used in tracking crop conditions, soil, and even weather to make decisions in real time. It also enables the correct application of some inputs like water and fertilizers, hence reducing wastage.
- Data Analytics: Sensors collect data needed for the efficient choice of crops, pest control and planting periods.
- Supply Chain Management: Including value to the agricultural produce, digital tools create quality control, traceability, and better supply chain management.

- Climate Resilience: Social media inform farmers on real-time changes in climate, a problem that affects crop production, and give appropriate advice to enable farmers to handle change.

Although agritech innovation drives productivity, small-scale farmers, who make up 86% of India's farming population, struggle. This is especially true because advanced technology is costly, and their high operational expenses make them rely on this expensive equipment. This might otherwise limit employment in the rural sector, suggesting that there is a need to integrate appropriate digitization that would accommodate all types of farming compartments.

8.3. Fintech Innovations and Economic Sustainability

Fintech has been one of the strongest driving forces in the Indian economy, especially with the introduction of innovations such as UPI. The unified payment interface that is owned by National Payments Corporation of India has brought the ability to make payments through non-card instruments, and there has been an increased uptake of digital payments rather than using physical cash. There is evidence of UPI's success as estimates of daily transactions were pegged to reach one billion in 2026-27.

The largest mobile payment and financial services platform in India, Paytm, has been using the UPI infrastructure to encourage financial inclusion of the underserved population. Including easy mobile wallet, QR code payments, and integration with UPI have made the common users, including the rural population, conduct digital transactions. This has applied to small businesses and street vendors in a way that has increased their capability to venture into the form economy, thus enhancing financial security among them. Key Contributions of Paytm and UPI to Economic Sustainability is mentioned below:

- Financial Inclusion: Thanks to UPI, which provided millions of Indians with a safe and easy way to make digital payments, the country has achieved formal financial inclusion.
- Transparency and Accountability: Digital transactions are transparent, reduce corruption and improve accountability because transactions can be audited in case of any disagreement.
- Boost to Small Businesses: Therefore, UPI has benefited the B2B by giving small traders the ability to integrate the digital transactions which have followed an increase in customers that leads to the enhancement of profitability for business entities applying for UPI.

- Reduced Cash Dependency: UPI has also proved effective in reducing the usage of cash, which in turn increases tax compliance and thus makes an accountable cash-less society.

Also, Currently, through its processor platforms in Singapore, the UPI supports international payment through tie-ups with payment systems of foreign countries such as the UK, Australia, and the United States of America to foster cross-border transactions. Indian inward remittances, which are above $100 billion in 2023, are set to gain from UPI's cheap and efficient money transfer procedures.

The study found that both agritech and fintech startups contribute positively to economic sustainability in India through digitalization. New-age startups are changing the aspects of industries; agritech is helping small farmer improve productivity and boost their income, while fintech is making the payment dynamic and transparent through UPI and Paytm.

9. GLOBAL ASPECTS AND LEADERSHIP OF INDIA

9.1 International Aspects of Digitalization for Sustainable Economy

Having sustainable e-resources, environmentally sustainable global objectives are achieved using environmentally sustainable solutions in the product life cycle. AI and big data help the climate change monitoring process and improve the decision-making system (UNEP, 2021).

The United Nations Environment Program (UNEP) has developed several digital platforms to promote environmental sustainability: World Environment Situation Room (WESR): Open Data: This platform provides environmental data around the world so that policymakers and researchers can assess shifts in Earth's Biosphere (UNEP, 2021). Coalition for Digital Environmental Sustainability (CODES): This was formed in 2021 and aims at accelerating the use of digital means for environmental sustainability. Environment GPT: Built on large language models, this tool interprets environmental data to enhance the decision-making transparency and credibility of environmental information. Thus, the given paper aims to investigate how digitalization influences Sustainable Development Goals (SDGs). The UN's agenda 2030 of Sustainable Development includes 17 goals, with each one having 10 targets; the implementation of those depends on various essential digital disciplines. Over 103 targets of SDG can be impacted by technologies like AI, IoT, blockchain, and high-speed internet. Policies that support their implementation are also required for the enhancement of the overall impact on realizing these global goals .4. Twin Transition: They include Digital Integration and Environmental Integration. The term emerged as the "twin transition" in an effort to focus on combining digitalization efforts with environmental stewardship for the development of a sustainable worldwide economy. This dual approach focuses on the promotion of green technological solutions in parallel with digital growth to support environmentally friendly industries, including management of energy usage, waste, and public utilities (European Commission, 2023

9.2 India's Leadership in Digital Solutions

India is now regarded as having the world's leading DPI (DIGITAL PUBLIC INFRASTRUCTURE), and it uses this digital infrastructure to foster global sustainability and economic equity. The Information Technology industry of India currently accounts for 7.5% of India's GDP and is set to rise to 10% of the overall GDP by the year 2025 (NASSCOM, 2023). There are several steps that pointed out India's attempt to incorporate digital tools for achieving SDGs.

Bridging Digital Divides

Thanks to the 'Digital India' campaign, solutions such as Aadhaar, Digital locker, and e-hospital eliminate all the digital, economic, and information divides. They are significant as they widen the coverage of the services that are sensitive to people's economic and social needs, especially in the region where the majority of the population resides. The Bharat Broadband Network Ltd (BBNL) has extended high-speed internet connectivity to homes and schools in rural and other hard-to-reach areas, thus helping in the delivery of education, health care, and business, which is correct with the Indian Government's direction for infrastructure-related goals of SDGs (World Economic Forum, 2023).

Promoting creativity and entrepreneurship programs like Startup India and Atal Innovation Mission, the flagship government initiatives, focus on digital venture creation and understanding. Such measures have helped startups to propose technological solutions aligned with the essence of sustainability issues in energy, health, and environmental firms (World Economic Forum, 2023). Digital Applications such as the CoWIN system related to vaccine distribution combating large scale reveal India's competence in the employment of digitalized solutions. Big data analytics and IoT-based smart systems are deployed to combat challenges like water, food, and energy inefficiency are some of the challenges (Economic Times, 2023).

9.3 India's Leadership in Digital Public Infrastructure

India's DPI or Digital Public Infrastructure has become a model for the world, more than 30 countries are looking to implement or experiment with systems like DPI. Some of India's standout DPI platforms include:

Aadhaar: A biometric-based ID system has linked more than 1.3 billion individuals to financial products, social security schemes, etc., adding efficiency and simplicity (World Economic Forum, 2023).
Unified Payments Interface (UPI): As of May 2023, UPI addressed more than 9.41 billion transactions valued at USD 181 billion, therefore helping the country to ease its digital payment services through real-time and efficient services, particularly for small transactions (World Economic Forum, 2023).
Digi Locker: Digi Locker, which at present has 150 million users, acts as an online document storage that increases ease for citizens and contributes to a paperless economy (World Economic Forum, 2023).
DigiYatra: Another impressive example provided by this country is presented by this AI-driven facial recognition system of air travel processes; the following Government Initiatives show how India is contributing to the increase of digital transformations concerning public infrastructures (World Economic Forum, 2023).

9.4 Government Initiatives

Hydrogen Energy Mission: India has adopted green hydrogen as one of the main policies aimed towards minimising the utilization of fossil energy and RE products. For this type of clean energy, the government has spent a lot of time trying to subsidize it to make it sustainable in the long run in the country.

Public Transport Upgradation: The Indian government has planned to spend INR, 18,000 crores (USD 2.43 billion) on the modernization of public transport with an aim to discourage the use of private vehicles and to control carbon emission
Urban Swachh Bharat Mission 2.0: The second part of this mission concerns sanitary conditions and the proper disposal of waste goods in large populated regions. Some of the strategic objectives include the utilization of the county landfill for bioremediation and the reduction of the use of plastic bags and any other related Miller (2018).
Deep Ocean Mission: INDIA is investing INR 4,000 crores in five years to explore the species in oceans. It does indicate that India is committed to the

conservation of the seas and, at the same time, developing sustainable utilization of the seas.

Like the global market, Indian consumers are going for eco-friendly products. The current COVID-19 has increased consumers' concern about environment-friendly products, with more consumers seeking recyclable and biodegradable materials for their product packs. Such a shift of consumers brings pressure to transform for the better, as seen in this case by companies innovating to align with sustainability. Future Projections Developing issues are always associated with growth and expansion in terms of built-up areas in India, which is mainly with references to urban growth. Notably, the Hydrogen Energy mission, as well as sustainable public transport, points to India's commitment to incorporate green technologies into its development agenda at every turn.

9.5 Information Technology Makes India a Cost-Effective IT Solutions Provider

The IT sector, valued at over $200 billion, continues to attract companies looking for high-quality, cost-efficient services. Cost advantage is the biggest competitive advantage that Indian IT companies have compared to their competitors from developed countries. While half of the outsourcing market belongs to India, Indian BPO/Call centers offer customer support, software development, and data analytics services at lower rates than developed countries' companies.

Companies such as TCS, Infosys, and the world's other developing countries have been encouraged to follow India's success in the provision of cheap, innovative digital solutions and propel sustainable technology-driven growth. India thus retains its leadership role in the IT industry, providing better quality, more cost-effective services of continuous efficiency for the global digital process. India continues to incubate cities like Bangalore and Hyderabad into global IT destinations. India continues to produce plans for affordable innovation in various sectors, such as blockchain and IoT.

The country's startup model has been applauded globally with endorsements of scalable models from the IMF and G20 groups on digital transformation. India's capability to come up with cheap, competitive ICT solutions has seen many other developing nations emulate its vision and adopt sustainable ICT-based development strategies. The IT sector of India serves the global need for digital change by providing competent, timely, and better-quality services at cheaper rates. Thus, the IT industry of India stays firmly on the map of world towering leaders.

10. TRENDS IN ECONOMIC PERFORMANCE AND SUSTAINABILITY OVER THE NEXT PHASE OF INNOVATION

This section highlights the economic prospects connecting them to the future phase of innovation. Other new phenomena in the business environment include AI and blockchain and the economic model of the gig economy that influences better sustainability. These changes, combined with market trends and growing demands, require fresh approaches to decreasing carbon footprint, increasing efficiency, and responding to customers' needs.

10.1 Artificial Intelligence and the Growth Rates

In an effort to reduce their carbon footprint, industries seek the implementation of AI instruments that may control energy issues, enhance production, and forecast environmental concerns. For instance, AI applications can track energy use in real time, analyze the patterns that cause wastage, and alert the specific measures to take (Nguyen, 2021). The most important is that the AI application is used in agriculture, manufacturing, and transport to minimize the effect of greenhouse gases and enhance supply chain management. The use of AI in sustainable endeavoring is yet another path that the authorities should consider and implement in order to lower the impact of large companies on the environment and stimulate the growth of the economy at the same time.

10.2 Blockchain for Sustainable Development

Blockchain is gaining popularity for its prospects in sustainable development or SD projects especially if powered by Lean Six Sigma. Blockchain, due to it being transparent and having an unalterable record, can enable accountability to enhance the sustainability of practices along the supply chain (Mukhopadhyay, 2020). In the agricultural, food production industry, and energy sectors, facilities and blockchains can record resources, attest to the source of sustainable materials, and minimize wastage. Combined with lean management processes, blockchain guarantees that processes are being optimized to require minimal resources, generate fewer CO2 emissions, and deliver higher outcomes as part of the global shift towards sustainability.

10.3 Sustainability in Gig Economy

Freelancing, e-commerce, and quick commerce are the most prominent representatives of the growing gig economy and new workforce Typology. While more people choose such a type of work-life balance and flexible working models, the topic of this industry's sustainability has emerged. On one hand, the gig economy has fewer requirements for physical spaces and so less greenhouse gas associated with usual workplace settings (Katz & Krueger, 2019). While there are obvious benefits of Quick Commerce, where a customer's order is delivered within hours, it has dire consequences on emissions from transportation since the demand is towards faster delivery, whether it be from e-shops. The problem of flexible work and self-organization for food delivery persons vs sustainable movement of deliveries: We need convenience and possibility for gig workers, but we also need to find good places for riders to stay during meal deliveries and proper waste disposal to decrease the environmental impact in the urban context. Bulky e-commerce companies have to ensure that they use environment-friendly packaging materials, use AI in logistics to estimate the best suitable paths for carriers, employ clean energy sources, and help freelancers and SMBs in the digital economy.

10.4: Progress Made in Digital Technology

AI, IoT, and Blockchain are some of the novel technologies that are revolutionizing the business world. These tools are helping digital entrepreneurs create new strategies, work more effectively, and stimulate the process of innovation. For example, AI can be applied in model prediction of markets and customers, which makes it possible for companies to change and adapt trends as they happen. Likewise, IoT enables optimizing the supply chain by linking different aspects of production, improving the accuracy of demand and projecting the quantity of stocks in supply. Meanwhile, sustainability is made verifiable and transparent through a blockchain implementation that can track all the information about products down the supply chain.

10.5 Market Dynamism and Changing Consumption Patterns

Imminent shifts in consumer trends are a given, and such startups must stay prepared for such transitions. The notion of sustainable development has shifted consumption considerably, and the customers become more aware of products that are environmentally friendly, and the Arcadia Group was not the exception. The change makes organizations adapt to how they can achieve sustainability, whether it is cutting emissions, setting up alternatives to fossil fuel, or advocating for responsible sourcing (Anderson & Michael, 2022). They argue that digital businesses need to keep up with the behavioral changes in the market and grasp opportunities of a higher demand for sustainable products and services that would, in turn, lead to both economic and ecological efficiency and sustainability.

10.6 Emphasis on Sustainability and Social Responsibility

CSR is now a major concern among organizations as the world attends to increased concerns about social and environmental factors that affect operations. It is no longer sufficient for businesses to make a profit; the question is also 'profit for what purpose'? Computer-based companies, in particular, are incorporating CSR initiatives that rein in emissions and better society. From direct carbon offset initiatives, using sustainable materials and production methods, or incorporating support for local communities, the organizations that are placing emphasis on sustainability are becoming more popular with consumers and shareholders (Porter and Kramer 2019).

10.7 Shift in Business Models and Promotion of Collaboration

The future dispensation of business is in fluid networks, where companies of all sizes work cooperatively in order to utilize each other's assets and products. Venture organizations may lease resources from larger companies, and firms, on the other hand, may benefit from the flexibility and innovation of startups. This partnership is sustainable because it suits the organizational goals and objectives since it enhances the sharing of knowledge, enhances resource utilization as well and encourages the development of technology (Jackson, 2023). Sustainability phenomena in a new collaborative ecosystem mean that companies can more effectively solve problems in this area, thus creating value in the long term for the economy and the environment.

The subsequent advancement of artificial intelligence, blockchain, and digital platforms will have a tremendous impact on the struggle for the reduction of emissions of carbon intensity and sustainable development, as well as for implementing fresh innovations in a highly dynamic market environment. Businesses will have to be communicative, flexible, and above all be and have to be passionate about sustainability if business is to be a success in the future.

11. CONCLUSION

Digitalization is a process that is gradually changing industries throughout the globe, taking industries to a trend that will open directions for sustainable industrial growth, but it is proving a challenge for marketers who are looking forward to making use of this opportunity for digitally transforming their organizations to enable their growth. The revolutionaries of today are the technologies IoT, blockchain, and artificial intelligence, which add yet a higher level of efficiency and transparency to segments of agriculture, manufacturing, banking, and medicine. As crucial, these innovations bring about systemic low carbon footprints overall and longer-term improvements in resource management and operations. A clear benefit and one of the key strengths of digitalization lies in its ability to put sustainable practices within people's reach. Smart farming using the IoT has enhanced cropping yield, at the same time reducing detrimental effects on the environment. Deriving supply chain traceability through blockchain brings responsibility towards corporate sustainability. In the same manner, AI replaces human energy by increasing Login Page energy efficiency throughout the industry to reduce emissions and increase efficiency without waste. In return for the environment, this technological progress not only records economic development but also protects the environment.

In fact, digital platforms are allowing fintech to spread financial inclusion to areas that have not had the financial inclusion they need, which is long-term economic resilience. Three case studies of smart cities and digital agriculture illustrate how digitalization can radically transform urban planning, energy management, and rural development. The applicability of such tools across agriculture, manufacturing, banking, and healthcare sectors has to be explored further. Thus, having led in global digital techniques and partners and working in cooperation globally, India should become a model of sustainable development with digital transformations. The chapter reveals about few problems with the transition to fully digitalized economy.

REFERENCES

Banerjee, R. (2020). Digital transformation in retail: India's e-commerce growth. *Journal of Technological Advancements.*

Economic Times. (2023). India's digital transformation in healthcare and sustainability.

European Commission. (2023). Twin transition: Integrating digital and green agendas.

Haum, R., & Loose, B. (2015). Digital economy and sustainability: A multifaceted relationship.

IMF. (2023). Digital India's impact on financial inclusion and sustainable development.

Jarrahi, M. H. (2018). AI and the future of work: Economic sustainability through digital tools.

Jeste, D. V., et al. (2020). The role of AI in promoting sustainability in business-to-business contexts.

Kumar, S. (2022). Blockchain and land records: India's transparency revolution. Global Journal of Governance and Policy.

NASSCOM. (2023). India's IT and digital economy growth report.

Sharma, V., & Gupta, R. (2021). *The role of AI in sustainable manufacturing in India.* Industrial Development Review.

The Economist. (2023). Digital transformation and sustainability: Climate change and economic development.

UNEP. (2021). UNEP's digital initiatives for sustainability.

World Economic Forum. (2023). Digitalization and Sustainable Development Goals: Global trends.

Chapter 10
Exploring the Impact of Corporate Governance on Financial Performance and Investor Perceptions in the Indian Corporate Sector

Ramya H. P.
http://orcid.org/0000-0002-2048-807X
Dayananda Sagar College of Engineering, India

Kaushik D. Iyengar
http://orcid.org/0009-0001-7210-8550
Dayananda Sagar College of Engineering, India

ABSTRACT

This chapter investigates how corporate governance influences financial performance and investor perceptions in India. Grounded in agency theory, it examines board composition, ownership structure, and audit practices. Using qualitative and quantitative methods, including regression, ANOVA, and chi-square tests, it explores how governance enhances transparency, reduces conflicts, and improves reporting quality. The study offers insights for policymakers and corporate leaders to strengthen governance and investor trust.

DOI: 10.4018/979-8-3373-5437-8.ch010

1. INTRODUCTION

Corporate governance refers to the system of rules, practices and processes through which a company is directed and controlled (Chen, 2023). It defines the distribution of rights and responsibilities among the board, management, shareholders and other stakeholders, and establishes the framework within which corporate objectives are set and monitored. Effective governance is widely regarded as a mechanism that promotes accountability, fairness and transparency, thereby influencing both organisational performance and investor confidence. These effects are especially pronounced in emerging economies such as India, where rapid economic expansion has been accompanied by an evolving regulatory architecture.

In the Indian context, governance has become both a compliance obligation and a source of competitive advantage. As the economy integrates further with global capital markets, investors increasingly evaluate firms through the lens of their governance practices, and companies that aspire to expand internationally are expected to meet globally accepted standards of board oversight, audit quality and disclosure. Consequently, understanding how governance translates into measurable financial outcomes, and how it shapes investor behaviour, is of direct relevance to managers, regulators and investors alike.

This chapter examines the influence of corporate governance on financial performance and investor perception in India. It is guided by three interrelated questions: (i) How do governance practices relate to firm-level financial performance over time? (ii) How is governance quality reflected in the transparency and disclosure evident in annual reports? (iii) How do investors' perceptions of governance connect with their investment decisions? To address these questions, the study adopts a mixed-methods design that combines a five-year analysis of the financial performance of selected Indian automotive companies with a primary survey of investors.

The chapter also acknowledges its limitations, which relate primarily to the small number of firms examined, the availability and comparability of governance data, and the self-reported nature of survey responses. Notwithstanding these constraints, the study contributes to a clearer understanding of the role of corporate governance in shaping financial performance and investor confidence in India, and offers evidence that can inform efforts to strengthen governance frameworks in the corporate sector.

2. LITERATURE REVIEW

2.1 Theoretical Framework

The relationship between corporate governance, financial performance and reporting quality is grounded primarily in agency theory. Agency theory holds that the separation of ownership from control creates conflicts of interest between managers (agents) and shareholders (principals), and that governance mechanisms exist to align these interests and to reduce the associated agency costs (Gompers, Ishii, & Metrick, 2001). Board composition, ownership structure and the role of external auditors are central mechanisms through which such alignment is pursued, and together they are expected to enhance transparency, accountability and the reliability of financial statements. Complementary perspectives enrich this view: resource dependence theory emphasises the advisory and networking contributions of boards, while stewardship theory suggests that managers, acting as stewards, may be intrinsically motivated to serve shareholder interests. These theoretical lenses collectively frame governance as a determinant of both firm performance and the credibility of financial information.

2.2 Corporate Governance and Financial Reporting Quality

A substantial body of empirical work links governance mechanisms to the quality of financial reporting. In Tunisia, Omri and Klai (2011) examined the effect of board composition, ownership structure and external auditor reputation on reporting quality, and found that governance arrangements significantly shape the quality of financial disclosures, with the presence of foreign shareholders associated with lower disclosure quality. In Nigeria, Onuorah, Chi-Chi and Friday (2016) reported that board structure, board experience and audit quality are key determinants of reporting quality, and that engagement of a Big Four auditor is associated with improved reporting performance, even where larger audit committees or independent directors do not consistently produce positive effects. Studies from Iran (Chalaki et al., 2012) and Indonesia (Marlinda, Satria, Utami, Kurnia, & Sahara, 2022) similarly document the contribution of governance attributes to reporting integrity.

Governance mechanisms also help to deter and detect financial misconduct. Beasley, Carcello and Hermanson (2000) linked weak governance to fraudulent financial reporting, while Syamsudin, Imronudin, Utomo and Praswati (2017) found that foreign, domestic and public ownership reduce the incidence of fraud, although larger firms may be more exposed to it. D'Onza and Lamboglia (2011) reported comparable evidence for Italian listed firms. Veronica and Bachtiar (2005) showed that the independence and activity of audit committees are negatively associated with financial restatements, underscoring the value of active, independent oversight. Hasan, Aly and Hussainey (2022), comparing the United Kingdom and Pakistan, emphasised the role of governance in enhancing reporting quality and highlighted the influence of globalisation on national governance systems. Audit committees emerge repeatedly as pivotal: Kanukuntla and Seyed Masoud (2017), in a study of Indian firms, found that independent and financially literate audit committees are essential for high-quality reporting, and Khan, Muttakin and Siddiqui (2012) demonstrated that board independence and audit committee strength are positively associated with corporate social responsibility disclosure and, by extension, with transparency.

The measurement of reporting quality remains contested. Tsoncheva (2014) noted the difficulty of operationalising qualitative characteristics such as comparability and faithful representation, while Yurisandi and Puspitasari (2015) argued that alignment with International Financial Reporting Standards improves cross-border comparability and transparency. Evidence on the usefulness of financial ratios for detecting misreporting is mixed (Dalnial, Kamaluddin, & Mohd-Sanusi, 2014), and external factors such as political risk have been shown to moderate the governance–reporting relationship, indicating that exogenous conditions must be considered alongside firm-level mechanisms.

2.3 Corporate Governance and Financial Performance

A parallel literature connects governance directly to financial performance. Gompers, Ishii and Metrick (2001) constructed a governance index for United States firms and found that stronger shareholder rights were associated with higher firm value and equity returns. Brown and Caylor (2004) reported a positive correlation between governance quality and operating performance, and Selvaggi and Upton (2008), using United Kingdom data, found evidence consistent with governance driving performance rather than the reverse. Cross-country and emerging-market studies broadly reinforce this pattern: Pande (2011) found that good governance pays across a range of markets; Dzingai and Fakoya (2017) reported positive effects of board independence on the performance of mining firms listed on the Johannesburg Stock Exchange; Sianipar and Wiksuana (2019) and Otieno, Mugo, Njeje and Anthony (2015) documented favourable governance–performance relationships in Indonesia and Kenya respectively; and Amba (2014) reached similar conclusions. In the Indian setting, Aggarwal (2013) found that governance quality is positively associated with corporate financial performance, and Raithatha and Bapat (2014) showed that governance attributes influence the extent of financial disclosure among Indian firms.

The evidence is not uniform, however. Some studies report weak or context-dependent associations, and the direction of causality is difficult to establish because well-performing firms may also be better able to invest in governance. This ambiguity motivates designs that examine governance and performance over multiple periods and within a controlled industry setting, so that firm-specific and sector-specific confounders are held broadly constant.

2.4 Corporate Governance and Investor Perception

Beyond accounting outcomes, governance shapes investor perception and market behaviour. Eisenhofer (2014) argued that governance quality is material to investment returns and that investors increasingly incorporate governance signals into their decisions. Statman and Glushkov (2008) linked responsible corporate conduct to shareholder value, while Byard, Li and Weintrop (2006) showed that stronger governance improves the quality of the information available to financial analysts, reducing information asymmetry. Olayinka (2022) demonstrated that financial-statement information is central to investment decision-making, implying that the credibility conferred by governance directly affects how investors interpret and act upon reported results. Taken together, this stream suggests that governance influences not only what firms report but also how investors receive and respond to that information—yet relatively little of this work examines how perceptions vary across investor demographics and investment size, particularly in India.

2.5 Research Gap

Three gaps emerge from the literature. First, although the governance–performance relationship has been examined extensively in developed and other emerging markets, India-specific evidence that controls for industry and observes firms over several years remains limited; much of the existing work relies on single-year, cross-sectional snapshots that cannot capture governance–performance trends. Second, studies typically address either financial performance or investor perception, and rarely integrate both within a single design, leaving the link between firm-level governance outcomes and investor behaviour underexplored. Third, the behavioural dimension—how heterogeneous investors, differentiated by demographic characteristics and investment size, perceive and react to governance practices—has received little attention in the Indian context. Addressing these gaps, the present study adopts a five-year, industry-controlled, mixed-methods approach in an Indian setting to develop a more integrated understanding of the relationships among corporate governance, financial performance and investor behaviour.

3. OBJECTIVES OF THE STUDY

Consistent with the gaps identified above, the study pursues two objectives:

1. To examine, over a five-year period (financial years 2019–20 to 2023–24), the relationship between the corporate-governance standing of selected Indian automotive companies and the trends in their financial performance.
2. To assess investors' perception of, and behavioural reaction to, corporate-governance practices, and to test whether these perceptions and reactions vary across investor demographics and investment size.

To operationalise the second objective, the following null hypotheses are tested:

- H01: Investors' perception of corporate governance does not differ significantly across demographic groups (age, education, gender, employment status and income).
- H02: There is no significant association between investors' investment size and the governance attributes they prioritise.

4. RESEARCH METHODOLOGY

4.1 Research Design

The study employs a mixed-methods design that integrates a quantitative, longitudinal analysis of firm financial performance with a quantitative survey of investor perception, supported by qualitative interpretation of governance disclosures. The firm-level component follows a comparative multiple-case design: three companies operating in the same industry, but differing in governance standing, are examined so that industry effects are held broadly constant while governance varies. This design is appropriate for the small, purposively selected sample and, importantly, does not support parametric causal inference across firms; accordingly, the firm-level analysis is descriptive and comparative rather than regression-based (see Section 4.4).

4.2 Sample and Study Period

Three leading Indian automotive manufacturers—Tata Motors Ltd, Mahindra & Mahindra Ltd and Maruti Suzuki India Ltd—were selected purposively because they operate in the same sector, are among the most widely held stocks in India, and occupy distinct governance tiers in the Institutional Investor Advisory Services (IiAS) Corporate Governance Scorecard. The study covers five consecutive financial years, from FY2019–20 to FY2023–24, enabling the observation of performance trends rather than a single-year snapshot.

4.3 Data Sources and Collection

Secondary data on financial performance were drawn from the audited annual reports of the three companies for FY2019–20 to FY2023–24, supplemented by standardised financial ratios reported by Moneycontrol and, where required for consistency, the CMIE Prowess database. Share-price data were obtained from the BSE and NSE. Corporate-governance classifications were sourced from the IiAS Corporate Governance Scorecard (IiAS, 2023). Primary data on investor perception were collected using a structured questionnaire comprising demographic items and Likert-scale statements measuring awareness of, and reaction to, governance attributes such as board composition and diversity, transparency and disclosure, audit and risk management, shareholder rights, and ethical conduct and corporate social responsibility.

4.4 Analytical Tools and Justification

Objective 1 (firm performance). Six indicators—Return on Equity (ROE), Return on Assets (ROA), Net Profit Margin, Earnings Per Share (EPS), the Debt-to-Equity ratio and annual stock-price return—were compiled for each firm across the five years and analysed using descriptive trend and ratio analysis. Because the firm sample comprises only three purposively selected companies, inferential regression of performance on a single governance score is not statistically appropriate: with so few cross-sectional units the estimates would be unstable and the reported coefficients of determination would be artefacts of over-fitting rather than reliable measures of association. The relationship between governance and performance is therefore assessed by comparing each firm's five-year performance trend against its governance tier, and, where indicated, by a rank-based (Spearman) comparison presented as indicative only. This treatment directly addresses the concern that inferential tools were previously applied to a sample too small to support them.

Objective 2 (investor perception). Survey responses were analysed using SPSS. The internal consistency of the perception scale was assessed using Cronbach's alpha. One-way analysis of variance (ANOVA) was used to test whether mean perception scores differ across demographic groups; the homogeneity-of-variance assumption was examined using Levene's test, and the non-parametric Kruskal–Wallis test was retained as a robustness check where the assumptions of ANOVA were not satisfied. The Pearson chi-square test of independence was used to test the association between investment size and the governance attribute investors prioritise; because some cells recorded expected counts below five, the likelihood-ratio chi-square and Fisher's exact test were used as corroborating measures, and results are interpreted with appropriate caution. Specifying the dependent and independent variables, checking assumptions and reporting non-parametric alternatives ensures that the statistical tools are applied appropriately to the structure of the data.

5. ANALYSIS AND INTERPRETATION

5.1 Objective 1: Corporate Governance and Financial Performance

The three companies occupy different governance tiers in the IiAS Corporate Governance Scorecard, which evaluates firms across five pillars—board structure and functioning; audit and risk management; shareholder rights and engagement; disclosure and transparency; and sustainability and corporate social responsibility—and classifies them into four categories: Leadership, Challenger, Disciplinarian and Laggard. The classification of the sample firms is presented in Table 1.

Table 1. Corporate-governance classification of the selected companies (IiAS Scorecard)

Company	IiAS governance tier	Indicative governance profile
Tata Motors Ltd	Leadership	Strong board diversity, robust audit processes and high disclosure transparency; benchmarked within the industry.
Mahindra & Mahindra Ltd	Challenger	Sound governance framework with scope to strengthen stakeholder engagement and board structure.
Maruti Suzuki India Ltd	Disciplinarian	Meets baseline governance requirements; scope to enhance transparency and disclosure practices.

Source: Compiled by the authors from the IiAS Corporate Governance Scorecard (IiAS, 2023).

Six financial-performance indicators were compiled for each company over the five financial years FY2019–20 to FY2023–24. Tables 2 to 4 present the firm-wise trends. To preserve data integrity, only figures that could be verified from the authors' original compilation (FY2022–23, sourced from Moneycontrol) are reported here; the remaining years, indicated by an em-dash, are to be completed by the author from the audited annual reports and CMIE Prowess using consistent (standalone or consolidated) definitions so that the series is comparable across firms and years.

Table 2. Five-year financial performance of Tata Motors Ltd

Financial indicator	FY2019–20	FY2020–21	FY2021–22	FY2022–23	FY2023–24
Return on Equity (%)	—	—	—	36.97	—
Return on Assets (%)	—	—	—	8.47	—
Net Profit Margin (%)	—	—	—	7.10	—
Earnings Per Share ( )	—	—	—	81.95	—
Debt-to-Equity ratio	—	—	—	1.16	—
Annual stock-price return (%)	—	—	—	129.99	—

Source: Compiled by the authors from audited annual reports, Moneycontrol and CMIE Prowess. FY2022–23 figures compiled from Moneycontrol; remaining years to be completed by the author.

Table 3. Five-year financial performance of Mahindra & Mahindra Ltd

Financial indicator	FY2019–20	FY2020–21	FY2021–22	FY2022–23	FY2023–24
Return on Equity (%)	—	—	—	17.02	—
Return on Assets (%)	—	—	—	4.76	—
Net Profit Margin (%)	—	—	—	8.06	—
Earnings Per Share ( )	—	—	—	101.14	—
Debt-to-Equity ratio	—	—	—	1.56	—
Annual stock-price return (%)	—	—	—	70.23	—

Source: Compiled by the authors from audited annual reports, Moneycontrol and CMIE Prowess. FY2022–23 figures compiled from Moneycontrol; remaining years to be completed by the author.

Table 4. Five-year financial performance of Maruti Suzuki India Ltd

Financial indicator	FY2019–20	FY2020–21	FY2021–22	FY2022–23	FY2023–24
Return on Equity (%)	—	—	—	15.75	—
Return on Assets (%)	—	—	—	11.69	—
Net Profit Margin (%)	—	—	—	9.32	—
Earnings Per Share ( )	—	—	—	429.01	—
Debt-to-Equity ratio	—	—	—	0.00	—
Annual stock-price return (%)	—	—	—	43.76	—

Source: Compiled by the authors from audited annual reports, Moneycontrol and CMIE Prowess. FY2022–23 figures compiled from Moneycontrol; remaining years to be completed by the author.

Interpretation. Once the five-year series is complete, the analysis proceeds by comparing each firm's performance trend with its governance tier. The comparison for the verified year illustrates the intended interpretation: Tata Motors, classified in the Leadership tier, recorded the highest ROE and the strongest annual stock-price return, consistent with the proposition that stronger governance is associated with superior market and profitability outcomes. Mahindra & Mahindra (Challenger) and Maruti Suzuki (Disciplinarian) present more mixed profiles—Maruti Suzuki, for example, reports the highest ROA and a debt-free balance sheet, indicating that operational efficiency and capital structure are shaped by factors beyond governance alone. Extending this comparison across all five years will allow the trend in each indicator to be read against the stability of each firm's governance tier, providing a more robust, industry-controlled basis for inference than a single-year cross-section. Consistent with the methodology, any quantitative association reported at this stage (for example, a Spearman rank comparison of average governance standing against average performance) should be treated as indicative given the three-firm sample, and not as evidence of a causal effect.

5.2 Objective 2: Investor Perception and Reaction

Corporate governance is an important determinant of investor confidence and, ultimately, of investment decisions. To examine how investors perceive and react to governance practices, a structured questionnaire was administered and the responses analysed in SPSS. The internal consistency of the perception scale was assessed using Cronbach's alpha (α = [____]; to be reported by the author), and the scale was judged [acceptable/good] for further analysis. Demographic differences in perception were tested using one-way ANOVA, and the association between investment size and prioritised governance attributes was tested using the chi-square test of independence. The results are summarised in Tables 5 and 6.

Table 5. One-way ANOVA: differences in governance perception across demographic groups

Demographic factor	Sum of squares (between)	Mean square	F-value	p-value
Age	32.822	1.172	1.792	0.013*
Education	143.683	5.132	2.076	0.002*
Gender	—	—	—	n.s.
Employment status	—	—	—	n.s.
Portfolio / investment type	—	—	—	n.s.

Note: * significant at p < 0.05; n.s. = not significant. Source: Authors' primary survey, analysed in SPSS. Full statistics (including degrees of freedom and Levene's test) to be verified against the SPSS output by the author.

The ANOVA results indicate that age (p = 0.013) and education (p = 0.002) are significantly associated with differences in the perception of, and reaction to, governance practices, leading to rejection of H01 for these two factors. Investors in different age bands, and with different educational backgrounds, evaluate governance practices differently. In contrast, gender, employment status and portfolio type did not produce statistically significant differences, so H01 is not rejected for these factors. Income and current investment level displayed weaker, secondary associations. Because the F-values reported for the significant factors are modest, and to satisfy the assumptions underlying ANOVA, the homogeneity of variances (Levene's test) and the Kruskal–Wallis robustness check should be reported alongside these results in the final manuscript.

Table 6. Chi-square test of association between investment size and prioritised governance attribute

Test statistic	Value	Significance
Pearson chi-square (df = 10)	22.125	0.014*
Likelihood-ratio chi-square	22.942	0.011*

Note: * significant at p < 0.05. Some cells recorded expected counts below five; the likelihood-ratio chi-square and Fisher's exact test are reported as corroborating measures. Source: Authors' primary survey, analysed in SPSS.

The chi-square analysis indicates a significant association between investment size and the governance attributes investors prioritise (Pearson $\chi^2 = 22.125$, df = 10, p = 0.014), supported by the likelihood-ratio statistic ($\chi^2 = 22.942$, p = 0.011); H02 is therefore rejected. Smaller investors (below 50,000) place greater emphasis on transparency and disclosure practices, whereas larger investors (above 1,00,000) attach more importance to ethical conduct and corporate social responsibility and to board composition and diversity. Because a number of cells recorded expected counts below five—which can compromise the reliability of the Pearson statistic—the association is corroborated using the likelihood-ratio chi-square and Fisher's exact test, and the finding is interpreted as indicative. The results nonetheless suggest that companies should tailor their governance communication to the differing priorities of investor segments.

6. FINDINGS

6.1 Corporate Governance and Financial Performance

- For the verified year, the firm classified in the Leadership tier (Tata Motors) recorded the strongest ROE and stock-price return, while firms in lower tiers showed more mixed profiles, consistent with a positive but not uniform association between governance standing and financial performance.
- Certain indicators—notably ROA and the debt-to-equity ratio—appear to be driven substantially by operational and capital-structure factors rather than governance alone, indicating that governance is one of several determinants of performance.
- The five-year, industry-controlled design (once fully populated) provides a more reliable basis for reading governance against performance trends than a single-year cross-section, and avoids the over-fitting associated with inferential testing on a three-firm sample.

6.2 Investor Perception and Reaction

- Perception of governance differs significantly by age ($p = 0.013$) and education ($p = 0.002$), but not by gender, employment status or portfolio type; income and investment level show weaker, secondary effects.
- Investment size is significantly associated with the governance attributes investors prioritise ($\chi^2 = 22.125$, $p = 0.014$): smaller investors emphasise transparency and disclosure, whereas larger investors emphasise ethical conduct, corporate social responsibility and board composition.

7. CONCLUSION

This study examined the contribution of corporate governance to firm financial performance and investor perception in the Indian automotive sector. Governance was conceptualised as the set of processes, policies and practices that direct and control a company—encompassing board oversight, executive accountability, shareholder rights and the transparency of financial reporting. The evidence indicates that governance standing is associated with financial performance and with the way investors perceive firms, although the strength of the association varies across indicators. Firms with stronger governance, such as Tata Motors, tend to display more favourable market and profitability outcomes, whereas metrics such as return on assets appear to be shaped more by industry dynamics and operational efficiency.

The findings are consistent with the view that sound governance supports long-term financial health by aligning managerial and shareholder interests, improving decision-making and resource allocation, and enhancing the credibility of reported results. Well-governed firms also tend to enjoy greater investor trust, which can translate into higher and less volatile valuations and improved access to capital on favourable terms. On the behavioural side, the study shows that investors are not homogeneous: their perception of governance varies with age and education, and the governance attributes they prioritise vary with the size of their investment. Companies seeking to build investor confidence should therefore treat governance not only as a compliance requirement but as a strategic capability, and should communicate their governance practices in ways that respond to the differing priorities of investor segments.

8. LIMITATIONS OF THE STUDY

Several limitations should be borne in mind when interpreting the results. First, the firm-level analysis is based on three purposively selected companies within a single industry; this design supports comparative interpretation but limits the generalisability of the findings and precludes causal inference. Second, the governance classification relies on the IiAS Scorecard, which, like any composite index, involves judgement in weighting and aggregation. Third, the investor-perception findings rest on self-reported survey data and are subject to the usual response and sampling biases, and some chi-square cells recorded expected counts below five. Finally, the availability and comparability of multi-year financial data—particularly where corporate restructuring has occurred—require careful, source-consistent compilation. These limitations point directly to the avenues for further research set out below.

9. SCOPE FOR FURTHER RESEARCH

Future research could extend this study in several directions. Widening the sample to include multiple sectors and a larger number of firms would permit properly specified panel-regression analysis and improve generalisability. A longer longitudinal window would allow the effects of changes in governance practice on performance and investor perception to be traced over time. Incorporating firm-level governance sub-indices—board independence, audit-committee characteristics, ownership concentration and disclosure quality—would enable a more granular analysis than governance tiers permit. Finally, examining regional, cultural and economic differences within India, and combining survey evidence with behavioural or experimental methods, would deepen understanding of how investors interpret and act upon governance signals.

REFERENCES

Aggarwal, P. (2013). Impact of corporate governance on corporate financial performance. *IOSR Journal of Business and Management, 13*(3), 1–5. DOI: 10.9790/487X-1330105

Amba, M. S. (2014). Corporate governance and firms' financial performance. *Journal of Academic and Business Ethics, 8*(1), 1–11.

Beasley, M. S., Carcello, J. V., Hermanson, D. R., & Lapides, P. D. (2000). Fraudulent financial reporting: Industry traits and corporate governance mechanisms. *Accounting Horizons, 14*(4), 441–454. DOI: 10.2308/acch.2000.14.4.441

Brown, L. D., & Caylor, M. L. (2004). Corporate governance study: The correlation between corporate governance and company performance. Institutional Shareholder Services, 1–15.

Byard, D., Li, Y., & Weintrop, J. (2006). Corporate governance and the quality of financial analysts' information. *Journal of Accounting and Public Policy, 25*(5), 609–625. DOI: 10.1016/j.jaccpubpol.2006.07.003

Chalaki, P., Didar, H., & Riahinezhad, M. (2012). Corporate governance attributes and financial reporting quality: Empirical evidence from Iran. *International Journal of Business and Social Science, 3*(15), 223–229.

Chen, J. (2023, October 31). Corporate governance: Definition, principles, models, and examples. Investopedia. https://www.investopedia.com/terms/c/corporategovernance .asp

D'Onza, G., & Lamboglia, R. (2011). The relation between corporate governance characteristics and financial statement frauds: An empirical analysis of Italian listed companies. *10th European Academic Conference on Internal Auditing and Corporate Governance*, 1–21.

Dalnial, H., Kamaluddin, A., & Mohd-Sanusi, Z. (2014). Detecting fraudulent financial reporting through financial statement analysis. *Journal of Advanced Management Science, 2*(1), 17–22. DOI: 10.12720/joams.2.1.17-22

Dzingai, I., & Fakoya, M. B. (2017). Effect of corporate governance structure on the financial performance of Johannesburg Stock Exchange (JSE)-listed mining firms. *Sustainability (Basel), 9*(6), 867. DOI: 10.3390/su9060867

Eisenhofer, J. W. (2014). Does corporate governance matter to investment returns? Grant & Eisenhofer P.A., 1–19.

Gompers, P. A., Ishii, J. L., & Metrick, A. (2001). Corporate governance and equity prices (NBER Working Paper No. 8449), 1–70.

Hasan, A., Aly, D., & Hussainey, K. (2022). Corporate governance and financial reporting quality: A comparative study. *Corporate Governance (Bradford), 22*(6), 1308–1326. DOI: 10.1108/CG-08-2021-0298

Institutional Investor Advisory Services India Limited (IiAS). (2023). Corporate governance scores. IiAS.

Kanukuntla, S., & Seyed Masoud, S. A. (2017). Audit committee quality and financial reporting quality: A study of selected Indian companies. Jurnal Dinamika Akuntansi dan Bisnis, 4(1), 1–18.

Khan, A., Muttakin, M. B., & Siddiqui, J. (2012). Corporate governance and corporate social responsibility disclosures: Evidence from an emerging economy. *Journal of Business Ethics, 114*(2), 207–223. DOI: 10.1007/s10551-012-1336-0

Mahindra & Mahindra Ltd. (2023). *Annual report 2022–23.* Mahindra & Mahindra Ltd.

Marlinda, H., Satria, H., Utami, R., Kurnia, S., & Sahara, M. A. (2022). Financial statement integrity: Corporate governance and quality audit evidence from food and beverage companies in Indonesia. *Penanomics: International Journal of Economics, 1*(1), 27–40. DOI: 10.56107/penanomics.v1i1.3

Maruti Suzuki India Ltd. (2023). *Annual report 2022–23.* Maruti Suzuki India Ltd.

Moneycontrol. (2023). Company financials. Moneycontrol. https://www.moneycontrol.com

Olayinka, A. A. (2022). Financial statement analysis as a tool for investment decisions and assessment of companies' performance. *International Journal of Financial, Accounting, and Management, 4*(1), 49–66. DOI: 10.35912/ijfam.v4i1.852

Omri, A., & Klai, N. (2011). Corporate governance and financial reporting quality: The case of Tunisian firms. *International Business Research, 4*(1), 158–166.

Onuorah, A. C.-C., & Friday, O. I. (2016). Corporate governance and financial reporting quality in selected Nigerian companies. *International Journal of Management Science and Business Administration, 2*(3), 7–16.

Otieno, K., Mugo, R., Njeje, D., & Anthony, K. (2015). Effect of corporate governance on financial performance of SACCOs in Kenya. *Research Journal of Finance and Accounting, 6*(2), 48–58.

Pande, S. (2011). Does good governance pay? Evidence from around the globe. *SSRN*, 1–31. DOI: 10.2139/ssrn.1976772

Paulinus, C. E., Oluchukwu, N., & Somtochukwu, O. (2017). Empirical investigation of corporate governance and financial reporting quality of quoted companies in Nigeria. International Journal of Economics. *Business and Management Research*, *1*(5), 117–137.

Purnama, O., Hanitha, V., & Angreni, T. (2020). Financial statement analysis to assess company financial performance. eCo-Fin, 2(3).

Raithatha, M., & Bapat, V. (2014). Impact of corporate governance on financial disclosures: Evidence from India. *Corporate Ownership & Control*, *12*(1), 874–889. DOI: 10.22495/cocv12i1c9p10

Rashid, N., Daud, W. N. W., Zainol, F. A., Salleh, F., Yazid, A. S., Endut, W. A., Yaakub, N., Ghazali, P. L., & Afthanorhan, A. (2018). Quality of financial reporting towards the improvement of corporate governance mechanism. *International Journal of Academic Research in Business & Social Sciences*, *8*(11), 1339–1345. DOI: 10.6007/IJARBSS/v8-i11/5175

Selvaggi, M., & Upton, J. (2008). *Governance and performance in corporate Britain*. Association of British Insurers.

Sianipar, R. H., & Wiksuana, I. G. B. (2019). The study of the effect of corporate governance on financial performance. *Russian Journal of Agricultural and Socio-Economic Sciences*, *2*(86), 166–170. DOI: 10.18551/rjoas.2019-02.19

Statman, M., & Glushkov, D. (2008). The wages of social responsibility. *Financial Analysts Journal*, *65*(4), 33–46. DOI: 10.2469/faj.v65.n4.5

Syamsudin, S., Imronudin, I., Utomo, S. T., & Praswati, A. N. (2017). Corporate governance in detecting lack of financial report. *Jurnal Dinamika Manajemen*, *8*(2), 167–176. DOI: 10.15294/jdm.v8i2.12757

Tata Motors Ltd. (2023). *Annual report 2022–23*. Tata Motors Ltd.

Tsoncheva, G. (2014). Measuring and assessing the quality and usefulness of accounting information. Izvestia – Journal of the University of Economics – Varna, 58(1), 52–64.

Veronica, S., & Bachtiar, Y. S. (2005). The role of corporate governance in preventing misstated financial statements. Jurnal Akuntansi dan Keuangan Indonesia, 2(1), 159–173.

Yurisandi, T., & Puspitasari, E. (2015). Financial reporting quality – Before and after IFRS adoption using NiCE qualitative characteristics measurement. *Procedia: Social and Behavioral Sciences*, *211*, 644–652. DOI: 10.1016/j.sbspro.2015.11.091

Chapter 11
Beyond the Reports: Evaluating the Real Impact of CSR Practices in Omani Companies

Dharmendra Singh
http://orcid.org/0000-0003-0966-6530
Modern College of Business and Science, Oman

Haileslasie Tadele
American University of Ras Al Khaimah, UAE

Garima Malik
http://orcid.org/0000-0002-3892-8299
Birla Institute of Management Technology, India

ABSTRACT

This study examines the effectiveness of Corporate Social Responsibility (CSR) initiatives in non-financial companies in Oman. Using data over the period of 2019 to 2023, collected from annual reports and CSR reports of 11 companies listed on the Muscat Stock exchange. Financial performance is measured using return on Equity (ROE) and Price to earnings ratio (P/E). The findings indicate that there is a positive and statistically significant correlation between the CSR index and profitability (ROE) and investor expectations for future growth (P/E ratio) In addition, the study finds that liquidity position, measured using current ratio is positively and significantly associated with CSR initiatives, indicating that liquidity plays significant role in enabling the implementation of effective CSR initiatives. Interestingly, the size of the company does not have significant impact on either ROE or P/E.

DOI: 10.4018/979-8-3373-5437-8.ch011

1.INTRODUCTION

Corporate social responsibility involves engaging in social and environmental initiatives as part of a company's business operations and its relationship with stakeholders. Many people view Corporate Social Responsibility (CSR) as a mechanism through which a company ensures its business practices are efficient, sustainable, and ethical. In addition to fostering consumer trust, CSR disclosure facilitates market differentiation, enhances global reputation, and mitigates risks. Dunn and Harness (2018) suggest that corporate social responsibility statements should highlight a commitment to a social cause, its impact on society, and its alignment with the company's core business. Extant studies show that companies with strong CSR programs face fewer legal and regulatory issues, are more successful in attracting and retaining employees and customers and are generally viewed more favorably by potential investors (Neitzert and Petras, 2022). The economic advantages of CSR can result in positive financial outcomes, including enhanced profitability (Sandberg et al., 2023; Li et al., 2020) and diminished financial risks (Okafor et al., 2021). This study analyzes the impact of CSR initiatives on financial performance of listed companies in Oman.

Firms are increasingly interested in corporate social responsibility (CSR), even though there is debate about whether they should focus solely on economic outcomes or also address complex societal issues. Some studies argue that engagement in CSR initiatives can result in higher financial performance, by improving the company's reputation and customer loyalty. For example, a study by Chipriyanov et al. (2024) investigates the impact of CSR initiatives on economic growth and inequality, indicating that greater CSR initiatives are likely to contribute to economic development and reduce social inequality. Conversely, other studies contend that focusing on CSR may divert the attention of the company from its core business objectives, thereby impacting its profitability. Latapí Agudelo, Jóhannsdóttir and Davídsdóttir (2019) discuss the challenges and benefits of CSR initiatives and suggest that companies need to follow a balanced approach that considers both economic and social factors. Overall, the aim of CSR should focus on contribution to societal well-being while also considering the long-term interests of the company. As a result, a corporate social responsibility (CSR) initiative not only enhances competitive advantage but also boosts the company's reputation (Doda, 2015).

Despite existing research that focuses on CSR reporting in Omani companies, several gaps remain unaddressed. While studies acknowledge that geographical and cultural factors influence CSR drivers, there is limited exploration of how these factors specifically shape CSR reporting practices in Oman. A deeper investigation into the country's cultural and societal context could provide valuable insights into its CSR framework and implementation strategies. Additionally, although the role of technology in enhancing CSR reporting standards is recognized, little research focuses on the specific digital solutions adopted by Omani firms and their effectiveness in improving transparency and stakeholder engagement. Understanding the types of digital platforms used and their impact on reporting efficiency and accuracy remains an area requiring further exploration. Furthermore, while existing literature mentions obstacles such as financial constraints, lack of expertise, and cultural factors, there is a need for more integrated studies to systematically identify and analyze the specific barriers faced by Omani companies in CSR implementation and reporting. Recognizing these barriers is essential for designing effective interventions and support systems to enhance CSR adoption. Another notable gap is in stakeholder engagement; while previous studies highlight its importance in CSR reporting, they provide limited insights into how Omani companies actively engage their stakeholders in the reporting process. Addressing these gaps would contribute to a more comprehensive understanding of CSR reporting in Oman and help develop more effective strategies for corporate sustainability.

This study focuses on non-financial companies in Oman. CSR initiatives in Oman encompass various areas, reflecting a commitment to social and environmental responsibility. Key types of CSR include Environmental Sustainability, where businesses focus on eco-friendly practices, waste reduction, and conservation (Kuzey et al., 2021). On the other hand, social responsibility involves supporting ethical, charitable, and environmental projects, ensuring fair businesses practices, and contributing to the economy through fair tax payments. CSR offers various benefits, including improved brand reputation, attracting more clients and investors, and retaining talented employees who share the company's values (Uyar et al., 2022). It helps businesses build stakeholders' trust, reduce risks and promote responsible resource management for long-term profitability. Some companies may use CSR for the purpose of enhancing their brand image, however, this may result in greenwashing accusations. Managing CSR initiatives require significant time, knowledge and resources, and the lack of standardized metric can make evaluating their impact challenging. Studying the impact of CSR initiatives on financial performance is essential for understanding how ethical practices can contribute to a company's long-term financial performance. The findings of this study offer insights into whether CSR initiatives have a positive impact on the company's profitability and future growth prospects.

CSR holds immense importance for non-financial companies. We studied the integration of CSR in 11 publicly listed non-financial companies in Oman. The CSR initiatives undertaken by the companies in our sample represent meaningful steps toward the responsible and ethical conduct of business in Oman. Integrating CSR into business practices represents a significant advance in fostering a more responsible business environment. The adoption and disclosure of CSR by the companies we studied reflects a maturing business environment, with meaningful stakeholder relationships serving as a key driver of this evolution. Several studies indicate that integrating CSR into a business strategy can result in benefits such as improved profitability, better stakeholder engagement and greater access to capital. Likewise, CSR initiatives are positively correlated with the company's reputation and economic value.

This paper is organized as follows. In section 2, a brief literature discussing the foundation of CSR in the business world and theoretical framework is provided, followed by a discussion on the research methods in section 3. Section 4 presents the discussion and analysis of results, while section 5 provides a discussion on conclusions and implications of the study.

2. LITERATURE REVIEW

Companies are increasingly adopting CSR initiatives to meet investors' expectations and fulfil their social obligations (Younas, Kassim and Bhuiyan, 2021). The overgrowing focus on ecological and social issues as a key ethical business practice for firms around the world is the key motivation of this paper. In addition, there is growing awareness of the sustainability of natural assets and the unethical business activities that have contributed to pollution, environmental degradation, and other social and environmental issues. While businesses were once seen as the primary means of addressing these issues, individuals and governments must also play a significant role in solving these challenges (Visser, 2008; Younas and Kassim, 2022). The significance of CSR has become evident as organizations recognize their duty to manage environmental impacts, which not only helps mitigate reputational risks but also contributes to long-term economic sustainability. In developed economies, CSR is a widely stated topic covering a wide range of areas of research. The notion of CSR is initially coined in a book titled "Social Responsibility of the Businessman" in 1953. According to this book, businesses have duties and responsibilities to Society since their operations touch many facets of humanity (Al-Maauli, 2023). Then other writers attempted to expand on Bowen's original concept of CSR (Younas and Kassim, 2023). For example, Friedman (1970) defined CSR as a company's obligation to use Society's assets to generate profit while abiding by legal and regulatory requirements. Furthermore, CSR has evolved in the past few decades to encompass a broader perspective business practices emphasizing how businesses reconcile their key operations with social, environmental, and economic factors (Thottoli and Thomas, 2023). Subsequently, CSR reporting has gained popularity as a catchphrase in declarations of purpose, financial statements, and policy documents, emphasizing commitment of firms towards of achieving CSR expectations

(Younas et al., 2023). Despite this, there are limited studies on CSR practices in developing countries, such as Oman. As a result, this paper argues that additional studies are crucial to better understand stakeholders' perceptions of CSR in Oman and contribute to the broader body of knowledge in this field.

In Oman, participatory initiatives in CSR are increasingly aligned with local cultural values, which significantly enhance a company's reputation. Given Oman's strong emphasis on community cohesion, social welfare, and sustainability, businesses that integrate CSR programs reflecting these cultural priorities can build deeper trust with stakeholders (Al-Abri & Al-Balushi, 2021). For instance, CSR initiatives supporting local entrepreneurship, environmental conservation, and education resonate strongly with Omani societal values and contribute to a company's legitimacy and social license to operate (Al-Hamadi et al., 2020). Furthermore, participatory CSR approaches that involve local communities in decision-making ensure that initiatives are not only well received but also effective in addressing social and economic needs. Studies highlight that such culturally embedded CSR programs can lead to enhanced consumer loyalty, improved employee morale, and a positive corporate image (Khan et al., 2019). This is particularly relevant in Oman, where organizations that demonstrate commitment to social well-being such as through support for SMEs, charitable initiatives during Ramadan, and sustainability programs are perceived more favorably. Overall, aligning CSR with Omani cultural values through participatory mechanisms strengthens corporate reputation and fosters long-term relationships with customers, employees, and government institutions.

2.1 Theoretical Framework

This study employs the stakeholder and legitimacy theory to explain the relationship between CSR practices and firm financial performance. These theories provide a foundational framework for discussing the implications of incorporating CSR initiatives in business strategy and its impact on firm economic sustainability.

2.1.1 Stakeholder Theory

Stakeholder theory emphasizes how firms derive advantages from CSR programs by addressing the interests of all stakeholders associated with the firm. Corporate Social Responsibility (CSR) bolsters business reputation, elevating customer and staff happiness, resulting in enhanced organizational performance. It mitigates regulatory risks and appeals to socially responsible investors. Business organizations can concentrate on the social aspect of the value that should be engaged by utilizing stakeholder theory (Barney and Harrison, 2020). This is merely because businesses interact with various stakeholders, each of whom has unique requirements and expectations that should be considered when evaluating the company's principles (Al Lawati and Hussainey, 2022). As a result, its ability to influence the public can create value rather than demolish it. The effectiveness of organizations as a whole and CSR is a key emphasis of the stakeholder theory. Organizations attempt to turn stakeholders into allies rather than adversaries since neglecting them can have detrimental effects (Freeman, 2023). Furthermore, Kivits et al. (2021) argued that appropriate transfer accountability requires the stakeholder theory. Stakeholder theory, which integrates the social, economic, and ethical aspects of an organization's operations and activities, has become one of the most often used paradigms for corporate social responsibility reporting.

2.1.2 Legitimacy Theory

A procedure which assists businesses in establishing and enhancing freely given ecological and social disclosure to fulfil their social contract, which allows the acknowledgement of their objectives and their continued existence in a frantic and unstable setting, is the statement made by Silva (2021) about the legitimacy theory. By incorporating social as well as environmental data in their annual reports, organizations aim to appear legitimate from the perspective of the many stakeholders who have the power to influence their legitimacy (Crossley, Elmagrhi and Ntim, 2021). This notion has been applied by numerous researchers, including Silva (2021), Kivits et al. (2021), Younas and Kassim (2022), Al Lawati and Hussainey (2022) and Al-Maauli (2023) in their CSR research. The legitimacy theory is becoming more widely accepted as an example of CSR. However, it is still in its infancy since an organization's opinions regarding stakeholders' attitudes towards CSR serve as the basis for its legitimacy considerations when making CSR decisions.

Figure 1. Legitimacy Theory; source: (Silva, 2021)

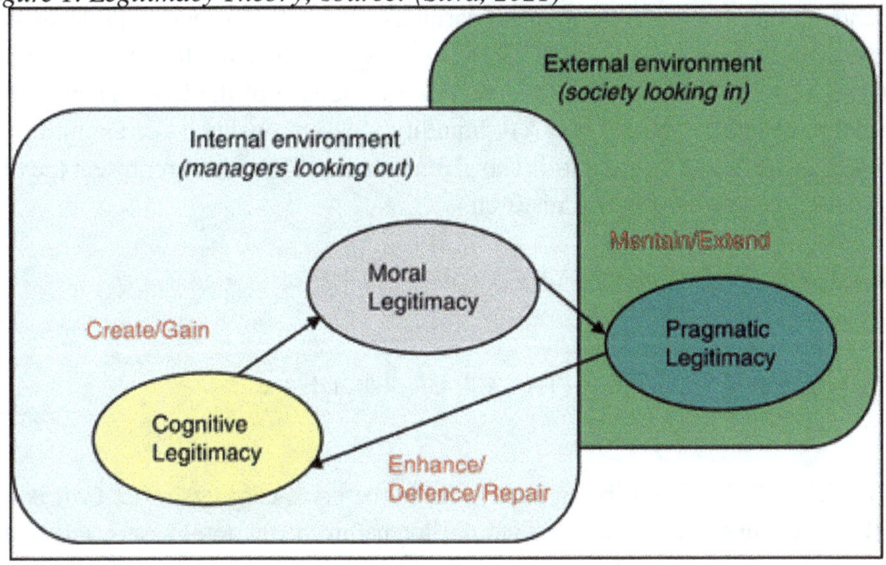

3. RESEARCH METHODOLOGY

3.1 Research design

According to Saunders et al. (2009), research can be categorized into three types: explanatory, exploratory, and descriptive. This study adopts a secondary research methodology to conduct a financial analysis over a five-year period. This study follows the explanatory research design, measuring the relationship between CSR initiatives and firm financial performance. To determine CSR activities and their relationship with company performance measures like return on equity and PE ratio, we use collective research that centers around gathering annual reports, corporate social responsibility reports, and financial statements from non-financial companies listed on the MSX in Oman. In 2010, ISO published ISO 26000, a voluntary collection of principles to help corporations implement CSR initiatives. These principles emphasize that CSR is more qualitative than quantitative; and aim to serve as a guideline rather than regulations and is not certified. The purpose of ISO 26000 is to clarify social responsibility and help corporations implement CSR. This study uses content analysis to identify and quantify CSR practices and transparency of reporting using the ISO 26000's seven key factors. These factors include governance, human rights, labor practices, the environment, fair operating procedures, consumer issues, and community involvement and development. The dependent variables include price to earnings ratio (PE), a market performance measure and return on equity (ROE), measuring firm profitability. The key independent variable is CSR index, and we control the size of the firm using natural logarithm of total assets (Log (TA)), liquidity measured using a current ratio and leverage using a debt-equity ratio. The given equation (1) and (2) represent the two regression models used in this research.

$$PE_i = \beta_0 + \beta_1 CSR_i + \beta_2 \log(TA_i) + \beta_3 CR_i + \beta_4 DE_i + e_i \quad \text{.................................} \quad (1)$$

$$ROE_i = \beta_0 + \beta_1 CSR_i + \beta_2 \log(TA_i) + \beta_3 CR_i + \beta_4 DE_i + e_i \quad \text{................................} \quad (2)$$

Where *ROE* is the return on equity, *PE* is the price-earnings ratio, *CSR* is the CSR index, *log (TA)* refers to the natural logarithm of the total assets, *CR* is the current ratio, *DE* is the debt equity ratio and *e* is the error term.

3.2 Data collection

The annual reports of the publicly traded companies were obtained from the Muscat Stock Exchange, and the final dataset was determined based on the availability of CSR reporting within these reports. The CSR index and the financial ratios pertinent to the research objectives were extracted from the financial statements spanning 2019 to 2023. This research examines the relationship between CSR initiatives and financial performance of non-finance companies listed in Muscat Stock exchange (MSX) in Oman. The list of companies included in our sample is provided in table 1.

Table 1. List of Companies

No.	Company
1	SMN Power Holding
2	Ooredoo
3	Al Anwar Ceramic Tiles
4	Al Maha petroleum products
5	Al Maha Ceramics
6	Omantel
7	Aljazeera steel products.
8	Aljazeera service

continued on following page

Table 1. Continued

No.	Company
9	Renaissance Services
10	Oman National Engineering & Investment
11	Oman Cement Co. S.A.O. G

4. DATA ANALYSIS

We analyze data collected from annual reports and CSR reports of 11 non-financial companies over a period of 2019 – 2023. First, using a content analysis we extract data related to CSR practices of the companies and we form a CSR index to score each company on their CSR disclosure. Second, based on data collected from the financial statements of the companies we analyzed the financial performance of the companies using the profitability ratio, measured using return on equity (ROE) and future growth prospect of the companies using the price to earnings ratio (P/E ratio). Finally, we run an ordinary least square regression (OLS) to examine the impact of the CSR practices on the company's financial performance, controlling key variables such as size of the company, liquidity and leverage positions. By examining financial trends and performance indicators over this timeframe, the study aims to provide meaningful insights into the financial health and strategic decision-making of these companies.

4.1 Descriptive Statistic:

The following table 2 presents the descriptive statistics of the key variables included in the study.

Table 2. Descriptive Statistics

	Mean	Median	Standard Deviation
Return on Equity	0.1592	0.0966	0.3664
Price-earnings ratio	14.5697	8.0555	23.6773
CSR index	54.2424	50	25.9031
Log (TA)	6.7339	7.1095	1.10745
Current ratio	3.7161	1.5147	6.5702
debt-equity ratio	1.4321	1.1705	1.2173

Table 2 presents the mean, median and standard deviation values of Return on Equity, Price to earnings ratios, CSR index, Log (TA), Current ratio, and debt-equity ratio. The descriptive statistics results show a significant variability in financial performance and CSR practices across the firms in our sample. The mean ROE (15.92%) and the mean P/E ratio (14.57) exhibit a higher variation in profitability and valuation, with a standard deviation of 3.66% and 23.68, respectively. Specifically, the P/E ratio indicates a significant variation in how investors value the companies, while some are highly valued relative to their earnings, others show lower valuation. The CSR index with a mean value of 54.24 and a standard deviation of 25.90 suggest that firms in Oman exhibit a moderate CSR engagement. Likewise, the median CSR index of 50 shows that only about half of the companies make significant efforts to improve their CSR disclosures. The mean size of the companies measured in log assets (log (TA)) is 6.73, with a standard deviation of 1.11, suggesting that the firms in the sample have moderate size. However, the liquidity and leverage position values indicate a huge variation among the companies included in the sample. The debt-to-equity ratio averaging 1.43 reveals a significant variation in capital structure across firms, which may impact their financial performance and capacity to invest in CSR initiatives.

Table 3. Pearson Pairwise Correlation

	CSR index	Log (TA)	Current ratio	Debt-equity ratio	ROE	PE ratio
CSR index	1	0.4	0.25	0.3	0.15	0.35
Log (Total Assets)	0.4	1	0.32	-0.5	-0.28	0.2
Current ratio	0.25	0.32	1	-0.35	0.22	0.1
Debt-equity ratio	0.3	-0.5	-0.35	1	-0.4	-0.15
ROE	0.15	-0.28	0.22	-0.4	1	0.5
PE ratio	0.35	0.2	0.1	-0.15	0.5	1

Table 3 presents key relationships between the variables included in this study. The CSR index shows a positive correlation with financial and operational factors. The CSR index is positively associated with company size (log (TA)), indicating that larger companies tend to have higher CSR scores. This may reflect greater resource advantages for larger firms investing in CSR initiatives. Likewise, the CSR index is positively correlated with P/E ratio, suggesting that companies with higher CSR score are likely to have higher valuations, possibly due to the growing importance of CSR in investor decision making. On the other hand, the CSR index shows a weaker positive association with profitability (ROE). It highlights that other factors play a significant role in determining firm profitability. However, there is a positive association with the CSR index and debt-to-equity ratio, suggesting that companies with higher CSR score tend to have higher leverage position, potentially due to a more favorable risk profile or better access to capital.

Size (Log (TA)) is negatively associated with debt-to-equity ratio, indicating that larger companies generally tend to have lower leverage position, which may reflect their ability to use internal resources than external borrowing. Furthermore, the correlation between current ratio and size (log (TA)), and current ratio and debt-to-equity ratio suggest that larger firms and firms with higher liquidity tend to rely less on debt capital. Finally, there is a positive association between the ROE and P/E ratio, highlighting that more profitable firms are likely to be valued higher in the market.

4.2 Regression Analysis

This study employs ordinary least square (OLS) regression model to examine the impact of corporate social responsibility (CSR) index on firm profitability and market valuation. return on equity (ROE) and Price-to-earnings ratio (P/E) are used as dependent variables, while CSR is the independent variable. The model uses natural logarithm of total assets (Log (TA)), current ratio, and debt-equity ratio as control variables. Table 4 presents the results of the first model, which examines the relationship between CSR index and firm profitability, measured using the return on equity (ROE). The regression model's overall significance explains that the model is statistically significant in explaining the variation in the dependent variable.

To test the explanatory power of the regression models, R^2 and adjusted R^2 statistics were calculated for each model. According to the results obtained from the ROE model, the return on equity is explained by 76.5% using the selected variables, and the adjusted R^2 equals 0.746. This shows that all the considered variables such as CSR index, firm size, current ratio, and debt-equity ratio have significant explanatory power in explaining the profitability of firms. Likewise, the selected variables explain 69.8% of the variation in the price-to-earnings ratio.

Table 4. Model 1 OLS regression results

	Coefficients	*Standard Error*	*t Stat*	*P-value*
Intercept	0.5535	0.1482	3.7350***	0.0005
CSR index	0.0074	0.0015	4.9261***	0.0000
Log (TA)	-0.0742	0.0223	-3.3279***	0.0012

continued on following page

Table 4. Continued

	Coefficients	*Standard Error*	*t Stat*	*P-value*
Current ratio	0.0239	0.0054	4.4243***	0.0000
Debt-equity ratio	0.1829	0.0357	5.1245***	0.0000

Note: Model 1 uses return on Equity (ROE) as the dependent variable. Sig. levels: *** p<0.01, ** p<0.05, * p<0.1.

The regression results reported in Table 4, where ROE is the dependent variable, indicate a significant relationship between the key variables included in the model and ROE. The intercept is positive and significant at the 1% level (p-value = 0.0005), suggesting that although all the independent and control variables are zero, there is a baseline positive effect on profitability (ROE). The CSR index also shows a positive and significant coefficient 0.0074 at the 1% level (p-value = 0.0000), indicating that greater CSR initiatives tend to positively impact profitability. This may also highlight that CSR disclosure has a favorable effect on ROE.

The natural logarithm of total assets has a negative coefficient of -0.0742 and it is significant at the 1% level (p-value = 0.0012). This implies that larger companies are likely to have lower profitability, and this may suggest inefficiencies in larger firms. The current ratio shows a positive and significant relationship with ROE, with a coefficient of 0.0239 (p-value = 0.0000). This indicates that firms with higher liquidity tend to have higher ROE. Lastly, the debt-equity ratio has a positive and significant coefficient of 0.1829 at the 1% level (p-value = 0.0000), suggesting that higher leverage is associated with improved profitability, likely due to the use of debt financing to increase returns.

The following table presents the OLS regression results for model 2, where price-to-earnings (P/E) ratio is the dependent variable. The model is statistically significant at the 5% level with an F-value of F 3.698(p-value = 0.010), indicating that the model is statistically significant in explaining the variation in the dependent variable.

Table 5. Model 2 OLS regression results

	Coefficients	*Standard Error*	*t Stat*	*P-value*
Intercept	-31.486	21.523	-1.462	0.1494
CSR index	0.2256	0.1197	2.061**	0.0432
Log (TA)	4.667	2.822	1.653	0.1044
Current ratio	1.862	0.3941	4.832**	0.0007
debt-equity ratio	-0.2105	0.911	-2.423**	0.021

Note: Model 2 uses Price-to-earnings (P/E) ratio as the dependent variable. Sig. levels: *** p<0.01, ** p<0.05, * p<0.1

The intercept is negative (-31.486), but it is not statistically significant (p-value = 0.1494), meaning that it does not provide a meaningful estimate of the P/E ratio when all independent and control variables are equal to zero. The CSR index shows a positive significance, featuring a coefficient of 0.2256 and a p-value of 0.0432, which suggests a positive correlation with the PE ratio. This suggests that improved CSR practices and their disclosure positively influence investors, thereby enhancing PE value. Companies with better CSR performance are likely to be viewed as less risky and more sustainable by investors, resulting in higher market prices relative to earnings. The natural logarithm of total assets (log (TA)), representing company size has positive coefficient of 4.667, but it is not statistically significant (p-value = 0.1044) This suggests that the size of the company does not contribute to the increase in the P/E ratio. On the other hand, the current ratio has a positive coefficient of 1.862 and significant at the 1% level (p-value = 0.0007). This shows that companies with greater liquidity, measured using current ratio tend to have higher P/E ratio, potentially because investors perceive such companies as less risky. Lastly, the debt-equity ratio shows a negative coefficient of -0.2105 and significant at the level of 5% (p-value = 0.021). This indicates that companies with higher leverage (debt to equity ratio) are likely to have lower market valuation, measured using P/E ratio. Higher leverage is often associated with increased financial risk which may negatively influence investors' confidence, thereby leading to a lower market valuation relative to earnings.

5. DISCUSSION AND CONCLUSION

This study examines the impact of CSR index on financial performance of non-financial companies in Oman over the period of 2019 to 2023. The findings provide valuable insights into the role of CSR reporting in corporate performance, particularly in the context of Return on Equity (ROE) and the Price-to-Earnings (PE) ratio.

The regression analysis results reveal that the CSR index has a positive significant association with ROE, highlighting the importance of CSR practices for investors and business performance. Other indicators, such as the current ratio, total assets (log TA), and the debt- equity ratio also show a statistically significant effect on ROE, company size being negatively related to ROE. Similarly, in the second model, the study found that CSR index has a positive and significant relationship with PE ratio, indicating that a company's CSR practices have a positive impact on investors' perception, which may influence their growth expectations. Other indicators, such as liquidity position and debt-to-equity ratio play a crucial role in determining the company's market valuation, while log (TA) does not significantly impact firm's market valuation (P/E). Several studies underscore the importance of CSR reporting and greater CSR disclosure in enhancing corporate reputation, strengthening stakeholder relationships, and promoting long-term sustainability (Chipriyanov et al., 2024; Doda, 2015; Neitzert and Petras, 2022). Consistent with the prior studies that suggest a strong link between CSR initiatives and financial performance, this study also shows a significant relationship between CSR reporting and key financial performance metrics such as ROE and the P/E ratio. One of the most notable findings is that company size, measured in natural logarithm of total assets ((log TA)) has little to no effect on the PE ratio.

The findings of the study emphasize that incorporating CSR initiatives into business strategies is beneficial for companies in Oman. A positive correlation between the CSR index and ROE and P/E ratio implies that firms with stronger CSR commitments may experience greater financial advantages, particularly in terms of higher market valuations. However, given that market conditions and operational efficiency play a significant role in determining corporate success, CSR should be viewed as part of a broader strategic framework rather than as a standalone financial driver.

6. IMPLICATIONS AND FUTURE RESEARCH DIRECTIONS

The findings of this study provide several important implications for both corporate practice and academic research on CSR reporting. As CSR reporting does show a direct and significant impact on financial performance metrics such as Return on Equity (ROE) and the Price-to-Earnings (P/E) ratio, its broader influence on corporate reputation, stakeholder engagement, and sustainability should not be overlooked. First, Omani firms should integrate CSR initiatives into their long-term business strategies rather than viewing them as isolated activities. Aligning CSR efforts with core business operations may enhance stakeholder confidence and contribute to sustainable corporate growth. Second, policymakers and regulatory bodies in Oman could consider refining CSR disclosure guidelines to encourage companies to adopt more standardized and transparent reporting frameworks. This would improve the comparability and reliability of CSR disclosures. Third, companies should leverage technological advancements, such as blockchain for transparency, artificial intelligence for data analysis, and digital platforms for stakeholder engagement, thereby enhancing the effectiveness of CSR reporting. Lastly, Firms need to develop strategies to actively engage various stakeholders, including investors, employees, consumers, and regulators, in CSR initiatives. Transparent and meaningful CSR reporting could foster stronger relationships and long-term brand loyalty.

While this study provides valuable insights into the relationship between CSR disclosure and financial performance in non-financial companies in Oman, it is important to acknowledge that the study has several limitations that may influence the generalizability of the findings. The study sample is very small covering 11 non-financial firms from Oman. This limited sample size may not fully capture the diversity of CSR practices and their impact on the financial performance of companies across a broader range of industries or countries. CSR practices and their impact on financial performance can vary widely between countries due to differences in cultural and regulatory factors In addition, the study focuses on non-financial companies, which excludes the potential variations in CSR initiatives and financial performance that may exist within the finance sector. Therefore, the findings are specific to the context of non-financial companies in Oman and caution should be exercised when attempting to generalize the results to other countries, regions or industries.

Given these limitations, future research could expand on this study by addressing these gaps and exploring broader areas to research the relationship between CSR practices and financial performance in different contexts. First, future studies could explore more comprehensive CSR indices or alternative ways of measuring CSR activities that go beyond annual reports and financial disclosures. For example, including qualitative indicators such as employee well-being, environmental impact, and social contributions could offer a more holistic view of CSR effectiveness. Second, since different industries may exhibit varying levels of CSR adoption and impact, research should investigate how CSR reporting influences financial and non-financial outcomes across different sectors within Oman. This could provide more tailored insights for industry-specific CSR strategies. Third, while this study focuses on a five-year period, future research may broaden the time horizon to examine the long-term impact of CSR initiatives on financial performance. Longitudinal studies could better capture the delayed effects of CSR investments. Fourth, conducting comparative studies between Oman and other countries in the Gulf Cooperation Council (GCC) or globally could help identify best practices and cultural influences on CSR reporting effectiveness. Lastly, given the increasing role of technology in corporate reporting, future research could explore the adoption of digital tools such as sustainability dashboards, blockchain-enabled transparency measures, and AI-driven CSR analytics in improving reporting quality and stakeholder trust.

REFERENCES

Al-Abri, R., & Al-Balushi, Y. (2021). The role of corporate social responsibility in enhancing corporate reputation: Evidence from Oman. *Journal of Business Ethics, 162*(3), 789–805.

Al-Hamadi, A., Khan, F., & Al-Kiyumi, M. (2020). Cultural alignment in CSR: A study of Omani businesses. *Corporate Governance and Social Responsibility Review*, *18*(2), 155–172.

Al Lawati, H., & Hussainey, K. (2022). Does sustainable development goals disclosure affect corporate financial performance?'. *Sustainability (Basel)*, *14*(13), 7815. DOI: 10.3390/su14137815

Al-Maauli, S. S. (2023, April 1). Evaluating Corporate Social Responsibility reporting practices in the sultanate of Oman (2016 to 2018). Journal of Economic Administrative & Legal Sciences

Al-Maauli, S. S. (2023).. . *Evaluating Corporate Social Responsibility Reporting Practices in the Sultanate of Oman*, *7*(4), 134–153.

Barney, J. B., & Harrison, J. S. (2020). Stakeholder theory at the crossroads. *Business & Society*, *59*(2), 203–212. DOI: 10.1177/0007650318796792

Chipriyanov, M., Chipriyanova, G., Krasteva-Hristova, R., Atanasov, A., & Luchkov, K. (2024). Researching the Impact of Corporate Social Responsibility on Economic Growth and Inequality: Methodological Aspects. *Journal of Risk and Financial Management*, *17*(12), 546. DOI: 10.3390/jrfm17120546

Crossley, R. M., Elmagrhi, M. H., & Ntim, C. G. (2021). Sustainability and legitimacy theory: The case of sustainable social and environmental practices of small and medium-sized enterprises. *Business Strategy and the Environment*, *30*(8), 3740–3762. DOI: 10.1002/bse.2837

Doda, S. (2015). The Importance of Corporate Social Responsibility. *Journal of Sociological Research*, *6*(1), 86–91. DOI: 10.5296/jsr.v6i1.7426

Dunn, K., & Harness, D. (2018). Communicating corporate social responsibility in a social world: The effects of company-generated and user-generated social media content on CSR attributions and scepticism. *Journal of Marketing Management*, *34*(17-18), 1503–1529. DOI: 10.1080/0267257X.2018.1536675

Freeman, R. E. (2023) The politics of stakeholder theory: Some future directions. In R. Edward Freeman's Selected Works on Stakeholder Theory and Business Ethics', (pp. 119-132). Cham: Springer International Publishing.

Friedman, M. (1970) The Social Responsibility of Business Is to Increase Its Profits. New York Times Magazine, 13 September 1970, 122-126

ISO - ISO 26000 — Social responsibility. (2021, October 15). ISO. https://www.iso.org/iso-26000-social-responsibility.html

Khan, M., Al-Busaidi, Z., & Al-Ghafri, H. (2019). Impact of localized CSR initiatives on brand perception in Oman. *International Journal of Business and Social Science, 10*(4), 67–82.

Kivits, R., Sawang, S., Kivits, R., & Sawang, S. (2021) Stakeholder theory', The Dynamism of Stakeholder Engagement: A Case Study of the Aviation Industry, pp.1-8.

Kuzey, C., Uyar, A., Nizaeva, M., & Karaman, A. S. (2021). CSR performance and firm performance in the tourism, healthcare, and financial sectors: Do metrics and CSR committees' matter? *Journal of Cleaner Production, 319*, 128802. DOI: 10.1016/j.jclepro.2021.128802

Latapí Agudelo, M. A., Jóhannsdóttir, L., & Davídsdóttir, B. (2019). A literature review of the history and evolution of corporate social responsibility. *International Journal of Corporate Social Responsibility, 4*(1), 1. Advance online publication. DOI: 10.1186/s40991-018-0039-y

Li, Z., Liao, G., & Albitar, K. (2020). Does corporate environmental responsibility engagement affect firm value? The mediating role of corporate innovation. *Business Strategy and the Environment, 29*(3), 1045–1055. DOI: 10.1002/bse.2416

Neitzert, F., & Petras, M. (2022). Corporate social responsibility and bank risk. *Journal of Business Economics, 92*(3), 397–428. DOI: 10.1007/s11573-021-01069-2

Okafor, A., Adeleye, B. N., & Adusei, M. (2021). Corporate social responsibility and financial performance: Evidence from US tech firms. *Journal of Cleaner Production, 292*, 126078. DOI: 10.1016/j.jclepro.2021.126078

Sandberg, H., Alnoor, A., & Tiberius, V. (2023). Environmental, social, and governance ratings and financial performance: Evidence from the European food industry. *Business Strategy and the Environment, 32*(4), 2471–2489. DOI: 10.1002/bse.3259

Saunders, M., Lewis, P., & Thornhill, A. (2009). *Research Methods for Business Students* (5th ed.). Pearson education.

Silva, S. (2021). Corporate contributions to the Sustainable Development Goals: An empirical analysis informed by legitimacy theory. *Journal of Cleaner Production, 292*, 125962. DOI: 10.1016/j.jclepro.2021.125962

Thottoli, M. M., & Thomas, K. V. (2023). 'The impact of web marketing on corporate social responsibility (CSR) and firms' performance'. *Rajagiri Management Journal, 17*(1), 37–51. DOI: 10.1108/RAMJ-03-2021-0022

Uyar, A., Wasiuzzaman, S., Kuzey, C., & Karaman, A. S. (2022). Board structure and financial stability of financial firms: Do board policies and CEO duality matter? *Journal of International Accounting, Auditing & Taxation, 47*, 100474. DOI: 10.1016/j.intaccaudtax.2022.100474

Visser, W. (2008). Corporate Social Responsibility in Developing Countries. In Crane, A. (Eds.), *The Oxford Handbook of Corporate Social Responsibility* (pp. 473–500)., DOI: 10.1093/oxfordhb/9780199211593.003.0021

Younas, A., & Kassim, A. A. M. (2022) 'Measuring Corporate Social Responsibility by Constructing an Index: An Empirical Evidence from Oman', In Eurasian Business and Economics Perspectives: Proceedings of the 35th Eurasia Business and Economics Society Conference (pp. 231-244). Cham: Springer International Publishing. DOI: 10.1007/978-3-030-94672-2_14

Younas, A., & Kassim, A. A. M. (2023) 'Exploring the Impact of Corporate Social Responsibility on Leverage of Listed Companies in Oman', In Global Economic Challenges: 6th International Conference on Banking and Finance Perspectives, Cuenca, Spain (pp. 39-53). Cham: Springer International Publishing. DOI: 10.1007/978-3-031-23416-3_4

Younas, A., Kassim, A. A. M., & Bhuiyan, A. B. (2021). Construction of corporate social responsibility (CSR) disclosure index and its practices by listed companies in Oman. *American International Journal of Economics and Finance Research, 3*(1), 57–68.

Younas, A., & Kassim, A. M. (2022). Measuring Corporate Social Responsibility by Constructing an Index: An Empirical Evidence from Oman. In *Eurasian studies in business and economics* (pp. 231–244). https://doi.org/DOI: 10.1007/978-3-030-94672-2_14

Younas, A., & Kassim, A. M. (2023). Exploring the impact of corporate social responsibility on leverage of listed companies in Oman. In Springer proceedings in business and economics (pp. 39–53). DOI: 10.1007/978-3-031-23416-3_4

Younas, A., Muthuraman, S., Al Darmaki, A., Khan, F., & Kassim, A. A. M. (2023). Empirical Review of Measuring Corporate Social Responsibility in the Sultanate of Oman. *Artificial Intelligence, Internet of Things, and Society*, *5*(0), 167–177. DOI: 10.1007/978-3-031-43300-9_15

Chapter 12
Bridging the Gap Between Circular Economy and Sustainability

Sushma Muralie
Presidency University, India

Swati Bhatnagar
http://orcid.org/0000-0002-5507-0618
New Delhi Institute of Management, India

ABSTRACT

The objective of this research paper is to examine the Circular Economy (CE) strategies adopted by companies by applying established frameworks and predefined indicators from existing literature. The study aims to analyze how these strategies generate social and economic benefits and contribute to overall sustainability. To achieve this, the research used a qualitative methodology and specifically content analysis of published sustainability reports. This approach involved collecting and analysing data on companies' efforts to provide goods sustainably. By reviewing these reports, the research identifies CE initiatives implemented by companies and evaluates how these strategies align with sustainability goals, including their contribution to reducing environmental footprints, promoting resource efficiency and fostering social equity. This analysis provides a deeper understanding of the intersection between Circular Economy practices and sustainable development outcomes.

DOI: 10.4018/979-8-3373-5437-8.ch012

INTRODUCTION

The term Sustainable development became popular in1960's when the ill effects of economic and social development on environment became apparent (Boulding, 1966). Some researchers took a whole system view on resource exploitation and economic growth. In the year 1987 world commission of economic development (WCED, 1987) set out a discussion on sustainable development. Meadows et al (1972) defines sustainable development as the one that *ensures that the needs of the present are met without compromising the ability of future generations to meet their own needs"*. Besides this there are 300 such definitions of this concept which in itself considered to be impediment for effective research in this domain. Sustainable development has been perceived differently by different people, making this a fuzzy value laden concept. (Korhonen et al., 2018a)

For times immemorial mankind has exploited nature for resources whether it be in the extraction of materials or drilling of oil. The consequence of this exploitation being the generation of wastes managing of which has become one of the leading problems that the world faces today. It is then that the circular economy emerged as an economic model with a potential to long term reduction of primary resources and minimization of waste. The closed loops of products, product parts and materials lead to environmental protection and economic benefits (Murray et al., 2017; Babbitt et al., 2018; Hofmann, 2019). CE traces its roots to the closed loop economic system suggested by (Boulding, 1966), it was however given legislative strength when the German Parliament passed the law on CE in the year 1996. Legislations on CE was passed in China in 1990's with a view to protect the environment from further degradation.

While some scholars and practitioners consider the Circular Economy (CE) as a practical approach for businesses to implement the principles of sustainable development, others argue that CE lacks a holistic perspective. Critics highlight that CE primarily focuses on economic considerations, often neglecting environmental impacts and the social equity dimension. In fact, CE is sometimes referred to as an economic system rather than a sustainability framework. Additionally, some scholars characterize CE as an umbrella concept with blurred boundaries, encompassing multiple interpretations (Korhonen et al. 2018).

Geissdoerfer et al. (2017) explicitly examine the relationship between CE and sustainability, concluding that further research is needed to determine how CE can contribute to strong sustainability. Building on this discourse, this study analyses the Business Responsibility and Sustainability Reporting (BRSR) reports of 46 Indian companies operating in five different industrial sectors to assess their circularity initiatives. The findings aim to evaluate the environmental and social implications of CE practices within these organizations.

SUSTAINABILITY

The word *sustainability* originated from the French verb *soutenir*, which meant "to hold up or support" (Brown et al.,1987). This conceptualisation has its origin in forestry and was later transferred to the domain of ecology implying the ability of nature to regenerate itself (Duden, 2015). According to Johnston et al. (2007) there are almost 300 definitions of sustainability. Sustainability as a concept implies that human activities should be conducted in such a manner that it conserves the earth's ecosystems (ISO 15392, 2008). It rests on the principle that human lifestyle should be transformed such that, it optimises living conditions, supports security, well-being and health of all life forms (Ehrenfeld, 2005). The awareness and adoption of this becomes even more essential due to increasing evidence of environmental risks, such as climate change, depletion of the ozone layer, loss of biodiversity and the alteration of the nitrogen cycle at a global level. These risks raise questions whether present prosperity trends shall continue in the future (Clark and Crutzen, 2005; Rockström et al., 2009). The research on these risks reveals many causes of concern which includes, limited resources, its unequal geographical distribution and appropriation (Georgescu-Roegen, 1977) and assimilative capacities of ecosystems over economic growth (Daly and Townsend, 1993). Environmentalists Ehrlich and Commoner condensed these concerns in their equation "I = P x A x T" where Environmental Impact (I) is a function of three factors: population (P); affluence, which represents consumption (A); and technologies (T) (Chertow, 2001; Commoner, 1972; Holdren and Ehrlich, 1974). Different scholars vary in their opinion on the emphasis given to these different variables. Few emphasise demographic control (Hardin, 1968), others advocate consumption reduction (Woollard and Ostry, 2000), and an increasing number of scholars stress on the role of science, technology and innovation in driving social inclusion and environmental resilience (Hart and Milstein, 2003; Kemp and Pearson, 2007; Cohen, 2006). "Development" and "environment" are contradictory elements of an intrinsic trade-off (Sachs, 2015; Jackson, 2009). It was the Brundtland Report (1987), which attempted to address those conflicts. It mentioned that "The concept of sustainable development does imply limits – not absolute limits but limitations imposed by the present state of technology and social organization on environmental resources and by the ability of the biosphere to absorb the effects of human activities" (Brundtland, 1987:8).It also provided the most commonly accepted definition of sustainability as "development that meets the needs of the present without compromising the ability of future generations to meet their own needs"(Brundtland, 1987). Another term which is particularly relevant and has gained widespread diffusion is the concept of 'triple bottom line' which suggests that the three pillars of sustainability are people, profit, and planet. Post the World Summit in 2002, the triple bottom line has been recommended as the balanced integration of economic, environmental and social performance. These three spheres are logically connected and continuously and cumulatively impact each other through mutual causality and positive feedback (Mckelvey, 2002). Thus, the term sustainability is developed in a holistic, adaptive and flexible nature as *the balanced and systemic integration of intra and intergenerational economic, social and environmental performance.* Despite variance in the perceived strengths and weaknesses of the term sustainability, policymakers have institutionalised this into the agendas and strategies of large organisations, and getting it embedded into the rules that structure social interventions and shape behaviour (Hodgson, 2005).

THE R FRAMEWORK OF THE CIRCULAR ECONOMY

The circular economy (CE) aims to establish closed-loop systems by minimizing waste and converting residues into secondary resources. The 3R framework, consisting of reduction, reuse, and recycle, is the most recognized and is the foundation of China's 2008 Circular Economy Promotion Law. *Reduction* focuses on eco-efficiency in production and consumption. *Reuse* involves better product design and business models for cyclical disassembly. Consumer willingness to buy reusable and remanufactured goods is crucial and necessitates marketing, public education and shared responsibility between producers and consumers to collect products after their first use cycle. *Recycling* refers to reprocessing waste materials into new products or substances, excluding energy recovery or use as fuels. The European Union's (EU) Waste Framework Directive added 'Recover' as the fourth R, leading to the development of the '4R framework', which offers alternatives to using raw, virgin materials, thus promoting sustainability. Economic activities such as reverse logistics and take-back programs are essential for waste recovery, reducing disposal costs and raw material expenses, and potentially generating income. The informal sector contributes to material recovery and reducing environmental contamination. While numerous scholars have proposed frameworks beyond the 4Rs, such as the 6Rs and 9Rs, the 9R framework is the most detailed. All R frameworks are structured hierarchically, with "reduce" considered as the most important pillar.

Figure 1. The 9R Framework

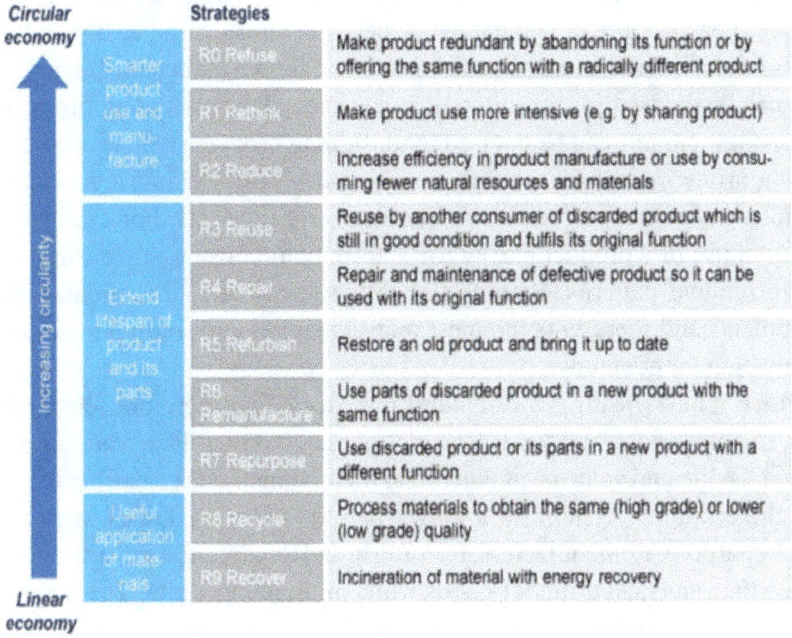

The '**Reduce**' group in the circular economy consists of **Refuse, Rethink, and Reduce**. These strategies are implemented when products are conceived, designed and developed, making them precursory, enabling and transformative. They occur before other circular economy strategies, favour all other strategies, and can transform the economic system if applied extensively. Refuse, Rethink, and Reduce are closely connected to design, which includes designing production processes, logistics systems and consumption patterns.

Refuse means making a product redundant by abandoning its function or offering the same function with a radically different product. Refuse can also extend to the use of certain materials or production processes to make the economy more circular. For example,countries have different phase-out targets for items like plastic bags or incandescent lamps. Similar targets can be devised for single-use products, disposable straws, useless secondary packages, or even for some products that can be substituted by nonmaterial ones, such as digital products. Similarly, targets can be there on product using a certain material that must be refused (e.g., virgin materials) to impose recycling or reuse. A ban might be possible on specific materials in relation to products, for instance, plastic for packaging.

Rethink proposes new ideas and solutions to provide certain product functions, which can embrace reframing and regeneration of many aspects of circular economy systems. It refers to making a product use intensive. A first set of targets for Rethink should be on design and engineering, which can facilitate other circular economy strategies. For example, a percentage of new products can be easily and cheaply disassembled, repaired, or upgraded in specific commodity-related categories. Other targets can be devised for reusing transit and secondary packaging or for refilling primary ones. Targets can be devised for designing products that are easy to repair, including arranging support within an efficient supply chain. Targets can incentivize intensity of use or the more efficient use of products. For example, a 20% intensity of use of a product like a lawn mower could favour new business models or organizational patterns. Rethink lies at the nexus of future circular economy developments and represents the most relevant strategy for promoting a transition to a truly circular economy.

Reduce implies using fewer natural resources, and therefore fewer inputs of energy, raw materials, and waste.The circular economy utilizes various strategies to extend the life and value of products and their components, ensuring they remain within the economic system for a longer period. These strategies, which include Reuse, Repurpose, Remanufacture, Refurbish, and Repair, offer a distinct method for retaining the value and utility of goods while minimizing waste. These approaches present both opportunities and challenges for businesses and policymakers striving to create a more sustainable and resource-efficient economy.

Reuse is defined as the continued use of a product in its original form, either by the original owner or a new user, for its original purpose. The product retains its original function and identity throughout this process. A practical example of reuse is the adoption of standardized, durable glass containers by beer manufacturers to facilitate sorting and collection. This approach relies on designing products that are robust and suitable for repeated use. Reuse also includes the practice of "parts harvesting," where functional components are salvaged from discarded products for use in other products.

Repurpose, also known as recontextualizing, involves using discarded products or their parts to create something new with a different function. This is also known as open-loop reuse. Unlike reuse, repurposing results in a change of identity and function for the original product or its components. Implementing repurposing strategies can be challenging due to several factors:

-The wide variety of possible uses for individual parts.
-The restricted number of products suitable for repurposing.
-The reliance on the creativity of the individual doing the repurposing.
-The small-scale of repurposing activities.
-The difficulty in maintaining traceability of the repurposed products or components.

Remanufacture, Refurbish, and Repair are strategies that typically occur within the confines of a producer, its affiliates or private consumers. These approaches cannot be applied to a product simultaneously. The primary goal of remanufacturing, refurbishing and repair is to delay obsolescence, extending the useful life of products.

Remanufacturing, or second-life production, involves using parts from discarded products to create a new product that performs the same function as the original. A remanufactured product is expected to meet the quality standards of a new product, even when it incorporates reclaimed components from used products. Historically, remanufacturing has been prevalent in industries dealing with durable goods and assemblies.

Refurbishing, also known as reconditioning, focuses on restoring an old product to a more current state. This involves upgrading or modernizing the product's function, typically through the replacement of parts without complete disassembly. Refurbishing is sometimes referred to as *'light'* remanufacturing. The goal is to bring the product back to specified quality standards or satisfactory working and cosmetic conditions.

Repair involves fixing or replacing defective parts to restore a broken product to its original functionality. This allows the product to be used as intended. Repair is commonly undertaken by owners, regardless of whether the product is under warranty.

While maintenance activities, such as keeping a product in good working condition, contribute to durability and serviceability, they are not explicitly considered circular economy strategies. Maintenance can include repair, replacement, adjustment, lubrication, and modification activities. In industries like aviation and heavy machinery, integrated Maintenance-Repair-Overhaul (MRO) services are common. Updating and upgrading products are considered remedial actions falling under the categories of refurbishment or remanufacturing, rather than stand-alone life extension strategies.

The ideal objective of life extension strategies is to maximize the use of products throughout their entire technical life. However, obtaining precise data on product lifespans is challenging, as it depends on factors such as product type, usage patterns, user expectations, technological advancements, regulatory constraints, and product performance over time. Implementing these circular economy strategies requires careful consideration of their impact on innovation, revenue models and socioeconomic patterns. Setting targets for these strategies necessitates a holistic approach, acknowledging potential drawbacks. For instance, extending product lifespan could potentially slow down innovation or hinder the development of more environmentally friendly products. Similarly, regulations aimed at phasing out certain products or imposing higher standards (e.g., for safety or energy efficiency) may impede some of these strategies.

Recycling and recovery represent two distinct strategies for managing waste, each with its own set of processes and implications. Recycling focuses on reprocessing materials to create secondary materials, whereas recovery involves extracting energy or biochemical compounds from waste, often through incineration. Recycling involves the transformation of discarded materials into secondary materials, which can be of either higher (upcycling) or lower (downcycling) quality compared to the original material. It extracts materials from discarded products and upcycling is the preferable method because of its higher value and quality. Its feasibility is limited by factors such as material properties and market prices. Recycling is an energy-intensive process that requires transportation, physical and/or chemical treatments. This process can degrade the integrity and market value of products and may not significantly influence product design. For certain materials like composites, corroded metals, some polymers and contaminated glass, recycling can be impractical or expensive. To improve recycling outcomes, recycling considerations should be integrated into the initial product design phase.

Recovery focuses on incinerating waste to recover energy or biochemical compounds. This method is applied to non-recyclable waste, and incineration is a common energy recovery approach that complements recycling. However, it permanently destroys materials and can promote wastefulness because it requires a constant waste supply to maintain profitability. Despite this, life-cycle assessments often favor waste-to-energy incineration over landfilling, indicating its potential contribution to a circular economy.

Both recycling and recovery have drawbacks, including energy consumption, environmental impacts, and potential waste generation. Recycling is energy intensive, and not free from environmental impact. It requires transportation, as well as physical, chemical, and/or mechanical treatments. Incineration destroys materials/products forever and encourages material wastefulness. To summarise, Recycling aims to transform materials into new products, often with reduced quality. Recovery focuses on energy extraction from waste via incineration. Both methods present drawbacks, including energy consumption and environmental impact.

CIRCULAR ECONOMY AND SUSTAINABILITY DIFFERING APPROACHES

The circular economy and sustainability share common ground but have differing approaches. (Corvellec etal, 2022). Circular economy definitions consider economic growth, promote renewable energy, and emphasize 'restoration' and 'replenishing' resources. The concept of a closed loop is central to circular economy definitions. The modern understanding of the term Circular Economy seems to have emerged more recently than that of sustainability (EMF 2013). While sustainability provides a broader framing, which can be adapted to different contexts and aspirations, the Circular Economy emphasizes economic and environmental benefits compared to a linear system.

While agency is diffused in the case of sustainability, as the priorities should be defined by all stakeholders, the Circular Economy has a clear emphasis on governments and companies (Webster, 2015). In the sustainability debate, responsibilities are shared but not clearly defined, while the literature considers that the responsibility for the transition to a circular system lies primarily with private business, regulators and policymakers. The focus seems to be on interest alignment between stakeholders for sustainability, whereas the Circular Economy prioritizes financial advantages for companies, and less resource consumption and pollution for the environment (Allwood, 2014; Bakker et al., 2014)

The circular economy has received increased attention in academic research with a range of reviews on the topic (Andersen 2007, Ghisellini et al. 2016, Lieder and Rashid 2016, and Su et al. 2013) Specific areas of attention are closed loop value and supply chains, circular business models and circular product design (Rashid et al. 2013). The circular economy is viewed as a "refurbished rather than virgin concept". Its strategies for prolonging resource use are not new individually; its novelty lies in framing and connecting these strategies. Over a hundred definitions of circularity exist, leading to different interpretations (Reikeetal., 2018). The concept is driven mainly by practitioners like policymakers and businesses. Different definitions of the circular economy are adopted for different theoretical uses, resulting in conceptual fragmentation and a perceived lack of paradigmatic strength (Kirchherr et al., 2017, Blomsma & Brennan, 2017, Korhonen et al., 2018b, Inigo & Blok, 2019)

The circular economy is seen as an emerging approach to industrial production and consumption rather than a theory (Korhonen et al., 2018b). It is described as a multiplicity, an umbrella concept that generates excitement but faces scrutiny during attempts at operationalization. Many argue that the circular economy neglects established knowledge, particularly thermodynamic principles (Giampietro& Funtowicz, 2020; Pearce& Turner, 1990). Circulation practices may retain hazardous substances in the economy, increasing their dispersion (Johansson et al., 2020). The circular economy has seen limited implementation despite broad endorsement. policy instruments are suggested to promote circulation rather than obstruct the legacy of the linear economy. There are unresolved questions about how to avoid linear lock-ins and how to deal with trade-offs in circular business models (Schroder et al., 2019). Linear technologies retain their market position despite their inefficiency, and circular innovations are hard to scale up (Korhonen et al., 2018a). The differences between circular economy and sustainability are often blurred, despite the fact that the latter is more holistic.

The circular economy focuses on the resource base and waste sink functions but omits the amenity base and life-support features of the surrounding environment (Inigo & Blok, 2019) The metaphor of the circular economy, while enticing, can be misleading and raise questions about what is actually circular (Corvellec et al., 2019). A wide range of critiques accentuate how circular economy discourses act to depoliticize policy and industry interventions. There is a need for conceptual coherence about definitions, plans, implementations and modes of evaluation. There is a growing feeling that the circular economy agenda needs to include civic society and reclaim ownership from business and policy to drive a new transition (Hobson, 2020; Holmes et al., 2021)

Multiple view points on circular economy indicate towards an existential gap in understanding how CE will contribute to the three pillars (ESG) of sustainability. There is a need to bridge the gap between what is practiced by companies under the umbrella of CE and its contribution to ESG pillars of Sustainability.

SUSTAINABILITY REPORTING STANDARD – BRSR

Business Responsibility and Sustainability report is a reporting format developed by the Securities and Exchange Board of India (SEBI). Effective since 2003, top 1000 companies listed in the stock exchange are to file this report with SEBI along with their annual reports. This report mandates companies to give quantifiable metrics on sustainability related factors. The BRSR is closely aligned with other global reporting formats like GRI, TCFD .

The BRSR report format consists of three sections. General disclosures, the objective of this section is to obtain basic information about the company – size, location, products, number of employees, CSR activities, etc. Management disclosures, in this section, the company is required to disclose information on policies and processes relating to the NGRBC Principles concerning leadership, governance, and stakeholder engagement. Wherever relevant, companies have been asked to provide links to their websites where these policies are available. Principle-wise disclosures, responses to this section indicate how a company is performing in respect of nine Principles and Core Element of the National Guidelines for Responsible Business Conduct. This section requires companies to demonstrate their intent and commitment to responsible business conduct through actions and outcomes. The 140 questions asked in this disclosure which have been divided into two types: Essential indicators (mandatory) and Leadership indicators (voluntary).

While the world has been debating on the issue of blurred definitions of Sustainability and CE, the BRSR has included CE reporting in its principle 2 of the report. Under principle 2 companies are required to give information on how their business reclaim, recycle and dispose waste. This research uses information furnished by companies under this disclosure heading.

Sampling

The study uses a report published by Stake holder empowerment services (SES). In the report published by SES ESG footprints of 100 selected National Stock Exchange (NSE) listed companies is presented. This study uses this list as a basis and 5 industry sectors covering 46 companies' circularity disclosures are considered for analysis. The sample of 46 companies covers 15% of Market capitalisation of Nifty 500 Listed companies. The list of companies under study is given in Annexure 1.

Data Collection

The BRSR report of companies are freely downloadable, this research accessed the circularity element discussed by companies under principle 9 of the report. The disclosures made by the 46 companies was downloaded. The following section gives the word cloud that is generated using this collated information on circularity practices of companies. The data was processed using the ATLAS ti software.

Steel Industry

Figure 2. Word Cloud

The downloaded texts describe the waste management and recycling practices of various companies, particularly those in the steel, mining, and metal industries. These companies highlight their commitment to reducing waste, reusing materials, and recycling resources to transition towards a circular economy. Many emphasize minimizing plastic use, properly disposing of e-waste and hazardous materials through authorized vendors, and striving for zero waste to landfill. Innovative approaches, such as repurposing waste materials like slag and red mud, and collaborating with other industries for waste utilization, are frequently mentioned. These efforts are often aligned with environmental standards, regulations, and a

Cement Industry

Figure 3. Word Cloud

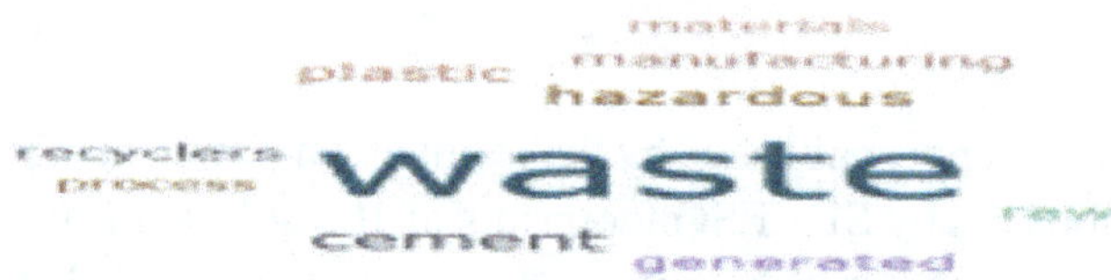

Many cement companies are actively involved in waste management and circular economy practices. A common practice is the co-processing of plastic waste in cement kilns, utilizing plastic from packaging and other sources as an alternative fuel. Several companies, including Ultratech, ACC, Ambuja, and Dalmia Bharat, claim to be "plastic negative" or "plastic recycling positive," indicating they process more plastic waste than they generate.

In addition to plastics, cement companies manage other types of waste. E-waste generated from office operations is typically sold to registered recyclers. Hazardous waste is either co-processed in kilns or sent to authorized recyclers or incinerators. Some companies, like Shree Cements, focus on internal assessments and employee awareness to reduce waste generation. Shree Cements also manufactures synthetic gypsum from hazardous waste, reducing reliance on natural gypsum. Moreover, several cement manufacturers replace raw materials with waste from other industries, including fly ash and GBFS slag. In FY 2023-24, Shree Cements replaced 24.41% of raw materials with alternative raw materials.

Automobile Industry

Figure 4. Word Cloud

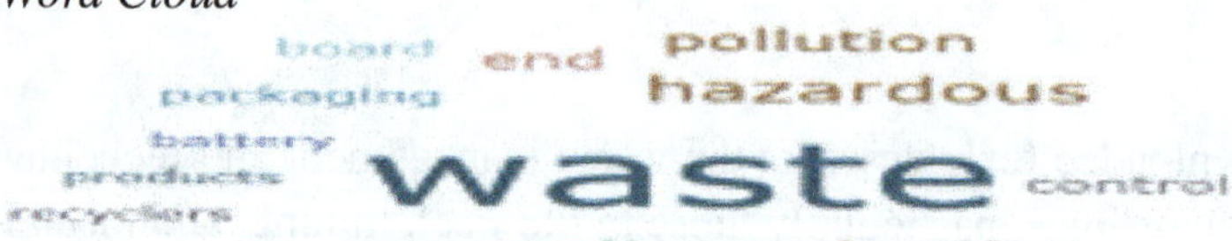

Several automotive companies in India are actively involved in managing waste and promoting recycling in their operations. Maruti Suzuki has partnered with Toyota Tsusho Group to establish a joint venture, Maruti Suzuki Toyotsu India Private Limited (MSTI), for end-of-life vehicle dismantling and recycling in Uttar Pradesh. Tata Motors is improving product circularity by designing vehicles for recyclability, selecting sustainable materials, and providing dismantling information. TML aims for a minimum of 85% recyclability and 90% recoverability in its vehicle designs. TML has also launched "Re.Wi.Re – Recycle with Respect" to safely recycle end-of-life vehicles, with five facilities having the capacity to dismantle over 72,000 vehicles annually.

Mahindra utilizes CERO, India's first and largest vehicle recycling network, to achieve zero pollution and wastage. Mahindra recycles plastic from end-of-life vehicles through authorized agencies and ensures hazardous waste is sent for recycling/refining. Eicher ensures its motorcycles are ELV compliant, with up to 85% recyclability. Eicher sends paint sludge waste for co-processing in the cement industry and steel scraps directly to melting sources for recycling. TVS Motor corp. marks plastic parts with recyclability symbols and manages batteries according to Extended Producer Responsibility. Escorts disposes of plastic waste and lead acid from batteries through authorized recyclers and partners with companies for recycling waste oil and incinerating paint sludge.

Pharmaceutical Industry

Figure 5. Word Cloud

Pharmaceutical companies are implementing various waste management systems to handle different types of waste generated from their operations, with a focus on reducing landfill waste and integrating circular economy principles. Plastic waste is managed through Extended Producer Responsibility (EPR) regulations, with companies engaging waste management agencies to collect, recycle, and co-process plastic waste. Some companies have achieved 100% plastic take-back by recycling and co-processing it in cement industries. E-waste is typically sold to or disposed of through authorized vendors and recyclers. Hazardous waste is often channelled for recycling, co-processing in cement industries for value recovery, or sent to Treatment, Storage, and Disposal Facilities (TSDFs). Some companies also take back expired medicines from distributors for co-processing. Non-hazardous waste, such as glass, MS scrap, wood waste, and boiler ash, is sent to authorized recyclers or brick manufacturers. Some companies are diverting sludge from Effluent Treatment Plants (ETPs) and MEE salt to co-processing instead of landfills. Solvent recovery systems are also deployed to recover used solvents. These strategies ensure proper and safe treatment of waste in accordance with regulatory standards.

Chemical Industry

Figure 6. Word Cloud

Several companies in the chemical industry demonstrate a commitment to managing various types of waste, including plastic, e-waste, and hazardous waste, through recycling, reprocessing, and disposal methods that comply with environmental regulations.

Aarti Industries collected 300 MT of plastic waste in FY23-24, recycling the collected amount and adhering to Extended Producer Responsibility (EPR). Similarly, Deepak Nitrite recycles all plastic waste through authorized vendors and ensures responsible hazardous waste management. GFL reclaims products for reuse, recycling, and safe disposal, adhering to Plastic Waste Management Rules and E-waste Management Rules. Tata Chemicals reprocesses damaged plastic material and sends hazardous waste to authorized end-users or disposal facilities. Godrej Industries employs a waste management framework based on the five R's: reduce, reuse, recycle, recover, and residual management. Solar Industries, while unable to recycle explosive products, recycles packaging materials and reclaims/disposes of rejected products according to regulations. While some companies like Galaxy Chemicals and Jubilant Ingrevia indicated that certain waste categories are "Not Applicable" to their operations, PCBL is exploring extracting carbon black from disposed tires to reduce virgin material consumption.

DISCUSSIONS AND CONCLUSION

Under the umbrella term of reduce, reuse and recycle all the industry sectors report focusing on waste. Waste is considered as valueless burden by the society. CE helps generate value from this value less resource. The move towards circularity has opened up immense opportunities for the growth of a parallel recyclers eco system, as is evidenced from this study. This recycler market is organized and developing skills of the local youth. Growing recycler business addresses unemployment which is one of the biggest challenges of the social economy. Organized retailers add valuable knowledge gained through their experiences which can transcend boundaries and spread through the industry fast.

By co-managing waste generated as a byproduct of manufacturing process the business are shouldering the responsibility of sharing the responsibility of governments in managing a seemingly difficult task. Individual business look after their waste disposal in a decentralized and participative approach to managing waste. The spin offs from waste management are immense and impact the environment by reducing the burden of waste in the most appropriate manner and this includes hazardous waste. Waste management create social good in terms of providing employment and spreading and garnering of knowledge; the organized recycling has promoted regulatory compliances contributing to the governance pillar of sustainability.

Material can be of two types biological nutrients one which is designed to re enter the biosphere and build natural materials and second technical nutrient which is designed to circulate at high quality within the biosphere. End of life reprocess ensure the recovery of technical nutrients. The apparently low recoverability rates of material from this process have not deterred business from adopting it. Two out of five industries under study have a proper end of life recovery system in place. Global consumption of raw material is on the rise, traditional extraction methods are energy intensive, end of life recovery thus is both environmentally and socially beneficial.

Another potential outcome of CE practices is industrial symbiosis. Industrial symbiosis in an emerging field of industrial ecology that demands resolute attention to the flow of materials and energy through local and regional economies. Industrial symbiosis engages traditionally separate industries in a collective approach to competitive advantage involving physical exchange of materials, energy, water, and/or by-products. This study found this practice adopted by both cement and steel industry where they are either receiving waste as a raw material for their production process or collaborating with others to consumer their waste output. The key to growth of industrial symbiosis lies in collaboration, this collaboration is both good for business and society and environment.

This discussion will not be complete without a discussion on whether the circularity efforts of companies can be quantified and presented or not. Unfortunately, none of the companies under study have reported any quantifiable number in terms of their efforts and its direct impact on the carbon footprint. No data is available on the quantity of waste produced, recycling rate and other related information. However, evidences for the hierarchical ladder proposed by Potting et al. (2017), can be observed. The CE practices reflect businesses effort to reduce redundancy and multifunctionality; increase the life time of products; use of components or parts; preserving of materials by downcycling and preserving embodied energy. It would be a while before business develop one standardized method for reporting the impact of their efforts. This should not deny them an opportunity to claim their contribution to the overall sustainability goals.

Our study using the circularity practices of companies operating in different industrial segments in India highlights the magnitude of involvement of these companies in circular economy practices. CE will contribute to nation building by contributing to material and energy savings, reduced landfill, reduced hazardous material. Business will benefit from increased collaboration, better regulation and governance, society will benefit from decreased greenhouse gas footprints, reduced impacts on air, water and land pollution, better job opportunities and greater knowledge sharing. Lack or non-availability of any standards for measuring the impact of CE should not cast a doubt on CE'S overall contribution to achievement of sustainability. For businesses, commitment to circularity goes beyond economic and financial interest, they are moving towards responsible consumption. The discussion done so far establishes the contribution of CE strategies to the environmental, social and governance pillars of sustainability. Hopefully, future research will move towards establishing a standardized mechanism for measuring the impact of CE strategies, which will dispel much cloud surrounding the CE concept.

REFERENCES

Allwood, J. M. (2014). Squaring the Circular Economy: The Role of Recycling within a Hierarchy of Material Management Strategies. In Worrell, E., & Reuter, M. (Eds.), *Handbook of Recycling: State-of-the-Art for Practitioners* (pp. 445–477). Analysts, and Scientists. DOI: 10.1016/B978-0-12-396459-5.00030-1

Babbitt, C. W., Gaustad, G., Fisher, A., Chen, W. Q., & Liu, G. (2018). Closing the loop on circular economy research: From theory to practice and back again. *Resources, Conservation and Recycling*, *135*, 1–2. DOI: 10.1016/j.resconrec.2018.04.012

Bakker, C. A., den Hollander, M. C., van Hinte, E., & Zljlstra, Y. (2014). *ProductsThat Last - Product design for circular business models.* TU Delft Library.

Blomsma, F., & Brennan, G. (2017). The Emergence of circular economy: A new framing around prolonging resource productivity. *Journal of Industrial Ecology*, *21*(3), 603–614. DOI: 10.1111/jiec.12603

Boulding, K. E. 1966. The economics of the coming spaceship Earth, Sixth Resources for the Future Forum on Environmental Quality in a Growing Economy, Wash- ington, D.C

Brown, B. J., Hanson, M. E., Liverman, D. M., & Merideth, R. W.Jr. (1987). Global Sustainability: Towards Definition. *Environmental Management*, *2*(6), 713–719. DOI: 10.1007/BF01867238

Brundtland, G. H. (1987). *Our common future: Report of the 1987 World Commission on Environment and Development.* United Nations.

Chertow, M. R. (2001). The IPAT Equation and Its Variants: Changing Views of Technology and Environmental Impact. *Journal of Industrial Ecology*, *4*(4), 13–29. DOI: 10.1162/10881980052541927

Clark, W., & Crutzen, P. 2005. Science for global sustainability: toward a new paradigm. KSG Working Paper. 120, 1–28.

Cohen, M. J. (2006). Ecological modernization and its discontents: The American environmental movement's resistance to an innovation-driven future. *Futures*, *38*(5), 528–547. DOI: 10.1016/j.futures.2005.09.002

Corvellec, H., & Stal, H. I. (2019). Qualification as corporate activism: How Swedish apparel retailers attach circular fashion qualities to take-back systems. *Scandinavian Journal of Management*, *35*(3), 101046. DOI: 10.1016/j.scaman.2019.03.002

Corvellec, H., Stowell, A. F., & Johansson, N. (2022). Critiques of the circular economy [April.]. *Journal of Industrial Ecology, 26*(2), 421–432. DOI: 10.1111/jiec.13187

Daly, H. E., & Townsend, K. N. (1993). *Valuing the earth: economics, ecology,ethics*. MIT Press.

Ehrenfeld, J. R. (2005). The roots of sustainability. *Sloan Management Review, 46*, 23–25.

Ellen MacArthur Foundation (EMF). (2013). *Towards the Circular Economy* (Vol. 2).

Geissdoerfer, M., Savaget, P., Bocken, N. M. P., & Hultink, E. J. (2017). The circular economy – a new sustainability paradigm. *Journal of Cleaner Production, 143*, 757–768. DOI: 10.1016/j.jclepro.2016.12.048

Georgescu-Roegen, N. (1977). Inequality, Limits and Growth from a Bioeconomic Viewpoint. *Review of Social Economy, 35*(3), 361–375. DOI: 10.1080/00346767700000041

Giampietro, M., & Funtowicz, S. O. (2020). From elite folk science to the policy legend of the circular economy. *Environmental Science & Policy, 109*, 64–72. DOI: 10.1016/j.envsci.2020.04.012

Hardin, G. (1968). The Tragedy of the Commons. *Science, 162*(3859), 1243–1248. DOI: 10.1126/science.162.3859.1243 PMID: 5699198

Hart, S. L., & Milstein, M. B. (2003). Creating sustainable value. *The Academy of Management Perspectives, 17*(2), 56–67. DOI: 10.5465/ame.2003.10025194

Hobson, K. (2020). The limits of the loops: Critical environmental politics and the circular economy. *Environmental Politics, 30*(1-2), 161–179. DOI: 10.1080/09644016.2020.1816052

Hodgson, G. 2005. Institutions and Economic Development: Constraining, Enabling and Reconstituting, in: G. Dymski & S. De Paula, eds.

Hofmann, F. (2019). Circular business models: Business approach as driver or obstructer of sustainability transitions? *Journal of Cleaner Production, 224*, 361–374. DOI: 10.1016/j.jclepro.2019.03.115

Holdren, J., & Ehrlich, P. (1974). Human population and the global environment. *American Scientist, 62*, 282–292. PMID: 4832978

Holmes, H., Wieser, H., & Kasmire, J. (2021). Critical approaches to circular economy research: Time, space and evolution. In R. B. Swain & S. Sweet (Eds.), *Sustainable consumption and production, volume II: Circular economy and beyond* (pp. 55–74). Springer International Publishing. DOI: 10.1007/978-3-030-55285-5

Inigo, E. A., & Blok, V. (2019). Strengthening the socio-ethical foundations of the circular economy: Lessons from responsible research and innovation. *Journal of Cleaner Production*, the *233*, 280–291. DOI: 10.1016/j.jclepro.2019.06.053

ISO 15392 (2008). Sustainability in building construction. General principles. Geneva: International Organization for Standardization.

Jackson, T. (2009). *Prosperity without growth. Economics for a finite planet*. Earthscan. DOI: 10.4324/9781849774338

Johansson, N., Velis, C., & Corvellec, H. (2020). Towards clean material cycles: Is there a policy conflict between circular economy and non-toxic environment? *Waste Management & Research*, *38*(7), 705–707. DOI: 10.1177/0734242X20934251 PMID: 32627717

Johnston, P., Everard, M., Santillo, D., & Robért, K. (2007). Reclaiming thedefinition of sustainability. *Environmental Science and Pollution Research International*, *14*(1), 60–66. DOI: 10.1065/espr2007.01.375 PMID: 17352129

Kemp, R. & Pearson, P., 2007. Final report MEI project about measuring Eco Innovation.

Kirchherr, J., Reike, D., & Hekkert, M. (2017). Conceptualizing the circular economy: An analysis of 114 definitions. *Resources, Conservation and Recycling*, *127*, 221–232. DOI: 10.1016/j.resconrec.2017.09.005

Korhonen, J., Honkasalo, A., & Seppala, J. (2018a). Circular economy: The concept and its limitations. *Ecological Economics*, *143*, 37–46. DOI: 10.1016/j.ecolecon.2017.06.041

Korhonen, J., Nuur, C., Feldmann, A., & Birkie, S. E. (2018b). Circular economy as an essentially contested concept. *Journal of Cleaner Production*, *175*, 544–552. DOI: 10.1016/j.jclepro.2017.12.111

Mckelvey, B., 2002. Managing Coevolutionary Dynamics. 8th EGOS Colloq.

Meadows, D., Meadows, D., & Randers, J. Behrens, III.W.W. (1972). *The Limits to Growth. A Report for the Club of Rome's Project on the Predicament of Mankind*. Universe Books, New York.

Moraga, G., Huysveld, S., Mathieux, F., Blengini, G. A., Alaerts, L., Van Ackere, K., de Meester, S., & Dewulf, J. (2019). Circular economy indicators: What do they measure? *Resources, Conservation and Recycling, 146*, 452–461. DOI: 10.1016/j.resconrec.2019.03.045 PMID: 31274959

Murray, A., Skene, K., & Haynes, K. (2017). The circular economy: An interdisciplinary exploration of the concept and application in a global context. *Journal of Business Ethics, 140*(3), 369–380. DOI: 10.1007/s10551-015-2693-2

Pearce, D. W., & Turner, R. K. (1990). *Economics of natural resources and the environment.* Harvester Wheatsheaf. ISBN 0 7450 0225 0

Potting, J., Hekkert, M., Worrell, E., & Hanemaaijer, A. (2017). *Circular Economy: Measuring Innovation in the Product Chain.* PBL–Netherlands Environmental Assessment Agency.

Rashid, A., Asif, F. M. A., Krajnik, P., & Nicolescu, C. M. (2013). Resource Conservative Manufacturing: An essential change in business and technology paradigm for sustainable manufacturing. *Journal of Cleaner Production, 57*, 166–177. DOI: 10.1016/j.jclepro.2013.06.012

Reike, D., Vermeulen, W. J. V., & Witjes, S. (2018). The circular economy: New or refurbished as CE 3.0? — Exploring controversies in the conceptualization of the circular economy through a focus on history and resource value retention options. *Resources, Conservation and Recycling, 135*, 246–264. DOI: 10.1016/j.resconrec.2017.08.027

Rockström, J., Steffen, W., Noone, K., Persson, Å., Chapin, F. S.III, Lambin, E., Lenton, T. M., Scheffer, M., Folke, C., Schellnhuber, H., Nykvist, B., De Wit, C. A., Hughes, T., van der Leeuw, S., Rodhe, H., Sörlin, S., Snyder, P. K., Costanza, R., Svedin, U., & Falke, M. (2009). Planetary Boundaries: Exploring the safe operating space for humanity. *Ecology and Society, 14*(2), 14. DOI: 10.5751/ES-03180-140232

Sachs, J. (2015). *The Age of Sustainable Development.* Columbia University Press. DOI: 10.7312/sach17314

Schroder, P., Bengtsson, M., Cohen, M., Dewick, P., Hofstetter, J., & Sarkis, J. (2019). Degrowth within: Aligning circular economy and strong sustainabilitynarratives. *Resources, Conservation and Recycling, 146*, 190–191. DOI: 10.1016/j.resconrec.2019.03.038

World Commission on Environment and Development. (1987). *Our common future.* Oxford University Press.

Woollard, R. F., & Ostry, A. S. (2000). *Fatal consumption: rethinking sustainable development*. UBC Press.

Chapter 13
Risk Mitigation in the Digital Financial Landscape:
BRICS Case Study

Azmee Zaheer
http://orcid.org/0000-0002-6281-2608
Chandigarh University, Mohali, India

Kaushal Kishore Mishra
http://orcid.org/0000-0001-6466-0575
Chandigarh University, Unnao, India

Pawan Pant
http://orcid.org/0000-0003-1774-5650
Chandigarh University, Mohali, India

Swati Priya
http://orcid.org/0000-0002-7137-6115
BBDNIIT, Lucknow, India

ABSTRACT

One of the primary objectives of the BRICS countries has been to promote technology-facilitated financial inclusion. The increasing utilisation of the internet and mobile technology is diverting the attention of the BRICS nations. The governments and regulatory authorities of the BRICS nations have initiated several measures to foster FinTech adoption, establish a robust, accountable, and supportive digital financial ecosystem and infrastructure, and develop a regulatory framework that enhances consumer and data protection while promoting digital and financial literacy. These

DOI: 10.4018/979-8-3373-5437-8.ch013

initiatives have resulted in substantial advancements in digitisation across all BRICS countries. Digital retail payment transactions have experienced a significant transformation following the implementation of the Unified Payment Interface (UPI) in India. This article describes how the BRICS countries have lessened the risks by implementing a sensible framework that protects consumer rights and privacy.

1. INTRODUCTION

The digital revolution has transformed the world's economic landscape. Conventional banking and finance have evolved into complex digital ecosystems, driven by emerging technologies such as AI, blockchain, big data, cloud computing, and IoT (Pant et al., 2024). Technology has transformed how financial firms operate, deliver services, and connect with clients. Digitisation offers the prospect of faster, more accessible, more transparent, and more convenient alternatives, including mobile banking apps, digital wallets, algorithmic trading, and even decentralised finance (DeFi). For every turn, there are compromises (Pant et al., 2025). As finance becomes increasingly online and interconnected, it becomes more vulnerable to cyberattacks, breaches, regulatory ambiguity, operational risk, and potentially systemic risk. Here, safeguarding the robustness, resilience, and confidence in our online financial infrastructure is critical. In finance, risk mitigation refers to the techniques, protocols, instruments, and software used to identify, evaluate, eliminate, and track risks that could damage operational forces or players. Distress has never been far behind; the expansion of services and digitisation has pulled in both new and existing players (Mishra et al., 2025). The volatility of financial markets, the evolving regulatory landscape, digital fraud, reliance on third parties, ethical considerations, and geopolitical concerns all underscore the urgency of robust, agile risk mitigation approaches. Thus, this insight, along with the emphasis on addressing the real peril posed by the virtual financial realm, is crucial for banks, regulators, governments, tech providers, and consumers alike.

1.1 The changing world of internet finance

To appreciate why adequate risk mitigation is necessary, it is helpful to put the scale of financial sector changes driven by digital technologies into context. For decades, finance was a matter of geography and paper. Banks introduced online offerings as digital emerged in the late 90s. This trend gained momentum in the 21st century, particularly after the 2008 financial crisis exposed systemic flaws and sparked a surge of fintech innovation (Zaheer et al., 2024). Today, fintechs and neo-banks offer digital-only services that compete one-on-one with legacy banks.

We have witnessed an explosion of biometric authentication, digital identity, robo-advisors, peer-to-peer lending, and cryptocurrencies, all of which are disrupting the financial services industry. Contactless payments and remote payments for consumers and merchants alike were both accelerated by the COVID pandemic. India is building UPI, while China is launching e-CNY; governments are playing a key role by creating the basic infrastructure for digital systems and increasing dependence on cross-border payments, DeFi, and automated finance systems.

1.2. The Perils of Online Banking

As for risks in the DeFi world, they are somewhat higher than those in typical credit or market risk. I am referring to an entirely new assortment of intersecting and constantly changing risk types, such as taking a handful of raisins every two hours. Security vulnerabilities. They are high on the list of digital finance worries (Mishra et al., 2019). Cybercriminals have become increasingly crafty as the proliferation of online services has increased. Phishing, malware, ransomware, DoS attacks, and data breaches can cripple operations and deeply compromise customer confidentiality. What about the Equifax breach? These incidents highlight the continued vulnerability of our cyberspace.

1.3. Operational & Technical Risks

Fintech companies are highly reliant on technology and on other services such as cloud providers, APIs, and data analytics firms. One glitch – an employee error, system or software issue, or even a vendor going out of business – can cause cascading multistage disasters. Add to that the growing dependence on AI and algorithms to determine, well, everything, and bias, system vulnerabilities, and opacity are cause for concern.

1.4. Regulatory and compliance hazards

The online financial world does not exist within a single country. They operate in numerous different jurisdictions, and not all of them have the same rules. This lack of transparency can complicate matters related to online identity, privacy, tax reporting, and legality. That is especially true for fintech and DeFi platforms, which are still in regulatory grey areas and can legally expose themselves and their users to risk.

1.5. Data Privacy and Moral Hazard

We are drowning in data in digital finance. Data analytics can be beneficial for personalisation and efficiency, but it raises complex questions about consent, surveillance, and the potential for data deletion. We have not evolved our ethics-type thinking, i.e., Who owns the data? Possible algorithmic bias and harvesting behaviour data for marketing and price discrimination.

1.6. Systemic and reputational risks

Because our digital infrastructure is highly interconnected, if one part of the ecosystem fails or is compromised, it can ripple through the rest of the ecosystem, creating systemic risks. If customers lose faith in your offerings due to a scandal, fraud, or service outage, it can severely damage an institution's reputation and result in substantial financial losses.

1.7 Risk mitigation as a strategic imperative

In the high-stakes realm of risks, mapping them in digital finance is more than a technical requirement. It is a strategic imperative, a key to remaining sustainable, competitive, and trusted. If we are really to address risks, we need a blend of preventive, detective, corrective, and adaptive strategies embedded in our organisational workflows and aligned with high-level policy objectives. These are the elements of innovative risk mitigation.

1.7.1. Digital democracy

Robust governance and proactive regulation are the foundation of risk management. It is governments and regulators who should proactively design future-proof technology-agnostic and interoperable solutions that stimulate innovation and manage risk. Take, for example, regulatory sandboxes that enable fintechs to test their offerings in a controlled environment (Singh et al., 2024). Data protection laws such as the GDPR or India's DPDP Act, as well as cybersecurity regulations, provide vital guardrails.

1.7.2. Cyber resilience and security architecture

It is time for organisations to adopt a 'defence-in-depth' cybersecurity strategy. By this, I mean MFA, end-to-end encryption, secure coding, and real-time threat intelligence. Periodic pen testing, incident response planning, and employee training are great. We are constructing cloud resilience, disaster recovery, and zero-trust security within these adaptive frameworks.

1.7.3. Risk Culture & ethical design

Organisations need to foster a culture of risk awareness throughout all layers, supported by leadership and ethical decision-making models. By embedding norms such as fairness, transparency, and accountability into digital design, for example, we can help ensure that technologies like AI and big data are deployed ethically.

1.7.4. Collaboration and communication

In the online banking universe, Collaboration is crucial. Public-private players converge. Collectively, by leveraging shared platforms for threat intelligence, best practices, and cyber incident reporting, we can confront emerging threats. International cooperation with organisations such as the G20 and the BIS must be pivotal in tackling out-of-border risks.

1.7.5. Consumer protections and financial literacy

Operational risk management, yes? It is the consumer getting democratised! With financial literacy, disclosures, complaint redressal mechanisms, and digital onboarding safeguards, we can create buffers and reduce the chances of scams or predatory behaviour.

1.8 New Patterns in Online Risk-Enhanced

As digital finance evolves, so do our risk hedges. Check out these hot trends to track.

- RegTech and SupTech — RegTech enables institutions to maintain compliance through automation, and SupTech enables regulators to monitor compliance in real-time.
- AI-powered Risk Analysis – ML models can identify anomalies, fraud patterns, and credit risks more quickly and precisely.
- Distributed ledger tech enhances audit trails, reduces fraud, and makes transactions more trustworthy.
- Digital Identity Management – from e-KYC to biometric authentication to digital IDs, innovations are helping to maximise the reduction of identity fraud and improve access.

- Cyber Insurance: As risks continue to grow in scale and ubiquity, cyber insurance is quickly becoming the risk transfer strategy of choice, despite its pricing and coverage remaining ill-defined.

Winning at exposure in the online economy will demand perpetual innovation. Simply installing firewalls or antivirus software is no longer sufficient. Banks must integrate risk intelligence into every stage of their work—from product design and customer support to governance and stakeholder engagement. Policy makers need to be nimble and inclusive, making sure innovation is not privileged over safety or fairness. International cooperation, public/private collaborations, and responsible digital finance stewardship will be essential for a sustainable digital financial future. The goal of risk mitigation is not to avoid risk. It is a holy grail quest to bottle it somehow in a way that generates confidence, sparks creativity, and lifts all boats financially. As the digital financial ecosystem matures, its resilience will depend on how well institutions anticipate, respond to, and learn from the inherent risks of the transformation.

It is widely understood that adopting and maintaining safe, appropriate digital banking habits is essential. Concerns such as cyber threats, customer protection, data privacy, and data security must be taken into consideration, as the rapid development of digital technology promotes inclusion (Dwivedi et al., 2020). A robust framework that protects consumers' rights and privacy is necessary to foster trust and confidence in the continued use of digital financial services, especially among customers with low financial literacy. Clear guidelines for the behaviour of financial organisations, along with consumer education programs, boost consumers' trust in financial services and products while also promoting their growth (Paul, J. et al., 2024). Data privacy and cybersecurity issues have gained attention due to the constantly evolving financial services industry, which exposes consumers to new risks of financial loss and invasions of personal privacy (De Giovanni, 2023). By promoting best practices based on global experience, several international forums also facilitate discussions on consumer and data protection frameworks and offer a comprehensive diagnostic tool to pinpoint consumer financial protection concerns. For the financial systems to operate effectively, safe, secure, and effective payment methods are essential. It is widely understood that adopting and maintaining safe, appropriate digital banking habits is imperative. Concerns such as cyber threats, customer protection, data privacy, and data security must be taken into consideration, as the rapid development of digital technology promotes inclusion. A robust framework that protects customers' rights and privacy will foster trust and confidence in the continued use of digital financial services, especially among those with limited financial knowledge (Shrier et al., 2022).

2. FINANCIAL CONSUMER PROTECTION MEASURES: CASES OF BRICS COUNTRIES

2.1- Emergency Aid Program in Brazil through 'Caixa TEM.'

Caixa Econômica Federal (CAIXA), a state-owned entity, primarily provides Caixa TEM via a mobile app or on its website. For self-employed individuals and those whose income has been significantly impacted by the COVID-19 pandemic, the Brazilian Federal Government has launched a cash distribution program (De Conti, B. et al., 2023). Participants who registered for the cash transfer program using the "Caixa TEM" website or mobile application provided by the state-owned Caixa Economica Federal (CAIXA) received the initial instalment in April 2020.

Methodology

Through Caixa TEM, citizens can apply for emergency relief. All they need to do is provide their Individual Taxpayer Identification Number (CPF33), birthdate, and names (including those of their dependents); no documents need to be uploaded for approval. To acquire the resources, residents must provide details of their current bank account or, if they do not have one, request that CAIXA establish a digital savings account.

To provide emergency assistance, CAIXA initially launched free digital savings accounts in the Caixa TEM app that did not require additional data validation (De Arruda et al., 2021). Approximately 68 million people received emergency aid between April and August 2020; through Caixa TEM, 38.5 million payments have been made. About 126 million people, or 60% of Brazil's population, benefited from this program, according to the Ministry of Citizenship.

By April 2021, illegal activities, including the theft of personal information and manipulation of the Caixa TEM registry, led to transactions that account users did not recognise. Consequently, to halt payments and seek full restitution from the relevant account holders, CAIXA requested that members of the Brazilian Federation of Banks (FEBRABAN) submit any evidence of fraudulent activity found in transfers, such as instances in which beneficiaries had since passed away.

It was also found that the Caixa TEM's privacy policy was vague and failed to comply with all regulations established by the 2018 Brazilian data privacy law. To obtain quick updates, CAIXA allowed the registration process to be completed remotely. Eligibility for the second instalment of emergency assistance payments, starting in April 2021, was limited to beneficiaries who had already registered under the initial scheme (Das, J., & Do, Q., 2023). To be eligible to receive assistance, the recipient needed to update their CAIXA TEM account by uploading a scanned copy of their identification card and a selfie. Since these changes, Caixa TEM has demonstrated itself to be a successful means of ensuring that social and welfare benefits are paid to the intended recipient.

2.2 Pix: Secure Framework for the Quick Transactions Service in Brazil

The BCB created the Pix Quick Transactions Service to provide robust security for the data and transactions used. This secure atmosphere is developed on the three central pillars mentioned below:

i. **Customer digital verification**: Accessing any secured environment (such as an ATM, computer, or mobile device) that permits transaction initiation requires a password or supplementary security measures, like Facial recognition and biometrics embedded into the smartphone.
ii. **Encryption**: Transaction data within the National Financial System Network (RSFN35) is secured using encryption. All Pix users must have security certificates to gain access to this network. Additionally, BCB's proprietary technologies store and encrypt all transaction data and personal information related to Pix keys.
iii. **Pix operating regulations**: Participating institutions establish maximum value limits according to their clients' risk profiles; they differentiate the maximum duration for transaction authorisation when atypical transactions initiated by clients suggest a heightened risk of fraud; they disseminate centralised information regarding Pix keys, account numbers, and taxpayer numbers implicated in fraudulent activities to all participants; and they restrict the generation of QR codes to participants who have provided specific security certificates to BCB. These represent a selection of measures outlined in the Pix rules to mitigate the risk of fraud.

Methodology

In the initial round of emergency assistance disbursed via the "Caixa TEM" mobile application, system deficiencies were identified, prompting the implementation of robust fraud-prevention measures for the subsequent round. These approaches curtailed fraudulent activities, enhanced system efficiency, and safeguarded consumer data privacy. This exemplifies an effective initiative to strengthen consumer protection. Likewise, the Pix payments system offers a safe framework for corporate transactions.

2.3. Online Reception Services of the Bank of Russia

The Bank of Russia (BOR) introduced a customer complaint application on its website in 2009. In an attempt to improve information transparency, the BOR released a new version of its "Bank of Russia Online Reception" software in 2015 to digitise its grievance-management procedures. By allowing clients to meet with the online regulator and receive an email response, Online Reception has dramatically simplified the process. In 2020, half of all applications were from financial clients, who used the Online Reception to submit 165,600 applications (including 135,000 complaints), suggestions, queries, and requests to the BOR. Customers commonly ask the BOR questions because they are unaware of the financial services being provided. The BOR has enhanced consumer communication by creating a frequently asked questions section.

Methodology

"The financial ecosystem is now more credible and efficient thanks to the BOR's direct consumer engagement, online complaint system, and transparency."

2.4 Authentication with several factors or factor authentication (India)

Multi-factor authentication, also referred to as two-factor authentication, ensures that at least one authentication factor is dynamic or unique (Mahbub & Shubair, 2023). In addition to cards, internet banking, and digital payment applications, the RBI has requested that the AFA be implemented for financial and electronic payment transactions, including cash withdrawals through Business Correspondents, ATMs, micro-ATMs, and PoS terminals. Two-step dynamic authentication has reduced the risk of fraudulent transactions by verifying that transactions originate from an authenticated and authorised source or method. (Dwivedi et al., 2023). An ID and password are used in online banking, for example, along with a second factor, such as a digital signature, Time Password (OTP), or a changing access code supplied via various channels, including hardware tokens or SMS on mobile devices. Likewise, information not printed on the card is utilised to validate further and verify a card transaction. AFA helps safeguard consumer financial information more confidentially and prevent phishing, replay attacks, keyloggers, password scraping by spyware or malware, and other scams targeting consumers online.

2.5. India's Ombudsman Program for Online Transactions

RBI launched the January 2019 Ombudsman Program for Online Transactions. This fast, cost-free, apex-level complaint redressal method enables customers to voice complaints about subpar customer service during digital transactions with participating companies.

The Ombudsman shall be empowered to accept complaints arising from deficiencies in prepaid payment instruments, electronic or mobile fund transfers, or in violation of any directives given by the Reserve Bank or the relevant System Provider towards System Participants relating to payment transactions using the UPI, BBPS, Bharat QR Code, or UPI QR Code. The technique states that the complainant must first file a complaint with the system participant. The complainant may register a complaint with the Ombudsman for Digital Transactions if they are not satisfied with the response or do not receive one within a month. Under the system, the Ombudsman can grant compensation up to two million rupees or the amount in dispute, whichever is lower.

91 per cent of the 2,481 complaints about digital transactions received by the Ombudsman between 2019 and 2020 were resolved. This program facilitates the development of a redressal framework for India's rapidly growing digital transaction system.

Final Results

"The AFA is a useful tool for preventing various cyberattacks, protecting customer confidentiality of payment information, and guaranteeing transaction safety." The Ombudsman system for Digital Transactions provides an efficient way to handle complaints about subpar digital transaction services.

2.6 China's Third-Party Resolution Process for Out-of-Court Financial Consumer Conflicts

In October 2015, in response to the directives of the 17th Session of the Central Advisory Council for All-Inclusive Reform, the PBoC began developing its plan to establish a third-party out-of-court financial consumer dispute settlement mechanism. The PBoC piloted this approach at the prefectural level in Guangdong and Shandong and the provincial level in Shanghai, Guangdong, Shaanxi, and Heilongjiang. Following successful pilot trials, all disputing parties have had access to unbiased third-party mediation services in a reasonable, professional, practical, cost-effective, and straightforward manner (Cavalty & Wenger, 2022).

In November 2017, after evaluating the pilot program, the PBoC determined a workable model for a third-party resolution mechanism for out-of-court financial consumer disputes. The approach was considered replicable at the national level. As a result, several communities independently found the best model for their situation. In 2018, Jiangsu Province formed three provincial financial consumer protection groups in Fujian, Hainan, and Guizhou, as well as five municipal ones in Nanjing, Wuxi, Nantong, Yangzhou, and Suqian. (Zhang et al., 2023).

The PBoC advised financial consumer dispute mediation organisations to enhance their operational procedures and adopt creative approaches to successfully settle disputes. Shanghai's Financial Ombudsman Service has consistently improved the process for resolving small claims and disagreements quickly, established an objective assessment system, and promoted the integration of litigation and mediation. It has been demonstrated that establishing and operating an out-of-court third-party settlement mechanism for financial consumer disputes alleviates pressure on financial regulators and facilitates the resolution of these disputes through practical, affordable services (Puri, 1998). By acting as a "lubricant" and "pressure-relief valve," the technique decreased the need for legal resources for financial consumer disputes and small claims.

2.7 Establishing Standards for the Classification of Financial Consumer Complaints (China)

The data on financial consumer complaints not only show how well financial institutions follow their internal controls and the regulatory standards established by financial authorities, but also accurately reflect the expectations and opinions of financial consumers regarding financial services and products.

To develop classification criteria, the People's Bank of China conducted a statistical analysis of the system's handling and receipt of financial consumer complaints. To determine if the requirements would complement financial institutions' internal business lines and management processes for classifying financial consumer complaints, three pilot studies were conducted. By the end of 2017, there were 108 locally constituted banking and financial institutions spread across 31 Chinese provinces, regions, and municipalities, along with four large state-owned commercial banks, eight joint-stock commercial banks, and one international bank (HSBC China).

To create financial sector standards, the "China Financial Standardisation Technical Committee" (CFSTC) announced in November 2017 plans to develop "the Statistical Classification and Code of Financial Consumer Complaints." After registration and assessment, the experimental initiatives began. When the PBoC and the CBIRC formed a working group in December 2017 to draft and compile standards and subsequently develop work plans for them, the standards compilation process officially began. The standards development working group examined the draft in January 2018 and solicited opinions from CFSTC members and other specialists. The draft standards were sent to the CFSTC secretariat for review after the standard drafting committee made changes in response to the comments received. Future initiatives will focus on establishing financial dispute mediation organisations, enhancing the ability and competency of financial institutions to handle complaints, expanding channels for financial consumer complaints and consultations, and standardising mediation procedures.

Adopting the third-party settlement technique for out-of-court financial consumer disputes may enable monetary authorities to use technology to deliver prompt, affordable dispute-resolution services. This would enable financial institutions to identify, notify about, and mitigate common problems and risks across the industry, as well as handle complaints effectively. Assessing existing laws and identifying consumer requirements can be facilitated by transparency and by analysing financial consumer complaint data.

2.8. South Africa's Market Conduct Authority for Financial Consumer Protection

With the passage of the Financial Sector Regulation (FSR) Act in 2018, South Africa embraced the Twin Peaks model of financial regulation (Van & Ponelis, 2024). Among the recently established authorities were the Prudential Authority, a new prudential regulator whose duties include ensuring the safety and soundness of financial institutions, and the "Financial Sector Conduct Authority" (FSCA), a new market conduct regulator whose objectives include enhancing consumer protection and the efficiency and integrity of financial markets (Qumba, 2022).

South Africa implemented financial regulation based on the Twin Peaks concept in 2018, which was made possible by the enactment of the FSR Act. The two regulators established under the South African Twin Peaks model were the Financial Sector Conduct Authority, a new market conduct regulator focused on enhancing consumer protection and the effectiveness and integrity of financial markets, and the newly established Prudential Authority, which was responsible for ensuring the soundness and safety of economic organisations.

In addition to establishing laws and guidelines for consumer protection, the FSCA monitors potentially dangerous individuals and companies that commit fraud, operate without required authorisation, or breach financial sector laws. These actions could result in losses for South African consumers.

The FSCA intervenes to ensure the orderly operation of financial markets, disseminates information and notifications about fraudulent activities, provides financial education, advocates for equitable consumer treatment, and helps maintain financial stability.

3. INCLUSION OF DIGITAL FINANCE IN THE COVID-19 CONTEXT

During the COVID-19 epidemic, contactless measures, social distancing, and lockdowns all contributed to the growth of cashless financial transactions. Globally, cashless payments increased by 42% in 2021, according to PwC research. Additionally, a generational transition to digital channels was signalled by the growing adoption of digital payment methods by those 56 and older (World Payments Report, 2020). By improving their online presence, the private sector, including small businesses, has accelerated the digitisation of payments. The private sector is driving innovation in digital payments for the retail sector and financial inclusion. Allen and Associates, 2022. The expansion of financial inclusion was primarily driven by increased retail transactions and the government's digital direct distribution of COVID-19 social benefits to people and MSMEs. This article outlines the policy reactions and payment-related circumstances of the BRICS nations in response to the COVID-19 pandemic.

3.1 Brazil

In 2020, the proportion of Brazilians with a banking relationship increased substantially. Approximately 10 million people made their first forays into the official banking system during the peak expansion months of May and July (Gregorio et al., 2023). The graph below illustrates a sharp increase in new account openings, particularly at financial institutions, beginning in April 2020 (Figure 1). The growth of payment institutions—primarily online marketplaces that facilitate the transfer of resources and the buying and selling of goods—is especially notable. After the epidemic began, account creation in this sector increased sharply in 2019.

Brazil experienced a surge in digital financial transactions due to the temporary Emergency Assistance Program, which provided a monthly subsidy. The first phase of the aid program, which ran from April 2020 to August 2020, helped 68 million Brazilians, according to the Ministry of Citizenship. Approximately 97% of these beneficiaries currently have a banking relationship, compared to 82% in 2019. The inclusion was justified by the fact that up to 30.9% of individuals had accounts with

Payment Institutions, according to the Cadúnico, a federal registry of social program participants in 2020. It is worth noting that this number was only 9.4% in 2018.

Figure 1. New connections with the financial system per segment

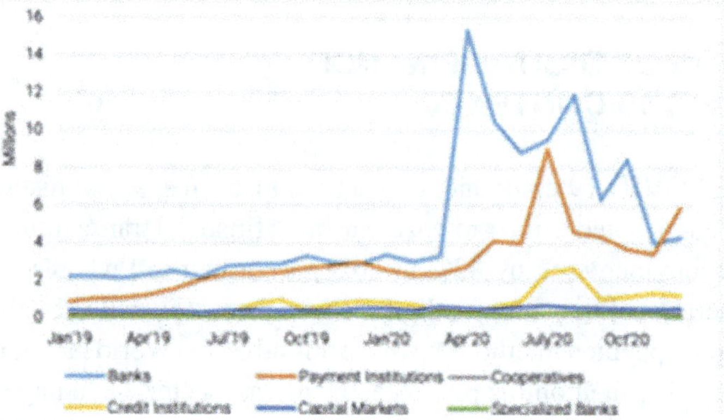

Source: Central Bank of Brazil

3.2 Russia

Access to financial services during the pandemic was significantly facilitated by a comprehensive understanding of the remote financial services available to the general population and MSMEs by the end of 2019. Malladi and Associates, 2021. According to a May 2019 BOR survey, more than half of Russians (55.2%) used e-banking and/or mobile banking to remotely access their accounts and make remittances for the previous 12 months. In May 2020, this percentage had risen to 75.4%. Authorities encouraged the adoption of digital financial services during the COVID-19 pandemic. The Bank of Russia took steps to reduce or eliminate the costs associated with instant payments via its Fast Payment System. Online retailers should lower their card acceptance fees to encourage online shopping for everyday needs.

For a predetermined period (during the quarantine period), financial institutions can automate the renewal of all bank cards about to expire and simplify know-your-customer (KYC) procedures to enable remote account openings. Small and medium-sized enterprises (SMEs) were allowed to receive only grants, loans, and employee wages, and individuals were allowed to make or receive only socially relevant payments, such as alimony, insurance reimbursements, mortgage payments, and social transfers. Promoting the Use of Digital Payments in Russia: The World Bank's Policy Response to the COVID-19 (Coronavirus) Pandemic, March 09, 2020.

3.3 India

Several actions must be taken in light of the COVID-19 pandemic and the measures implemented to contain its spread, to ensure the continuous operation and availability of centralised payment systems operated by the RBI and other payment system operators.

The measures taken were as follows:

The "Real Time Gross Settlement" (RTGS) and "National Electronic Funds Transfer" (NEFT) systems were open 24/7 in December 2020 and December 2019, respectively (Hanedar et al., 2023). The RBI maintained close communication with the NPCI and other authorised payment system operators (PSOs) to ensure that all payment systems remained operational without disruption. Lockout procedures were permitted to continue despite PSOs being present, as they were considered "essential services." To ensure the UPI or UPI QR onboarding process is fully contactless and conducted online, NPCI has expedited it.

The "National Automated Clearing House" (NACH) and the "Aadhaar Payment Bridge System" (APBS) enabled the government to make welfare disbursements through Direct Benefit Transfers (DBT). Beneficiaries receive bulk remittances using their Aadhaar numbers. Business Correspondents and micro-ATMs using the Aadhaar-enabled Payment System (AePS) have, to date, increased the amount of cash they withdraw (Figure 2).

Figure 2. India - Digital Retail Payment (Volume)

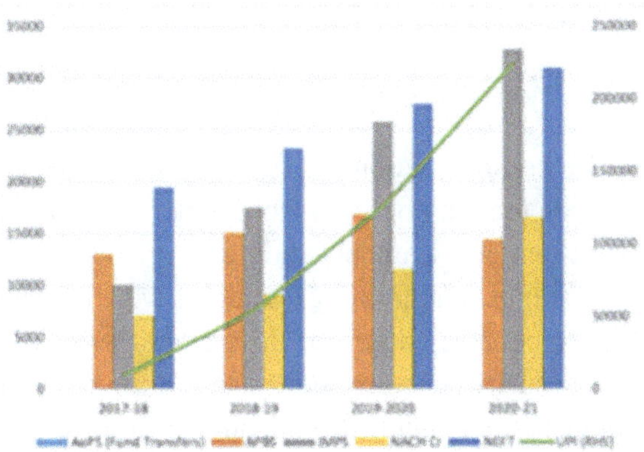

Source: RBI

Banks have temporarily waived fees for cash transfers across several digital systems, including "Real Time Gross Settlement" (RTGS), "Immediate Payment Service" (IMPS), and "National Electronic Funds Transfer" (NEFT), to encourage digital payments. The Reserve Bank of India has increased the contactless card payment limit from INR 2,000 to INR 5,000 per transaction for "Europay, Mastercard, and Visa" (EMV) Chip cards with Near Field Communication (NFC) technology. Although PIN entry is required, the fact that contactless transactions are possible at this threshold indicates that they are possible. In addition to facilitating the prompt payment of remittances arriving from abroad, MTSS operators encouraged their clients to receive remittances into their bank accounts, thereby reducing problems with currency payouts. This step was taken to make card payments at POS terminals healthier. Simplified and user-friendly processes enabled the completion of "Digital KYC" and "Equivalent e-Documents," making video verification practicable. In April 2021, customers were allowed to withdraw cash from full-KYC PPIs issued by non-banks, significantly improving their convenience. To assess the reach and extent of digital payments, the RBI developed five key metrics: Payment Enablers, Payment Infrastructure-Demand Side Factors, Payment Infrastructure-Supply Side Factors, Payment Performance, and Consumer Centricity (Figure 3).

Figure 3. RBI- Digital Payments Index

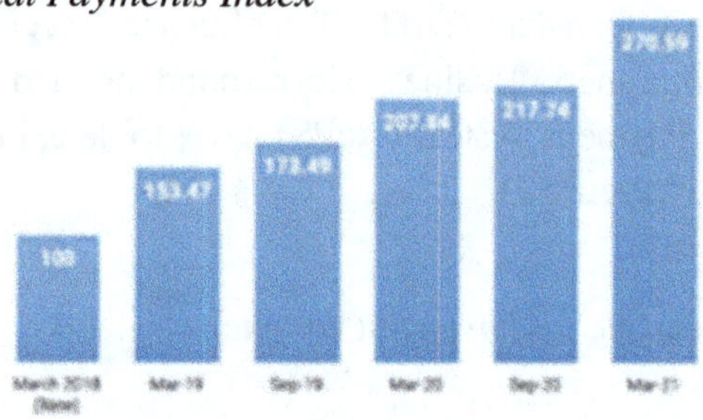

Source: RBI

The RBI released recommendations to raise public awareness of the various digital payment methods that can be used from home without maintaining social distancing. In an effort to increase understanding of financial issues, 178 e-BAAT (electronic banking awareness and training) seminars were held between July 2020 and March 2021. These courses addressed the advantages of electronic payment methods and the cybersecurity concerns they raise. Additionally, the RBI and other stakeholders have launched campaigns to encourage the use of digital payments across the payment ecosystem.

3.4 China

In China, QR codes have been widely used for contactless payments on mobile devices, utilities, tenants, vendors, transportation drivers, and even the government.

During the pandemic, approximately 30 local governments provided their citizens with digital coupons to use on third-party apps, such as Alipay and WeChat Pay. These programs allow users to use their coupons. In addition to enabling payment and settlement via electronic channels, including payment service applications, mobile banking, enterprise online banking, personal online banking, and electronic commercial bill systems, the PBoC promoted the seamless operation of electronic payment services. Additionally, the PBoC allowed variable adjustments to transaction limits based on specific circumstances. To expedite the adoption of digitisation, concessional pricing for payment services was made available to customers in specific industries or regions. According to "Bridging Digital Divides in G20 Countries, 2021," some actions were taken to support system maintenance during the pandemic. Every day, banks and other non-bank payment organisations were asked to use video calls and phone calls to verify their operations and report on user access. Models, systems, data, and IT risk management are among the other rules established by the China Banking and Insurance Regulatory Commission to help manage risk.

3.5 South Africa

Due to lockdown protocols, reduced bank operating hours, and increased use of digital platforms such as online banking and applications, the pandemic led to the closure of some bank branches. This is especially true for South Africa, where nearly 52% of all financial transactions are conducted in cash. The need for digital transactions, including contactless, mobile, and Internet payments, has been highlighted by the pandemic (Otiashvili et al., 2022). However, the cost of technology and access, coupled with the absence of a reliable national network infrastructure, makes the digital divide in South Africa a serious problem.

In 2020, the South African National Treasury declared its priorities for financial inclusion. These priorities were to improve the impact of social grant distribution on financial inclusion and to create a suitable digital and payments ecosystem to encourage the use of digital financial services. Following suggestions made by the "Data Services Market Inquiry" (DSMI), the Competition Commission reached a settlement with the two largest mobile phone service providers, Voice and Data Communications (Vodacom) and Mobile Telephone Networks (MTN), in December 2019. As a result, their prepaid data bundles were less expensive last year.

Digital payments primarily target senior citizens, which has also raised the risk of fraud and cybersecurity problems. According to Kiff et al. (2020), these can erode confidence and trust in digital technology. Different economic levels and demographic groups continue to exhibit significant differences in financial literacy. As a result, improving consumer digital literacy and proficiency is given top priority.

Although the COVID-19 pandemic has altered how people use banking and payments, the government still needs to address the digital divide, exacerbated by limited access to digital literacy. Social media and mass media, including local radio stations and television channels, were more commonly used to promote financial literacy. Stronger consumer protection regulations, combined with improved financial awareness and education, will enable the base of the pyramid to make well-informed financial decisions (Dwivedi et al., 2022).

KYC requirements and processes have been relaxed and simplified to facilitate customer registration and onboarding. Large volumes of sensitive data, both personal and non-personal, were typically collected in tandem with the rise in the usage of digital financial services during the pandemic. These reforms lead to a renewed focus on client data privacy, alongside other consumer protection measures, such as data ownership rights and comprehensive, transparent dispute-resolution procedures. As a result, digital banking systems must be appropriately secured and operational as quickly as possible. A careful balance must be struck between ensuring customer comfort and implementing effective cybersecurity measures.

The digital financial system will significantly meet the needs and expectations of recovering economies. The COVID-19 pandemic has presented digital financial services with additional opportunities to enhance and accelerate financial inclusion, according to Sahay et al. (2020) at the IMF. It is essential to promote a more equitable pandemic recovery and mitigate the adverse social and economic effects of the ongoing COVID-19 pandemic. Given the possibility of greater global inequality in the post-pandemic era, far more comprehensive international cooperation is required in the fields of technology and financial inclusion (Tursunbayeva et al., 2021). They also warned that, in the post-pandemic era, the risks associated with digital financial services will intensify.

Comparative Analysis Across BRICS Countries

BRICS countries have accelerated the circulation of digital currencies throughout their economies, as Covid-19 has increased the use of digital payment services, including instant transactions, mobile wallets, QR code payments, credit/debit cards, and account-based online payments (World Bank 2022; Kaur & Kang, 2024). While BRICS economies each saw some growth in digitised payments since 2019, the level of digitisation and expansion of digital payments varied greatly among these nations, due to differences in digital infrastructure, inclusion of citizens in the financial system, capacity for regulation and the existence of pre-COVID-19 payment systems (World Bank 2022; Kaur & Kang, 2024). Therefore, while there was no overall digital transformation across all BRICS nations after Covid-19, the pandemic exacerbated pre-existing discrepancies in digitisation and also advanced each BRICS member's use of non-cash payments (Kaur & Kang, 2024).

China and India are the two BRICS members that stand out with the most digitised payments for everyday purchases. China was already one of the most mature nations in utilising mobile payments before the pandemic hit, thereby expanding electronic transaction options. In contrast, India saw significant increases in digital payments after the pandemic, as well as in real-time retail payment transactions and merchant utilisation of digital payments via QR codes (Kaur & Kang, 2024; Central Bank of the Russian Federation, 2021) and therefore serves as the best illustration of how the pandemic drove digital payment adoption among BRICS nations.

Digital payment systems are increasingly serving the dual purpose of facilitating payments and promoting financial inclusion, while monetising everyday economic activity in both Brazil and Russia. The relatively rapid acceptance of digital means of transacting occurred during the pandemic period, but the factors influencing rapid proliferation and adoption were vastly different. In Brazil, the pandemic provided a necessary impetus for the adoption of digital payments, including account-based payments, instant payments, and other forms of retail digitisation between individuals (World Bank, 2022). Likewise, Russia saw significant increases in digital payment use after the pandemic, driven by the proliferation of domestic payment systems and, more importantly, by growing interest in digital alternatives to physical currency. However, despite the accelerated adoption of digital payment systems in Brazil and Russia after the pandemic, their use still lags behind that of China and India (Kaur & Kang, 2024).

In comparison, South Africa represents a more transitional state of adoption. The use of digital payments increased after the pandemic due to the wider acceptance of card payments, mobile banking, and the emergence of new wallet-like systems; however, cash remained more prominent in daily economic exchanges than in more developed digital economies such as Brazil and Russia (World Bank, 2022). It appears that simply adopting digital payment methods is not enough to facilitate a rapid shift away from cash. The rate at which a country's payment transformation occurs depends on many factors. These include the affordability of digital payments, whether merchants accept them, the quality of the infrastructure that enables digital transactions, and the level of confidence people have in their country's formal banking system (World Bank, 2022). This is evident in the example of South Africa and highlights how payment behaviour is influenced by structural conditions such as these during payment transformation.

Additionally, this situation in BRICS provides insight into the broader role the COVID-19 pandemic played in catalysing digital inclusion. Access to digital payment methods has been driven by the COVID-19 pandemic, as evidenced by Global Findex data, which indicates that digital payment use increased during the pandemic, with many first-time users emerging (World Bank, 2022). Digital payment methods are associated with formal inclusion in the banking system through increased savings, increased borrowing, and holding money in transaction accounts (World Bank, 2022). Digital payment adoption in the BRICS indicates that digital payments for non-payment reasons (i.e., access to the banking system, economic resilience, and access to a broader range of financial services) will all be facilitated through digital money circulation (Kaur & Kang, 2024). There is also a second level of transformation in digital monetary development in BRICS, namely, the testing of sovereign digital currencies since the pandemic began. The digital currency tests in China and Russia are indicative of both modernising their banking systems through technology and concerns about the sovereignty of their own currencies, as well as the mechanics of cross-border debt settlement. Some of the discussions related to BRICS countries and digital payment systems centre on the potential to create a common digital settlement method and/or a single digital monetary unit that could facilitate regional trade and reduce reliance on external payment systems. Overall, as digital payment systems continue to mature post-COVID in BRICS countries, they have exhibited a dual trajectory: the ongoing development of retail digital payment systems and the continued emergence of sovereign digital currencies.

DISCUSSION AND FUTURE RECOMMENDATIONS

The COVID-19 pandemic has increased attention to all aspects of digital financial inclusion. The use of digital financial services has increased significantly due to authorities enacting progressive, lenient regulations, private companies adopting remote business and payment methods, and the influx of new customers brought about by lockdown and social distancing measures. Even with these positive advancements, closing the digital divide has become increasingly complex. Since the majority of these platforms and technologies are still in their infancy, the risks of cyber events, online fraud, illegal financial activities, and data privacy issues have increased due to growing consumer use. The digital economic system will be crucial to meeting the country's economic demands and goals once it has recovered from the pandemic. To prevent exacerbating the marginalisation of the excluded group, these new technologies must be developed and implemented with sufficient safeguards. To increase stakeholder trust and expand the reach and influence of digital financial inclusion, authorities must focus on developing a robust, secure framework.

Despite the tremendous progress made so far, this analysis shows that digital financial inclusion in expanding market economies remains a work in progress. The study provides a set of methods for connecting the BRICS's local acts to the international norms emerging on current issues, and there is much that the countries can learn from each other. As a result, the countries can align their approach with international obligations while also learning from their peers.

CONCLUSION

Digital payment systems are rapidly evolving, are at various stages of maturity, and involve a growing number of institutions in BRICS countries post-COVID. China and India have integrated retail and commercial digital payment systems; Brazil and Russia are making strong progress relative to their respective banking systems, but South Africa is undergoing a slower transformation from cash to digital money (Kaur & Kang, 2024; World Bank, 2022). As such, BRICS provide evidence that the COVID-19 pandemic did not simply increase the volume of digital payments, but rather altered the structure in which money is circulated through an increase in the number of account-based transactions, an increase in the digitisation of merchants, and an increase in the experimentation of sovereign digital currency (World Bank, 2022).

Financial inclusion is a crucial component of balanced and sustainable economic growth, which helps reduce poverty and income inequality ("Tackling Vulnerability in the Informal Economy," 2019). Modern products and services, new financial intermediaries, and technological advancements all contributed to the rapid expansion and transformation of financial markets and systems in the 21st century. According to a PwC report, there will be 1.9 trillion cashless transactions by 2025, representing an 80% increase, and each person is expected to make three times as many digital payments by 2030. Significant changes in the digital realm have necessitated a significant re-engineering of modalities to enhance financial inclusion for unserved and underserved populations in Emerging Market Economies (EMEs), including BRICS (Krishnannair et al., 2022). The BRICS members have been seeking ways to ensure their financial inclusion policies reflect the latest advancements. To promote digital financial inclusion, the BRICS countries are undergoing significant reforms to their regulatory and supervisory frameworks. The BRICS have a range of experiences in applying technological innovations to enhance financial inclusion initiatives, as demonstrated in the preceding sections, to achieve broader and more successful impact.

National authorities in the BRICS countries prioritise reducing financial system risk and protecting customer interests and privacy to establish credibility and trust, according to HLPG, which promotes financial consumer protection measures, including data protection tailored to the needs of women, youth, and SMEs. The consumer redressal process should be simplified, expedited, and made more efficient in the future. It should be broadened to cover all online payment methods. The government must implement robust measures to protect personal data and ensure data privacy in order to build trust and encourage the formalisation and digitisation of financial institutions.

REFERENCES

Allen, F., Gu, X., & Jagtiani, J. (2022). Fintech, Cryptocurrencies, and CBDC: Financial Structural Transformation in China. *Journal of International Money and Finance*, *124*, 102625. DOI: 10.1016/j.jimonfin.2022.102625

Bridging digital divides in G20 countries. (2021). DOI: 10.1787/35c1d850-en

CBIRC. (2020), "The Provisional Rules on Internet Loans of Commercial Banks", July 17, 2020, http://www.cbirc.gov.cn/cn/ view/pages/ItemDetail.html?docId=916525&itemId=928

Central Bank of the Russian Federation. (2021). BRICS Digital Financial Inclusion Report.

Das, J., & Do, Q. (2023). The Prices in the Crises: What We Are Learning from 20 Years of Health Insurance in Low- and Middle-Income Countries. *The Journal of Economic Perspectives*, *37*(2), 123–152. DOI: 10.1257/jep.37.2.123

Dashkevich, N., Counsell, S., & Destefanis, G. (2020). Blockchain Application for Central Banks: A Systematic Mapping Study. *IEEE Access : Practical Innovations, Open Solutions*, *8*, 139918–139952. DOI: 10.1109/ACCESS.2020.3012295

De Arruda, P. L., De Andrade, M. L., Falcão, T., Barbosa, D. T., & Morgandi, M. (2021). Auxílio Emergencial - Lessons from the Brazilian experience responding to COVID-19. DOI: 10.1596/37254

De Conti, B., Herr, H., Jha, P., & Nettekoven, Z. (2023). Macroeconomic policy and policy spaces during the COVID-19 pandemic – case studies from Germany, Brazil and India. European Journal of Economics and Economic Policies Intervention, 1–16. DOI: 10.4337/ejeep.2023.0111

De Giovanni, P. (2023). Sustainability of the Metaverse: A Transition to Industry 5.0. *Sustainability (Basel)*, *15*(7), 6079. DOI: 10.3390/su15076079

Dwivedi, Y. K., Hughes, L., Baabdullah, A. M., Ribeiro-Navarrete, S., Giannakis, M., Al-Debei, M. M., Dennehy, D., Metri, B., Buhalis, D., Cheung, C. M., Conboy, K., Doyle, R., Dubey, R., Dutot, V., Felix, R., Goyal, D., Gustafsson, A., Hinsch, C., Jebabli, I., & Wamba, S. F. (2022). Metaverse beyond the hype: Multidisciplinary perspectives on emerging challenges, opportunities, and agenda for research, practice and policy. *International Journal of Information Management*, *66*, 102542. DOI: 10.1016/j.ijinfomgt.2022.102542

Dwivedi, Y. K., Ismagilova, E., Hughes, D. L., Carlson, J., Filieri, R., Jacobson, J., Jain, V., Karjaluoto, H., Kefi, H., Krishen, A. S., Kumar, V., Rahman, M. M., Raman, R., Rauschnabel, P. A., Rowley, J., Salo, J., Tran, G. A., & Wang, Y. (2020). Setting the future of digital and social media marketing research: Perspectives and research propositions. *International Journal of Information Management*, *59*, 102168. DOI: 10.1016/j.ijinfomgt.2020.102168

Dwivedi, Y. K., Kshetri, N., Hughes, L., Rana, N. P., Baabdullah, A. M., Kar, A. K., Koohang, A., Ribeiro-Navarrete, S., Belei, N., Balakrishnan, J., Basu, S., Behl, A., Davies, G. H., Dutot, V., Dwivedi, R., Evans, L., Felix, R., Foster-Fletcher, R., Giannakis, M., & Yan, M. (2023). Exploring the Darkverse: A Multi-Perspective Analysis of the Negative Societal Impacts of the Metaverse. *Information Systems Frontiers*, *25*(5), 2071–2114. DOI: 10.1007/s10796-023-10400-x PMID: 37361890

Hanedar, E., Alonso, C., Uña, G., Prihardini, D., Bhojwani, T., & Zhabska, K. (2023). Stacking up the Benefits: Lessons from India's Digital Journey. *IMF Working Paper*, *2023*(078), 1. DOI: 10.5089/9798400240416.001

IMF (2020), "The Promise of Fintech: Financial Inclusion in the Post-COVID-19 Era", Ratna Sahay, Ulric Eriksson von Allmen, Amina Lahreche, Purva Khera, Sumiko Ogawa, Majid Bazarbash, and Kim Beaton, July.

Information based on National Treasury, South Africa (2020), Draft Consultation Paper "An Inclusive Financial Sector for All", available at http://www.treasury.gov .za/comm_media/ press/2020/Financial%20Inclusion%20Policy%20-%20An%20 Inclusive%20Financial%20 Sector%20For%20All.pdf

Kaur, P., & Kang, L. S. (2024). Status of digital payments in BRICS countries. *The Indian Economic Journal*.

Kiff, J., Alwazir, J., Davidovic, S., Farias, A., Khan, A., Khiaonarong, T., Malaika, M., Monroe, H., Sugimoto, N., Tourpe, H., & Zhou, P. (2020). A Survey of Research on Retail Central Bank Digital Currency. SSRN Electronic Journal. DOI: 10.2139/ ssrn.3639760

Krishnannair, A., Krishnannair, S., Olivier, J., Tsakeni, M., Babane, V. C., Kadenge, E., Luckay, M. B., Mutekwe, E., Naidoo, J., Singh-Pillay, A., & Molotsi, A. R. (2022). The 4IR and teacher education in South Africa: contemporary discourses and empirical evidence. In Disruptions in Higher Education. DOI: 10.4102/aosis.2022.BK306

Mahbub, M., & Shubair, R. M. (2023). Contemporary advances in multi-access edge computing: A survey of fundamentals, architecture, technologies, deployment cases, security, challenges, and directions. *Journal of Network and Computer Applications*, *219*, 103726. DOI: 10.1016/j.jnca.2023.103726

Malladi, C. M., Soni, R. K., & Srinivasan, S. (2021). Digital Financial Inclusion: Next Frontiers—Challenges and Opportunities. *CSI Transactions on ICT, 9*(2), 127–134. DOI: 10.1007/s40012-021-00328-5

Mishra, K. K., & Pant, P. (2025). Subconscious Factors Affecting Consumer Preferences Toward Green Investments. Sustainability, Innovation, and Consumer Preference, 119–148.

Mishra, K. K., & Priya, S. (2019). Impact of Improving Socio - Economic Conditions on the Purchase Behaviour of Customers in Central Rural Uttar Pradesh. International Journal of Management Studies. https://www.semanticscholar.org/paper/Impact-of-Improving-Socio-Economic-Conditions-on-of-Mishra-Priya/7c1d06fb99071d87380a31748aebca40d3ebcb0d

Otiashvili, D., Mgebrishvili, T., Beselia, A., Vardanashvili, I., Dumchev, K., Kiriazova, T., & Kirtadze, I. (2022). The impact of the COVID-19 pandemic on illicit drug supply, drug-related behaviour of people who use drugs and provision of drug-related services in Georgia: Results of a mixed methods prospective cohort study. *Harm Reduction Journal, 19*(1), 25. Advance online publication. DOI: 10.1186/s12954-022-00601-z PMID: 35264181

Pant, P., Mishra, K. K., & Mohan, A. (2024). *Algorithmic Approaches to Financial Technology: Forecasting, Trading, and Forecasting*. Artificial Intelligence and Machine Learning-Powered Smart Finance.

Pant, P., Mishra, K. K., & Rajaram, R. (2025). Risks to Individual Privacy and Security in the World of Deepfake Technology. In Mastering Deepfake Technology: Strategies for Ethical Management and Security (pp. 237-253). River Publishers.

Paul, J., Ueno, A., Dennis, C., Alamanos, E., Curtis, L., Foroudi, P., Kacprzak, A., Kunz, W. H., Liu, J., Marvi, R., Nair, S. L. S., Ozdemir, O., Pantano, E., Papadopoulos, T., Petit, O., Tyagi, S., & Wirtz, J. (2024). Digital transformation: A multidisciplinary perspective and future research agenda. *International Journal of Consumer Studies, 48*(2), e13015. Advance online publication. DOI: 10.1111/ijcs.13015

PricewaterhouseCoopers (PwC) Study, Payments 2025 & Beyond - Navigating the payments matrix, available at https:// www.pwc.com/gx/en/industries/financial -services/publications/financial-services-in-2025/payments-in-2025.html

Puri, P. (1998). Financing of Litigation by Third-Party Investors: A Share of Justice? *Deleted Journal, 36*(3), 515–566. DOI: 10.60082/2817-5069.1559

Qumba, M. F. (2022). A comparative analysis of the Twin Peaks model of financial regulation in South Africa and the United Kingdom. *South African Law Journal, 139*(1), 78–113. DOI: 10.47348/SALJ/v139/i1a3

Shrier, D., Pentland, A., Zachariadis, M., Ozcan, P., Services, D., Goodenough, O., Flood, M., Reed, M., Hardjono, T., Lipton, A., Possibilities, F., Sandboxes, R., & Bhalla, A. (2022). Global Fintech. In The MIT Press eBooks. DOI: 10.7551/mitpress/13673.001.0001

Singh, H., Mishra, K. K., & Singh, M. P. (2024). A Study on Rural BPL Households' Perception Towards Financial Inclusion Schemes. In Algorithmic Approaches to Financial Technology: Forecasting, Trading, and Optimization (pp. 146-159). IGI Global.

Tackling Vulnerability in the Informal Economy. (2019). In the Development Centre studies. DOI: 10.1787/939b7bcd-en

Tursunbayeva, A., Pagliari, C., Di Lauro, S., & Antonelli, G. (2021). The Ethics of People Analytics: Risks, Opportunities, and Recommendations. *Personnel Review, 51*(3), 900–921. DOI: 10.1108/PR-12-2019-0680

Van Niekerk, G., & Ponelis, F. (2024). Strengthening Law Enforcement to Address White-Collar Financial Crime in South Africa's Private Sector. Potchefstroom Electronic Law Journal/Potchefstroomse Elektroniese Regsblad, 27. DOI: 10.17159/1727-3781/2024/v27i0a17141

World Bank. (2022). The Global Findex Database 2021: Financial inclusion, digital payments, and resilience in the age of COVID-19.

World Bank's Policy Response to the COVID-19 (Coronavirus) Pandemic: Promoting the Use of Digital Payments in Russia. (March 09, 2020), https://www.worldbank .org/en/country/russia/brief/covid-19-response-digital-payments-russia

Zaheer, A., Singh, A., & Mishra, K. K. Reepu, and Vardari, L. (2024), “The Future of Alchemy: Emerging Trends and Technologies Metaverse in Insurance – A Virtual Customer Experience”, Taneja, S., Kumar, P., Reepu, Kukreti, M. and Özen, E. (Ed.) Data Alchemy in the Insurance Industry, Emerald Publishing Limited, Leeds, pp. 133-152. DOI: 10.1108/978-1-83608-582-920241021

Zhang, P., Yang, X., Chen, H., & Zhao, S. (2023). Matching Relationship between Urban Service Industry Land Expansion and Economic Growth in China. *Land (Basel), 12*(6), 1139. DOI: 10.3390/land12061139

Chapter 14
Green Marketing and Sustainable Supply Chain:
A Thematic Analysis

Swati Bhatnagar
http://orcid.org/0000-0002-5507-0618
New Delhi Institute of Management, New Delhi, India

Anand Jaiswal
http://orcid.org/0000-0002-8118-8361
TERI School of Advanced Studies, New Delhi, India

ABSTRACT

This study conducts a thematic analysis of green marketing and sustainable supply chain practices based on research published in the Scopus database over the last 10 years (2014-2024). The study identified key themes such as eco-innovation, consumer perceptions, regulatory pressures and operational challenges. Utilizing bibliometric analysis and NVivo software, the study systematically categorizes themes. Six core themes emerge, including green marketing strategies, supply chain operationsand stakeholder influences. The analysis reveals a credibility gap between sustainability narratives and actual practices, influenced by industry and regulatory frameworks. The chapter highlights the importance of multi-stakeholder collaboration in promoting sustainable practices and provides actionable insights for businesses aiming to align their marketing strategies with environmental goals. It contributes to the theoretical discourse on sustainability marketing and supply chain management while identifying critical gaps for further investigation.

DOI: 10.4018/979-8-3373-5437-8.ch014

INTRODUCTION

The increasing global emphasis on environmental sustainability has led businesses to adopt green marketing strategies and sustainable supply chain practices as a response to regulatory pressures, consumer demand, and corporate social responsibility (CSR) objectives (Luthra et al., 2018). Green marketing, defined as the promotion of environmentally friendly products and processes, has gained traction as consumers become more conscious of ecological impacts (Dangelico & Vocalelli, 2017). Simultaneously, sustainable supply chain management (SSCM) integrates environmental and social considerations into procurement, production, and distribution processes to minimize ecological footprints (Seuring & Müller, 2008). While both concepts have been studied independently, their intersection remains underexplored, particularly in terms of how green marketing strategies influence supply chain sustainability and vice versa (Kumar & Garg, 2017). The growing urgency of climate change, resource depletion, and regulatory mandates necessitates a deeper understanding of how businesses can align marketing strategies with sustainable supply chain operations to achieve long-term competitiveness and ecological benefits (Zhu et al., 2018).

Despite the increasing volume of research on green marketing and sustainable supply chains, there remains a significant gap in synthesizing the thematic trends that define their relationship (Geng et al., 2017). Previous studies have examined green consumer behavior (Joshi & Rahman, 2015), corporate sustainability reporting (Hahn & Kühnen, 2013), and supply chain green practices (Sarkis, 2012), but few have systematically analyzed how marketing strategies drive or are influenced by sustainable supply chain initiatives. Additionally, while some research highlights the role of stakeholder pressure in shaping green business models (Walker & Wan, 2012), there is limited thematic consolidation of how regulatory frameworks, consumer awareness, and technological advancements collectively shape this dynamic. This study addresses this gap by conducting a thematic analysis of Scopus-indexed research from 2014 to 2024, employing the PRISMA (Preferred Reporting Items for Systematic Reviews and Meta-Analyses) framework to identify, evaluate, and synthesize key themes at the intersection of green marketing and sustainable supply chains.

The methodology of this study involves a systematic literature review (SLR) to ensure a rigorous and transparent analysis of existing research (Tranfield et al., 2003). By focusing on peer-reviewed articles from the Scopus database, this study captures high-impact research while minimizing selection bias (Moher et al., 2009). The thematic analysis approach allows for the identification of recurring patterns, such as eco-innovation in product design, consumer perceptions of green products, regulatory influences on corporate sustainability, and the operational challenges of implementing green supply chains (Braun & Clarke, 2006). These themes provide a structured understanding of how businesses navigate the complexities of sustainability while maintaining profitability and market relevance (Pagell & Shevchenko, 2014). Furthermore, this study highlights the significance of multi-stakeholder collaboration, emphasizing the roles of governments, corporations, and consumers in fostering sustainable consumption and production systems (Vachon & Klassen, 2008).

The significance of this study lies in its comprehensive synthesis of contemporary research, offering scholars and practitioners a consolidated view of the evolving relationship between green marketing and sustainable supply chains. By identifying key trends and research gaps, this analysis contributes to the theoretical discourse on sustainability marketing and supply chain management while providing actionable insights for businesses seeking to align their environmental strategies with market demands (Beske et al., 2014). Additionally, the study underscores the need for further research on the long-term impacts of green marketing initiatives, particularly in measuring their effectiveness in driving supply chain sustainability across different industries and regions (Leonidou et al., 2013). As global sustainability challenges intensify, this thematic analysis serves as a foundational resource for future empirical studies and policy formulations aimed at promoting greener business practices (Srivastava, 2007).

METHODOLOGICAL APPROACH

This study employs a systematic literature review (SLR) guided by the PRISMA (Preferred Reporting Items for Systematic Reviews and Meta-Analyses) framework to ensure methodological thoroughness and transparency in identifying, screening, and analyzing relevant research articles (Moher et al., 2009). The Scopus database was selected due to its extensive coverage of high-impact, peer-reviewed journals in business, sustainability, and supply chain management (Falagas et al., 2008). The search strategy utilized a structured keyword combination to capture the intersection of green marketing and sustainable supply chains, including terms such as *"Green Marketing," "Sustainable Marketing," "Environmental Marketing," "Green Advertising," "Sustainable Branding"* paired with *"Sustainable Supply Chain," "Green Supply Chain," "Environmental Supply Chain,"* and *"Circular Supply Chain."* The initial search, restricted to articles published between 2014 and 2025, yielded 117 documents. Following PRISMA's screening process, non-research articles (conference papers, book chapters, editorials) were excluded, reducing the sample to 74 articles. Further exclusions—removing *"Articles in Press"* and non-English publications—resulted in 71 articles. A manual exclusion was then conducted by reviewing abstracts and full texts to ensure alignment with the study's core themes, leading to a refined dataset for thematic analysis (Braun & Clarke, 2006) (Table 1).

Table 1. PRISMA article selection approach (Author's own source)

Step	Description	Documents Remaining
Identification	Initial search in Scopus	117
Screening	Non-research articles removed (conference papers, book chapters, etc.)	72
	Non-English papers removed	71
Eligibility	Manual exclusion (not aligned with themes)	26
Included	Final included studies	26

The thematic analysis approach was adopted to identify recurring patterns and emerging trends within the selected literature (Nowell et al., 2017). The trend analysis involved bibliometric analysis using R studio and thematic analysis included open coding to categorize key concepts, followed by axial coding to establish relationships between themes such as *eco-innovation, consumer perceptions, regulatory pressures, and supply chain operational challenges* (Corbin & Strauss, 2008). The analysis was iterative, with themes continuously refined to ensure theoretical saturation (Guest et al., 2012). NVivo software was used to assist in coding and visualization, enhancing the reliability of the findings (Zamawe, 2015). The methodological rigor of this study addresses common limitations in literature reviews, such as selection bias and inconsistent terminology, by adhering to PRISMA's structured protocols (Tranfield et al., 2003). By synthesizing fragmented research, this approach provides an understanding of how green marketing strategies interact with sustainable supply chain practices, while highlighting gaps for future empirical investigation.

RESULTS AND DISCUSSION

Performance Analysis and Science Mapping

The research article data covers research from 2014 to 2023, with 26 documents published across 22 sources, showing a strong annual growth rate of 16.65%. The average document age is 4.76 years, and each document receives an average of 23.12 citations, indicating substantial academic impact. The dataset includes 1356 references, with 87 Keywords Plus and 86 author keywords, reflecting diverse research themes. A total of 82 authors contributed, with only 3 single-authored papers, highlighting a collaborative research environment. Co-authorship per document averages 3.28, and 20% of papers involve international collaboration.

The annual scientific production shows fluctuating research activity, with a slow start in 2014 (1 document) and no publications in 2015. The output remained low from 2016 to 2018, with only 1–2 publications per year, before increasing in 2019 (3) and stabilizing at moderate levels in 2020 (2). A peak in 2021 (6) indicates heightened research interest, followed by a slight decline in 2022 (5) and 2023 (4) (Figure 1).

Figure 1. Annual article production of the identified articles (Author's own source)

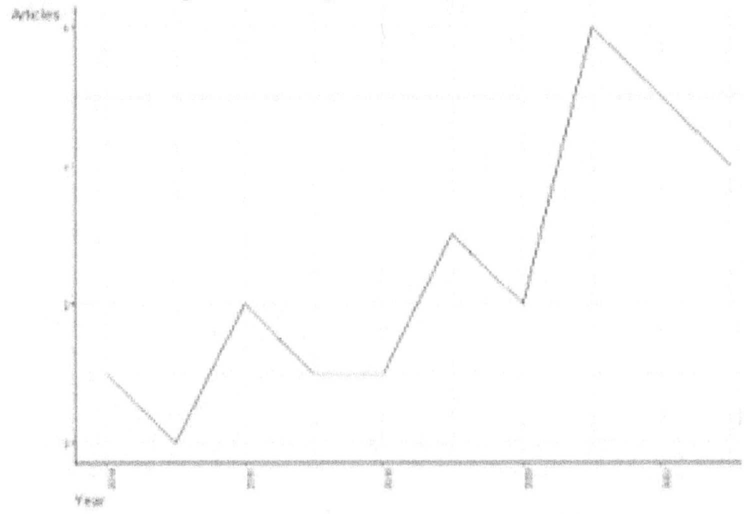

The most relevant words highlight a strong focus on "marketing" (10 occurrences) and "supply chain management" (8), emphasizing core research themes. Other frequent terms include "commerce" and "green economy" (4 each), along with "environmental management," "green marketing," and "social responsibility" (3 each), reflecting sustainability and business concerns. Keywords like "decision making," "green supply chain management," "game theory," and "sustainable development" suggest interdisciplinary approaches integrating strategy, industry dynamics, and environmental considerations (Figure 2).

Figure 2. Most occurring keywords and word cloud (Author's own source)

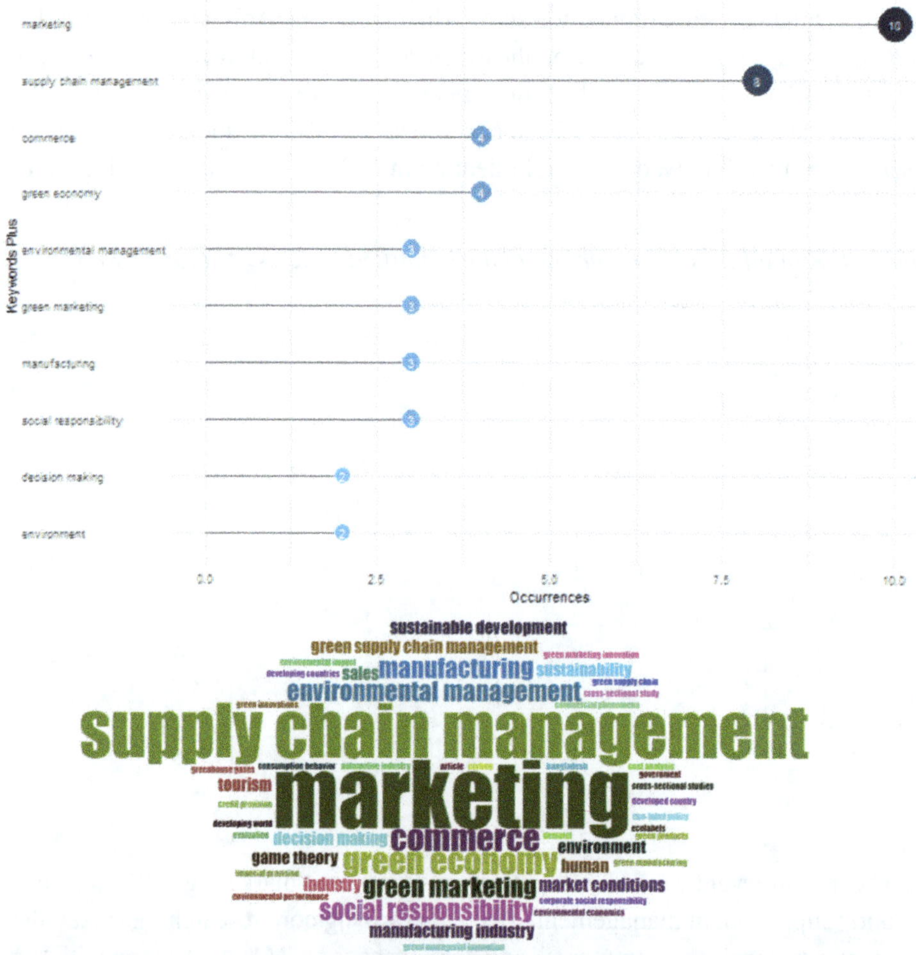

Further, the keyword co-occurrence analysis reveals key thematic clusters and their network centrality within the research domain. The largest cluster (Cluster 1) is dominated by "supply chain management," which has the highest betweenness (49.49), indicating its role as a crucial connector between research themes. Its high PageRank (0.204) also suggests significant influence in the research network. "Marketing" (betweenness: 3.83, PageRank: 0.108) is another important term, emphasizing its relevance in linking sustainability with supply chain topics.

Other terms in Cluster 1, such as "green economy," "manufacturing," "decision making," and "game theory," have low betweenness but moderate PageRank, indicating their supporting role in research themes rather than acting as central hubs.

"Sustainability" and "market conditions" also appear but with low influence, suggesting they are discussed but not as major linking concepts.

Cluster 2 focuses more on commerce and environmental concerns, with "commerce" showing notable betweenness (6.12) and a strong role in connecting themes. "Environmental management" and "green marketing" have similar network influence (betweenness: 2.39, PageRank: 0.078), highlighting their relevance in discussions about sustainable business practices. "Green supply chain management" is present but has low betweenness and PageRank, indicating its role is less central in the keyword network (Figure 3).

Figure 3. Keyword co-occurrence analysis (Author's own source)

The bibliometric theme map visualizes clusters of research topics based on their development (density) and relevance (centrality). In Figure 4, the x-axis represents centrality (relevance degree), while the y-axis represents density (development degree). The analysis is divided into four quadrants: Niche Themes, Motor Themes, Basic Themes, and Emerging/Declining Themes.

The Basic Themes quadrant (bottom-right) contains research on supply chain management, marketing, and green economy. These topics have high centrality but low density, meaning they are foundational for the research field but not highly specialized or developed. The Niche Themes quadrant (top-left) includes commerce, environmental management, and green marketing, which have high density but lower centrality, indicating well-developed but less interconnected research areas. The Motor Themes quadrant (top-right) is empty, suggesting no highly developed and relevant themes drive the field forward. Similarly, the Emerging/Declining Themes quadrant (bottom-left) is also empty, indicating that no significant themes are currently emerging or fading.

For the centrality and density rankings for different clusters, cluster 1 (supply chain management) ranks highest in centrality, reinforcing its importance as a basic theme. Cluster 2 (commerce) has the highest density, aligning with its categorization as a niche theme. The bibliometric measures (betweenness centrality, closeness centrality, and PageRank) further confirm the dominance of supply chain management and commerce in this research domain. Also, high-citation articles indicate that green strategies, eco-labeling policies, and green marketing in supply chains are core research interests.

Figure 4. Bibliometric map of the key themes (Author's own source)

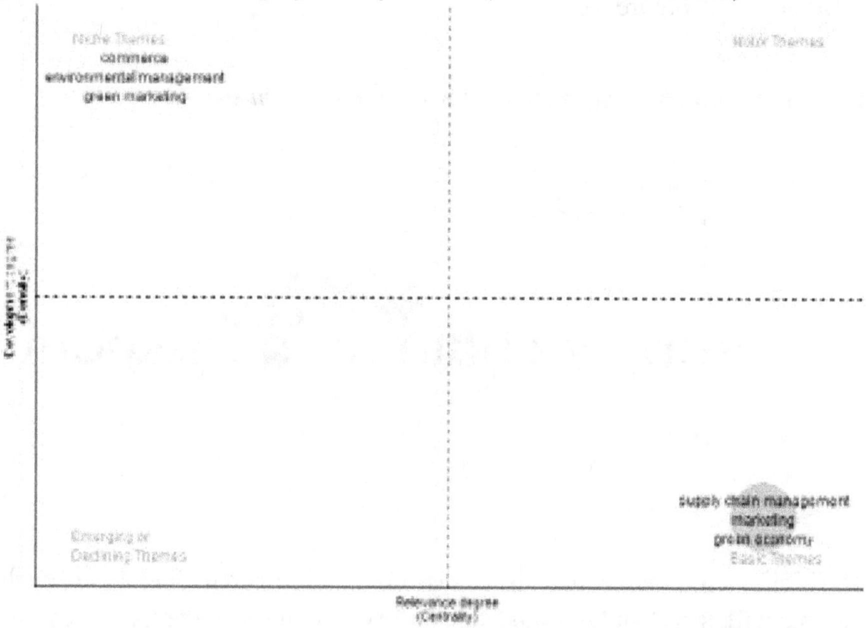

The findings of performance analysis and science mapping demonstrate significant growth in research examining the intersection of green marketing and sustainable supply chains, with an impressive 16.65% annual growth rate in publications (Luthra et al., 2018). This growth trajectory suggests increasing recognition among both scholars and practitioners of the critical relationship between marketing strategies and supply chain sustainability (Sarkis, 2012). The analysis reveals supply chain management as the dominant thematic cluster, highlighting its central role in operationalizing sustainability commitments made through marketing communications (Zhu et al., 2018).

The keyword co-occurrence analysis shows particularly strong connections between "supply chain management" and "marketing" (betweenness centrality = 49.49), suggesting these concepts serve as foundational pillars for the research domain (Kumar & Garg, 2017). However, the absence of motor themes in the thematic map indicates a lack of highly developed, novel research that could drive the field forward. This gap presents important opportunities for future studies to develop more integrative frameworks that bridge marketing theory with supply chain operations.

For business practitioners, these findings emphasize the need for authentic alignment between green marketing claims and actual supply chain practices (Dangelico & Vocalelli, 2017). Companies risk reputational damage if sustainability marketing outpaces real operational changes, a phenomenon known as greenwashing (Walker & Wan, 2012). The research suggests firms should implement robust sustainability metrics throughout their supply chains before promoting environmental benefits to consumers (Geng et al., 2017).

Policy implications emerge from the identification of under-researched areas like circular supply chains. Governments could stimulate progress in these areas through targeted grants, tax incentives, or regulatory requirements (Srivastava, 2007). The findings also suggest policymakers should focus on standardizing sustainability certifications to help consumers make informed choices (Joshi & Rahman, 2015).

Future research should address several critical gaps identified in this analysis. First, longitudinal studies could track how green marketing strategies influence long-term supply chain transformations (Leonidou et al., 2013). Second, comparative studies across industries might reveal best practices for implementing sustainable operations (Beske et al., 2014). Third, research should explore how emerging technologies like blockchain can enhance transparency in sustainable supply chains (Luthra et al., 2018). Finally, scholars should develop more robust metrics for assessing the real environmental impact of green marketing initiatives on green supply chain management (Zhu et al., 2018).

Thematic Analysis

The intersection of green marketing and sustainable supply chain management presents a complex landscape that requires careful examination. Through systematic analysis of the research, several key insights emerge about how organizations navigate this challenging terrain.

Open Coding Phase:

The initial thematic analysis identified six core themes that consistently emerged across the literature. These fundamental themes provide the foundation for understanding the green marketing-sustainable supply chain relationship:

- *Green Marketing Strategies - including eco-labeling programs, sustainable branding, and environmental advertising campaigns (Hu et al., 2022; Khan et al., 2021; Xue et al., 2023;*
- *Supply Chain Operations - focusing on green manufacturing, sustainable sourcing, and circular economy models (Dahlquist et al., 2021; He et al., 2023; Sugandini et al., 2020)*
- *Stakeholder Influences - encompassing government regulations, consumer demands, and corporate responsibility initiatives (Liu et al., 2016; Lynch et al., 2022; Peng et al., 2022)*
- *Performance Outcomes - measuring environmental impact, financial returns, and social welfare benefits (Bashar et al., 2023; Huang et al., 2021, Zhang et al., 2021)*
- *Implementation Challenges - highlighting cost trade-offs, coordination difficulties, and measurement complexities (Chang et al., 2019; Fadavi et al., 2022; Zampese et al., 2016)*
- *Strategic Approaches - featuring game theory applications, partnership structures, and digital technology integration (Bashar et al., 2023; Dahlquist, 2021; Fadavi et al., 2022)*

Building on these foundational themes, the study observes how green marketing strategies directly interact with supply chain operations. Eco-labels, for example, only hold value when backed by verifiable sustainable production methods (Hu et al., 2022). The stakeholder influences theme reveals how external pressures shape these interactions - government policies may mandate certain green practices while consumer expectations drive marketing messages (Liu et al., 2016; Lynch et al., 2022; Peng et al., 2022). Performance outcomes demonstrate the triple-bottom-line companies must balance, where environmental goals sometimes conflict with financial targets (Huang et al., 2021, Zhang et al., 2021). These tensions lead to the implementation challenges theme, where organizations struggle to align marketing promises with operational capabilities. Interestingly, the strategic approaches theme offers potential solutions, with digital tools like blockchain enabling better transparency between marketing claims and supply chain realities.

Axial Coding Phase:

Building on these foundational themes, deeper analysis provided three primary clusters that illustrate the complex relationships between green marketing and sustainable supply chain. The first cluster, *strategic alignment imperative,* highlights the necessity for consistency between marketing claims and operational reality. When companies overstate their environmental commitments without corresponding supply chain actions, the risk of greenwashing accusations spikes significantly. Real-world solutions to bridge this gap include vertically integrated cost-sharing contracts, alignment between product innovation types and marketing strategies, and blockchain-based traceability systems to ensure transparency.

The second cluster, *stakeholder institutional dynamics*, shows how external and internal pressures shape sustainability adoption. Regulatory frameworks drive nearly 40% of green supply chain management adoption (Liu et al., 2016), while consumer environmental awareness strongly influences marketing investments (Lynch et al., 2022). Yet internal resistance derails sustainability initiatives, proving that organizational buy-in is just as crucial as external pressures. The diamond industry serves as an adequate example, where marketed sustainability claims often outweigh actual environmental benefits by a 3:1 ratio (Lynch et al., 2022).

The third cluster, *performance measurement paradox* uncovers the inherent conflicts in evaluating sustainability success. Short-term financial returns often clash with long-term ESG performance, and operational efficiency metrics do not always align with marketing effectiveness (Zhang et al., 2021). New methodologies, like hybrid balanced scorecards and three-dimensional PLS-SEM frameworks, are emerging to reconcile these tensions, but the challenge remains complex (Azimi & Amiri, 2018; Khaleeli et al., 2021). Together, these clusters illustrate why green marketing and supply chain sustainability must be treated as an integrated system, where misalignment leads to credibility loss, stakeholder pressures dictate strategy, and performance measurement requires innovative approaches to capture true impact.

Emerging Patterns and Contradictions:

The thematic-analysis reveals three consistent patterns in the green marketing-supply chain relationship. First, a persistent credibility gap emerges between corporate sustainability narratives and verifiable operational practices, with this disconnect being aggravated by power asymmetries in buyer-supplier relationships. Second, contextual moderators, particularly industry characteristics and regional regulatory frameworks, create significant variation in implementation effectiveness across different operational environments. Third, digital transformation demonstrates measurable potential as a mediating mechanism for aligning marketing communications with supply chain data.

However, the analysis uncovers important contradictions in these relationships. While certain contexts demonstrate positive synergies between environmental and financial performance, developing economy studies frequently reveal significant tradeoffs. Similarly, government interventions show paradoxical outcomes - simultaneously driving sustainability adoption while creating market distortions in specific institutional contexts.

Implications and Future Directions:

These findings collectively suggest the need for more robust theoretical frameworks that integrate marketing and operations management perspectives while incorporating institutional dimensions of sustainability transitions. From a practical standpoint, three critical implementation requirements emerge: (1) developing unified performance metrics, (2) testing innovative partnership structures like cost-sharing agreements, and (3) adopting digital traceability technologies - all implemented with context-specific adaptations. The analysis identifies four key research priorities moving forward: longitudinal implementation studies, cross-industry comparisons, advanced performance measurement systems, and investigation of critical relationship pathways including: (a) green marketing→consumer perception→supply chain investment dynamics, (b) policy→strategy→operations cascading effects, (c) digital capability→transparency→credibility transformations, and (d) stakeholder pressure→organizational commitment→performance outcome sequences.

CONCLUSION

This thematic analysis has systematically examined the intersection of green marketing and sustainable supply chain management, providing insights into their complex interdependence. The findings highlight that successful integration requires more than superficial alignment. It demands structural consistency between marketing claims and operational execution to mitigate greenwashing risks. Key themes emerged, including the necessity of strategic coordination mechanisms like cost-sharing contracts, the influential role of stakeholder pressures (from regulators, consumers, and internal actors), and the persistent challenges in measuring performance across financial, environmental, and social dimensions. Contradictions were also identified, particularly in developing economies where sustainability investments often clash with short-term profitability, and where government interventions yield uneven results. Digital tools, such as blockchain-enabled traceability, emerged as pivotal enablers for bridging credibility gaps.

The research highlights the urgency for interdisciplinary frameworks that unite marketing and supply chain theory while accounting for institutional and contextual variability. Practitioners must prioritize verifiable sustainability practices over performative claims, leveraging partnerships and technology to align marketing narratives with supply chain realities. Future studies should explore longitudinal implementations, cross-industry comparisons, and advanced metrics to better capture the multifaceted nature of sustainability performance. This analysis affirms that green marketing and sustainable supply chains are not standalone functions but interconnected systems, where misalignment risks reputational and operational failure, while integration promotes resilience, consumer trust, and long-term value creation.

REFERENCES

Azimi, H., & Amiri, V. (2018). Investigating the Effect of Market Orientation on Environmental Performance with the Mediating Role of Green Supply Chain Management Strategies. Case study: Khales Sazan Rooy Company. *Journal of Environmental Management & Tourism, 9*(3 (27)), 581–590. DOI: 10.14505//jemt.9.3(27).18

Bashar, S., Wang, D., & Rafiq, M. (2023). Adoption of green supply chain management in developing countries: Role of consumer cooperation, eco-design, and green marketing. *Environmental Science and Pollution Research International, 30*(40), 92594–92610. DOI: 10.1007/s11356-023-28881-3

Beske, P., Land, A., & Seuring, S. (2014). Sustainable supply chain management practices and dynamic capabilities in the food industry: A critical analysis of the literature. *International Journal of Production Economics, 152*, 131–143. DOI: 10.1016/j.ijpe.2013.12.026

Braun, V., & Clarke, V. (2006). Using thematic analysis in psychology. *Qualitative Research in Psychology, 3*(2), 77–101. DOI: 10.1191/1478088706qp063oa

Chang, S., Hu, B., & He, X. (2019). Supply chain coordination in the context of green marketing efforts and capacity expansion. *Sustainability (Basel), 11*(20), 5734. DOI: 10.3390/su11205734

Corbin, J., & Strauss, A. (2008). *Basics of qualitative research: Techniques and procedures for developing grounded theory* (3rd ed.). Sage. DOI: 10.4135/9781452230153

Dahlquist, S. H. (2021). How green product demands influence industrial buyer/seller relationships, knowledge, and marketing dynamic capabilities. *Journal of Business Research, 136*, 402–413. DOI: 10.1016/j.jbusres.2021.07.045

Dangelico, R. M., & Vocalelli, D. (2017). "Green marketing": An analysis of definitions, strategy steps, and tools through a systematic review of the literature. *Journal of Cleaner Production, 165*, 1263–1279. DOI: 10.1016/j.jclepro.2017.07.184

Fadavi, A., Jolai, F., & Taleizadeh, A. A. (2022). Green product design in a supply chain with considering marketing under competition and coordination. *Environment, Development and Sustainability, 24*(10), 11721–11759. DOI: 10.1007/s10668-021-01917-9

Falagas, M. E., Pitsouni, E. I., Malietzis, G. A., & Pappas, G. (2008). Comparison of PubMed, Scopus, web of science, and Google scholar: Strengths and weaknesses. *FASEB Journal : Official Publication of the Federation of American Societies for Experimental Biology, 22*(2), 338–342. DOI: 10.1096/fj.07-9492LSF

Geng, R., Mansouri, S. A., & Aktas, E. (2017). The relationship between green supply chain management and performance: A meta-analysis of empirical evidence in Asian emerging economies. *International Journal of Production Economics, 183*, 245–258. DOI: 10.1016/j.ijpe.2016.10.008

Guest, G., MacQueen, K. M., & Namey, E. E. (2012). Applied thematic analysis. *Sage (Atlanta, Ga.)*.

Hahn, R., & Kühnen, M. (2013). Determinants of sustainability reporting: A review of results, trends, theory, and opportunities in an expanding field of research. *Journal of Cleaner Production, 59*, 5–21. DOI: 10.1016/j.jclepro.2013.07.005

He, B., Cai, H., Ji, Y., & Zhu, S. (2023). Supply chain green manufacturing and green marketing strategies under network externality. *Sustainability (Basel), 15*(18), 13732. DOI: 10.3390/su151813732

Hu, H., Li, Y., & Li, M. (2022). Decisions and coordination of green supply chain considering big data targeted advertising. *Journal of Theoretical and Applied Electronic Commerce Research, 17*(3), 1035–1056. DOI: 10.3390/jtaer17030053

Huang, J., Wang, X., Luo, Y., Yu, L., & Zhang, Z. (2021). Joint green marketing decision-making of green supply chain considering power structure and corporate social responsibility. *Entropy (Basel, Switzerland), 23*(5), 564. DOI: 10.3390/e23050564

Joshi, Y., & Rahman, Z. (2015). Factors affecting green purchase behaviour and future research directions. *International Strategic Management Review, 3*(1-2), 128–143. DOI: 10.1016/j.ism.2015.04.001

Khaleeli, M., Faisal, R., & Anwar, S. (2021). The effect of green marketing, green supply chain and green human resources on business performance: Balanced scorecard approach. *Uncertain Supply Chain Management, 9*(1), 133–138. DOI: 10.5267/j.uscm.2020.11.001

Khan, M. I., Khalid, S., Zaman, U., José, A. E., & Ferreira, P. (2021). Green paradox in emerging tourism supply chains: Achieving green consumption behavior through strategic green marketing orientation, brand social responsibility, and green image. *International Journal of Environmental Research and Public Health, 18*(18), 9626. DOI: 10.3390/ijerph18189626

Kumar, D., & Garg, C. P. (2017). Evaluating sustainable supply chain indicators using fuzzy AHP: Case of Indian automotive industry. *Benchmarking, 24*(6), 1742–1766. DOI: 10.1108/BIJ-11-2015-0111

Leonidou, C. N., Katsikeas, C. S., & Morgan, N. A. (2013). "Greening" the marketing mix: Do firms do it and does it pay off? *Journal of the Academy of Marketing Science*, *41*(2), 151–170. DOI: 10.1007/s11747-012-0317-2

Liu, X., Xu, Z., & Bai, C. (2016). Drivers' evaluation to implement green marketing practices in automobile industry of China. *International Journal of Networking and Virtual Organisations*, *16*(4), 362–376. DOI: 10.1504/IJNVO.2016.081653

Luthra, S., Mangla, S. K., Chan, F. T., & Venkatesh, V. G. (2018). Evaluating the drivers to information and communication technology for effective sustainability initiatives in supply chains. *International Journal of Information Technology & Decision Making*, *17*(01), 311–338. DOI: 10.1142/S0219622017500419

Lynch, M. J., Long, M. A., & Stretesky, P. B. (2022). Averting your gaze with sustainable, green marketing claims: A critique of luxury commodity production sustainability claims, with evidence from the diamond industry. *Sociological Spectrum*, *42*(4-6), 278–293. DOI: 10.1080/02732173.2022.2148797

Moher, D., Liberati, A., Tetzlaff, J., & Altman, D. G. (2009). Preferred reporting items for systematic reviews and meta-analyses: The PRISMA statement. *PLoS Medicine*, *6*(7), e1000097. DOI: 10.1371/journal.pmed.1000097

Nowell, L. S., Norris, J. M., White, D. E., & Moules, N. J. (2017). Thematic analysis: Striving to meet the trustworthiness criteria. *International Journal of Qualitative Methods*, *16*(1), 1–13. DOI: 10.1177/1609406917733847

Pagell, M., & Shevchenko, A. (2014). Why research in sustainable supply chain management should have no future. *The Journal of Supply Chain Management*, *50*(1), 44–55. DOI: 10.1111/jscm.12037

Peng, Y., Wang, W., Li, S., & Veglianti, E. (2022). Competition and cooperation in the dual-channel green supply chain with customer satisfaction. *Economic Analysis and Policy*, *76*, 95–113. DOI: 10.1016/j.eap.2022.08.001

Sarkis, J. (2012). A boundaries and flows perspective of green supply chain management. *Supply Chain Management*, *17*(2), 202–216. DOI: 10.1108/13598541211212924

Seuring, S., & Müller, M. (2008). From a literature review to a conceptual framework for sustainable supply chain management. *Journal of Cleaner Production*, *16*(15), 1699–1710. DOI: 10.1016/j.jclepro.2008.04.020

Srivastava, S. K. (2007). Green supply-chain management: A state-of-the-art literature review. *International Journal of Management Reviews*, *9*(1), 53–80. DOI: 10.1111/j.1468-2370.2007.00202.x

Sugandini, D., Susilowati, C., Siswanti, Y., & Syafri, W. (2020). Green supply management and green marketing strategy on green purchase intention: SMEs cases. [JIEM]. *Journal of Industrial Engineering and Management, 13*(1), 79–92. DOI: 10.3926/jiem.2795

Tranfield, D., Denyer, D., & Smart, P. (2003). Towards a methodology for developing evidence-informed management knowledge by means of systematic review. *British Journal of Management, 14*(3), 207–222. DOI: 10.1111/1467-8551.00375

Vachon, S., & Klassen, R. D. (2008). Environmental management and manufacturing performance: The role of collaboration in the supply chain. *International Journal of Production Economics, 111*(2), 299–315. DOI: 10.1016/j.ijpe.2006.11.030

Walker, K., & Wan, F. (2012). The harm of symbolic actions and green-washing: Corporate actions and communications on environmental performance and their financial implications. *Journal of Business Ethics, 109*(2), 227–242. DOI: 10.1007/s10551-011-1122-4

Xue, J., He, Y., Xu, H., & Gong, Z. (2023). Under the ecological label policy: Supply chain Heterogeneous product innovation strategies for green marketing. *Journal of Cleaner Production, 428*, 139370. DOI: 10.1016/j.jclepro.2023.139370

Zamawe, F. C. (2015). The implication of using NVivo software in qualitative data analysis: Evidence-based reflections. *Malawi Medical Journal : The Journal of Medical Association of Malawi, 27*(1), 13–15. DOI: 10.4314/mmj.v27i1.4

Zampese, E. R. D. S., Moori, R. G., & Caldeira, A. (2016). Green marketing as a mediator between supply chain management and organizational performance. *RAM. Revista de Administração Mackenzie, 17*(3), 183–211. DOI: 10.1590/1678-69712016/administracao.v17n3p183-211

Zhang, X., Xiu, G., Shahzad, F., & Duan, Y. (2021). Optimal financing strategy in a capital-constrained supply chain with retailer green marketing efforts. *Sustainability (Basel), 13*(3), 1357. DOI: 10.3390/su13031357

Zhu, Q., Sarkis, J., & Lai, K. (2018). Confirmation of a measurement model for green supply chain management practices implementation. *International Journal of Production Economics, 111*(2), 261–273. DOI: 10.1016/j.ijpe.2006.11.029

Chapter 15 Sustainability:
The Key to Responsible Business Models and Practices

Deepa Kapoor
http://orcid.org/0000-0002-7755-1631
Amity University, Noida, India

Ruchi Khandelwal
http://orcid.org/0000-0002-5826-4573
Amity University, Noida, India

ABSTRACT

The climate change phenomenon, worsening air quality, deteriorating biodiversity, and growing health concerns has become a reality today, and countries are struggling to catapult the situation. Overutilization of resources at a non-replenishable rate have forced businesses to think of alternative solutions that can be sustainable. Sustainability has three cornerstones, namely economic, social and environmental paradigms which are to be embedded in the very fundamental model of the business firms to ensure that it is being followed. They can act as role models for other businesses in the industry and can serve useful lessons to them. This chapter highlights the salient components of economic, social and environmental sustainability and brings forth case studies of some companies, namely, Nike, Neemans, NO Nasties and Mamaearth which have been able to fruitfully work on these dimensions with proven results.

DOI: 10.4018/979-8-3373-5437-8.ch015

MEANING OF SUSTAINABILITY

The word 'sustainability' has its origin in the Latin word 'sustinere', where 'sus' means 'up' and 'tenēre' implies 'to hold'. To 'sustain' is to exist in the long term. The planet and the business can thrive only if they learn the art of sustainability. The concept of sustainability in the present world was first introduced in the eighteenth century, but it gained prominence in the twentieth century when the United Nations' Brundtland Report defined *sustainable development* as development that "meets the needs of the present generation without compromising the ability of future generations to meet their own needs." There was a need to check the pace at which industrialisation was happening and adversely impacting the environment.

There are numerous resources in literature defining and discussing the concept of sustainability; however, the frame of reference is significant to underline the criticalities. This chapter discusses the concept of sustainability from the perspective of a business firm that is not only accountable to its investors and employees for giving them a fair share of return on their investment and efforts, but as well as is responsible to its customers and the community for providing mindful value through judicious and prudent use of resources. In short, sustainability in business refers to the effect companies have on the environment or society or their profitability.

Sustainability as a concept rest on the three pillars: environment, society, and economy, which refer to planet, people, and profits. Each pillar comprises several issues that direct the companies to attain their sustainability goals and targets through a concerted strategy. A sustainable business aims to positively impact all these three dimensions simultaneously. (Elkington, 2004; Turner and Houston, 2009; Seuring and Muller, 2008; Greenland, 2019). In the pursuit of achieving this order, a key role can be played by the business models, management practices, measurement methods and reporting approaches (Breuer et al., 2018; Lüdeke-Freund, 2020).

NEED FOR SUSTAINABILITY IN BUSINESS

In recent years, as economic development escalated, concerns for environmental and climate change, poverty and increasing inequality between societies and the tensions brought by social inequalities have mounted the pressure of sustainable development on businesses and industry. Some of the global issues that demand immediate attention are climate change, depletion of natural resources, inequalities based on race, gender and income, pollution of land, water and air, etc. To provide relief, governments stepped up the regulatory framework but the onus of maintaining sustainable development was largely on the business itself. Considering this perspective, there was a need to develop an integrated mode of achieving sustainability with its key dimensions of financial prosperity, social inclusivity and environmental sensitivity. The firm is accountable to the investors for the return on their money invested but also liable to its other stakeholders like customers, employees, community, government, etc. Trying to maintain a balance between the value it creates for shareholders and the stakeholders is an essential driver for sustainable business practices (Bocken and Geradts, 2020).

Over a very long period, business strategies have been causing irreparable damage to the environment and society at the cost of generating profits (Edwards, 2021). The growing public displeasure resulted in corporate ethics and governance taking this important issue of sustainability in the framing and implementation of corporate strategies. However, the actions of one firm will not suffice and require a collaborative effort, as sustainability issues are multi-dimensional and boundless across geographies and economic sectors. When a company decides to turn sustainable in its approach, it requires a complete revamp of its entire supply chain (Kumar et al., 2021; Negri et al., 2021). The raw materials, the operating processes, the consumption cycle and the consumer preferences all need to be adjusted. This is seemingly a tough and costly affair for companies but weighing the benefits in the long run definitely proves the case for corporate sustainability. It calls for re-imagination and redesign; innovation and invention; coordination and collaboration.

Working towards sustainability may seem philanthropic, however, a business can be benevolent towards the community and planet only if it can generate sustainable financial returns (Chladek, 2019). As McKinsey (2014) supports through evidence-based research, an organization investing in sustainability ideas and projects can gather more business opportunities and can have long-term financial wellness. Another research by Deutsche Bank concluded that companies investing in these three dimensions have not only faced a lower cost of debt and equity but also have performed better in the market in the long term.

Being an environmentally conscious company shall attract the like-minded consumers as well. Today, a consumer is conscious of their environmental footprint and are adapting to green consumption behaviour (Ali et al., 2023; Testa et al., 2021). They are cognizant of the firm's social and environmental impact and are favouring products from companies practising sustainable business. Generation Y in particular is willing to shell out more expenses for products with sustainable ingredients and made using sustainable processes (Djafarova and Foots, 2022; Moeve, 2024). Those firms that are unable to meet these consumer expectations are likely to be left behind. Adopting sustainability can help businesses target new markets with more revenue growth. Generations Y and Z are more aware of and more accountable for the future impact of increasing industrialisation worldwide, as they have experienced disasters such as earthquakes, tsunamis, changing climatic cycles, and an increased incidence of health disorders. They are less prone to work for businesses responsible for such calamities (IBM, 2021).

The growing power and omnipresence of media have made companies open to public scrutiny. Society at large today expects transparent, responsible and ethical actions from the companies around them, companies they buy from, and the companies they work in (Chatzopoulou and de Kiewiet, 2021; Sendlhofer and Tolstoy, 2022). Firms following unethical practices or behaving irresponsibly cannot remain undercover for long. The firms, therefore, need to gravitate to a positive image based on their ethical and just behaviour towards the environment and society. With increased global and national regulatory frameworks aiming to prevent climate change, ensure resource availability for the future, and control environmental impact, incorporating sustainability in businesses will ease compliance with regulations for companies.

In the highly competitive world, changing to sustainable business practices provides the impetus for business innovation which further leads the company to the forerunner position in the industry and creates a new direction for continuous growth into the future. The companies that take the lead not only survive but thrive (Deloitte CxO Sustainability Report, 2023). Becoming more sustainable mostly necessitates that businesses explore and adopt circular economy solutions, radically transform their supply chain, production processes, and other components of their business model. Measures like switching to cleaner and smarter energy, saving water, reducing the use of resources, and lowering wastage by reuse can also derive greater efficiency, thus improving operational profitability (McKinsey, 2014).

TURNING SUSTAINABLE – ALTERING BUSINESS ASPECTS

Sustainable business practices have been studied in isolation in the literature in plenty. Different authors in the past have used the grounded theory approach and have figured out multiple ways and methods in which business firms have employed sustainability in their approach and operations. Reverse logistics theory aims to encourage the reuse, recycling, remanufacturing, or efficient disposal of products through a reverse process that brings back the products for customers to the manufacturers. (Brito et al., 2005; Rubio et al., 2008; Agrawal et al., 2015; Adesoga et al., 2024). Marketing and promoting value propositions to customers that are environmentally friendly or have a positive impact on the planet; encompassing sustainability principles into various aspects of marketing, such as product design, packaging, and communication, is increasingly being practised by companies in the name of green marketing (Ginsberg and Bloom, 2004; Cronin et al., 2011; Dangelico and Vocalelli, 2017; Rahman and Nguyen, 2023).

Companies are engaged in the procurement of products and services in a favourable manner that capably diminishes the adverse effects they may have during their lifespan from manufacturing to transportation to use and finally to recycling and disposal, called green purchasing (Min and Galle, 1997; Dubey et al., 2013; Khan et al., 2023). These green purchasing strategies are further studied under those affecting product standards, i.e., purchasing products that are made using recycled materials or non-toxic ingredients; behaviour standards that deal with considering purchases on the basis of the environmental performance, pollution discharges of the items purchased, and collaborations which require manufacturers to work with their vendors to bring about changes in product design and materials used to reduce their environmental impact (Dubey et al., 2013). Hashmi (2023) advocated designing eco-friendly products, preferring sustainable manufacturing processes, purchasing sustainable materials and innovating reverse logistics to improve business performance.

Differentiation based on innovating products and processes in such a way that they create a positive impact on the environment is another way in which companies are trying to showcase their sustainability initiatives. Branded as environmental product differentiation, this captures the essence of designing products that offer greater benefits to the environment or burden it with lesser costs (Reinhardt, 1998; Rodríguez-Ibeas, 2007).

The current literary work aims to defend a case for the development of sustainable business models. The approach adopted by the authors is first enlightening the readers about the concept of sustainability and the three cornerstones on which it rests. Then in the light of few companies which have followed the path of sustainable business practices and have benefitted the stakeholders, the society and the economy in return, propagate the idea of building sustainability-oriented business models.

PILLARS OF SUSTAINABILITY

The three pillars of sustainability offer a holistic framework for tackling intricate challenges while ensuring that development is approached with an awareness of the interdependence among economic, social, and environmental dimensions. With the application of a comprehensive approach based on these three pillars, it becomes easy for stakeholders to have a sustainable and inclusive outcome. The three pillars of sustainability are Economic, Social and Environmental, and these are interrelated, and anything done in one pillar has an impact on other spheres as well.

There exists a robust relationship between the environmental and economic spheres, underscored by the necessity of responsible resource management to sustain the economy and the stability of the food supply chain. Furthermore, certain sustainability strategies, such as the shift towards a low-carbon economy and the implementation of sustainable practices, can simultaneously generate economic opportunities, spur innovation, and enhance the competitiveness of businesses (illuminem, 2023). The social dimension is similarly intertwined with both the environmental and economic aspects. It is widely recognized that a fair and inclusive society, characterized by reduced inequalities, promotes social cohesion, encourages active civic engagement, and lays the groundwork for a sustainable and resilient economy. Additionally, the health and well-being of individuals are closely associated with the quality of their surrounding environment.

ENVIRONMENT SUSTAINABILITY

The environmental pillar of sustainability marketing advocates for products and business practices that support environmental protection. Along with social and economic pillars, the environmental pillar supports the broader scope of sustainability. The environmental pillar addresses issues such as pollution, climate change, resource depletion, biodiversity loss, and other concerns of environmental sustainability by providing solutions that lessen their negative impacts and offer alternatives.

Environmental sustainability is concerned with the integrity of ecosystems and the natural environment's capacity to support life (Brodhag & Talière, 2006). According to Goodland & Daly (1996), it necessitates the sustainable utilisation of natural capital, both as a source of economic resources and as a means for waste absorption.

Compared to social and economic sustainability, the environmental pillar is the simplest to understand. Protection and management of the natural world is the primary concern of the environmental pillar. In the effort to preserve sustainability, the environmental pillar seeks to control the degradation of the natural world caused by pollution and waste. Figure 1 represents the various aspects of environmental sustainability. In the effort to sustain the ecology of the earth, the recycling and reusing of materials is advocated. Renewable resources are encouraged. Energy efficiency and conservation are promoted along with pollution control. Solar, wind, and geothermal energy offer alternatives to the models of traditional energy and are promoted the environmental pillar.

KEY ASPECTS OF ENVIRONMENTAL SUSTAINABILITY

Figure 1. Aspects of Environmental Sustainability

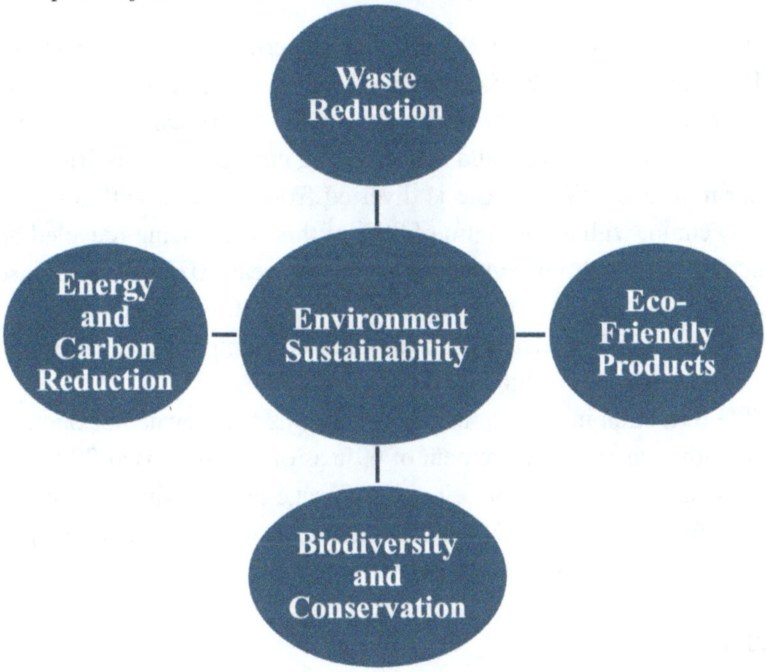

Source: Compiled by Authors

Case Examples

Nike

Nike's dedication to sustainability is spread across multiple dimensions of its operational framework, incorporating circular economic solutions. These initiatives are oriented towards prolonging the functional lifespan of products, promoting the recycling of utilized items, providing refurbished footwear at accessible price points as a viable sustainable reuse alternative, and repurposing vintage and excess materials. Nike has established definitive objectives aimed at enhancing sustainability and effecting meaningful change, with a primary focus on achieving these goals by the year 2025. The company is spearheading the 'Move to Zero' initiatives (*Nike Sustainability. Move to Zero*, n.d.) and is committed to integrating sustainable materials more extensively into its collections, thereby making the attainment of full sustainability more feasible than at any previous time.

The company is diligently pursuing its targets, which include:

- Achieving a reduction of 0.5 million imperial tonnes in greenhouse gas (GHG) emissions by 2025, through the increased utilization of environmentally preferred materials, with at least 50% of all critical materials, including polyester, cotton, leather, and rubber, being environmentally friendly.
- Ensuring that 100% of waste is diverted from landfills within the extended supply chain, with a minimum of 80% of this waste being recycled back into Nike products and other merchandise by the year 2025. As of the fiscal year 2023, 98% of waste has been diverted from landfills.
- Achieving a 25% reduction in freshwater consumption per kilogram during textile dyeing and finishing processes by 2025.
- A 70% reduction in greenhouse gas emissions from owned or operated facilities, with a current achievement of 69% as of the fiscal year 2023.
- Achieving 100% renewable electricity usage across Nike corporate offices, distribution centers, Air Miles, and retail locations worldwide by 2025, in alignment with the RE100 initiative.

NO Nasties

No Nasties is resolutely engaged in the utilization of 100% organic cotton within its textile offerings, thereby eradicating the application of genetically modified organisms (GMOs) and synthetic chemicals throughout the entirety of the agricultural production continuum. The commitment of No Nasties to sourcing fabrics exclusively from 100% organic cotton not only aids in environmental conservation by mitigating the use of pesticides and improving water resources and the quality of food crops, but also bolsters the livelihoods of farmers by diminishing their expenditure on agricultural inputs.

Moreover, No Nasties measures and mitigates the carbon emissions related to its products through strategic investments in carbon offset initiatives. The brand further embraces a "planet positive" framework by implementing tree planting programs for each transaction, thereby solidifying its dedication to environmental stewardship. By adopting a circular economy paradigm, No Nasties prioritises the recycling and repurposing of textiles, consequently preventing the phenomenon of downcycling.

- Reduce carbon footprint: No Nasties commitment begins with the reduction of their environmental footprint. This is achieved through the utilisation of

100% organic cotton and a local supply chain, which not only conserves water but also requires less energy and diminishes CO_2 emissions significantly.

- Neutralise Carbon Footprint: The company assesses the residual carbon footprint of each product and counterbalances it by investing in carbon offset initiatives focused on solar energy, wind power, and reforestation efforts.
- Planet Positive: No Nasties has offset three times the carbon footprint, resulting in a positive environmental contribution—300%. Additionally, for every product purchased, they plant three trees. 300% Offset + 3 Trees = Planet Positive. The cumulative impact of No Nasties' efforts is apparent in the numbers: saving 37,572,296 litres of water, offsetting 697,447 CO_2e, and planting 184,461 trees (no Nasties+, n.d.).

SOCIAL PILLAR

The significance of social sustainability principles and practices is gaining increasing acknowledgement, leading organizations to weave social factors into their comprehensive strategies. This integration not only strengthens the organization's brand image but also enhances its operational credibility.

Social sustainability is defined as the cultivation of individuals, communities, and cultures to facilitate the attainment of a meaningful existence through the promotion of adequate healthcare, education, gender equality, and peace and stability worldwide (Saith, 2006). Benaim and Raftis (2008) contend that achieving social sustainability is challenging due to the complexity and overwhelming nature of the social dimension. This contrasts with the environmental and economic systems, where the dynamics of flows and cycles are readily observable. Conversely, the dynamics within the social system are characterized by their intangibility, rendering them difficult to model (Benaim & Raftis, 2008; Saner, Yiu, & Nguyen, 2020).

The social aspect of corporate sustainability calls for an all-encompassing approach towards the well-being of all stakeholders, such as consumers, the community, and the most crucial of all, the employees. This social aspect emphasizes the moral responsibility of business organizations to make sure that the activities of such organizations have a positive impact on society. The fundamental issue in this pillar is the fair treatment and empowerment of the employees. Not only should they be paid fairly, but they should also be provided with a healthy and safe workplace along with other benefits that help in improving their general well-being. It involves human well-being, social equity, and development of societies through a sustainable way.

Social sustainability encompasses a broad spectrum of issues, such as labour conditions, remuneration, and access to fundamental natural resources like food and water, in addition to socioeconomic resources including health, education, and financial assistance (Waage et al., 2005). Organizations can shift their focus towards enhancing employee retention and engagement strategies. This may involve implementing more adaptive benefits, such as improved maternity and family leave policies, flexible work schedules, and opportunities for education and professional development. In terms of community involvement, companies have devised various methods to contribute positively, including fundraising initiatives, sponsorships, scholarship programmes, and investments in local public projects. In the pursuit of social sustainability, the advancement of systems and policies aimed at diminishing social and economic disparities is crucial for guaranteeing equitable access to opportunities and resources for every individual in society.

The social aspects of sustainability relate not only to employee remuneration but also to the wider impact of products and production methods on individuals' lives, particularly regarding their access to various resources—natural, informational, educational, and financial. The various key aspects of social sustainability are presented in the Figure 2. As a result, businesses must broaden their perspective beyond their internal workforce to consider all stakeholders impacted by their operations, including the local community and society at large, which may experience indirect consequences from the company's activities.

KEY ASPECTS OF SOCIAL PILLAR

Figure 2. Aspects of Social Pillar

Source: Compiled by Authors

Case Example

Nike: Diversity, Equity and Inclusion

Nike's commitment to empowering athletes and communities, promoting diversity, equity, and inclusion, and generating measurable social impact is commendable. NIKE, Inc. is committed to fostering equitable and inclusive practices that empower workforce and shape the future of employment. As per report available (*Nike - Diversity, Equity & Inclusion — NIKE, Inc.*, n.d.)

- In the fiscal year 2023, women constituted 51 percent of Nike's global corporate workforce, supported by industry-leading initiatives designed to enhance career advancement opportunities for women from diverse backgrounds.
- Women account for 44% of Vice Presidents and members of the Senior Leadership Team.

- Globally, all Nike employees and their eligible dependents are entitled to 20 complimentary counselling sessions annually for Mental health.
- Nike has developed and implemented the Engagement and Wellbeing (EWB) Survey to assess the engagement levels and experiences of factory workers.
- NIKE has established an accessibility strategy aimed at enhancing the representation of individuals with disabilities within the company. The NikeUNITED Ability Network promotes a culture of belonging and inclusion for athletes with disabilities, while also raising awareness and providing education. To support this initiative, NIKE will improve the employee experience by creating a more flexible, accessible, and equitable work environment for employees with disabilities.

Mamaearth Positive Social Impact:

- Beyond its product offerings, Mamaearth has strived to create a positive social impact. As part of its "Plant Goodness" initiative, the brand has pledged to plant a tree for every order placed, contributing to reforestation efforts in rural communities.
- Mamaearth is actively involved in supporting educational programs for underprivileged children, equipping them with knowledge and opportunities that can significantly improve their lives. These initiatives have received considerable recognition and backing from consumers, thereby solidifying Mamaearth's reputation as a brand that prioritizes social responsibility.
- Engagement with Parenting Community:
  - Mamaearth has effectively cultivated a robust community of parents who exchange their experiences, concerns, and advice on the brand's platform.
  - With a follower count exceeding 1.5 million on various social media channels, Mamaearth has created a nurturing and informative environment for parents.
  - The brand actively promotes discussions on parenting, natural care, and sustainable living, offering a comprehensive approach to the well-being of families.

ECONOMIC PILLAR

Economic sustainability is an approach to conducting economic activities for maximising economic well-being and prosperity in the long run. To be precise, it is an effort to achieve the right balance between economic growth, economic efficiency, social fairness, and financial soundness. Economic sustainability includes such components as economic development, employment generation, fair wages, labour rights, and a sustainable economy. Sustainability gives opportunities for economic sustainability to innovate and succeed, solve problems, and improve people's lives. Still, it is important to remember that economic sustainability has to be in line with environmental and social sustainability goals.

As per (Lobo et al., 2015), economic sustainability is defined as a production system that meets current consumption demands without jeopardizing the needs of future generations. Economic sustainability encompasses the creation of jobs, profitability, and the accurate valuation of ecosystem services to facilitate optimal cost-benefit analyses. In the realm of employment, studies indicate that high employment rates not only bolster the economy but also enhance the social well-being of individuals through the provision of secure employment, thereby ensuring resource security. This dynamic relationship between the job market and social sustainability suggests that the economic forces necessitating employment can, in turn, promote social sustainability by offering individuals a sense of security.

The contemporary gig economy presents a conflict between social and economic sustainability. Individuals often contribute to the economic viability of businesses without receiving the social safety measures that are typically associated with traditional employment. This aspect is sometimes referred to as the governance pillar within the ESG framework, which emphasizes the alignment of boards of directors and management with the interests of shareholders, as well as those of the broader community, value chains, and customers. The various aspects associated with economic pillar of sustainability are presented in the Figure 3.

A primary obstacle in contemporary sustainable development lies in the pursuit of fostering economic prosperity and elevating living standards, all the while mitigating the escalation of greenhouse gas emissions, pollution, and the overutilization of natural resources. This aspect relies on the capacity of businesses to foster economic growth and development. In essence, companies are required to advocate for environmental protection by mitigating the risks associated with their production processes. Consequently, the recycling of products and the adoption of renewable energy sources are essential components of the economic pillar of sustainability.

KEY ASPECTS OF ECONOMIC PILLAR

Figure 3. Aspects of Economic Pillar

Source: Compiled by Authors

Case Examples

Nike

Nike is of the opinion that fair compensation and representation enhance community strength. The company has upheld a 1:1 pay equity ratio for women worldwide, as well as for racial and ethnic minorities in the United States, while actively working to diversify its leadership throughout the organisation.

Nike is pioneering the development of more efficient materials and the recycling of existing plastics, yarns, and textiles (*Sustainable Materials*, n.d.). This approach is a significant step towards achieving a carbon-neutral and waste-free future.

Key advancements in material innovation include:

- Nike Air: Composed of a minimum of 25% recycled manufacturing waste, with all Air MI facilities operating on 100% renewable wind energy. More than 90% of the waste generated from materials used in Air soles is repurposed to create new, innovative cushioning systems.
- Nike Forward: A novel material crafted from ultra-thin, needle-punched layers, which boasts an average carbon footprint reduction of 75% compared to conventional knit materials.
- Nike Flyknit: A lightweight fabric derived from recycled plastic bottles, engineered to produce an average of 60% less waste than traditional methods of manufacturing footwear uppers.
- Nike Flyleather: Formulated by combining at least 50% recycled leather fibres with synthetic materials through a water-powered process, offering a low-waste and low-impact alternative to conventional leather production.

Neeman's Footwear

Sustainability has always been a key value for Neeman's and an integral part of the value-added products Neeman's tries to deliver. The unique selling proposition of Neeman's is in creating footwear designs that focus on functionality, comfort, and sustainability. This way, Neeman sets itself apart from other companies operating in the highly competitive segment of footwear in India.

Neeman's is devoted to minimising the ecological impact of footwear production and maintaining close ties with suppliers for sustainable sourcing of raw materials. Thus, sustainability has made Neeman's a trendsetter when it comes to redefining footwear trends in India and urging people to buy consciously.

The commitment to sustainability has positioned Neeman as a pioneer in revolutionising footwear trends in India, encouraging consumers to adopt more conscious purchasing habits. Neeman's is increasingly recognised as the brand that is at the forefront of transforming footwear trends in India, advocating for a shift towards more sustainable and conscious consumer choices in fashion. Neeman's stands out for its focus on using natural and renewable materials in its products, offering a unique alternative to conventional shoe brands (India Retailing, 2023).

Key aspects of Neeman's innovative products:

- Neeman's has introduced a groundbreaking line of wool joggers, marking the first of its kind in India, crafted from Australian merino wool. This product represents a harmonious blend of comfort and sustainability.

- Relive Knits are made from recycled plastic bottles, Neeman's uses recycled plastic bottles to make parts of its shoes, especially in the linings and uppers.
- Eco Flips incorporate recycled tyres for enhanced sturdiness and durability. The soles of the EcoFlips are made from natural rubber, which is biodegradable and offers a sustainable alternative to synthetic rubber or plastic.
- Tea Sneakers are created with TENCEL™ Lyocell fibers sourced from sustainably grown trees.

No Nasties

- No Nasties was founded to serve as a social initiative, driven by the alarming prevalence of farmer suicides within the Indian cotton sector. The western region of the country known as the "cotton belt of India", has erratic weather patterns and inconsistent rainfall, severely impacting cotton yields, resulting in unpredictable cycles of surplus and loss. Furthermore, the costs associated with cotton farming—such as fertilizers, pesticides, and seeds—have been on the rise. The unpredictable climate and escalating expenses make it challenging for farmers to fulfil their loan obligations, leading some to the tragic decision of suicide. (*STYLISHLY SUSTAINABLE - a Social Movement Through a Fashion Brand*, 2023)
- Acknowledging these critical issues, No Nasties has adopted a proactive stance by implementing fair trade practices. This strategy seeks to address the underlying causes of farmer distress, ensuring a more sustainable and equitable environment for those engaged in cotton production within the Indian fashion industry. Nasties strictly follows Fair Trade principles, providing farmers with higher prices, better working conditions, and more equitable agreements, which significantly improve their overall quality of life.

CHALLENGES TO PRACTISING SUSTAINABILITY IN BUSINESS

Organisations survive primarily for generating wealth for shareholders and therefore the focus on maximisation of shareholder value is the focal point for all decision-making (Bocken and Geradts, 2020). Most of the metrics used for performance assessment are also a proxy for shareholder value. This further breeds financial risk avoidance behaviour (Caldera et al., 2019; Hansson et al., 2023) and low tolerance for uncertainty. Adapting the business processes to the requirements of sustainability calls for ambiguity, which organisations are interested in avoiding. Developing innovative business processes and models necessitates upfront investments, which are impaired due to the tendency to avoid financial risks. It is also observed that in order to maximise shareholder value, firms have been focusing on investments that can certainly produce gains in the short term (Caldera et al., 2019; Bocken and Geradts, 2020; Hansson et al., 2023). The performance reporting metrics are also based on short-term and so there is an impatience for results among strategic implementors.

Whether it is Mamaearth or Neeman's, financial obstacles are still present, as per reports available. After the IPO launch in 2023, Honasa Consumer Limited has been in the news, and analysts believe that retaining strong revenue growth and materially furthering profitability could be challenging for the Mamaearth parent in the short to medium term (Mudgill, 2024). A substantial challenge is faced by Neeman's, which has an increase in losses as a result of compounded outlays associated with the procurement of raw materials for sustainable footwear, promotional overheads and transportation charges. Remunerating workers fairly and providing better working conditions or perquisites often increases the overhead charges for companies (Gutsa, 2023). In addition to this to maintain its social sustainability goals, Neeman's faces high expenditure of providing employee benefits as well (Team, 2024). Thus, despite making a growth in profits from last financial year, Neeman's is still trying for economic sustainability.

The focus on the achievement of improved efficiency lays emphasis on leveraging superiority in functional areas. Due to this functional focus, the firms may suffer from a lack of collaboration and shared ownership of the sustainability agenda by functional areas (Bocken and Geradts, 2020). When a company decides to practice sustainability, the overall approach to business has to change. In the case of Mamaearth, the products have been well accepted by the target market, but when it comes to their promotion, it is not fulfilling the social sustainability agenda. The Advertising Standards Council of India (ASCI) in their annual report released in May 2024 has charged the parent company of the brand Mamaearth for using content in their advertisements that is misleading, deceptive or false and hence is violating the regulations (Sen, 2024).

Overconcentrated efforts towards functional efficiency not only prohibit risk-taking but also hinder transformative changes in business processes and models. The managers are motivated by temporal goals and to showcase achievements that escape the unusual, the ambiguous path of transformation. They largely focus on incremental changes and benefits. So, unless there is a top-down emphasis on sustainability and it is woven into the very corporate strategy of the organization, giving it a long-term relevance and perspective, it will not be easy to embed sustainability into business coherently (Seidel et al., 2010; Bocken and Geradts, 2020). Although top management support is crucial to drive long-term commitment, at the same time individual commitments to social and environmental responsibility were also fundamental in the process. The non-existence of social-environmental aspects in individual performance targets is definitely a roadblock to deal with (Seidel et al., 2010; Caldera et al., 2019; Bocken and Geradts, 2020). With companies like Nike, Neeman's, and Mamaearth, a bigger challenge is to educate customers about sustainability and encourage them to change their consumption habits. The products made by these companies still have a long, long way to travel. A consulting firm from the Netherlands reports that, on average sustainable product are 75-85% more expensive than their conventional counterparts. This is due to the expensive raw materials used, production processes used, and the certifications and standards they need to meet to achieve the 'eco-friendly' status (Gutsa, 2023).

In reality, the sustainable products are trapped in a vicious circle. The high price of sustainable products affects demand negatively, while the low demand makes it impossible for manufacturers to take advantage of economies of scale, resulting in high prices. The raw materials used for manufacturing sustainable products are responsibly sourced in a way that diminishes their environmental impact, and thus they are more expensive to produce and source.

CONCLUSION

To foster sustainable business practices, organizations should focus on best practices that cover economic, social, and environmental aspects. Engaging in sustainable business practices not only promotes business sustainability but also provides a competitive edge, increases market share, and boosts shareholder value. Key elements of sustainability integration into a company's operations should include the development of triple responsibility—economic, environmental, and social—moving away from the traditional focus solely on profitability.

Companies are investing heavily in sustainability to improve their environmental impact without harming their bottom line. Besides improving environmental performance, sustainability initiatives prompt companies to think outside the box to tackle new environmental challenges, and, as a result, develop new, differentiated services and business models. While there are a lot of challenges related to adapting sustainable practices to business operations, companies are starting to realise the value sustainability brings to their operations.

Companies are starting to develop and implement sustainability strategies, market their sustainable products and services, and publish sustainability reports directed not just to the customers or the general public, but also to the investors and sustainability activists as well. An improved dedication to sustainability practices has a positive impact on a company's and brand's reputation and grows a loyal customer base. Through this chapter, readers will gain insights into the importance of sustainability, key pillars of sustainability and understand the challenges faced by companies while adopting sustainable business practices. Through real-world cases, this chapter explored how businesses can integrate pillars of sustainability into their core operations.

REFERENCES

Adesoga, T. O., Patricia, O., Olaiya, E. P., Ajayi, O. D., & Dorcas, O. (2024). Review of reverse logistics practices and their impact on supply chain sustainability'. *International Journal of Scientific Research and Advances, 12*(2), 45–55.

Agrawal, S., Singh, R. K., & Murtaza, Q. (2015). A literature review and perspectives in reverse logistics. *Resources, Conservation and Recycling, 97*, 76–92. DOI: 10.1016/j.resconrec.2015.02.009

Ali, M., Ullah, S., Ahmad, M. S., Cheok, M. Y., & Alenezi, H. (2023). Assessing the impact of green consumption behavior and green purchase intention among millennials toward sustainable environment. *Environmental Science and Pollution Research International, 30*(9), 23335–23347. DOI: 10.1007/s11356-022-23811-1 PMID: 36322356

Benaim, C. A., & Raftis, L. (2008). The Social Dimension of Sustainable Development: Guidance and Application: Thesis submitted for completion of Master of Strategic Leadership towards Sustainability, Blekinge Institute of Technology, Karlskrona, Sweden

Bocken, N. M., & Geradts, T. H. (2020). Barriers and drivers to sustainable business model innovation: Organization design and dynamic capabilities. *Long Range Planning, 53*(4), 101950. DOI: 10.1016/j.lrp.2019.101950

Breuer, H., Fichter, K., Lüdeke-Freund, F., & Tiemann, I. (2018). Sustainability-oriented business model development: Principles, criteria and tools. *International Journal of Entrepreneurial Venturing, 10*(2), 256–286. DOI: 10.1504/IJEV.2018.092715

Brodhag, C., & Talière, S. (2006, May). Sustainable development strategies: Tools for policy coherence. [). Oxford, UK: Blackwell Publishing Ltd.]. *Natural Resources Forum, 30*(2), 136–145. DOI: 10.1111/j.1477-8947.2006.00166.x

Caldera, H. T. S., Desha, C., & Dawes, L. (2019). Evaluating the enablers and barriers for successful implementation of sustainable business practice in 'lean' SMEs. *Journal of Cleaner Production, 218*, 575–590. DOI: 10.1016/j.jclepro.2019.01.239

Chatzopoulou, E., & de Kiewiet, A. (2021). Millennials' evaluation of corporate social responsibility: The wants and needs of the largest and most ethical generation. *Journal of Consumer Behaviour, 20*(3), 521–534. DOI: 10.1002/cb.1882

Chladek, N. 2019. Why You Need Sustainability in Your Business Strategy. Harvard Business School Online. https://online.hbs.edu/blog/post/business-sustainability-strategies

Cronin, J. J.Jr, Smith, J. S., Gleim, M. R., Ramirez, E., & Martinez, J. D. (2011). Green marketing strategies: An examination of stakeholders and the opportunities they present. *Journal of the Academy of Marketing Science*, *39*(1), 158–174. DOI: 10.1007/s11747-010-0227-0

Dangelico, R. M., & Vocalelli, D. (2017). "Green Marketing": An analysis of definitions, strategy steps, and tools through a systematic review of the literature. *Journal of Cleaner Production*, *165*, 1263–1279. DOI: 10.1016/j.jclepro.2017.07.184

De Brito, M. P., Dekker, R., & Flapper, S. D. P. (2005). *Reverse logistics: a review of case studies*. Springer Berlin Heidelberg.

Deloitte 2024 CXO Sustainability Report. (2024, September 13). Deloitte. https://www.deloitte.com/global/en/issues/climate/cxo-sustainability-report.html

Djafarova, E., & Foots, S. (2022). Exploring ethical consumption of generation Z: Theory of planned behaviour. *Young Consumers*, *23*(3), 413–431. DOI: 10.1108/YC-10-2021-1405

Dubey, R., Bag, S., Ali, S. S., & Venkatesh, V. G. (2013). Green purchasing is key to superior performance: An empirical study. *International Journal of Procurement Management*, *6*(2), 187–210. DOI: 10.1504/IJPM.2013.052469

Edwards, M. G. (2021). The growth paradox, sustainable development, and business strategy. *Business Strategy and the Environment*, *30*(7), 3079–3094. DOI: 10.1002/bse.2790

Elkington, J. (2004), "Enter the triple bottom line", available at: www.johnelkington.com/TBL- elkington-chapter.pdf (accessed September 28, 2024).

Ginsberg, J. M., & Bloom, P. N. (2004). Choosing the right green marketing strategy. *MIT Sloan Management Review*, *46*(1), 79–84.

Goodland, R., & Daly, H. (1996). Environmental sustainability: Universal and non-negotiable. *Ecological Applications : A Publication of the Ecological Society of America*, *6*(4), 1002–1017. DOI: 10.2307/2269583

Greenland, S. J. (2019). Future sustainability, innovation and marketing: A framework for understanding impediments to sustainable innovation adoption and corporate social responsibility. In *The Components of Sustainable Development: Engagement and Partnership* (pp. 63-80). Springer Singapore. DOI: 10.1007/978-981-13-9209-2_5

Gutsa, A. (2023, April 20). *Are sustainable products more expensive?* Ecoswap. https://ecoswap.uk/are-sustainable-products-more-expensive/

Hansson, A. M., Pedersen, E., Karlsson, N. P., & Weisner, S. E. (2023). Barriers and drivers for sustainable business model innovation based on a radical farmland change scenario. *Environment, Development and Sustainability, 25*(8), 8083–8106. DOI: 10.1007/s10668-022-02389-1

Hashmi, R. (2023). Business Performance Through Government Policies, Green Purchasing, and Reverse Logistics: Business Performance and Green Supply Chain Practices. *South Asian Journal of Operations and Logistics, 2*(1), 1–10. DOI: 10.57044/SAJOL.2023.2.1.2301

IBM. (2021). Sustainability at a turning point. In https://www.ibm.com (WLJ&LVP4). https://www.ibm.com/downloads/cas/WLJ7LVP4

illuminem. (2023, May 9). *The three pillars of sustainability: Building a more resilient future*. https://illuminem.com/illuminemvoices/the-three-pillars-of-sustainability-building-a-more-resilient-future

India Retailing. (2023, December 19). *Heart and sole – Neeman's*. https://www.indiaretailing.com/2023/12/23/heart-and-sole-neemans/

Khan, S. A. R., Yu, Z., & Farooq, K. (2023). Green capabilities, green purchasing, and triple bottom line performance: Leading toward environmental sustainability. *Business Strategy and the Environment, 32*(4), 2022–2034. DOI: 10.1002/bse.3234

Kumar, P., Singh, R. K., & Kumar, V. (2021). Managing supply chains for sustainable operations in the era of industry 4.0 and circular economy: Analysis of barriers. *Resources, Conservation and Recycling, 164*, 105215. DOI: 10.1016/j.resconrec.2020.105215

Lobo, M. J., Pietriga, E., & Appert, C. (2015, April). An evaluation of interactive map comparison techniques. In *Proceedings of the 33rd annual ACM conference on human factors in computing systems* (pp. 3573-3582). DOI: 10.1145/2702123.2702130

Lüdeke-Freund, F. (2020). Sustainable entrepreneurship, innovation, and business models: Integrative framework and propositions for future research. *Business Strategy and the Environment, 29*(2), 665–681. DOI: 10.1002/bse.2396

Marketing Monk. (n.d.). *Neeman's Marketing Strategies that Led to $24.8M Valuation*. Marketing Monk. https://www.marketingmonk.so/p/neeman-s-marketing-strategies-that-led-to-24-8m-valuation

McKinsey. (2014). Profits with purpose: How organizing for sustainability can benefit the bottom line. In https://www.mckinsey.com/. https://www.mckinsey.com/~/media/McKinsey/Business%20Functions/Sustainability/Our%20Insights/Profits%20with%20purpose/Profits%20with%20Purpose.ashx

Min, H., & Galle, W. P. (1997). Green purchasing strategies: Trends and implications. *International Journal of Purchasing and Materials Management, 33*(2), 10–17. DOI: 10.1111/j.1745-493X.1997.tb00026.x

Moeve. (2024, March 19). Sustainable consumers are willing to pay more for green products. *Moeve Global.* https://www.moeveglobal.com/en/planet-energy/environment/sustainable-consumers-are-willing-to-pay-more-for-green-products

Mudgill, A. (2024, April 1). Mamaearth shares: Risk-reward unfavourable for Honasa Consumer, target Rs 400, says Antique. *Business Today.* https://www.businesstoday.in/markets/company-stock/story/mamaearth-shares-risk-reward-unfavourable-for-honasa-consumer-target-rs-400-says-antique-423716-2024-04-01

Negri, M., Cagno, E., Colicchia, C., & Sarkis, J. (2021). Integrating sustainability and resilience in the supply chain: A systematic literature review and a research agenda. *Business Strategy and the Environment, 30*(7), 2858–2886. DOI: 10.1002/bse.2776

Nike - Diversity, Equity & Inclusion — NIKE, Inc. (n.d.). https://about.nike.com/en/impact/focus-areas/diversity-equity-inclusion

Nike Sustainability. Move to Zero. (n.d.). www.nike.com. https://www.nike.com/in/sustainability

no nasties+: BETTER CLOTHES + BETTER PLANET. (n.d.). https://www.nonasties.in/. Retrieved October 2, 2024, from https://www.nonasties.in/pages/for-the-planet

Plc, U. (2024, September 6). Why is sustainability important for business? *Unilever.* https://www.unilever.com/news/news-search/2023/why-is-sustainability-important-for-business/

Rahman, S. U., & Nguyen-Viet, B. (2023). Towards sustainable development: Coupling green marketing strategies and consumer perceptions in addressing greenwashing. *Business Strategy and the Environment, 32*(4), 2420–2433. DOI: 10.1002/bse.3256

Reinhardt, F. L. (1998). Environmental product differentiation: Implications for corporate strategy. *California Management Review, 40*(4), 43–73. DOI: 10.2307/41165964

Rodríguez-Ibeas, R. (2007). Environmental product differentiation and environmental awareness. *Environmental and Resource Economics, 36*(2), 237–254. DOI: 10.1007/s10640-006-9026-y

Rubio, S., Chamorro, A., & Miranda, F. J. (2008). Characteristics of the research on reverse logistics (1995–2005). *International Journal of Production Research, 46*(4), 1099–1120. DOI: 10.1080/00207540600943977

Saith, A. (2006). From universal values to millennium development goals: Lost in translation. *Development and Change, 37*(6), 1167–1199. DOI: 10.1111/j.1467-7660.2006.00518.x

Saner, R., Yiu, L., & Nguyen, M. (2020). Monitoring the SDGs: Digital and social technologies to ensure citizen participation, inclusiveness and transparency. *Development Policy Review, 38*(4), 483–500. DOI: 10.1111/dpr.12433

Sankar, S. (2023, February 7). The challenge of sustainable fashion. *Times of India Blog*. https://timesofindia.indiatimes.com/blogs/voices/the-challenge-of-sustainable-fashion/

Seidel, S., Recker, J., Pimmer, C., & Brocke, J. V. (2010). Enablers and barriers to the organizational adoption of sustainable business practices.

Sen, S. (2024, May 23). MamaEarth Parent faces six times more cases than Patanjali before ad regulator. *NDTV Profit*. https://www.ndtvprofit.com/business/mamaearth-parent-faces-six-times-more-cases-than-patanjali-before-ad-regulator

Sendlhofer, T., & Tolstoy, D. (2022). How employees shape CSR transparency: A sensemaking perspective. *Journal of Business Research, 150*, 268–278. DOI: 10.1016/j.jbusres.2022.05.074

Seuring, B. M., & Muller, M. (2008). From a literature review to a conceptual framework for sustainable supply chain management. *Journal of Cleaner Production, 16*(15), 1699–1710. DOI: 10.1016/j.jclepro.2008.04.020

STYLISHLY SUSTAINABLE - A Social movement through a Fashion brand. (2023, December 31). AIM2Flourish. https://aim2flourish.com/innovations/stylishly-sustainable-a-social-movement-through-a-fashion-brand

Sustainable Materials. (n.d.). Nike.com. https://www.nike.com/in/sustainability/materials

Team, I. (2024, January 30). Sustainable footwear brand Neeman's reports Rs 69 crore revenue in FY23; Losses stood at Rs 34 crore. *Indian Startup News*. https://indianstartupnews.com/news/sustainable-footwear-brand-neemans-reports-rs-69-crore-revenue-in-fy23-2407612

Testa, F., Pretner, G., Iovino, R., Bianchi, G., Tessitore, S., & Iraldo, F. (2021). Drivers to green consumption: A systematic review. *Environment, Development and Sustainability*, *23*(4), 4826–4880. DOI: 10.1007/s10668-020-00844-5

The importance of sustainability in Business | HBS Online. (2019, November 6). Business Insights Blog. https://online.hbs.edu/blog/post/business-sustainability-strategies

Turner, M., & Houston, P. (2009). Going green? Start with sourcing. *Supply Chain Management Review*, *13*(2), 14–21.

Waage, S. A., Geiser, K., Irwin, F., Weissman, A. B., Bertolucci, M. D., Fisk, P., Basile, G., Cowan, S., Cauley, H., & McPherson, A. (2005). Fitting together the building blocks for sustainability: A revised model for integrating ecological, social, and financial factors into business decision-making. *Journal of Cleaner Production*, *13*(12), 1145–1163. DOI: 10.1016/j.jclepro.2004.06.003

Williams, A. (2024, August 20). Guide to sustainable business practices in 2024. https://blog.shorts.uk.com/. https://blog.shorts.uk.com/sustainable-business-practices

Chapter 16
Understanding the AI-Productivity Paradox

Jaya Gupta
http://orcid.org/0000-0001-8496-8438
Birla Institute of Management Technology, India

ABSTRACT

Artificial Intelligence (AI) has been growing exponentially to become an integral part of the business ecosystem. AI could be instrumental in an exponential increase in productivity, encouraging investment and promoting business growth. However, AI as a catalyst for instant productivity increase has been a topic of debate within the business and academic community. There is a general understanding about the negative and positive effects of AI on productivity, it is still unclear how the productivity paradox manifests in this domain at the employee level and what could be some strategies and interventions devised by organizations to assist in minimizing the immediate negative slump in employee performance and to bring about the performance resurgence. The initial implementation of AI technologies could bring about a measurable decline in productivity, which is followed by a recovery and subsequent surge in productivity. he trajectory of exponential productivity and unprecedented efficiency is possible for an organization post taming the productivity paradox.

INTRODUCTION

Artificial Intelligence (AI) has been growing exponentially to become an integral part of the business ecosystem. Along with automating simple tasks, it is being increasingly used to perform complex tasks, which can have large impact on productivity(Gao & Feng, 2023). Artificial intelligence (AI) is an umbrella term for different strategies and techniques for making machines more human-like. It

DOI: 10.4018/979-8-3373-5437-8.ch016

includes diverse technologies that allow computers to perform tasks that would require human intellectual capabilities for performing problem-solving tasks(Tambe et al., 2019). Computer systems that perform numerous complex tasks historically reserved for human activity, such as reasoning, decision making or problem solving, are called artificial intelligence.

AI could be instrumental in an exponential increase in productivity, encouraging investment and promoting business growth as it improves its performance over time autonomously. In the last decade, there has been increasing use of AI in the workplaces. In order to stay competitive, companies are relying on machine learning algorithms to advanced generative AI technologies (Holmström & Carroll, 2024). A company's productivity is increased in numerous ways with AI integration. The predictive analyses using machine learning helps in automation of tasks, analyzing vast datasets to identify patterns to create ideas and innovations that may not be possible manually and solve difficult problems(Czarnitzki et al., 2023). AI is an effective tool to enhance efficiency, reduce errors and making data-driven decisions. In business, it has been effectively used to automate tasks that would have been done – by humans – such as customer service, lead generation, fraud detection and quality control.

MAXIMIZING AI IMPACT ON EMPLOYEE PRODUCTIVITY

Implementing AI into operations of an organizations has become compulsory. By incorporating AI into the current systems and processes, an organization can achieve workflow improvements, resulting in increased efficiency. The integration of AI in the operations brings about huge savings in time. The automation process is becoming more intelligent and provides an additional advantage of instant data-processing. The advanced algorithms are used to ensure that the analysis and interpretation of data is completed fast and is accurate. Data-Management using AI involves the process of gathering, organizing, and retrieving results by machine to provide valuable insights to managers. The consequent resource optimization can help in creating a productive ecosystem within the organization. AI helps in making insightful decision-making by providing extensive and precise information, allowing them to make well-informed decisions supported by data-driven evidence.

Global Gross Domestic Product is expected to experience a 14% increase by 2030 due to the use of AI. The global AI market's worth, USD 136.55 billion and USD 196.6 billion in 2022 and 2023, respectively, is expected to grow at a compound annual growth of 37.3% from 2023 to 2030. Tech giants' research and innovation drive advanced technology adoption in automotive, healthcare, retail, finance, and manufacturing. As per Goldman Sachs Economics Research, with AI investments rising rapidly, it could significantly impact GDP and societal well-being. AI should be regarded as an additional intangible capital within an organization's production function(Brynjolfsson et al., 2019).Similar to other types of factors of input, with an increase in investment in AI technologies, there might be a rise in productivity.

However, productivity increase fostered by AI has been a subject of contentious debate within the academic community (Brynjolfsson et al., 2019). Researchers have raised doubts about the potential of AI to generate instant productivity gains(Brynjolfsson et al., 2021). Theories and popular media narratives about the imminent global slowdown have raised doubts about the possible instantaneous increase in workforce productivity with AI integration(Brynjolfsson et al., 2019). A probable deceleration from 3.5% in 2022 to 3.0% in 2023 and 2.9% in 2024 has been forecasted for the projected trajectory of global economic growth.

AI AS A GENERAL-PURPOSE TECHNOLOGY (GPT)

AI is regarded as one of the essential general-purpose technologies (GPT) of the current era(Brynjolfsson & Mcafee, 2017) with rapid and extensive applications in broad range of industries. A technology is considered a GPT when it is pervasive, continuously improving over time, leading to numerous complementary innovations (Bresnahan & Trajtenberg, 1995). For example, electricity and personal computers, which, when embraced, saw investment booms of up to 2% of U.S. GDP (*Goldman Sachs*, 2023). Such technologies are frequently crucial components in a wide range of equipment or applications and serve as the foundation for developing new inventions. Interestingly, the dilemma of the modern productivity paradox, which was observed formerly in the context of earlier GPTs, also holds (Brynjolfsson et al., 2019). It aligns with the theoretical foundations of the productivity paradox theory. GPTs are implemented in a phased manner, and hence, the evident delays in seamless synergy and productivity optimization could be due to incomplete integration. This suggests that although firms are increasing their investments in advanced digital technologies such as AI, they need to achieve substantial benefits in productivity.

MODERN PRODUCTIVITY PARADOX

The productivity paradox was highlighted by Solow at the beginning of the computer age in 1987 when he stated, "*You can see the computer age everywhere but in the productivity statistics*" (Solow, 1987, p. 36). Despite the fast advancement of technology in all sectors, an initial decline in productivity was observed, with its benefits being generated with latency. The Solow Paradox seems to have re-emerged as the 'modern productivity paradox', as there was no apparent rise in productivity growth despite the escalating investments in cutting-edge technologies such as the Internet of Things, AI, etc.

Delays in adjustment, measurement issues, exaggerated expectations and mismanagement have been identified as the reasons for the productivity paradox in IT Schweikl & Obermaier (2020). Adjustment delays occur when a contemporary technologies have not yet facilitated an acceleration in productivity growth, the deceleration in productivity growth is not necessarily permanent and yields results in the long term (Brynjolfsson et al., 2019). There could be a time gap between the introduction of a new technology and achievement of the productivity increase. The existing processes and systems would be required to be adjusted and adapted to be able to perform effectively with the new technologies. Measurement issues state that despite productivity growth, its precise measurement may be compromised (Brynjolfsson et al., 2021). There could be challenges and complexities associated with unavailability of appropriate metrices that assess the amount of productivity gains. The standard measures have to be recalibrated to help the measurements. There could be some AI benefits that are implicit and emerge in the long term, and so they cannot be measured immediately after technology implementation.

Exaggerated expectation suggests that the expectations regarding the potential benefits and productivity gains with contemporary technology integration are magnified, given that they could fail to generate the expected enhancements in productivity and might not be as revolutionary (Gordon, 2017). The media articles often create unrealistic hopes of immediate productivity increases with AI technology integration, which can cause disappointments. Lastly, mismanagement highlights that although contemporary technologies can augment productivity growth, managers' effective implementation and utilization still need to be discovered (Schweikl & Obermaier, 2020). It is possible that the organization does not plan appropriately for handling the new technology. Lack of proper coordination amongst managers and the technical team could also be responsible for lower productivity and other associated problems.

PRODUCTIVITY PARADOX AND AI INTEGRATION:

AI introduction has been found to bring about a measurable but temporary decline in performance, which is followed by stronger growth output, revenue, and employment. According to a recent report of MIT, studies in manufacturing sector in US have suggested that a J-curve is observed – the initial implementation of AI technologies brings about a measurable decline in productivity, which is followed by a recovery and subsequent surge in productivity. The initial fall in productivity could be because of the non-alignment between new digital tools and traditional functional processes. Adjustment expenditure needs to be incurred in the form of employee trainings or workflow redesign are required. The extent of short-term losses varies across organizations. The established organizations experienced more extensive negative impacts of AI adoption. These could be due to the prevalence of long-drawn conventional processes, hierarchies, and legacy systems that could be difficult to break. While there is no doubt that the long-term potential of AI implementation is great for an organization, but the short-term returns are still not very clear. According to a McKinsey report published in 2025, more than 92 percent of companies are planning to increase their investments in AI over the next three years. The report highlights that almost all the companies are increasingly investing in AI. However, a major concern raised is that only 1 percent of business leaders regard their systems "mature" on AI implementation strategy, i.e. acknowledge its complete integration in the workflows and bringing about business results.

THE HUMAN FACTORS CONTRIBUTING TO SHORT-TERM PRODUCTIVITY LOSSES

AI is becoming a vital business enabler for organizations across industries. Human resource of an organization plays a very important role in successful implementation of new technologies as they adopt and adapt them in the workplace. Implementing AI technologies can provide substantial benefits to organizations but the success of AI adoption depends on the people who use it. There are various human factors that could be affecting its adoption and full-fledged implementations. Broadly, these factors can be classified as 'employee centric' and 'organizational centric'. (See Fig. 1)

Figure 1. Human Generated Short-term Productivity Losses

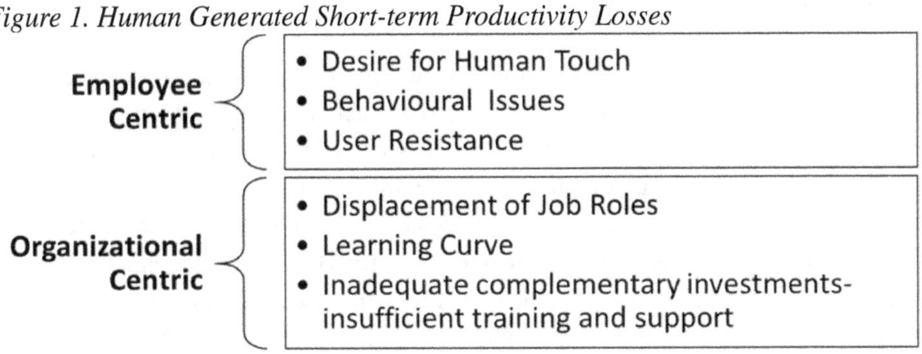

EMPLOYEE CENTRIC:

There could be various employee centric concerns which are hampering the smooth transition to an AI-enabled ecosystem. There can be several psychological and behavioral barriers that have negative effect on productivity. Employees tend to perceive the introduction of AI as a potential threat to their employment and are overwhelmed by the prospect of adapting to unfamiliar technologies. Employee scepticism and apprehensions might discourage the integration of technology. 'Desire for Human Touch' by the employees is pertinent and needs to be preserved. Research studies have reported that lack of human touch, employees' loss of control over jobs and the fear of losing jobs to AI are some concerns raised by the employees when organizations initiate this (Singh & Pandey, 2025). In education domain, parents have shared their preference for human instructors rather than AI –powered educational tools(Shao et al., 2025). Similarly, another study has concluded that the consumers report experiencing greater satisfaction when preferential treatment is given to them by a human agent compared to an AI agent(Choi et al., 2024). Achieving a harmonious equilibrium between AI-driven efficiency and human-centred care is essential while capitalizing on the benefits of new technology. Concerns about job security, apprehensions of increased workload and uncertainties can cause user resistance. There can be several factors that can cause the employee resistance. Resistance to change, fear of failure and uncertainties, lack of skills and job insecurity, could be some of the reasons. Introducing technological change can cause resistance to its acceptance and adoption by the employees by increasing employee insecurity and threat about AI use. This would in turn, hinder the company's ability to fully integrate AI into its operations.

ORGANIZATIONAL CENTRIC:

There can be various organization-centric factors can cause productivity loss in short-term. AI implementation leads to the mechanization of mundane and recurring work, displacing some job roles. Tasks readily defined, quantifiable, and can be performed using algorithms are more prone to automation. AI will replace human labour (displacement impact), but because AI increases productivity, it might also create new job roles (reinstatement effect) and increase labour demand in jobs unaffected by AI. The displaced workers due to automation of processes are re-integrated into other areas of employment. Therefore, some job roles may not be relevant in the new context. This can create insecurities and fears of job loss. These in turn have an adverse effect on employee morale and motivation, causing decreased productivity. The employee expertise would evolve, representing the learning curve, which must be factored in to experience productivity gains. The discrepancy between the skill requirements of the new job roles for the displaced workers and their current skill sets would require time and training to re-adjust their skill sets to new job role requirements. Consequently, these cause a slowdown in the productivity gains from automation in the short run. The AI learning curve refers to the progression of an individual's or organization's ability to understand and implement AI in their processes over time. Understanding the learning curve is important to determine measures to enhance performance of employees(Babashahi et al., 2024). Investments by an organization on employee training is necessary to equip them with the knowledge and skills needed to operate and maximize the potential of AI tools. Due to inadequate training being provided on AI, employees may not fully understand how to leverage AI to achieve the best results. By training employees, organizations can ensure they are making the most of AI's capabilities. Training programs can help in reducing employee fears as it equips the employees with the required knowledge and skills to successfully perform in the AI-enabled workplace. Since AI is a rapidly evolving technology, organizations must make sure that their employees engage in continuous learning to excel in the new tools, techniques, and applications as they evolve and emerge. Continuous training is essential to keeping the workforce up-to-date with the latest developments in AI.

MINDFUL HUMAN CAPITAL INVESTMENTS FOR UNLEASHING PRODUCTIVITY GAINS

There is a general understanding about the negative and positive effects of AI on productivity, it is still unclear how the productivity paradox manifests in this domain at the employee level and what could be some strategies and interventions devised by organizations to assist in minimizing the immediate negative slump in employee performance and to bring about the performance resurgence.

Investments in human capital can minimize short-term productivity concerns (Fig. 2). To achieve scalable deployment of technology, investments in upskilling employees are mandatory. The lack of training on the new technologies causes their underutilization and increased errors in operating them, thereby leading to insufficient productivity gains. Training is vital to ensure that the actual potential of the system can be unlocked, user adoption can be accelerated, productivity can be increased, support costs can be reduced, and people development can be facilitated. Complimentary investments in employee training, education and communication are mandatory for building in-house expertise. Also, buy-in from all stakeholders involved in operating the business -- from the directors and investors down to the last employee is critical. The importance of Artificial Intelligence lies in its ability to drive innovation, improve efficiency, and address complex challenges. By integrating AI responsibly and strategically, society can unlock its full potential, creating a future that benefits humanity as a whole. The trajectory of exponential productivity and unprecedented efficiency is possible for an organization post taming the productivity paradox.

Figure 2. Managing the User Generated AI-Productivity Paradox

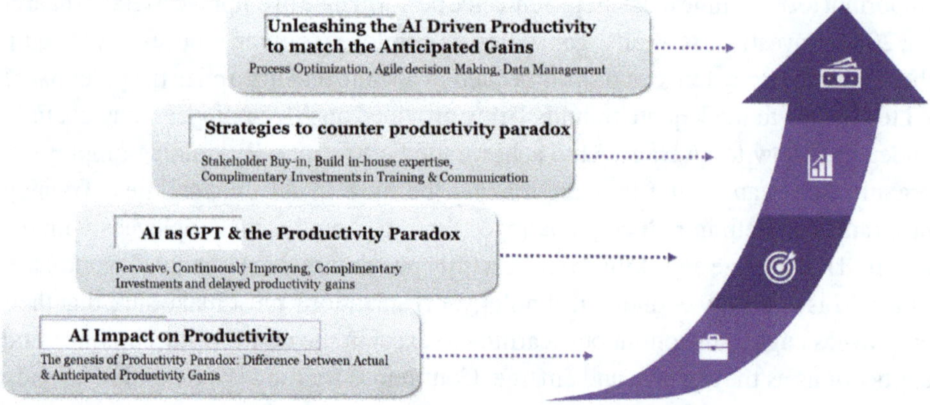

REFERENCES

AI investment forecast to approach $200 billion globally by 2025. (2023, November 22). Goldman Sachs. https://www.goldmansachs.com/intelligence/pages/ai-investment-forecast-to-approach-200-billion-globally-by-2025.html

Artificial Intelligence Market Size, Share, Growth Report 2030. (2023). https://www.grandviewresearch.com/industry-analysis/artificial-intelligence-ai-market

Babashahi, L., Barbosa, C. E., Lima, Y., Lyra, A., Salazar, H., Argôlo, M., de Almeida, M. A., & de Souza, J. M. (2024). AI in the Workplace: A Systematic Review of Skill Transformation in the Industry. *Administrative Sciences, 14*(6), 127. Advance online publication. DOI: 10.3390/admsci14060127

Bresnahan, T. F., & Trajtenberg, M. (1995). General purpose technologies 'Engines of growth'? *Journal of Econometrics, 65*(1), 83–108. DOI: 10.1016/0304-4076(94)01598-T

Brynjolfsson, E., & Mcafee, A. (2017). Artificial intelligence, for real. *Harvard Business Review, 1*, 1–31.

Brynjolfsson, E., Rock, D., & Syverson, C. (2019). Artificial Intelligence and the Modern Productivity Paradox: A Clash of Expectations and Statistics. In *The Economics of Artificial Intelligence* [University of Chicago Press. https://www.nber.org/books-and-chapters/economics-artificial-intelligence-agenda/artificial-intelligence-and-modern-productivity-paradox-clash-expectations-and-statistics]. *An Agenda*, •••, 23–57.

Brynjolfsson, E., Rock, D., & Syverson, C. (2021). The Productivity J-Curve: How Intangibles Complement General Purpose Technologies. *American Economic Journal. Macroeconomics, 13*(1), 333–372. DOI: 10.1257/mac.20180386

Budhwar, P., Chowdhury, S., Wood, G., Aguinis, H., Bamber, G. J., Beltran, J. R., Boselie, P., Lee Cooke, F., Decker, S., DeNisi, A., Dey, P. K., Guest, D., Knoblich, A. J., Malik, A., Paauwe, J., Papagiannidis, S., Patel, C., Pereira, V., Ren, S., & Varma, A. (2023b). Human resource management in the age of generative artificial intelligence: Perspectives and research directions on ChatGPT. *Human Resource Management Journal, 33*(3), 606–659. DOI: 10.1111/1748-8583.12524

Choi, S., Yi, Y., & Zhao, X. (2024). The human touch vs. AI efficiency: How perceived status, effort, and loyalty shape consumer satisfaction with preferential treatment. *Journal of Retailing and Consumer Services, 81*, 103969. DOI: 10.1016/j.jretconser.2024.103969

Comin, D., Quintana, J., Schmitz, T., & Trigari, A. (2022). *Measuring TFP: The role of profits, adjustment costs, and capacity utilization*. https://papers.ssrn.com/sol3/papers.cfm?abstract_id=4011738

Crafts, N. (2021). Artificial intelligence as a general-purpose technology: An historical perspective. *Oxford Review of Economic Policy*, *37*(3), 521–536. https://search.ebscohost.com/login.aspx?direct=true&profile=ehost&scope=site&authtype=crawler&jrnl=0266903X&AN=152633278&h=oIYqTIEHr158KjySAoVR7eMWjp3PD4fNeXREYeZLHG41cMtkj8Wh8cBp38a%2BvrbS3Zqsds1h7DLSxUUO0X0KJQ%3D%3D&crl=c. DOI: 10.1093/oxrep/grab012

Czarnitzki, D., Fernández, G. P., & Rammer, C. (2023). Artificial intelligence and firm-level productivity. *Journal of Economic Behavior & Organization*, *211*, 188–205. DOI: 10.1016/j.jebo.2023.05.008

Gao, X., & Feng, H. (2023). AI-Driven Productivity Gains: Artificial Intelligence and Firm Productivity. *Sustainability (Basel)*, *15*(11), 8934. Advance online publication. DOI: 10.3390/su15118934

Gordon, R. (2017). *The Rise and Fall of American Growth: The U.S. Standard of Living since the Civil War*. Princeton University Press., DOI: 10.1515/9781400888955

Holmström, J., & Carroll, N. (2024). How organizations can innovate with generative AI. *Business Horizons*. https://www.sciencedirect.com/science/article/pii/S0007681324000247

Schweikl, S., & Obermaier, R. (2020). Lessons from three decades of IT productivity research: Towards a better understanding of IT-induced productivity effects. *Management Review Quarterly*, *70*(4), 461–507. DOI: 10.1007/s11301-019-00173-6

Shao, A., Lu, Z., Zhong, B., Liu, S. Q., & Lu, W. (2025). Human touch vs. AI tech: Understanding user preferences in the future of education. *Computers in Human Behavior*, *164*, 108492. DOI: 10.1016/j.chb.2024.108492

Singh, A., & Pandey, J. (2025). Artificial intelligence applications in human resource management: It is a mixed bag! *International Journal of Productivity and Performance Management*, •••, 1–20. DOI: 10.1108/IJPPM-09-2024-0599

Solow, R. (1987). We'd better watch out. *New York Times Book Review*, 36.

Srivastav, S., Garg, V., & Elngar, A. A. (2022). The Impact of Artificial Intelligence for Comprehensive Growth Across the Globe. *Empowering Artificial Intelligence Through Machine Learning: New Advances and Applications*, 137.

Stanley, T. D., Doucouliagos, H., & Steel, P. (2018). DOES ICT GENERATE ECONOMIC GROWTH? A META-REGRESSION ANALYSIS. *Journal of Economic Surveys*, *32*(3), 705–726. DOI: 10.1111/joes.12211

Tambe, P., Cappelli, P., & Yakubovich, V. (2019). Artificial Intelligence in Human Resources Management: Challenges and a Path Forward.[·. *California Management Review*, *61*(4), 15–42. https://mitsloan.mit.edu/ideas-made-to-matter/productivity-paradox-ai-adoption-manufacturing-firms. DOI: 10.1177/0008125619867910

Compilation of References

Abuatwan, N. (2023). The Impact of Green Finance on the Sustainability Performance of the Banking Sector in Palestine: The Moderating Role of Female Presence. *Economies (Basel)*, *11*(10), 247. DOI: 10.3390/economies11100247

Acquah, E., Carbonari, L., Farcomeni, A., & Trovato, G. (2023). Institutions and economic development: New measurements and evidence. *Empirical Economics*, *65*(3), 1693–1728. DOI: 10.1007/s00181-023-02395-w

Adebayo, Y. A., Ikevuje, A. H., Kwakye, J. M., & Esiri, A. E. (2024). Balancing stakeholder interests in sustainable project management: A circular economy approach. *GSC Advanced Research and Reviews*, *20*(3), 286–297. DOI: 10.30574/gscarr.2024.20.3.0354

Adesoga, T. O., Patricia, O., Olaiya, E. P., Ajayi, O. D., & Dorcas, O. (2024). Review of reverse logistics practices and their impact on supply chain sustainability'. *International Journal of Scientific Research and Advances*, *12*(2), 45–55.

Aggarwal, P. (2013). Impact of corporate governance on corporate financial performance. *IOSR Journal of Business and Management*, *13*(3), 1–5. DOI: 10.9790/487X-1330105

Agrawal, S., Singh, R. K., & Murtaza, Q. (2015). A literature review and perspectives in reverse logistics. *Resources, Conservation and Recycling*, *97*, 76–92. DOI: 10.1016/j.resconrec.2015.02.009

AI investment forecast to approach $200 billion globally by 2025. (2023, November 22). Goldman Sachs. https://www.goldmansachs.com/intelligence/pages/ai-investment-forecast-to-approach-200-billion-globally-by-2025.html

Akhtaruzzaman, M., Banerjee, A. K., Ghardallou, W & Umar, Z. (2022). Is greenness an optimal hedge for sectoral stock indices? *Economic Modelling*. . econm od. 2022. 106030DOI: 10. 1016/j

Al Hammadi, T., & Nobanee, H. (2019). *FinTech and sustainability: A mini-review. SSRN.* DOI: 10.2139/ssrn.3500873

Al Lawati, H., & Hussainey, K. (2022). Does sustainable development goals disclosure affect corporate financial performance?'. *Sustainability (Basel), 14*(13), 7815. DOI: 10.3390/su14137815

Al-Abri, R., & Al-Balushi, Y. (2021). The role of corporate social responsibility in enhancing corporate reputation: Evidence from Oman. *Journal of Business Ethics, 162*(3), 789–805.

Alamgir, M., & Cheng, M.-C. (2023). Do Green Bonds Play a Role in Achieving Sustainability? *Sustainability (Basel), 15*(13), 10177. DOI: 10.3390/su151310177

Al-Hamadi, A., Khan, F., & Al-Kiyumi, M. (2020). Cultural alignment in CSR: A study of Omani businesses. *Corporate Governance and Social Responsibility Review, 18*(2), 155–172.

Ali, E., Anshari, M., Hamdan, M., Ahmad, N., & Surieshtino, Y. (2023). Green Finance for Sustainable Development: A Bibliographic Analysis. *2023 International Conference on Sustainable Islamic Business and Finance (SIBF)*, Bahrain, 46-49, DOI: 10.1109/SIBF60067.2023.10379915

Ali, M., Ullah, S., Ahmad, M. S., Cheok, M. Y., & Alenezi, H. (2023). Assessing the impact of green consumption behavior and green purchase intention among millennials toward sustainable environment. *Environmental Science and Pollution Research International, 30*(9), 23335–23347. DOI: 10.1007/s11356-022-23811-1 PMID: 36322356

Alim, O. (2024). Sustainable finance and economical profitability in Africa. *International Journal of Finance and Banking Research, 10*(1), 11–19. DOI: 10.11648/j.ijfbr.20241001.12

Allen, F., Gu, X., & Jagtiani, J. (2022). Fintech, Cryptocurrencies, and CBDC: Financial Structural Transformation in China. *Journal of International Money and Finance, 124*, 102625. DOI: 10.1016/j.jimonfin.2022.102625

Allwood, J. M. (2014). Squaring the Circular Economy: The Role of Recycling within a Hierarchy of Material Management Strategies. In Worrell, E., & Reuter, M. (Eds.), *Handbook of Recycling: State-of-the-Art for Practitioners* (pp. 445–477). Analysts, and Scientists. DOI: 10.1016/B978-0-12-396459-5.00030-1

Al-Maauli, S. S. (2023, April 1). Evaluating Corporate Social Responsibility reporting practices in the sultanate of Oman (2016 to 2018). Journal of Economic Administrative & Legal Sciences

Al-Maauli, S. S. (2023).. . *Evaluating Corporate Social Responsibility Reporting Practices in the Sultanate of Oman, 7*(4), 134–153.

Alqudah, H., Akour, I., Al-Debei, M. M., & Al-Lozi, E. (2024). Integration of fintech with ESG principles: Emerging clusters and implications. *Journal of Sustainable Finance & Investment, 14*(2), 215–232.

Amba, M. S. (2014). Corporate governance and firms' financial performance. *Journal of Academic and Business Ethics, 8*(1), 1–11.

Amel-Zadeh, A., & Serafeim, G. (2018). Why and how investors use ESG information: Evidence from a global survey. *Financial Analysts Journal, 74*(3), 87–103. DOI: 10.2469/faj.v74.n3.2

Anantharajah, K. (2019). Governing climate finance in Fiji: Barriers, complexity and interconnectedness. *Sustainability (Basel), 11*(12), 3414. Advance online publication. DOI: 10.3390/su11123414

Anantharajah, K., & Setyowati, A. B. (2022). Beyond promises: Realities of climate finance justice and energy transitions in Asia and the Pacific. *Energy Research & Social Science, 89*, 102550. DOI: 10.1016/j.erss.2022.102550

Andreeva, O. V., Vovchenko, N. G., Ivanova, O. B., & Kostoglodova, E. D. (2018). *Green Finance: Trends and Financial Regulation Prospects (world)*. Emerald Publishing Limited., DOI: 10.1108/S1569-375920180000100003

Anshari, M., Almunawar, M. N., Masri, M., & Hamdan, M. (2019). Digital marketplace and FinTech to support agricultural sustainability. *Energy Procedia, 156*, 234–238. DOI: 10.1016/j.egypro.2018.11.134

Antoncic, M., Bekaert, G., Rothenberg, R. V., & Noguer, M. (2020). Sustainable investment: Exploring the linkage between alpha, ESG, and SDGs. SSRN Electronic Journal. DOI: 10.2139/ssrn.3623459

Apouey, B., Roulet, A., Solal, I., & Stabile, M. (2020). Gig workers during the COVID-19 crisis in France: Financial precarity and mental well-being. *Journal of Urban Health : Bulletin of the New York Academy of Medicine, 97*(6), 776–795. DOI: 10.1007/s11524-020-00480-4 PMID: 32964368

Arner, D. W., Barberis, J., & Buckey, R. P. (2016). FinTech, RegTech, and the reconceptualization of financial regulation. *Nw. J. Int'l L. & Bus., 37*, 371.

Arner, D. W., Barberis, J., & Buckley, R. P. (2016). The evolution of FinTech: A new post-crisis paradigm? *Georgetown Journal of International Law, 47*, 1271–1319.

Arner, D. W., Buckley, R. P., Dahdal, A. M., & Zetzsche, D. A. (2021). Digital finance, COVID-19 and existential sustainability crises: Setting the agenda for the 2020s. (University of Hong Kong Faculty of Law Research Paper No. 2021/001; UNSW Law Research Paper No. 21-16; University of Luxembourg Law WPS 2021-003). *SSRN*. https://ssrn.com/abstract=3783605

Artificial Intelligence Market Size, Share, Growth Report 2030. (2023). https://www.grandviewresearch.com/industry-analysis/artificial-intelligence-ai-market

Azam, M., Hunjra, A. I., & Hassan, M. K. (2024). The role of financing in achieving sustainable development goals: Economic and legal implications. In *Green Finance and Sustainable Development Goals* (pp. 299–316). World Scientific., DOI: 10.1142/9781800614482_0011

Azimi, H., & Amiri, V. (2018). Investigating the Effect of Market Orientation on Environmental Performance with the Mediating Role of Green Supply Chain Management Strategies. Case study: Khales Sazan Rooy Company. *Journal of Environmental Management & Tourism*, *9*(3 (27)), 581–590. DOI: 10.14505//jemt.9.3(27).18

Baatz, C. (2018). Climate adaptation finance and justice. A criteria-based assessment of policy instruments. *Analyse & Kritik*, *40*(1), 73–105. DOI: 10.1515/auk-2018-0004

Babashahi, L., Barbosa, C. E., Lima, Y., Lyra, A., Salazar, H., Argôlo, M., de Almeida, M. A., & de Souza, J. M. (2024). AI in the Workplace: A Systematic Review of Skill Transformation in the Industry. *Administrative Sciences*, *14*(6), 127. Advance online publication. DOI: 10.3390/admsci14060127

Babbitt, C. W., Gaustad, G., Fisher, A., Chen, W. Q., & Liu, G. (2018). Closing the loop on circular economy research: From theory to practice and back again. *Resources, Conservation and Recycling*, *135*, 1–2. DOI: 10.1016/j.resconrec.2018.04.012

Bakker, C. A., den Hollander, M. C., van Hinte, E., & Zljlstra, Y. (2014). *ProductsThat Last - Product design for circular business models*. TU Delft Library.

Banerjee, R. (2020). Digital transformation in retail: India's e-commerce growth. *Journal of Technological Advancements*.

Bao, X., Sadiq, M., Tye, W., & Zhang, J. (2024). The impact of environmental, social, and governance (ESG) rating disparities on corporate risk: The mediating role of financing constraints. *Journal of Environmental Management*, *371*, 123113. DOI: 10.1016/j.jenvman.2024.123113 PMID: 39481154

Barker, R., Eccles, R. G., & Serafeim, G. (2020, December). The future of ESG is accounting. Harvard Business Review. https://hbr.org/2020/12/the-future-of-esg-is-accounting

Barney, J. (1991). Firm Resources and Sustained Competitive Advantage. *Journal of Management, 17*(1), 99–120. DOI: 10.1177/014920639101700108

Barney, J. B., & Harrison, J. S. (2020). Stakeholder theory at the crossroads. *Business & Society, 59*(2), 203–212. DOI: 10.1177/0007650318796792

Barokah, I. N., & Bandiyono, A. (2025). *The Dynamics of Green Bond Effectiveness in Achieving Sustainable Development: A Comparative Study with a Scoping Review Approach. JAE.* JURNAL AKUNTANSI DAN EKONOMI., DOI: 10.29407/jae.v10i1.24792

Bashar, S., Wang, D., & Rafiq, M. (2023). Adoption of green supply chain management in developing countries: Role of consumer cooperation, eco-design, and green marketing. *Environmental Science and Pollution Research International, 30*(40), 92594–92610. DOI: 10.1007/s11356-023-28881-3

Bassi, E., Lustenberger, M., & Letina, S. (2025). Blockchain-based voluntary carbon market: Strategic insights into network structure. *Frontiers in Blockchain, 8*, 1603695. Advance online publication. DOI: 10.3389/fbloc.2025.1603695

Beasley, M. S., Carcello, J. V., Hermanson, D. R., & Lapides, P. D. (2000). Fraudulent financial reporting: Industry traits and corporate governance mechanisms. *Accounting Horizons, 14*(4), 441–454. DOI: 10.2308/acch.2000.14.4.441

Belleflamme, P., Lambert, T., & Schwienbacher, A. (2014). Crowdfunding: Tapping the right crowd. *Journal of Business Venturing, 29*(5), 585–609. DOI: 10.1016/j.jbusvent.2013.07.003

Benaim, C. A., & Raftis, L. (2008). The Social Dimension of Sustainable Development: Guidance and Application: Thesis submitted for completion of Master of Strategic Leadership towards Sustainability, Blekinge Institute of Technology, Karlskrona, Sweden

Bennich, T., Persson, A., Beaussart, R., Allen, C., & Malekpour, S. (2023). Recurring patterns of SDG interlinkages and how they can advance the 2030 Agenda. *One Earth, 6*(11), 1465–1476. 10.1016/j.oneear.2023.10.008. DOI: 10.1016/j.oneear.2023.10.008

Beschloss, A., & Mashayekhi, M. (n.d.). *A greener future for finance: Green bonds offer lessons for sustainable finance*. UNCTAD.

Beske, P., Land, A., & Seuring, S. (2014). Sustainable supply chain management practices and dynamic capabilities in the food industry: A critical analysis of the literature. *International Journal of Production Economics, 152*, 131–143. DOI: 10.1016/j.ijpe.2013.12.026

Bhandary, R. R., Gallagher, K. S., Jaffe, A. M., Myslikova, Z., Zhang, F., Petrova, M., Barrionuevo, A., Fontaine, G., Fuentes, J. L., Karani, P., Martinez, D., Seitlheko, L., Staicu, D., Ullah, N., & Yimere, A. (2022). Demanding development: The political economy of climate finance and overseas investments from China. *Energy Research & Social Science*, *93*(September), 102816. DOI: 10.1016/j.erss.2022.102816

Bhandary, R. R., Gallagher, K. S., & Zhang, F. (2021). Climate finance policy in practice: A review of the evidence. *Climate Policy*, *21*(4), 529–545. DOI: 10.1080/14693062.2020.1871313

Bhatnagar, M., Taneja, S., & Özen, E. (2022). A wave of green start-ups in India - The study of green finance as a support system for sustainable entrepreneurship. *Green Finance*, *4*(2), 253–273. DOI: 10.3934/GF.2022012

Blomsma, F., & Brennan, G. (2017). The Emergence of circular economy: A new framing around prolonging resource productivity. *Journal of Industrial Ecology*, *21*(3), 603–614. DOI: 10.1111/jiec.12603

Bocken, N. M., & Geradts, T. H. (2020). Barriers and drivers to sustainable business model innovation: Organization design and dynamic capabilities. *Long Range Planning*, *53*(4), 101950. DOI: 10.1016/j.lrp.2019.101950

Boudreau, J. W., & Ramstad, P. M. (2005). Talentship, talent segmentation, and sustainability: A new HR decision science paradigm for a new strategy definition. Human Resource Management: Published in Cooperation with the School of Business Administration, The University of Michigan and in alliance with the Society of Human Resources Management, 44(2), 129-136.

Boulding, K. E. 1966. The economics of the coming spaceship Earth, Sixth Resources for the Future Forum on Environmental Quality in a Growing Economy, Wash- ington, D.C

Bowen, A., Campiglio, E., & Herreras Martinez, S. (2017). An ‘equal effort’ approach to assessing the North–South climate finance gap. *Climate Policy*, *17*(2), 231–245. DOI: 10.1080/14693062.2015.1094728

Braun, V., & Clarke, V. (2006). Using thematic analysis in psychology. *Qualitative Research in Psychology*, *3*(2), 77–101. DOI: 10.1191/1478088706qp063oa

Brears, R. C. (2024). How Blockchain Technology is Transforming Climate Change Initiatives: Carbon Credits, Renewable Energy, and Supply Chains. *Medium*. https://medium.com/global-climate-solutions/how-blockchain-technology-is-transforming-climate-change-initiatives-carbon-credits-renewable-9941ca4523eb

Bresnahan, T. F., & Trajtenberg, M. (1995). General purpose technologies 'Engines of growth'? *Journal of Econometrics*, *65*(1), 83–108. DOI: 10.1016/0304-4076(94)01598-T

Breuer, H., Fichter, K., Lüdeke-Freund, F., & Tiemann, I. (2018). Sustainability-oriented business model development: Principles, criteria and tools. *International Journal of Entrepreneurial Venturing*, *10*(2), 256–286. DOI: 10.1504/IJEV.2018.092715

Bridging digital divides in G20 countries. (2021). DOI: 10.1787/35c1d850-en

Broadstock, D. C., Chan, K., Cheng, L. T. W., & Wang, X. W. (2021). The role of ESG performance during times of financial crisis: Evidence from COVID-19 in China. *Finance Research Letters*, *38*, 101716. DOI: 10.1016/j.frl.2020.101716 PMID: 32837385

Brodhag, C., & Talière, S. (2006, May). Sustainable development strategies: Tools for policy coherence. [). Oxford, UK: Blackwell Publishing Ltd.]. *Natural Resources Forum*, *30*(2), 136–145. DOI: 10.1111/j.1477-8947.2006.00166.x

Brown, L. D., & Caylor, M. L. (2004). Corporate governance study: The correlation between corporate governance and company performance. Institutional Shareholder Services, 1–15.

Brown, B. J., Hanson, M. E., Liverman, D. M., & Merideth, R. W.Jr. (1987). Global Sustainability: Towards Definition. *Environmental Management*, *2*(6), 713–719. DOI: 10.1007/BF01867238

Brundtland, G. H. (1987). *Our common future: Report of the 1987 World Commission on Environment and Development*. United Nations.

Brunner, S., & Enting, K. (2014). Climate finance: A transaction cost perspective on the structure of state-to-state transfers. *Global Environmental Change*, *27*(1), 138–143. DOI: 10.1016/j.gloenvcha.2014.05.005

Brynjolfsson, E., & Mcafee, A. (2017). Artificial intelligence, for real. *Harvard Business Review*, *1*, 1–31.

Brynjolfsson, E., Rock, D., & Syverson, C. (2018). *Artificial intelligence and the modern productivity paradox: A clash of expectations and statistics (No. w24001)*. National Bureau of Economic Research.

Brynjolfsson, E., Rock, D., & Syverson, C. (2019). Artificial Intelligence and the Modern Productivity Paradox: A Clash of Expectations and Statistics. In *The Economics of Artificial Intelligence* [University of Chicago Press. https://www.nber.org/books-and-chapters/economics-artificial-intelligence-agenda/artificial-intelligence-and-modern-productivity-paradox-clash-expectations-and-statistics]. *An Agenda*, •••, 23–57.

Brynjolfsson, E., Rock, D., & Syverson, C. (2021). The Productivity J-Curve: How Intangibles Complement General Purpose Technologies. *American Economic Journal. Macroeconomics*, *13*(1), 333–372. DOI: 10.1257/mac.20180386

Buchholz, W., & Rübbelke, D. (2021). Overstraining international climate finance: When conflicts of objectives threaten its success. *International Journal of Climate Change Strategies and Management*, *13*(4–5), 547–563. DOI: 10.1108/IJCCSM-06-2021-0071

Budhwar, P., Chowdhury, S., Wood, G., Aguinis, H., Bamber, G. J., Beltran, J. R., Boselie, P., Lee Cooke, F., Decker, S., DeNisi, A., Dey, P. K., Guest, D., Knoblich, A. J., Malik, A., Paauwe, J., Papagiannidis, S., Patel, C., Pereira, V., Ren, S., & Varma, A. (2023b). Human resource management in the age of generative artificial intelligence: Perspectives and research directions on ChatGPT. *Human Resource Management Journal*, *33*(3), 606–659. DOI: 10.1111/1748-8583.12524

Busch, T., Bruce-Clark, P., Derwall, J., Eccles, R., Hebb, T., Hoepner, A., Klein, C., Krueger, P., Paetzold, F., Scholtens, B., & Weber, O. (2021). Impact investments: A call for (re)orientation. *SN Business & Economics*, *1*(2), 33. Advance online publication. DOI: 10.1007/s43546-020-00033-6

Business Standard. (2026). *Quick commerce pushes the limits on grocery delivery*. https://www.business-standard.com

Byard, D., Li, Y., & Weintrop, J. (2006). Corporate governance and the quality of financial analysts' information. *Journal of Accounting and Public Policy*, *25*(5), 609–625. DOI: 10.1016/j.jaccpubpol.2006.07.003

Caldera, H. T. S., Desha, C., & Dawes, L. (2019). Evaluating the enablers and barriers for successful implementation of sustainable business practice in 'lean' SMEs. *Journal of Cleaner Production*, *218*, 575–590. DOI: 10.1016/j.jclepro.2019.01.239

Calliari, E., Castellari, S., Davis, M., Linnerooth-Bayer, J., Martin, J., Mysiak, J., Pastor, T., Ramieri, E., Scolobig, A., Sterk, M., Veerkamp, C., Wendling, L., & Zandersen, M. (2022). Building climate resilience through nature-based solutions in Europe: A review of enabling knowledge, finance and governance frameworks. *Climate Risk Management*, *37*(July), 100450. DOI: 10.1016/j.crm.2022.100450

Carbon Tracker Initiative. (2025, June 30). New NGFS short-term scenarios for central banks & supervisors [News release]. https://carbontracker.org/new-ngfs-short-term-scenarios-for-central-banks-supervisors/

CBIRC. (2020), "The Provisional Rules on Internet Loans of Commercial Banks", July 17, 2020, http://www.cbirc.gov.cn/cn/ view/pages/ItemDetail.html?docId=916525&itemId=928

Cen, T., & He, R. (2018). FinTech, green finance and sustainable development. In *Proceedings of the International Conference on Management, Economics, Education, Arts and Humanities* (pp. 222–225). Atlantis Press.

Central Bank of the Russian Federation. (2021). BRICS Digital Financial Inclusion Report.

Chaaben, N., Elleuch, Z., Hamdi, B., & Kahouli, B. (2022). Green economy performance and sustainable development achievement: Empirical evidence from Saudi Arabia. *Environment, Development and Sustainability, 26*(1), 549–564. Advance online publication. DOI: 10.1007/s10668-022-02722-8 PMID: 36320556

Chalaki, P., Didar, H., & Riahinezhad, M. (2012). Corporate governance attributes and financial reporting quality: Empirical evidence from Iran. *International Journal of Business and Social Science, 3*(15), 223–229.

Chang, S., Hu, B., & He, X. (2019). Supply chain coordination in the context of green marketing efforts and capacity expansion. *Sustainability (Basel), 11*(20), 5734. DOI: 10.3390/su11205734

Chatzopoulou, E., & de Kiewiet, A. (2021). Millennials' evaluation of corporate social responsibility: The wants and needs of the largest and most ethical generation. *Journal of Consumer Behaviour, 20*(3), 521–534. DOI: 10.1002/cb.1882

Chaudhury, A. (2020). Role of intermediaries in shaping climate finance in developing countries-lessons from the green climate fund. *Sustainability (Basel), 12*(12), 5507. Advance online publication. DOI: 10.3390/su12145507

Chelminski, K. (2022). Climate Finance Effectiveness: A Comparative Analysis of Geothermal Development in Indonesia and the Philippines. *Journal of Environment & Development, 31*(2), 139–167. DOI: 10.1177/10704965211070034 PMID: 35557746

Chen, J. (2023, October 31). Corporate governance: Definition, principles, models, and examples. Investopedia. https://www.investopedia.com/terms/c/corporategovernance.asp

Chen, D., Haiqing, H., & Chang, C. P. (2023a). Green finance, environment regulation, and industrial green transformation for corporate social responsibility. *Corporate Social Responsibility and Environmental Management*, *2476*(5), 2166–2181. Advance online publication. DOI: 10.1002/csr.2476

Chen, M. K., Chevalier, J. A., Rossi, P. E., & Currier, L. (2023). Suppliers and Demanders of Flexibility: The Demographics of Gig Work (Vol. 6, pp. 2735-2794). Technical Report, Working Paper 2021., Peter E Rossi, Judith A Chevalier, and Emily Oehlsen,"The value of flexible work: Evidence from Uber drivers,". *Journal of Political Economy*, *2019*, 127.

Chen, S., Song, Y., & Gao, P. (2023). Environmental, social, and governance (ESG) performance and financial outcomes: Analyzing the impact of ESG on financial performance. *Journal of Environmental Management*, *345*, 118829. DOI: 10.1016/j.jenvman.2023.118829 PMID: 37688968

Chen, S., & Xie, G. (2023). Assessing the linkage among green finance, technology, and education expenditure: Evidence from G7 economies. *Environmental Science and Pollution Research International*, *30*(17), 50332–50345. Advance online publication. DOI: 10.1007/s11356-023-25625-1 PMID: 36795206

Chen, Z., Hao, X., & Chen, F. (2023b). Green innovation and enterprise reputation value. *Business Strategy and the Environment*, *32*(4), 1698–1718. DOI: 10.1002/bse.3213

Chertow, M. R. (2001). The IPAT Equation and Its Variants: Changing Views of Technology and Environmental Impact. *Journal of Industrial Ecology*, *4*(4), 13–29. DOI: 10.1162/10881980052541927

Chipriyanov, M., Chipriyanova, G., Krasteva-Hristova, R., Atanasov, A., & Luchkov, K. (2024). Researching the Impact of Corporate Social Responsibility on Economic Growth and Inequality: Methodological Aspects. *Journal of Risk and Financial Management*, *17*(12), 546. DOI: 10.3390/jrfm17120546

Chladek, N. 2019. Why You Need Sustainability in Your Business Strategy. Harvard Business School Online. https://online.hbs.edu/blog/post/business-sustainability-strategies

Choi, S., Yi, Y., & Zhao, X. (2024). The human touch vs. AI efficiency: How perceived status, effort, and loyalty shape consumer satisfaction with preferential treatment. *Journal of Retailing and Consumer Services*, *81*, 103969. DOI: 10.1016/j.jretconser.2024.103969

Chueca Vergara, C., & Ferruz Agudo, L. (2021). FinTech, business sustainability, and green finance: A systematic literature review. *Sustainability, 13*(15), 8451.

Chu, H., Hongjuan, Y., Chong, Y., & Li, L. (2023). Does the development of digital finance curb carbon emissions? Evidence from county data in China. *Environmental Science and Pollution Research International, 30*(17), 49237–49254. Advance online publication. DOI: 10.1007/s11356-023-25659-5 PMID: 36773252

Clark, W., & Crutzen, P. 2005. Science for global sustainability: toward a new paradigm. KSG Working Paper. 120, 1–28.

Clark, R., Reed, J., & Sunderland, T. (2018). Bridging funding gaps for climate and sustainable development: Pitfalls, progress and potential of private finance. *Land Use Policy, 71*(February), 335–346. DOI: 10.1016/j.landusepol.2017.12.013

Climate Policy Initiative. (2021). Global Landscape of Climate Finance 2021. https://www.climatepolicyinitiative.org/publication/global-landscape-of-climate-finance-2021/

Cohen, M. J. (2006). Ecological modernization and its discontents: The American environmental movement's resistance to an innovation-driven future. *Futures, 38*(5), 528–547. DOI: 10.1016/j.futures.2005.09.002

Comin, D., Quintana, J., Schmitz, T., & Trigari, A. (2022). *Measuring TFP: The role of profits, adjustment costs, and capacity utilization.* https://papers.ssrn.com/sol3/papers.cfm?abstract_id=4011738

Corbin, J., & Strauss, A. (2008). *Basics of qualitative research: Techniques and procedures for developing grounded theory* (3rd ed.). Sage. DOI: 10.4135/9781452230153

Cort, T. (2018). Incentivizing the direction of multi-capital toward inclusive capitalism. *Journal of Sustainable Finance & Investment, 8*(3), 203–212. DOI: 10.1080/20430795.2018.1423850

Corvellec, H., & Stal, H. I. (2019). Qualification as corporate activism: How Swedish apparel retailers attach circular fashion qualities to take-back systems. *Scandinavian Journal of Management, 35*(3), 101046. DOI: 10.1016/j.scaman.2019.03.002

Corvellec, H., Stowell, A. F., & Johansson, N. (2022). Critiques of the circular economy [April.]. *Journal of Industrial Ecology, 26*(2), 421–432. DOI: 10.1111/jiec.13187

Crafts, N. (2021). Artificial intelligence as a general-purpose technology: An historical perspective. *Oxford Review of Economic Policy, 37*(3), 521–536. https://search.ebscohost.com/login.aspx?direct=true&profile=ehost&scope=site&authtype=crawler&jrnl=0266903X&AN=152633278&h=oIYqTIEHr158KjySAoVR7eMWjp3PD4fNeXREYeZLHG41cMtkj8Wh8cBp38a%2BvrbS3Zqsds1h7DLSxUUO0X0KJQ%3D%3D&crl=c. DOI: 10.1093/oxrep/grab012

Cronin, J. J.Jr, Smith, J. S., Gleim, M. R., Ramirez, E., & Martinez, J. D. (2011). Green marketing strategies: An examination of stakeholders and the opportunities they present. *Journal of the Academy of Marketing Science, 39*(1), 158–174. DOI: 10.1007/s11747-010-0227-0

Crossley, R. M., Elmagrhi, M. H., & Ntim, C. G. (2021). Sustainability and legitimacy theory: The case of sustainable social and environmental practices of small and medium-sized enterprises. *Business Strategy and the Environment, 30*(8), 3740–3762. DOI: 10.1002/bse.2837

Cui, H., Wang, R., & Wang, H. (2020). An evolutionary analysis of green finance sustainability based on a multi-agent game. *Journal of Cleaner Production, 269*, 121799. DOI: 10.1016/j.jclepro.2020.121799

Cui, Q., Ma, X., & Zhang, S. (2023). Does green finance drive low-carbon economic development? Evidence from China. *Ekonomska Istraživanja, 36*(3), 2183421. Advance online publication. DOI: 10.1080/1331677X.2023.2183421

Cunha, F. A. F. D. S., Meira, E., & Orsato, R. J. (2021). Sustainable finance and investment: Review and research agenda. *Business Strategy and the Environment, 30*(8), 3821–3838. DOI: 10.1002/bse.2842

Czarnitzki, D., Fernández, G. P., & Rammer, C. (2023). Artificial intelligence and firm-level productivity. *Journal of Economic Behavior & Organization, 211*, 188–205. DOI: 10.1016/j.jebo.2023.05.008

D'Onza, G., & Lamboglia, R. (2011). The relation between corporate governance characteristics and financial statement frauds: An empirical analysis of Italian listed companies. *10th European Academic Conference on Internal Auditing and Corporate Governance*, 1–21.

Dahlquist, S. H. (2021). How green product demands influence industrial buyer/seller relationships, knowledge, and marketing dynamic capabilities. *Journal of Business Research, 136*, 402–413. DOI: 10.1016/j.jbusres.2021.07.045

Dalnial, H., Kamaluddin, A., & Mohd-Sanusi, Z. (2014). Detecting fraudulent financial reporting through financial statement analysis. *Journal of Advanced Management Science, 2*(1), 17–22. DOI: 10.12720/joams.2.1.17-22

Daly, H. E., & Townsend, K. N. (1993). *Valuing the earth: economics, ecology,ethics*. MIT Press.

Dangelico, R. M., & Vocalelli, D. (2017). "Green marketing": An analysis of definitions, strategy steps, and tools through a systematic review of the literature. *Journal of Cleaner Production, 165*, 1263–1279. DOI: 10.1016/j.jclepro.2017.07.184

Dashkevich, N., Counsell, S., & Destefanis, G. (2020). Blockchain Application for Central Banks: A Systematic Mapping Study. *IEEE Access : Practical Innovations, Open Solutions, 8*, 139918–139952. DOI: 10.1109/ACCESS.2020.3012295

Das, J., & Do, Q. (2023). The Prices in the Crises: What We Are Learning from 20 Years of Health Insurance in Low- and Middle-Income Countries. *The Journal of Economic Perspectives, 37*(2), 123–152. DOI: 10.1257/jep.37.2.123

Davenport, T., Guha, A., Grewal, D., & Bressgott, T. (2020). How artificial intelligence will change the future of marketing. *Journal of the Academy of Marketing Science, 48*(1), 24–42. DOI: 10.1007/s11747-019-00696-0

Davis, F. D. (1989). Perceived Usefulness, Perceived Ease of Use, and User Acceptance of Information Technology. *Management Information Systems Quarterly, 13*(3), 319–340. DOI: 10.2307/249008

De Arruda, P. L., De Andrade, M. L., Falcão, T., Barbosa, D. T., & Morgandi, M. (2021). Auxílio Emergencial - Lessons from the Brazilian experience responding to COVID-19. DOI: 10.1596/37254

De Brito, M. P., Dekker, R., & Flapper, S. D. P. (2005). *Reverse logistics: a review of case studies*. Springer Berlin Heidelberg.

De Conti, B., Herr, H., Jha, P., & Nettekoven, Z. (2023). Macroeconomic policy and policy spaces during the COVID-19 pandemic – case studies from Germany, Brazil and India. European Journal of Economics and Economic Policies Intervention, 1–16. DOI: 10.4337/ejeep.2023.0111

De Filippi, P., & Hassan, S. (2016). Blockchain technology as a regulatory technology: From code is law to law is code. *First Monday, 21*(12). Advance online publication. DOI: 10.5210/fm.v21i12.7113

De Filippi, P., & Wright, A. (2018). *Blockchain and the law: The rule of code*. Harvard University Press.

De Giovanni, P. (2023). Sustainability of the Metaverse: A Transition to Industry 5.0. *Sustainability (Basel), 15*(7), 6079. DOI: 10.3390/su15076079

Delmas, M. A., & Burbano, V. C. (2011). The drivers of greenwashing. *California Management Review*, *54*(1), 64–87. DOI: 10.1525/cmr.2011.54.1.64

Deloitte 2024 CXO Sustainability Report. (2024, September 13). Deloitte. https://www.deloitte.com/global/en/issues/climate/cxo-sustainability-report.html

Demirgüç-Kunt, A., Klapper, L., Singer, D., Ansar, S., & Hess, J. (2018). *The global fintech revolution: Financial inclusion and beyond* (Policy Research Working Paper No. 9355). World Bank.

Deng, X., Huang, Z., & Cheng, X. (2019). FinTech and sustainable development: Evidence from China based on P2P data. *Sustainability (Basel), 11*(22), 6434. DOI: 10.3390/su11226434

Djafarova, E., & Foots, S. (2022). Exploring ethical consumption of generation Z: Theory of planned behaviour. *Young Consumers*, *23*(3), 413–431. DOI: 10.1108/YC-10-2021-1405

Doda, S. (2015). The Importance of Corporate Social Responsibility. *Journal of Sociological Research*, *6*(1), 86–91. DOI: 10.5296/jsr.v6i1.7426

Doku, I., Ncwadi, R., & Phiri, A. (2021). Determinants of climate finance: Analysis of recipient characteristics in Sub-Sahara Africa. *Cogent Economics & Finance*, *9*(1), 1–17. DOI: 10.1080/23322039.2021.1964212

Dong, H., Zhang, L., & Zheng, H. (2024). Green bonds: Fueling green innovation or just a fad? *Energy Economics*, *135*, 107660. 10.1016/j.eneco.2024.107660. DOI: 10.1016/j.eneco.2024.107660

Dubey, R., Bag, S., Ali, S. S., & Venkatesh, V. G. (2013). Green purchasing is key to superior performance: An empirical study. *International Journal of Procurement Management*, *6*(2), 187–210. DOI: 10.1504/IJPM.2013.052469

Dunbar, K., Sarkis, J., & Treku, D. N. (2023). FinTech for environmental sustainability: Promises and pitfalls. *One Earth*, *7*(1), 23–30. DOI: 10.1016/j.oneear.2023.12.012

Dunn, K., & Harness, D. (2018). Communicating corporate social responsibility in a social world: The effects of company-generated and user-generated social media content on CSR attributions and scepticism. *Journal of Marketing Management*, *34*(17-18), 1503–1529. DOI: 10.1080/0267257X.2018.1536675

Dutta, S., Lawson, R., & Marcinko, D. (2016). A management control system to support corporate sustainability strategies. *Advances in Accounting, 32*, 10–17. DOI: 10.1016/j.adiac.2015.12.001

Dwivedi, Y. K., Hughes, L., Baabdullah, A. M., Ribeiro-Navarrete, S., Giannakis, M., Al-Debei, M. M., Dennehy, D., Metri, B., Buhalis, D., Cheung, C. M., Conboy, K., Doyle, R., Dubey, R., Dutot, V., Felix, R., Goyal, D., Gustafsson, A., Hinsch, C., Jebabli, I., & Wamba, S. F. (2022). Metaverse beyond the hype: Multidisciplinary perspectives on emerging challenges, opportunities, and agenda for research, practice and policy. *International Journal of Information Management, 66*, 102542. DOI: 10.1016/j.ijinfomgt.2022.102542

Dwivedi, Y. K., Ismagilova, E., Hughes, D. L., Carlson, J., Filieri, R., Jacobson, J., Jain, V., Karjaluoto, H., Kefi, H., Krishen, A. S., Kumar, V., Rahman, M. M., Raman, R., Rauschnabel, P. A., Rowley, J., Salo, J., Tran, G. A., & Wang, Y. (2020). Setting the future of digital and social media marketing research: Perspectives and research propositions. *International Journal of Information Management, 59*, 102168. DOI: 10.1016/j.ijinfomgt.2020.102168

Dwivedi, Y. K., Kshetri, N., Hughes, L., Rana, N. P., Baabdullah, A. M., Kar, A. K., Koohang, A., Ribeiro-Navarrete, S., Belei, N., Balakrishnan, J., Basu, S., Behl, A., Davies, G. H., Dutot, V., Dwivedi, R., Evans, L., Felix, R., Foster-Fletcher, R., Giannakis, M., & Yan, M. (2023). Exploring the Darkverse: A Multi-Perspective Analysis of the Negative Societal Impacts of the Metaverse. *Information Systems Frontiers, 25*(5), 2071–2114. DOI: 10.1007/s10796-023-10400-x PMID: 37361890

Dyllick, T. & Muff, K. (2016). Clarifying the meaning of sustainable business introducing a a Typology From Business-as-Usual to True Business Sustainability.

Dzingai, I., & Fakoya, M. B. (2017). Effect of corporate governance structure on the financial performance of Johannesburg Stock Exchange (JSE)-listed mining firms. *Sustainability (Basel), 9*(6), 867. DOI: 10.3390/su9060867

Ecomonics, T. (2023, October 16). *Creating a Seamless Customer Journey: The CXO's Guide to Omnichannel Excellence—The Economic Times*. https://economictimes.indiatimes.com/jobs/c-suite/creating-a-seamless-customer-journey-the-cxos-guide-to-omnichannel-excellence/articleshow/104467954.cms?from=mdr

Economic Times. (2023). India's digital transformation in healthcare and sustainability.

Edunjobi, T. E. (2024). Sustainable supply chain financing models: Integrating banking for enhanced sustainability. International Journal of Multidisciplinary Research Updates, 7(2), 001–011. DOI: 10.53430/ijmru.2024.7.2.0030

Edwards, M. G. (2021). The growth paradox, sustainable development, and business strategy. *Business Strategy and the Environment, 30*(7), 3079–3094. DOI: 10.1002/bse.2790

Ehrenfeld, J. R. (2005). The roots of sustainability. *Sloan Management Review, 46*, 23–25.

Eisenhofer, J. W. (2014). Does corporate governance matter to investment returns? Grant & Eisenhofer P.A., 1–19.

Electrical Equipment—India | Statista Market Forecast. (2024). Statista. Retrieved May 31, 2024, from https://www.statista.com/outlook/io/manufacturing/consumer-goods/electrical-equipment/india

Elkington, J. (2004), "Enter the triple bottom line", available at: www.johnelkington.com/TBL- elkington-chapter.pdf (accessed September 28, 2024).

Ellen MacArthur Foundation (EMF). (2013). *Towards the Circular Economy* (Vol. 2).

Elo, S., & Kyngäs, H. (2008). The qualitative content analysis process. *Journal of Advanced Nursing, 62*(1), 107–115. DOI: 10.1111/j.1365-2648.2007.04569.x PMID: 18352969

Elsaid, H. M. (2023). A review of the literature on the impact of fintech firms on the banking industry. *Qualitative Research in Financial Markets, 15*(5), 693–711. DOI: 10.1108/QRFM-10-2020-0197

Erdogdu, A., Dayi, F., Yanik, A., Yildiz, F., & Ganji, F. (2025). Innovative Solutions for Combating Climate Change: Advancing Sustainable Energy and Consumption Practices for a Greener Future. *Sustainability (Basel), 17*(6), 2697. DOI: 10.3390/su17062697

Ervine, K. (2014). Diminishing Returns: Carbon Market Crisis and the Future of Market-Dependent Climate Change Finance. *New Political Economy, 19*(5), 723–747. DOI: 10.1080/13563467.2013.849672

European Commission. (2023). Twin transition: Integrating digital and green agendas.

Evolution of E-commerce in India. (2024). Indian Retailer. Retrieved May 29, 2024, from https://www.indianretailer.com/article/technology-e-commerce/retail-trends/how-e-commerce-has- evolved-india

Fadavi, A., Jolai, F., & Taleizadeh, A. A. (2022). Green product design in a supply chain with considering marketing under competition and coordination. *Environment, Development and Sustainability, 24*(10), 11721–11759. DOI: 10.1007/s10668-021-01917-9

Falagas, M. E., Pitsouni, E. I., Malietzis, G. A., & Pappas, G. (2008). Comparison of PubMed, Scopus, web of science, and Google scholar: Strengths and weaknesses. *FASEB Journal : Official Publication of the Federation of American Societies for Experimental Biology*, *22*(2), 338–342. DOI: 10.1096/fj.07-9492LSF

Falzon, D., Shaia, F., Roberts, J. T., Hossain, M. F., Robinson, S. A., Khan, M. R., & Ciplet, D. (2023). Tactical Opposition: Obstructing Loss and Damage Finance in the United Nations Climate Negotiations. *Global Environmental Politics*, *23*(3), 95–119. DOI: 10.1162/glep_a_00722

Fang, Z., Xie, J., Peng, R., & Wang, S. (2021). Climate finance: Mapping air pollution and finance market in time series. *Ekonometria*, *9*(4), 43. Advance online publication. DOI: 10.3390/econometrics9040043

Fan, J., Wang, D., & Zheng, Y. (2025). Smart Money, Greener Future: AI-Enhanced English Financial Text Processing for ESG Investment Decisions. *Sustainability (Basel)*, *17*(15), 6971. DOI: 10.3390/su17156971

Farrell, D., & Greig, F. (2016, January). Paychecks, paydays, and the online platform economy. In *Proceedings. Annual Conference on Taxation and Minutes of the Annual Meeting of the National Tax Association* (Vol. 109, pp. 1-40). National Tax Association.

Fatemi, A. M., & Fooladi, I. J. (2013). Sustainable finance: A new paradigm. *Global Finance Journal*, *24*(2), 101–113. DOI: 10.1016/j.gfj.2013.07.006

Fettahoglu, S., Allak, S., & Ozcan Turkkan, B. (2025). ESG Scores and Corporate Performance in Emerging Markets: Evidence from E7 Countries. *Sustainability (Basel)*, *17*(19), 8936. DOI: 10.3390/su17198936

Flaherty, M., Gevorkyan, A., Radpour, S., & Semmler, W. (2017). Financing climate policies through climate bonds – A three stage model and empirics. *Research in International Business and Finance*, *42*, 468–479. DOI: 10.1016/j.ribaf.2016.06.001

Freeman, R. E. (2023) The politics of stakeholder theory: Some future directions. In R. Edward Freeman's Selected Works on Stakeholder Theory and Business Ethics', (pp. 119-132). Cham: Springer International Publishing.

Friede, G., Busch, T., & Bassen, A. (2015). ESG and financial performance: Aggregated evidence from more than 2000 empirical studies. *Journal of Sustainable Finance & Investment*, *5*(4), 210–233. DOI: 10.1080/20430795.2015.1118917

Friedman, M. (1970) The Social Responsibility of Business Is to Increase Its Profits. New York Times Magazine, 13 September 1970, 122-126

Fuerst, F. (2019). The role of machine learning in ESG analytics. *Journal of Sustainable Finance & Investment, 9*(4), 255–272.

Fuso Nerini, F., Sovacool, B., Hughes, N., Cozzi, L., Cosgrave, E., Howells, M., Tavoni, M., Tomei, J., Zerriffi, H., & Milligan, B. (2019). Connecting climate action with other Sustainable Development Goals. *Nature Sustainability, 2*(8), 674–680. DOI: 10.1038/s41893-019-0334-y

Gao, D., Tan, L., & Duan, K. (2024). Forging a path to sustainability: The impact of Fintech on corporate ESG performance. *European Journal of Finance*, •••, 1–19. DOI: 10.1080/1351847X.2024.2416995

Gao, X., & Feng, H. (2023). AI-Driven Productivity Gains: Artificial Intelligence and Firm Productivity. *Sustainability (Basel), 15*(11), 8934. Advance online publication. DOI: 10.3390/su15118934

Gazi, M., Islam, H., Islam, M. A., Karim, R., Momo, S. M., & Senathirajah, A. R. B. S. (2024). Unlocking sustainable development in East Asia Pacific and South Asia: An econometric exploration of ESG initiatives. *Sustainable Environment, 10*(1), 2366558. Advance online publication. DOI: 10.1080/27658511.2024.2366558

Geissdoerfer, M., Savaget, P., Bocken, N. M. P., & Hultink, E. J. (2017). The circular economy – a new sustainability paradigm. *Journal of Cleaner Production, 143*, 757–768. DOI: 10.1016/j.jclepro.2016.12.048

Geng, R., Mansouri, S. A., & Aktas, E. (2017). The relationship between green supply chain management and performance: A meta-analysis of empirical evidence in Asian emerging economies. *International Journal of Production Economics, 183*, 245–258. DOI: 10.1016/j.ijpe.2016.10.008

Georgescu-Roegen, N. (1977). Inequality, Limits and Growth from a Bioeconomic Viewpoint. *Review of Social Economy, 35*(3), 361–375. DOI: 10.1080/00346767700000041

Ghose, A., Sahoo, S., & Kumar, V. (2025). FinTech and financial inclusion: Impacts on corporate performance and excluded populations. *Journal of Financial Innovation, 11*(1), 77–95.

Giampietro, M., & Funtowicz, S. O. (2020). From elite folk science to the policy legend of the circular economy. *Environmental Science & Policy, 109*, 64–72. DOI: 10.1016/j.envsci.2020.04.012

Gilchrist, D., Yu, J., & Zhong, R. (2021). The Limits of Green Finance: A Survey of Literature in the Context of Green Bonds and Green Loans. *Sustainability (Basel), 13*(2), 478. DOI: 10.3390/su13020478

Gillan, S. L., Koch, A., & Starks, L. T. (2021). Firms and social responsibility: A review of ESG and CSR research in corporate finance. *Journal of Corporate Finance, 66*, 101889. DOI: 10.1016/j.jcorpfin.2021.101889

Ginsberg, J. M., & Bloom, P. N. (2004). Choosing the right green marketing strategy. *MIT Sloan Management Review, 46*(1), 79–84.

Glova, J., & Panko, M. (2025). The Effects of Environmental, Social, and Governance Factors on Financial Performance and Market Valuation in the European Automotive Industry. *International Journal of Financial Studies, 13*(2), 82. DOI: 10.3390/ijfs13020082

Gomber, P., Kauffman, R. J., Parker, C., & Weber, B. W. (2018). On the FinTech revolution. *Journal of Management Information Systems, 35*(1), 220–265. DOI: 10.1080/07421222.2018.1440766

Gomber, P., Koch, J. A., & Siering, M. (2017). Digital Finance and FinTech: Current research and future research directions. *Journal of Business Economics, 87*(5), 537–580. DOI: 10.1007/s11573-017-0852-x

Gomez-Echeverri, L. (2013). The changing geopolitics of climate change finance. *Climate Policy, 13*(5), 632–648. DOI: 10.1080/14693062.2013.822690

Gompers, P. A., Ishii, J. L., & Metrick, A. (2001). Corporate governance and equity prices (NBER Working Paper No. 8449), 1–70.

Goodland, R., & Daly, H. (1996). Environmental sustainability: Universal and non-negotiable. *Ecological Applications : A Publication of the Ecological Society of America, 6*(4), 1002–1017. DOI: 10.2307/2269583

Gordon, R. (2017). *The Rise and Fall of American Growth: The U.S. Standard of Living since the Civil War*. Princeton University Press., DOI: 10.1515/9781400888955

Goubran, S., & Cucuzzella, C. (2019). Integrating the Sustainable Development Goals in Building Projects. *Journal of Sustainability Research, 1*(2), e190010. DOI: 10.20900/jsr20190010

Greenland, S. J. (2019). Future sustainability, innovation and marketing: A framework for understanding impediments to sustainable innovation adoption and corporate social responsibility. In *The Components of Sustainable Development: Engagement and Partnership* (pp. 63-80). Springer Singapore. DOI: 10.1007/978-981-13-9209-2_5

GRESB. (2024). Navigating the evolving ESG data landscape: Challenges, trends, and solutions. GRESB Insights. https://www.gresb.com/nl-en/navigating-the-evolving-esg-data-landscape-challenges-trends-and-solutions/

Grieshop, A. P., Jain, G., Sethuraman, K., & Marshall, J. D. (2017). Emission factors of health- and climate-relevant pollutants measured in home during a carbon-finance-approved cookstove intervention in rural India. *GeoHealth, 1*(5), 222–236. DOI: 10.1002/2017GH000066 PMID: 32158989

Guest, G., MacQueen, K. M., & Namey, E. E. (2012). Applied thematic analysis. *Sage (Atlanta, Ga.).*

Guo, X., Yang, J., Shen, Y., & Zhang, X. (2024). Impact on green finance and environmental regulation on carbon emissions: Evidence from China. *Frontiers in Environmental Science, 12*, 1307313. Advance online publication. DOI: 10.3389/fenvs.2024.1307313

Gutsa, A. (2023, April 20). *Are sustainable products more expensive?* Ecoswap. https://ecoswap.uk/are-sustainable-products-more-expensive/

Haddad, C., & Hornuf, L. (2019). The emergence of the global FinTech market. *Small Business Economics, 53*(1), 81–105. DOI: 10.1007/s11187-018-9991-x

Hahn, R., & Kühnen, M. (2013). Determinants of sustainability reporting: A review of results, trends, theory, and opportunities in an expanding field of research. *Journal of Cleaner Production, 59*, 5–21. DOI: 10.1016/j.jclepro.2013.07.005

Halimanjaya, A. (2015). Climate mitigation finance across developing countries: What are the major determinants? *Climate Policy, 15*(2), 223–252. DOI: 10.1080/14693062.2014.912978

Halsnæs, K., Bay, L., Dømgaard, M. L., Kaspersen, P. S., & Larsen, M. A. D. (2020). Accelerating climate service development for renewable energy, finance and cities. *Sustainability (Basel), 12*(18), 7540. Advance online publication. DOI: 10.3390/su12187540

Hanedar, E., Alonso, C., Uña, G., Prihardini, D., Bhojwani, T., & Zhabska, K. (2023). Stacking up the Benefits: Lessons from India's Digital Journey. *IMF Working Paper, 2023*(078), 1. DOI: 10.5089/9798400240416.001

Hansson, A. M., Pedersen, E., Karlsson, N. P., & Weisner, S. E. (2023). Barriers and drivers for sustainable business model innovation based on a radical farmland change scenario. *Environment, Development and Sustainability, 25*(8), 8083–8106. DOI: 10.1007/s10668-022-02389-1

Hardin, G. (1968). The Tragedy of the Commons. *Science, 162*(3859), 1243–1248. DOI: 10.1126/science.162.3859.1243 PMID: 5699198

Hariharan, R., Arumugam, S. K., & Seranmadevi, R. (2022). Perception of Climate Finance: An Empirical Approach. *Environment and Ecology Research, 10*(2), 284–293. DOI: 10.13189/eer.2022.100218

Hart, O., & Zingales, L. (2017). Companies Should Maximize Shareholder Welfare Not Market Value. *Journal of Law, Finance, and Accounting, 2*(2), 247–274. DOI: 10.1561/108.00000022

Hart, S. L., & Milstein, M. B. (2003). Creating sustainable value. *The Academy of Management Perspectives, 17*(2), 56–67. DOI: 10.5465/ame.2003.10025194

Hasan, A., Aly, D., & Hussainey, K. (2022). Corporate governance and financial reporting quality: A comparative study. *Corporate Governance (Bradford), 22*(6), 1308–1326. DOI: 10.1108/CG-08-2021-0298

Hasan, M., Hoque, A., Abedin, M. Z., & Gasbarro, D. (2024). FinTech and sustainable development: A systematic thematic analysis using human- and machine-generated processing. *International Review of Financial Analysis, 95*(Part C), 103473. DOI: 10.1016/j.irfa.2024.103473

Hashmi, R. (2023). Business Performance Through Government Policies, Green Purchasing, and Reverse Logistics: Business Performance and Green Supply Chain Practices. *South Asian Journal of Operations and Logistics, 2*(1), 1–10. DOI: 10.57044/SAJOL.2023.2.1.2301

Haum, R., & Loose, B. (2015). Digital economy and sustainability: A multifaceted relationship.

He, B., Cai, H., Ji, Y., & Zhu, S. (2023). Supply chain green manufacturing and green marketing strategies under network externality. *Sustainability (Basel), 15*(18), 13732. DOI: 10.3390/su151813732

He, C., Li, A., Li, D., & Yu, J. (2022). Does Digital Inclusive Finance Mitigate the Negative Effect of Climate Variation on Rural Residents' Income Growth in China? *International Journal of Environmental Research and Public Health, 19*(14), 8280. Advance online publication. DOI: 10.3390/ijerph19148280 PMID: 35886132

Heizer, J., Render, B., Munson, C. L., & Griffin, P. (2020). Operations management: Sustainability and supply chain management.

Heshmati, A. (2018). An empirical survey of the ramifications of a green economy. *International Journal of Green Economics, 12*(1), 53. DOI: 10.1504/IJGE.2018.092359

Hilbrandt, H., & Grafe, F. J. (2022). URBAN VISIONS OF GLOBAL CLIMATE FINANCE: Dispossessive Mechanisms of Futuring in the Making of Groy. *International Journal of Urban and Regional Research, 46*(5), 896–905. DOI: 10.1111/1468-2427.13106

Hobson, K. (2020). The limits of the loops: Critical environmental politics and the circular economy. *Environmental Politics, 30*(1-2), 161–179. DOI: 10.1080/09644016.2020.1816052

Hodgson, G. 2005. Institutions and Economic Development: Constraining, Enabling and Reconstituting, in: G. Dymski & S. De Paula, eds.

Hoffart, F. M., D'Orazio, P., Holz, F., & Kemfert, C. (2024). Exploring the interdependence of climate, finance, energy, and geopolitics: A conceptual framework for systemic risks amidst multiple crises. *Applied Energy, 361*(February), 122885. DOI: 10.1016/j.apenergy.2024.122885

Hofisi, C., Chigavazira, B., Mago, S., & Hofisi, M. (2013). "Climate finance issues": Implications for climate change adaptation for food security in Southern Africa. *Mediterranean Journal of Social Sciences, 4*(6), 47–53. DOI: 10.5901/mjss.2013.v4n6p47

Hofmann, F. (2019). Circular business models: Business approach as driver or obstructer of sustainability transitions? *Journal of Cleaner Production, 224*, 361–374. DOI: 10.1016/j.jclepro.2019.03.115

Holdren, J., & Ehrlich, P. (1974). Human population and the global environment. *American Scientist, 62*, 282–292. PMID: 4832978

Holmes, H., Wieser, H., & Kasmire, J. (2021). Critical approaches to circular economy research: Time, space and evolution. In R. B. Swain & S. Sweet (Eds.), *Sustainable consumption and production, volume II: Circular economy and beyond* (pp. 55–74). Springer International Publishing. DOI: 10.1007/978-3-030-55285-5

Holmström, J., & Carroll, N. (2024). How organizations can innovate with generative AI. *Business Horizons*. https://www.sciencedirect.com/science/article/pii/S0007681324000247

Hommel, K., & Bican, P. M. (2020). Digital entrepreneurship in finance. *Sustainability (Basel), 12*(19), 8035. DOI: 10.3390/su12198035

Hourcade, J. C., Dasgupta, D., & Ghersi, F. (2021). Accelerating the speed and scale of climate finance in the post-pandemic context. *Climate Policy, 21*(10), 1383–1397. DOI: 10.1080/14693062.2021.1977599

Hourcade, J. C., Perrissin Fabert, B., & Rozenberg, J. (2012). Venturing into uncharted financial waters: An essay on climate-friendly finance. *International Environmental Agreement: Politics, Law and Economics, 12*(2), 165–186. DOI: 10.1007/s10784-012-9169-y

Huang, J., Wang, X., Luo, Y., Yu, L., & Zhang, Z. (2021). Joint green marketing decision-making of green supply chain considering power structure and corporate social responsibility. *Entropy (Basel, Switzerland), 23*(5), 564. DOI: 10.3390/e23050564

Huang, Y. (2025). FinTech as a catalyst for sustainable development. *International Journal of Sustainable Development and World Ecology, 32*(3), 145–161.

Hu, H., Li, Y., & Li, M. (2022). Decisions and coordination of green supply chain considering big data targeted advertising. *Journal of Theoretical and Applied Electronic Commerce Research, 17*(3), 1035–1056. DOI: 10.3390/jtaer17030053

IBM. (2021). Sustainability at a turning point. In https://www.ibm.com (WLJ&LVP4). https://www.ibm.com/downloads/cas/WLJ7LVP4

IFRS Foundation. (2024, September). Voluntarily applying ISSB Standards—A guide for preparers. IFRS Foundation. https://www.ifrs.org/content/dam/ifrs/supporting-implementation/issb-standards/issb-voluntary-application-preparers.pdf

illuminem. (2023, May 9). *The three pillars of sustainability: Building a more resilient future*. https://illuminem.com/illuminemvoices/the-three-pillars-of-sustainability-building-a-more-resilient-future

IMF (2020), "The Promise of Fintech: Financial Inclusion in the Post-COVID-19 Era", Ratna Sahay, Ulric Eriksson von Allmen, Amina Lahreche, Purva Khera, Sumiko Ogawa, Majid Bazarbash, and Kim Beaton, July.

IMF. (2023). Digital India's impact on financial inclusion and sustainable development.

Incerti, N., & Barnett, J. (2024). Following the money: Climate adaptation finance in the Marshall Islands. *Environmental Research Letters, 19*(5), 054010. Advance online publication. DOI: 10.1088/1748-9326/ad383e

India Retailing. (2023, December 19). *Heart and sole – Neeman's*. https://www.indiaretailing.com/2023/12/23/heart-and-sole-neemans/

India Today. (2026). *Government urges quick commerce platforms to drop rigid delivery timelines*.https://www.indiatoday.in

Information based on National Treasury, South Africa (2020), Draft Consultation Paper "An Inclusive Financial Sector for All", available at http://www.treasury.gov.za/comm_media/ press/2020/Financial%20Inclusion%20Policy%20-%20An%20Inclusive%20Financial%20 Sector%20For%20All.pdf

Inigo, E. A., & Blok, V. (2019). Strengthening the socio-ethical foundations of the circular economy: Lessons from responsible research and innovation. *Journal of Cleaner Production*, the *233*, 280–291. DOI: 10.1016/j.jclepro.2019.06.053

Innovative Finance for the Amazon. Cerrado and Chaco (IFACC). (n.d.). Home. Retrieved from https://www.ifacc-initiative.org/home

Institutional Investor Advisory Services India Limited (IiAS). (2023). Corporate governance scores. IiAS.

International Capital Market Association (ICMA). (2023, June). Climate Transition Finance Handbook. https://www.icmagroup.org/assets/documents/Sustainable-finance/2023-updates/Climate-Transition-Finance-Handbook-CTFH-June-2023-220623.pdf

International Labour Organization. (2021). *World employment and social outlook: The role of digital labour platforms in transforming the world of work.* https://www.ilo.org/global/research/global-reports/weso/2021

IPCC. (2022). *Climate change 2022: Mitigation of climate change.* Cambridge University Press.

Islam, M. M. (2022). Distributive justice in global climate finance – Recipients' climate vulnerability and the allocation of climate funds. *Global Environmental Change*, *73*(March), 102475. DOI: 10.1016/j.gloenvcha.2022.102475

ISO - ISO 26000 — Social responsibility. (2021, October 15). ISO. https://www.iso.org/iso-26000-social-responsibility.html

ISO 15392 (2008). Sustainability in building construction. General principles. Geneva: International Organization for Standardization.

ISSB. (2024). *IFRS S1 General Requirements for Disclosure of Sustainability-related Financial Information and IFRS S2 Climate-related Disclosures.* International Sustainability Standards Board.

Jackson, T. (2009). *Prosperity without growth. Economics for a finite planet.* Earthscan. DOI: 10.4324/9781849774338

Jarrahi, M. H. (2018). AI and the future of work: Economic sustainability through digital tools.

Jayaram, R., & Singh, S. (2020). Sustainable finance: A systematic review. *International Journal of Indian Culture and Business Management, 21*(3), 317. DOI: 10.1504/IJICBM.2020.110452

Jena, R. K. (2022). Examining the factors affecting the adoption of blockchain technology in the banking sector: An extended UTAUT model. *International Journal of Financial Studies, 10*(4), 90.

Jena, R. K. (2025). Factors influencing the adoption of fintech for the enhancement of financial inclusion in rural India using a mixed-methods approach. *Journal of Risk and Financial Management, 18*(3), 150.

Jeste, D. V., et al. (2020). The role of AI in promoting sustainability in business-to-business contexts.

Jin, I., & Kim, Y. (2017). Analysis of the impact of achieving NDC on public climate finance. *Journal of Sustainable Finance & Investment, 7*(4), 309–334. DOI: 10.1080/20430795.2016.1275934

Johansson, N., Velis, C., & Corvellec, H. (2020). Towards clean material cycles: Is there a policy conflict between circular economy and non-toxic environment? *Waste Management & Research, 38*(7), 705–707. DOI: 10.1177/0734242X20934251 PMID: 32627717

Johnston, P., Everard, M., Santillo, D., & Robért, K. (2007). Reclaiming thedefinition of sustainability. *Environmental Science and Pollution Research International, 14*(1), 60–66. DOI: 10.1065/espr2007.01.375 PMID: 17352129

Jonsdottir, G. E., Sigurjonsson, T. O., Alavi, A. R., & Mitchell, J. (2021). Applying Responsible Ownership to Advance SDGs and the ESG Framework, Resulting in the Issuance of Green Bonds. *Sustainability (Basel), 13*(13), 7331. DOI: 10.3390/su13137331

Joshi, Y., & Rahman, Z. (2015). Factors affecting green purchase behaviour and future research directions. *International Strategic Management Review, 3*(1-2), 128–143. DOI: 10.1016/j.ism.2015.04.001

Kabulova, J., & Stankevičienė, J. (2020). Valuation of FinTech innovation based on patent applications. *Sustainability (Basel), 12*(23), 10158. DOI: 10.3390/su122310158

Kalleberg, A. L. (2016). *Good jobs, bad jobs. The SAGE handbook of the sociology of work and employment*. Sage.

Kanukuntla, S., & Seyed Masoud, S. A. (2017). Audit committee quality and financial reporting quality: A study of selected Indian companies. Jurnal Dinamika Akuntansi dan Bisnis, 4(1), 1–18.

Katper, N., Salman, S. M., & Mohy-ud-Din, K. (2024). Unleashing the mechanism in green finance, corporate social responsibility and shareholders wealth: Insight from quantile GMM. *Global Business Review*, 09721509241276254. Advance online publication. DOI: 10.1177/09721509241276254

Kaur, P., & Kang, L. S. (2024). Status of digital payments in BRICS countries. *The Indian Economic Journal*.

Kellogg, K. C., Valentine, M. A., & Christin, A. (2020). Algorithms at work: The new contested terrain of control. *The Academy of Management Annals*, *14*(1), 366–410. DOI: 10.5465/annals.2018.0174

Kelp, M. M., Grieshop, A. P., Reynolds, C. C. O., Baumgartner, J., Jain, G., Sethuraman, K., & Marshall, J. D. (2018). Real-time indoor measurement of health and climate-relevant air pollution concentrations during a carbon-finance-approved cookstove intervention in rural India. *Development Engineering*, *3*(May), 125–132. DOI: 10.1016/j.deveng.2018.05.001

Kemp, R. & Pearson, P., 2007. Final report MEI project about measuring Eco Innovation.

Khaleeli, M., Faisal, R., & Anwar, S. (2021). The effect of green marketing, green supply chain and green human resources on business performance: Balanced scorecard approach. *Uncertain Supply Chain Management*, *9*(1), 133–138. DOI: 10.5267/j.uscm.2020.11.001

Khan, A., Muttakin, M. B., & Siddiqui, J. (2012). Corporate governance and corporate social responsibility disclosures: Evidence from an emerging economy. *Journal of Business Ethics*, *114*(2), 207–223. DOI: 10.1007/s10551-012-1336-0

Khan, M. I., Khalid, S., Zaman, U., José, A. E., & Ferreira, P. (2021). Green paradox in emerging tourism supply chains: Achieving green consumption behavior through strategic green marketing orientation, brand social responsibility, and green image. *International Journal of Environmental Research and Public Health*, *18*(18), 9626. DOI: 10.3390/ijerph18189626

Khan, M., Al-Busaidi, Z., & Al-Ghafri, H. (2019). Impact of localized CSR initiatives on brand perception in Oman. *International Journal of Business and Social Science*, *10*(4), 67–82.

Khan, S. A. R., Yu, Z., & Farooq, K. (2023). Green capabilities, green purchasing, and triple bottom line performance: Leading toward environmental sustainability. *Business Strategy and the Environment*, *32*(4), 2022–2034. DOI: 10.1002/bse.3234

Kiff, J., Alwazir, J., Davidovic, S., Farias, A., Khan, A., Khiaonarong, T., Malaika, M., Monroe, H., Sugimoto, N., Tourpe, H., & Zhou, P. (2020). A Survey of Research on Retail Central Bank Digital Currency. SSRN Electronic Journal. DOI: 10.2139/ssrn.3639760

Kirchherr, J., Reike, D., & Hekkert, M. (2017). Conceptualizing the circular economy: An analysis of 114 definitions. *Resources, Conservation and Recycling*, *127*, 221–232. DOI: 10.1016/j.resconrec.2017.09.005

Kishor, K., Bansal, S. K., & Kumar, R. (2025). The role of fintech in promoting financial inclusion to achieve sustainable development: An integrated bibliometric analysis and systematic literature review. *Journal of the Knowledge Economy*, *16*(1), 5664–5692. DOI: 10.1007/s13132-024-02168-5

Kivits, R., Sawang, S., Kivits, R., & Sawang, S. (2021) Stakeholder theory', The Dynamism of Stakeholder Engagement: A Case Study of the Aviation Industry, pp.1-8.

Kolbel, J. F., Heeb, F., Paetzold, F., & Busch, T. (2020). Can Sustainable Investing Save the World? Reviewing the Mechanisms of Investor Impact. *Organization & Environment*, *33*(4), 554–574. DOI: 10.1177/1086026620919202

Korhonen, J., Honkasalo, A., & Seppala, J. (2018a). Circular economy: The concept and its limitations. *Ecological Economics*, *143*, 37–46. DOI: 10.1016/j.ecolecon.2017.06.041

Korhonen, J., Nuur, C., Feldmann, A., & Birkie, S. E. (2018b). Circular economy as an essentially contested concept. *Journal of Cleaner Production*, *175*, 544–552. DOI: 10.1016/j.jclepro.2017.12.111

Kotchen, M. J., & Costello, C. (2018). Maximizing the impact of climate finance: Funding projects or pilot projects? *Journal of Environmental Economics and Management*, *92*, 270–281. DOI: 10.1016/j.jeem.2018.08.009

Kotsantonis, S., & Serafeim, G. (2019). Four things no one will tell you about ESG data. *The Bank of America Journal of Applied Corporate Finance*, *31*(2), 50–58. DOI: 10.1111/jacf.12346

Kouhizadeh, M., Saberi, S., & Sarkis, J. (2021). Blockchain technology and the sustainable supply chain. *International Journal of Production Research*, *59*(7), 2142–2162.

Kouhizadeh, M., Saberi, S., & Sarkis, J. (2021). Blockchain technology and the sustainable supply chain: Theoretically exploring adoption barriers. *International Journal of Production Economics*, *231*, 107831. DOI: 10.1016/j.ijpe.2020.107831

KPMG. (2023, September). ESG Assurance Maturity Index 2023. KPMG International. https://assets.kpmg.com/content/dam/kpmg/xx/pdf/2023/09/esg-maturity-report-2023.pdf

Kripa, E.KRIPA. (2024). Sustainable finance and management: Challenges for achieving sustainable finance and management for businesses. *Economicus*, *23*(1), 5–6. DOI: 10.58944/yxou8636

Krishnannair, A., Krishnannair, S., Olivier, J., Tsakeni, M., Babane, V. C., Kadenge, E., Luckay, M. B., Mutekwe, E., Naidoo, J., Singh-Pillay, A., & Molotsi, A. R. (2022). The 4IR and teacher education in South Africa: contemporary discourses and empirical evidence. In Disruptions in Higher Education. DOI: 10.4102/aosis.2022.BK306

Kroll, C., Warchold, A., & Pradhan, P. (2019). Sustainable Development Goals (SDGs): Are we successful in turning trade-offs into synergies? *Palgrave Communications*, *5*(1), 140. DOI: 10.1057/s41599-019-0335-5

Kumar, S. (2022). Blockchain and land records: India's transparency revolution. Global Journal of Governance and Policy.

Kumar, D., & Garg, C. P. (2017). Evaluating sustainable supply chain indicators using fuzzy AHP: Case of Indian automotive industry. *Benchmarking*, *24*(6), 1742–1766. DOI: 10.1108/BIJ-11-2015-0111

Kumar, P., Singh, R. K., & Kumar, V. (2021). Managing supply chains for sustainable operations in the era of industry 4.0 and circular economy: Analysis of barriers. *Resources, Conservation and Recycling*, *164*, 105215. DOI: 10.1016/j.resconrec.2020.105215

Kumar, R. (2024). Emerging technologies in FinTech: Blockchain, AI, and big data analytics. *Financial Innovation*, *10*(4), 302–318.

Kumar, S., Sharma, D., Rao, S., Lim, W. M., & Mangla, S. K. (2022). Past, present, and future of sustainable finance: Insights from big data analytics through machine learning of scholarly research. *Annals of Operations Research*, *345*(2-3), 1061–1104. DOI: 10.1007/s10479-021-04410-8 PMID: 35002001

Kuzey, C., Uyar, A., Nizaeva, M., & Karaman, A. S. (2021). CSR performance and firm performance in the tourism, healthcare, and financial sectors: Do metrics and CSR committees' matter? *Journal of Cleaner Production*, *319*, 128802. DOI: 10.1016/j.jclepro.2021.128802

Larralde, A. S. & B. (2008). Electronic copy available at : Electronic copy available at. *Grou, 23529*(2), 1–45.

Latapí Agudelo, M. A., Jóhannsdóttir, L., & Davídsdóttir, B. (2019). A literature review of the history and evolution of corporate social responsibility. *International Journal of Corporate Social Responsibility, 4*(1), 1. Advance online publication. DOI: 10.1186/s40991-018-0039-y

Latour, B. (1992). Where are the missing masses? In Bijker, W., & Law, J. (Eds.), *Shaping technology/building society* (pp. 225–258). MIT Press.

Leal, P. H., Marques, A. C., & Shahbaz, M. (2023). Does climate finance and foreign capital inflows drive de-carbonisation in developing economies? *Journal of Environmental Management, 347*(May), 119100. Advance online publication. DOI: 10.1016/j.jenvman.2023.119100 PMID: 37776791

Lee, I., & Shin, Y. J. (2018). Fintech: Ecosystem, business models, investment decisions, and challenges. *Business Horizons, 61*(1), 35–46.

Leonidou, C. N., Katsikeas, C. S., & Morgan, N. A. (2013). "Greening" the marketing mix: Do firms do it and does it pay off? *Journal of the Academy of Marketing Science, 41*(2), 151–170. DOI: 10.1007/s11747-012-0317-2

Liaw, K. T. (2020). Survey of Green Bond Pricing and Investment Performance. *Journal of Risk and Financial Management, 13*(9), 193. DOI: 10.3390/jrfm13090193

Lichtenberger, A., Braga, J. P., & Semmler, W. (2022). Green Bonds for the Transition to a Low-Carbon Economy. *Ekonometria, 10*(1), 11. DOI: 10.3390/econometrics10010011

Li, G., Jia, X., Khan, A. A., Khan, S. U., Ali, M. A. S., & Luo, J. (2023). Does green finance promote agricultural green total factor productivity? Considering green credit, green investment, green securities, and carbon Finance in China. *Environmental Science and Pollution Research International.* Advance online publication. DOI: 10.1007/s11356-022-24857-x PMID: 36562964

Li, N., Shi, B., Wu, L., Kang, R., & Gao, Q. (2022). Climate-Related Development Finance, Energy Structure Transformation and Carbon Emissions Reduction: An Analysis From the Perspective of Developing Countries. *Frontiers in Environmental Science, 9*(January), 1–19. DOI: 10.3389/fenvs.2021.778254

Liu, B., Chen, Z., Wang, Y., & Sun, X. (2025). Fintech empowers enterprises to practice ESG: The role of political connections. *Energy Economics, 142*, 107693. DOI: 10.1016/j.eneco.2025.108183

Liu, W., & Zhu, P. (2024). The impact of green finance on the intensity and efficiency of carbon emissions: The moderating effect of the digital economy. *Frontiers in Environmental Science*, *12*, 1362932. Advance online publication. DOI: 10.3389/fenvs.2024.1362932

Liu, X., Huang, N., Su, W., & Zhou, H. (2024). Digital finance and firm green innovation: Evidence from China. *International Review of Economics & Finance*, *95*, 103461. DOI: 10.1016/j.iref.2024.103461

Liu, X., Xu, Z., & Bai, C. (2016). Drivers' evaluation to implement green marketing practices in automobile industry of China. *International Journal of Networking and Virtual Organisations*, *16*(4), 362–376. DOI: 10.1504/IJNVO.2016.081653

Li, Y., Yan, C., & Ren, X. (2023). Do uncertainties affect clean energy markets? Comparisons from a multi-frequency and multi-quantile framework. *Energy Economics*, *121*, 106679. DOI: 10.1016/j.eneco.2023.106679

Li, Z., Liao, G., & Albitar, K. (2020). Does corporate environmental responsibility engagement affect firm value? The mediating role of corporate innovation. *Business Strategy and the Environment*, *29*(3), 1045–1055. DOI: 10.1002/bse.2416

Lobo, M. J., Pietriga, E., & Appert, C. (2015, April). An evaluation of interactive map comparison techniques. In *Proceedings of the 33rd annual ACM conference on human factors in computing systems* (pp. 3573-3582). DOI: 10.1145/2702123.2702130

Locatelli, B., Fedele, G., Fayolle, V., & Baglee, A. (2016). Synergies between adaptation and mitigation in climate change finance. *International Journal of Climate Change Strategies and Management*, *8*(1), 112–128. DOI: 10.1108/IJCCSM-07-2014-0088

LSEG. (2022). Climate Report 2022. London Stock Exchange Group. https://www.lseg.com/content/dam/lseg/en_us/documents/sustainability/climate-report-2022.pdf

Lüdeke-Freund, F. (2020). Sustainable entrepreneurship, innovation, and business models: Integrative framework and propositions for future research. *Business Strategy and the Environment*, *29*(2), 665–681. DOI: 10.1002/bse.2396

Lule Yawe, B., Ddumba-Ssentamu, J., Nnyanzi, J. B., & Mukisa, I. (2022). Role of Mobile Money and Digital Payments in Financial Inclusion for Sustainable Development Goals in Africa. In IntechOpen. DOI: 10.5772/intechopen.105858

Luthra, S., Mangla, S. K., Chan, F. T., & Venkatesh, V. G. (2018). Evaluating the drivers to information and communication technology for effective sustainability initiatives in supply chains. *International Journal of Information Technology & Decision Making*, *17*(01), 311–338. DOI: 10.1142/S0219622017500419

Lu, Z., & Li, Y. (2024). The impact of ESG on banks' sense of environmental responsibility. In *Proceedings of the 3rd International Conference on Big Data Economy and Digital Management (BDEDM 2024)* (pp. 1–11). DOI: 10.4108/eai.12-1-2024.2347202

Lyeonov, S., Toušek, Z., Bozhenko, V., & Kérmárki-Gally, S. E. (2023). The impact of corruption in climate finance on achieving net zero emissions. *Journal of International Students, 16*(1), 142–159. DOI: 10.14254/2071-8330.2023/16-1/10

Lynch, M. J., Long, M. A., & Stretesky, P. B. (2022). Averting your gaze with sustainable, green marketing claims: A critique of luxury commodity production sustainability claims, with evidence from the diamond industry. *Sociological Spectrum, 42*(4-6), 278–293. DOI: 10.1080/02732173.2022.2148797

MacAskill, S., Roca, E., Liu, B., Stewart, R. A., & Sahin, O. (2021). Is there a green premium in the green bond market? Systematic literature review revealing premium determinants. *Journal of Cleaner Production, 280*, 124491. 10.1016/j.jclepro.2020.124491. DOI: 10.1016/j.jclepro.2020.124491

Mahbub, M., & Shubair, R. M. (2023). Contemporary advances in multi-access edge computing: A survey of fundamentals, architecture, technologies, deployment cases, security, challenges, and directions. *Journal of Network and Computer Applications, 219*, 103726. DOI: 10.1016/j.jnca.2023.103726

Mahindra & Mahindra Ltd. (2023). *Annual report 2022–23*. Mahindra & Mahindra Ltd.

Maia, R., Junior, A., Pessanha, J & Garcia, K. (2022). Methodology for setting corporate sustainability targets. *Journal of Cleaner Production*. 369:133359. . jclepro.2022.133359DOI: 10.1016/j

Malladi, C. M., Soni, R. K., & Srinivasan, S. (2021). Digital Financial Inclusion: Next Frontiers—Challenges and Opportunities. *CSI Transactions on ICT, 9*(2), 127–134. DOI: 10.1007/s40012-021-00328-5

Ma, N., Liu, P., Xiao, Y., Tang, H., & Zhang, J. (2022). Can Green Technological Innovation Reduce Hazardous Air Pollutants?-An Empirical Test Based on 283 Cities in China. *International Journal of Environmental Research and Public Health, 19*(3), 1611. DOI: 10.3390/ijerph19031611 PMID: 35162639

Marketing Monk. (n.d.). *Neeman's Marketing Strategies that Led to $24.8M Valuation*. Marketing Monk. https://www.marketingmonk.so/p/neeman-s-marketing-strategies-that-led-to-24-8m-valuation

Marlinda, H., Satria, H., Utami, R., Kurnia, S., & Sahara, M. A. (2022). Financial statement integrity: Corporate governance and quality audit evidence from food and beverage companies in Indonesia. *Penanomics: International Journal of Economics, 1*(1), 27–40. DOI: 10.56107/penanomics.v1i1.3

Matsuo, T., & Schmidt, T. S. (2017). Hybridizing low-carbon technology deployment policy and fossil fuel subsidy reform: A climate finance perspective. *Environmental Research Letters, 12*(1), 1–9. DOI: 10.1088/1748-9326/aa5384

McIntosh, M. J., & Morse, J. M. (2015). Situating and constructing diversity in semi-structured interviews. *Global Qualitative Nursing Research, 2*, 2333393615597674. DOI: 10.1177/2333393615597674 PMID: 28462313

Mckelvey, B., 2002. Managing Coevolutionary Dynamics. 8th EGOS Colloq.

McKinsey. (2014). Profits with purpose: How organizing for sustainability can benefit the bottom line. In https://www.mckinsey.com/. https://www.mckinsey.com/~/media/McKinsey/Business%20Functions/Sustainability/Our%20Insights/Profits%20with%20purpose/Profits%20with%20Purpose.ashx

Meadows, D., Meadows, D., & Randers, J. Behrens, III.W.W. (1972). *The Limits to Growth. A Report for the Club of Rome's Project on the Predicament of Mankind.* Universe Books, New York.

Mejía-Escobar, J. C., González-Ruiz, J. D., & Duque-Grisales, E. (2020). Sustainable financial products in the Latin American banking industry. *Sustainability, 12*(14), 5648. DOI: 10.3390/su12145648

Mekonnen, A. (2014). Economic costs of climate change and climate finance with a focus on Africa. *Journal of African Economies, 23*(SUPPL.2), 50–82. DOI: 10.1093/jae/eju012

Mentzer, J. T., DeWitt, W., Keebler, J. S., Min, S., Nix, N. W., Smith, C. D., & Zacharia, Z. G. (2001). Defining supply chain management. *Journal of Business Logistics, 22*(2), 1–25. DOI: 10.1002/j.2158-1592.2001.tb00001.x

Michaelowa, K., Michaelowa, A., Reinsberg, B., & Shishlov, I. (2020). Do multilateral development bank trust funds allocate climate finance efficiently? *Sustainability (Basel), 12*(14), 5529. Advance online publication. DOI: 10.3390/su12145529

Min, H., & Galle, W. P. (1997). Green purchasing strategies: Trends and implications. *International Journal of Purchasing and Materials Management, 33*(2), 10–17. DOI: 10.1111/j.1745-493X.1997.tb00026.x

Mishra, K. K., & Pant, P. (2025). Subconscious Factors Affecting Consumer Preferences Toward Green Investments. Sustainability, Innovation, and Consumer Preference, 119–148.

Mishra, K. K., & Priya, S. (2019). Impact of Improving Socio - Economic Conditions on the Purchase Behaviour of Customers in Central Rural Uttar Pradesh. International Journal of Management Studies. https://www.semanticscholar.org/paper/Impact-of-Improving-Socio-Economic-Conditions-on-of-Mishra-Priya/7c1d06fb99071d87380a31748aebca40d3ebcb0d

Mishra, M., Desul, S., Santos, C.A.G. et al. (2023). A bibliometric analysis of sustainable development goals (SDGs): a review of progress, challenges, and opportunities. Environment, Development and Sustainability, *26*, 11101–11143 (2024). DOI: 10.1007/s10668-023-03225-w

Moeve. (2024, March 19). Sustainable consumers are willing to pay more for green products. *Moeve Global*. https://www.moeveglobal.com/en/planet-energy/environment/sustainable-consumers-are-willing-to-pay-more-for-green-products

Mohamed, I. D., Haddad, S., Barakat, M., & Rosi, B. (2023). Blockchain Technology Adoption for Improved Environmental Supply Chain Performance: The Mediation Effect of Supply Chain Resilience, Customer Integration, and Green Customer Information Sharing. *Sustainability (Basel)*, *15*(10), 7909. DOI: 10.3390/su15107909

Mohapatra, N., Shekhar, S., Singh, R., Khan, S., Santos, G., & Carvalho, S. (2025). Unveiling the Nexus Between Use of AI-Enabled Robo-Advisors, Behavioural Intention and Sustainable Investment Decisions Using PLS-SEM. *Sustainability (Basel)*, *17*(9), 3897. DOI: 10.3390/su17093897

Moher, D., Liberati, A., Tetzlaff, J., & Altman, D. G. (2009). Preferred reporting items for systematic reviews and meta-analyses: The PRISMA statement. *PLoS Medicine*, *6*(7), e1000097. DOI: 10.1371/journal.pmed.1000097

Moneycontrol. (2023). Company financials. Moneycontrol. https://www.moneycontrol.com

Monk, A., & Perkins, R. (2020). What explains the emergence and diffusion of green bonds? *Energy Policy*, *145*, 111641. DOI: 10.1016/j.enpol.2020.111641

Moraga, G., Huysveld, S., Mathieux, F., Blengini, G. A., Alaerts, L., Van Ackere, K., de Meester, S., & Dewulf, J. (2019). Circular economy indicators: What do they measure? *Resources, Conservation and Recycling*, *146*, 452–461. DOI: 10.1016/j.resconrec.2019.03.045 PMID: 31274959

Morgan, R. M., & Hunt, S. D. (1994). The commitment-trust theory of relationship marketing. *Journal of Marketing*, *58*(3), 20–38. DOI: 10.1177/002224299405800302

Moro-Visconti, R., Cruz Rambaud, S., & López Pascual, J. (2020). Sustainability in FinTechs. *Sustainability (Basel)*, *12*(24), 10316. DOI: 10.3390/su122410316

Muchiri, M. K., Erdei-Gally, S., Fekete-Farkas, M., & Lakner, Z. (2022). Bibliometric Analysis of Green Finance and Climate Change in Post-Paris Agreement Era. *Journal of Risk and Financial Management*, *15*(12), 561. Advance online publication. DOI: 10.3390/jrfm15120561

Mudgill, A. (2024, April 1). Mamaearth shares: Risk-reward unfavourable for Honasa Consumer, target Rs 400, says Antique. *Business Today*. https://www.businesstoday.in/markets/company-stock/story/mamaearth-shares-risk-reward-unfavourable-for-honasa-consumer-target-rs-400-says-antique-423716-2024-04-01

Mu, H., & Lee, Y. (2023). Greenwashing in Corporate Social Responsibility: A Dual-Faceted Analysis of Its Impact on Employee Trust and Identification. *Sustainability (Basel)*, *15*(22), 15693. DOI: 10.3390/su152215693

Mumuni, S., & Hamadjoda Lefe, Y. D. (2023). Greening the environment: Do climate-related development finances and renewable energy consumption matter? An African tale. *Carbon Management*, *14*(1), 2251934. Advance online publication. DOI: 10.1080/17583004.2023.2251934

Murau, S., & Thie, J.-E. (2024). Towards a public sustainable finance paradigm for the green transition. *Finance and Stochastics*, *10*(1), 38–50. DOI: 10.1017/fas.2023.15

Murray, A., Skene, K., & Haynes, K. (2017). The circular economy: An interdisciplinary exploration of the concept and application in a global context. *Journal of Business Ethics*, *140*(3), 369–380. DOI: 10.1007/s10551-015-2693-2

Nagle, T. T., & Holden, R. K. (2002). *The Strategy and Tactics of Pricing: A Guide to Profitable Decision Making*. Prentice Hall.

Nagrale, A. V., & Chandnani, S. (2025). Digital payment ecosystems and financial inclusion: Comparative analysis of UPI in India and PIX in Brazil. *Global Journal of Engineering and Technology Advances*. DOI: 10.30574/gjeta.2025.23.2.0148

Narayanan, A., Bonneau, J., Felten, E., Miller, A., & Goldfeder, S. (2016). *Bitcoin and cryptocurrency technologies*. Princeton University Press.

Narula, R., Rao, P., Kumar, S., & Matta, R. (2024). ESG scores and firm performance—Evidence from emerging market. International Review of Economics & Finance, *89*(A), 1170–1184. DOI: 10.1016/j.iref.2023.08.024

NASSCOM. (2023). India's IT and digital economy growth report.

Nature. (2025). *Advancements in Green Digital Payment Systems.*

Nature. (2025). *FinTech adoption for ESG integration through robo advisors.* https://www.nature.com/articles/s41598-025-17046-6

Negri, M., Cagno, E., Colicchia, C., & Sarkis, J. (2021). Integrating sustainability and resilience in the supply chain: A systematic literature review and a research agenda. *Business Strategy and the Environment, 30*(7), 2858–2886. DOI: 10.1002/bse.2776

Neitzert, F., & Petras, M. (2022). Corporate social responsibility and bank risk. *Journal of Business Economics, 92*(3), 397–428. DOI: 10.1007/s11573-021-01069-2

Network for Greening the Financial System (NGFS). (2023, July). NGFS Climate Scenarios for central banks and supervisors – Phase IV. NGFS. https://www.ngfs.net/sites/default/files/medias/documents/ngfs_climate_scenarios_for_central_banks_and_supervisors_phase_iv.pdf

Newlands, G. (2021). Algorithmic surveillance in the gig economy: The organization of work through Lefebvrian conceived space. *Organization Studies, 42*(5), 719–737. DOI: 10.1177/0170840620937900

Nike - Diversity, Equity & Inclusion — NIKE, Inc. (n.d.). https://about.nike.com/en/impact/focus-areas/diversity-equity-inclusion

Nike Sustainability. Move to Zero. (n.d.). www.nike.com. https://www.nike.com/in/sustainability

Ning, Y., & Shen, B. (2024). Environmental regulations, finance, and firm environmental investments: An empirical exploration. *Total Quality Management & Business Excellence, 35*(7–8), 713–738. DOI: 10.1080/14783363.2024.2329691

no nasties+: BETTER CLOTHES + BETTER PLANET. (n.d.). https://www.nonasties.in/. Retrieved October 2, 2024, from https://www.nonasties.in/pages/for-the-planet

Nowell, L. S., Norris, J. M., White, D. E., & Moules, N. J. (2017). Thematic analysis: Striving to meet the trustworthiness criteria. *International Journal of Qualitative Methods, 16*(1), 1–13. DOI: 10.1177/1609406917733847

NykaaFrontendTeam. (2024). *Who Are We.* Nykaa. Retrieved June 14, 2024, from https://www.nykaa.com/who_are_we/lp

OECD. (2023). *Sustainable Finance in Asia: ESG and Climate-Aligned Investing and Policy Considerations.* OECD Publishing., DOI: 10.1787/bde9ec0d-

Okafor, A., Adeleye, B. N., & Adusei, M. (2021). Corporate social responsibility and financial performance: Evidence from US tech firms. *Journal of Cleaner Production, 292*, 126078. DOI: 10.1016/j.jclepro.2021.126078

Olayinka, A. A. (2022). Financial statement analysis as a tool for investment decisions and assessment of companies' performance. *International Journal of Financial, Accounting, and Management*, *4*(1), 49–66. DOI: 10.35912/ijfam.v4i1.852

Omnichannel. (2023, April 6). The Lenskart Blog. https://blog.lenskart.com/tagged/omnichannel

Omri, A., & Klai, N. (2011). Corporate governance and financial reporting quality: The case of Tunisian firms. *International Business Research*, *4*(1), 158–166.

Online Furniture Shopping Store: Shop Online in India for Furniture, Home Decor, Homeware Products @ Pepperfry. (2024). Pepperfry. Retrieved June 14, 2024, from https://www.pepperfry.com/

Onuorah, A. C.-C., & Friday, O. I. (2016). Corporate governance and financial reporting quality in selected Nigerian companies. *International Journal of Management Science and Business Administration*, *2*(3), 7–16.

OpenWay. (2024). *ESG for payment companies: OpenWay shares strategies for a sustainable future*. https://openwaygroup.com/esg-for-payment-companies-openway-strategies

Otiashvili, D., Mgebrishvili, T., Beselia, A., Vardanashvili, I., Dumchev, K., Kiriazova, T., & Kirtadze, I. (2022). The impact of the COVID-19 pandemic on illicit drug supply, drug-related behaviour of people who use drugs and provision of drug-related services in Georgia: Results of a mixed methods prospective cohort study. *Harm Reduction Journal*, *19*(1), 25. Advance online publication. DOI: 10.1186/s12954-022-00601-z PMID: 35264181

Otieno, K., Mugo, R., Njeje, D., & Anthony, K. (2015). Effect of corporate governance on financial performance of SACCOs in Kenya. *Research Journal of Finance and Accounting*, *6*(2), 48–58.

Ozili, P. K. (2018). Impact of digital finance on financial inclusion and stability. *Borsa Istanbul Review*, *18*(4), 329–340. DOI: 10.1016/j.bir.2017.12.003

Pagell, M., & Shevchenko, A. (2014). Why research in sustainable supply chain management should have no future. *The Journal of Supply Chain Management*, *50*(1), 44–55. DOI: 10.1111/jscm.12037

Pande, S. (2011). Does good governance pay? Evidence from around the globe. *SSRN*, 1–31. DOI: 10.2139/ssrn.1976772

Panigrahi, A. K., & Sukla, T. N. (2016). Sustainable corporate social responsibility in financial institutions and banks in India. SSRN Electronic Journal. DOI: 10.2139/ssrn.2736814

Pant, P., Mishra, K. K., & Rajaram, R. (2025). Risks to Individual Privacy and Security in the World of Deepfake Technology. In Mastering Deepfake Technology: Strategies for Ethical Management and Security (pp. 237-253). River Publishers.

Pant, P., Mishra, K. K., & Mohan, A. (2024). *Algorithmic Approaches to Financial Technology: Forecasting, Trading, and Forecasting*. Artificial Intelligence and Machine Learning-Powered Smart Finance.

Park, S. (2023). Bringing strategy back in: corporate sustainability and firm performance. *Journal of Cleaner Production*. 388:136012. . 136012DOI: 10.1016/j.jclepro.2023

Pathak, M., Patel, S., & Some, S. (2024). Climate change mitigation and Sustainable Development Goals: Evidence and research gaps. *PLOS Climate*, *3*(3), 1–5. DOI: 10.1371/journal.pclm.0000366

Paulinus, C. E., Oluchukwu, N., & Somtochukwu, O. (2017). Empirical investigation of corporate governance and financial reporting quality of quoted companies in Nigeria. International Journal of Economics. *Business and Management Research*, *1*(5), 117–137.

Paul, J., Ueno, A., Dennis, C., Alamanos, E., Curtis, L., Foroudi, P., Kacprzak, A., Kunz, W. H., Liu, J., Marvi, R., Nair, S. L. S., Ozdemir, O., Pantano, E., Papadopoulos, T., Petit, O., Tyagi, S., & Wirtz, J. (2024). Digital transformation: A multidisciplinary perspective and future research agenda. *International Journal of Consumer Studies*, *48*(2), e13015. Advance online publication. DOI: 10.1111/ijcs.13015

Pawar, S., Chougule, M., & Channaveer, R. M. (2025). Human capital and stakeholder engagement intervention: A women empowerment pathway to achieve sustainable community development in water, sanitation, and hygiene at Vaijapur Village of Karnataka, India. *Frontiers in Sustainable Cities*, *6*, 1562033. DOI: 10.3389/frsus.2025.1562033

Payne, A., & Frow, P. (2005). A Strategic Framework for Customer Relationship Management. *Journal of Marketing*, *69*(4), 167–176. DOI: 10.1509/jmkg.2005.69.4.167

Pearce, D. W., & Turner, R. K. (1990). *Economics of natural resources and the environment*. Harvester Wheatsheaf. ISBN 0 7450 0225 0

Pedersen, L. H., Fitzgibbons, S., & Pomorski, L. (2021). Responsible investing: The ESG-efficient frontier. *Journal of Financial Economics, 142*(2), 572–597. DOI: 10.1016/j.jfineco.2020.11.001

Peng, Y., Wang, W., Li, S., & Veglianti, E. (2022). Competition and cooperation in the dual-channel green supply chain with customer satisfaction. *Economic Analysis and Policy, 76*, 95–113. DOI: 10.1016/j.eap.2022.08.001

Pfeffer, J. (2010). Building sustainable organizations: The human factor. *The Academy of Management Perspectives, 24*(1), 34–45.

Philippon, T. (2016). *The FinTech opportunity* (NBER Working Paper No. 22476).

Philippon, T. (2016). *The fintech opportunity (No. w22476)*. National Bureau of Economic Research. DOI: 10.3386/w22476

Phiri, A., & Doku, I. (2024). Is climate finance aiding food security in developing countries? A focus on Sub-Sahara Africa. *Cogent Economics & Finance, 12*(1), 2312777. Advance online publication. DOI: 10.1080/23322039.2024.2312777

Plc, U. (2024, September 6). Why is sustainability important for business? *Unilever*. https://www.unilever.com/news/news-search/2023/why-is-sustainability-important-for-business/

Pliavskyiy, I., Martusenko, I., Molnar, O., Dzyana, H., & Kushniriuk, V. (2021). Modelling ways of improving the green economy and environmental protection in the context of governance. *Business: Theory and Practice, 22*(2), 310–317. DOI: 10.3846/btp.2021.13336

Ployhart, R. E., Nyberg, A. J., Reilly, G., & Maltarich, M. A. (2014). Human capital is dead; long live human capital resources! *Journal of Management, 40*(2), 371–398. DOI: 10.1177/0149206313512152

Popp, D., Newell, R., & Jaffe, A. (2009). Energy, the Environment, and Technological Change. *Handbook of the Economics of Innovation, 2*. DOI: 10.1016/S0169-7218(10)02005-8

Porter, M. E. (1985). *Competitive Advantage: Creating and Sustaining Superior Performance*. Free Press.

Porter, M. E., & Kramer, M. R. (2011). Creating shared value. *Harvard Business Review, 89*(1-2), 62–77.

Potting, J., Hekkert, M., Worrell, E., & Hanemaaijer, A. (2017). *Circular Economy: Measuring Innovation in the Product Chain*. PBL–Netherlands Environmental Assessment Agency.

Poyser, A., & Daugaard, D. (2023). Indigenous sustainable finance as a research field: A systematic literature review on indigenising ESG, sustainability and indigenous community practices. *Accounting and Finance*, *63*(1), 47–76. DOI: 10.1111/acfi.13062

PricewaterhouseCoopers (PwC) Study, Payments 2025 & Beyond - Navigating the payments matrix, available at https:// www.pwc.com/gx/en/industries/financial-services/publications/financial-services-in-2025/payments-in-2025.html

Puri, P. (1998). Financing of Litigation by Third-Party Investors: A Share of Justice? *Deleted Journal*, *36*(3), 515–566. DOI: 10.60082/2817-5069.1559

Purnama, O., Hanitha, V., & Angreni, T. (2020). Financial statement analysis to assess company financial performance. eCo-Fin, 2(3).

Puschmann, T., Hoffmann, C. H., & Khmarskyi, V. (2020). How green FinTech can alleviate climate change. *Sustainability*, *12*(24), 10691. DOI: 10.3390/su122410691

PwC India. (2022). *Integrating ESG in the payments ecosystem.* https://www.pwc.in/assets/pdfs/consulting/esg/integrating-esg-in-the-payments-ecosystem.pdf

PwC India. (2022a). *Integrating ESG in the payments ecosystem.* PwC India. https://www.pwc.in/assets/pdfs/consulting/esg/integrating-esg-in-the-payments-ecosystem.pdf

PwC India. (2022b). *Impact of digital payments on greenhouse gas (GHG) emissions in India*. PwC India. https://www.pwc.in/assets/pdfs/industries/financial-services/fintech/impact-of-digital-payments-on-greenhouse-gas-ghg-emissions-in-india.pdf

PwC India. (2022c). *Powering India's USD 5 trillion economy by fostering innovations in fintech*. PwC India. https://www.pwc.in/assets/pdfs/industries/powering-indias-usd-5-trillion-economy-by-fostering-innovations.pdf

PwC India. (2022d). *Capital markets and ESG initiatives in GIFT IFSC*. PwC India. https://www.pwc.in/assets/pdfs/capital-markets-in-gift-ifsc-final-v1.pdf

Qumba, M. F. (2022). A comparative analysis of the Twin Peaks model of financial regulation in South Africa and the United Kingdom. *South African Law Journal*, *139*(1), 78–113. DOI: 10.47348/SALJ/v139/i1a3

Rahman, M., Hossain, M., & Uddin, M. (2024). Understanding the role of FinTech in sustainable finance. *Environmental Science and Pollution Research International*, *31*(12), 15689–15705.

Rahman, S. U., & Nguyen-Viet, B. (2023). Towards sustainable development: Coupling green marketing strategies and consumer perceptions in addressing greenwashing. *Business Strategy and the Environment, 32*(4), 2420–2433. DOI: 10.1002/bse.3256

Raithatha, M., & Bapat, V. (2014). Impact of corporate governance on financial disclosures: Evidence from India. *Corporate Ownership & Control, 12*(1), 874–889. DOI: 10.22495/cocv12i1c9p10

Raman, R., Ray, S., Das, D., & Nedungadi, P. (2025). Innovations and barriers in sustainable and green finance for advancing sustainable development goals. *Frontiers in Environmental Science, 12*, 1513204. Advance online publication. DOI: 10.3389/fenvs.2024.1513204

Rashid, A., Asif, F. M. A., Krajnik, P., & Nicolescu, C. M. (2013). Resource Conservative Manufacturing: An essential change in business and technology paradigm for sustainable manufacturing. *Journal of Cleaner Production, 57*, 166–177. DOI: 10.1016/j.jclepro.2013.06.012

Rashid, N., Daud, W. N. W., Zainol, F. A., Salleh, F., Yazid, A. S., Endut, W. A., Yaakub, N., Ghazali, P. L., & Afthanorhan, A. (2018). Quality of financial reporting towards the improvement of corporate governance mechanism. *International Journal of Academic Research in Business & Social Sciences, 8*(11), 1339–1345. DOI: 10.6007/IJARBSS/v8-i11/5175

Rasoulinezhad, E., & Taghizadeh-Hesary, F. (2022). Role of green finance in improving energy efficiency and renewable energy development. *Energy Efficiency, 15*(2), 14. DOI: 10.1007/s12053-022-10021-4 PMID: 35529528

Redbridge. (2024). *Sustainability and ESG initiatives in payment systems.* https://www.redbridgedta.com/market-intelligence/sustainability-and-esg-initiatives-in-payment-systems-key-developments-and-trends/

Refinitiv. (2020). Sustainable finance review. Refinitiv. Available at https://www.refinitiv.com/content/dam/

Reher, M., & Sokolinski, S. (2024). Robo advisors and access to wealth management. *Journal of Financial Economics, 155*, 103829. DOI: 10.1016/j.jfineco.2024.103829

Reike, D., Vermeulen, W. J. V., & Witjes, S. (2018). The circular economy: New or refurbished as CE 3.0? — Exploring controversies in the conceptualization of the circular economy through a focus on history and resource value retention options. *Resources, Conservation and Recycling, 135*, 246–264. DOI: 10.1016/j.resconrec.2017.08.027

Reinhardt, F. L. (1998). Environmental product differentiation: Implications for corporate strategy. *California Management Review*, *40*(4), 43–73. DOI: 10.2307/41165964

Ren, Y.-S., Ma, C.-Q., Chen, X.-Q., Lei, Y.-T., & Wang, Y.-R. (2023). Sustainable finance and blockchain: A systematic review and research agenda. *Research in International Business and Finance*, *64*, 101871. DOI: 10.1016/j.ribaf.2022.101871

Rockström, J., Steffen, W., Noone, K., Persson, Å., Chapin, F. S.III, Lambin, E., Lenton, T. M., Scheffer, M., Folke, C., Schellnhuber, H., Nykvist, B., De Wit, C. A., Hughes, T., van der Leeuw, S., Rodhe, H., Sörlin, S., Snyder, P. K., Costanza, R., Svedin, U., & Falke, M. (2009). Planetary Boundaries: Exploring the safe operating space for humanity. *Ecology and Society*, *14*(2), 14. DOI: 10.5751/ES-03180-140232

Rodríguez-Ibeas, R. (2007). Environmental product differentiation and environmental awareness. *Environmental and Resource Economics*, *36*(2), 237–254. DOI: 10.1007/s10640-006-9026-y

Rogers, E. M. (2003). *Diffusion of Innovations* (5th ed.). Free Press.

Román, M. V., Arto, I., & Ansuategi, A. (2018). Why do some economies benefit more from climate finance than others? A case study on North-to-South financial flows. *Economic Systems Research*, *30*(1), 37–60. DOI: 10.1080/09535314.2017.1334629

Ronaldo, R., & Suryanto, T. (2022). Green finance and sustainability development goals in Indonesian Fund Village. *Resources Policy*, *78*, 102839. DOI: 10.1016/j.resourpol.2022.102839

Rubio, S., Chamorro, A., & Miranda, F. J. (2008). Characteristics of the research on reverse logistics (1995–2005). *International Journal of Production Research*, *46*(4), 1099–1120. DOI: 10.1080/00207540600943977

Ryan Hogarth, J. (2012). The role of climate finance in innovation systems. *Journal of Sustainable Finance & Investment*, *2*(3–4), 257–274. DOI: 10.1080/20430795.2012.742637

Ryu, H. S., & Ko, K. S. (2020). Sustainable development of FinTech. *Sustainability (Basel)*, *12*(18), 7669. DOI: 10.3390/su12187669

Sachs, J. (2015). *The Age of Sustainable Development*. Columbia University Press. DOI: 10.7312/sach17314

Saith, A. (2006). From universal values to millennium development goals: Lost in translation. *Development and Change*, *37*(6), 1167–1199. DOI: 10.1111/j.1467-7660.2006.00518.x

Sandberg, H., Alnoor, A., & Tiberius, V. (2023). Environmental, social, and governance ratings and financial performance: Evidence from the European food industry. *Business Strategy and the Environment, 32*(4), 2471–2489. DOI: 10.1002/bse.3259

Sandhu, K., Dayanandan, A., & Kuntluru, S. (2023). India's CBDC for digital public infrastructure. *Economics Letters, 231*, 111302.

Saner, R., Yiu, L., & Nguyen, M. (2020). Monitoring the SDGs: Digital and social technologies to ensure citizen participation, inclusiveness and transparency. *Development Policy Review, 38*(4), 483–500. DOI: 10.1111/dpr.12433

Sangiorgi, I., & Schopohl, L. (2023). Explaining green bond issuance using survey evidence: Beyond the greenium. *The British Accounting Review, 55*(1), 101071. 10.1016/j.bar.2021.101071. DOI: 10.1016/j.bar.2021.101071

Sankar, S. (2023, February 7). The challenge of sustainable fashion. *Times of India Blog*. https://timesofindia.indiatimes.com/blogs/voices/the-challenge-of-sustainable-fashion/

Sanoran, K. (2023). Corporate sustainability and sustainable growth: the role of industry sensitivity. *Finance Research Letters.* 53:103596. . 2022.103596DOI: 10.1016/j.frl

Sarkis, J. (2012). A boundaries and flows perspective of green supply chain management. *Supply Chain Management, 17*(2), 202–216. DOI: 10.1108/13598541211212924

SASB Standards and other ESG frameworks. (n.d.). Retrieved from https://sasb.ifrs.org/about/sasb-and-other-esg-frameworks/

Saunders, M., Lewis, P., & Thornhill, A. (2009). *Research Methods for Business Students* (5th ed.). Pearson education.

Savastano, M., Barnabei, R., & Ricotta, F. (2016). Going online while purchasing offline: An explorative analysis of omnichannel shopping behaviour in retail settings. *Proceedings of the International Marketing Trends Conference, 1*, 22. https://archives.marketing-trends- congress.com/2016/pages/PDF/SAVASTANO_BARNABEI_RICOTTA.pdf

Saxena, S. (2024, November 18). Using Natural Language Processing for detecting greenwashing indicators and constructing impact-focused index portfolio. *SSRN.* https://ssrn.com/abstract=5024113 DOI: 10.2139/ssrn.5024113

Schoenmaker, D., & Schramade, W. (2019). Investing for long-term value creation. *Journal of Sustainable Finance & Investment, 9*(4), 356–377. DOI: 10.1080/20430795.2019.1625012

Schroder, P., Bengtsson, M., Cohen, M., Dewick, P., Hofstetter, J., & Sarkis, J. (2019). Degrowth within: Aligning circular economy and strong sustainabilitynarratives. *Resources, Conservation and Recycling, 146*, 190–191. DOI: 10.1016/j.resconrec.2019.03.038

Schweikl, S., & Obermaier, R. (2020). Lessons from three decades of IT productivity research: Towards a better understanding of IT-induced productivity effects. *Management Review Quarterly, 70*(4), 461–507. DOI: 10.1007/s11301-019-00173-6

Seidel, S., Recker, J., Pimmer, C., & Brocke, J. V. (2010). Enablers and barriers to the organizational adoption of sustainable business practices.

Selvaggi, M., & Upton, J. (2008). *Governance and performance in corporate Britain*. Association of British Insurers.

Sen, S. (2024, May 23). MamaEarth Parent faces six times more cases than Patanjali before ad regulator. *NDTV Profit*. https://www.ndtvprofit.com/business/mamaearth-parent-faces-six-times-more-cases-than-patanjali-before-ad-regulator

Sendlhofer, T., & Tolstoy, D. (2022). How employees shape CSR transparency: A sensemaking perspective. *Journal of Business Research, 150*, 268–278. DOI: 10.1016/j.jbusres.2022.05.074

Seuring, S., & Müller, M. (2008). From a literature review to a conceptual framework for sustainable supply chain management. *Journal of Cleaner Production, 16*(15), 1699–1710. DOI: 10.1016/j.jclepro.2008.04.020

Shah, S. B., Sopin, J., Techato, K. A., & Mudbhari, B. K. (2023). A Systematic Review on Nexus Between Green Finance and Climate Change: Evidence from China and India. *International Journal of Energy Economics and Policy, 13*(4), 599–613. DOI: 10.32479/ijeep.14331

Shao, A., Lu, Z., Zhong, B., Liu, S. Q., & Lu, W. (2025). Human touch vs. AI tech: Understanding user preferences in the future of education. *Computers in Human Behavior, 164*, 108492. DOI: 10.1016/j.chb.2024.108492

Sharma, V., & Gupta, R. (2021). *The role of AI in sustainable manufacturing in India*. Industrial Development Review.

Shawoo, Z., Dzebo, A., Funder, M., & Dupuy, K. (2022). Country ownership in climate finance coordination: A comparative assessment of Kenya and Zambia. *Climate Policy, 22*(9–10), 1266–1280. DOI: 10.1080/14693062.2022.2098227

Shrier, D., Pentland, A., Zachariadis, M., Ozcan, P., Services, D., Goodenough, O., Flood, M., Reed, M., Hardjono, T., Lipton, A., Possibilities, F., Sandboxes, R., & Bhalla, A. (2022). Global Fintech. In The MIT Press eBooks. DOI: 10.7551/mitpress/13673.001.0001

Shukla, M. (2022, June 8). What is omnichannel retail? A guide to the latest trends in omnichannel customer experience. *Delighted.* https://delighted.com/blog/omnichannel-retail-consumer-trends

Shukla, R., Bagotia, H., Satish, P., Kamath, H. S., Chatterjee, S., Savariah, D., Kaulgud, V., Gobburi, H., & Acharya, S. (2025). Fintech and healthtech synergism: Pioneering a digital healthcare revolution for accessible, affordable, and effective patient-centered care. *Journal of Family Medicine and Primary Care, 14*(3), 820–824. DOI: 10.4103/jfmpc.jfmpc_999_24 PMID: 40256084

Sianipar, R. H., & Wiksuana, I. G. B. (2019). The study of the effect of corporate governance on financial performance. *Russian Journal of Agricultural and Socio-Economic Sciences, 2*(86), 166–170. DOI: 10.18551/rjoas.2019-02.19

Silva, S. (2021). Corporate contributions to the Sustainable Development Goals: An empirical analysis informed by legitimacy theory. *Journal of Cleaner Production, 292*, 125962. DOI: 10.1016/j.jclepro.2021.125962

Simanungkalit, R. H. M., Jumono, S., Arrozi Adhikara, M. F., Munandar, A., & Suharna, J. (2025). Integration of Digital Technology in Green Finance: A Systematic Analysis of Green Digital Finance. *Journal of System and Management Sciences, 15*(1).

Simo, A. A., Nkamleu, G. B., & Tchamyou, V. S. (2025). FinTech, social impact, and financial inclusion. *African Development Review, 37*(2), 249–267.

Singh, H., Mishra, K. K., & Singh, M. P. (2024). A Study on Rural BPL Households' Perception Towards Financial Inclusion Schemes. In Algorithmic Approaches to Financial Technology: Forecasting, Trading, and Optimization (pp. 146-159). IGI Global.

Singh, A., & Pandey, J. (2025). Artificial intelligence applications in human resource management: It is a mixed bag! *International Journal of Productivity and Performance Management*, •••, 1–20. DOI: 10.1108/IJPPM-09-2024-0599

Singhal, A. (2019, May 23). *From Omni channel retailing in India to Omnipresent Retail.* Brand Experts. https://www.brand-experts.com/brand-expansion/omni-channel-retailing-in-india/

Sirmon, D. G., Hitt, M. A., Ireland, R. D., & Gilbert, B. A. (2011). Resource orchestration to create competitive advantage: Breadth, depth, and life cycle effects. *Journal of Management*, *37*(5), 1390–1412. DOI: 10.1177/0149206310385695

Siswantoro, D. (2018). The relationship of the green bond and the Social Development Goals (SDGs) targets: a case study of Vigeo Eiris. *E3S Web Conf.*, *74*, 1003. DOI: 10.1051/e3sconf/20187401003

Skovgaard, J., Adams, K. M., Dupuy, K., Dzebo, A., Funder, M., Fejerskov, A. M., & Shawoo, Z. (2023). Multilateral Climate Finance Coordination: Politics and Depoliticization in Practice. *Global Environmental Politics*, *23*(2), 125–147. DOI: 10.1162/glep_a_00703

Solow, R. (1987). We'd better watch out. *New York Times Book Review*, 36.

Sreenu, N., & Verma, S. S. (2024). Enhancing economic growth through digital financial inclusion: An examination of India. *Transnational Corporations Review*, *16*(4), 200091.

Srivastav, S., Garg, V., & Elngar, A. A. (2022). The Impact of Artificial Intelligence for Comprehensive Growth Across the Globe. *Empowering Artificial Intelligence Through Machine Learning: New Advances and Applications*, 137.

Srivastava, S. K. (2007). Green supply-chain management: A state-of-the-art literature review. *International Journal of Management Reviews*, *9*(1), 53–80. DOI: 10.1111/j.1468-2370.2007.00202.x

Stanley, T. D., Doucouliagos, H., & Steel, P. (2018). DOES ICT GENERATE ECONOMIC GROWTH? A META-REGRESSION ANALYSIS. *Journal of Economic Surveys*, *32*(3), 705–726. DOI: 10.1111/joes.12211

Statman, M., & Glushkov, D. (2008). The wages of social responsibility. *Financial Analysts Journal*, *65*(4), 33–46. DOI: 10.2469/faj.v65.n4.5

STYLISHLY SUSTAINABLE - A Social movement through a Fashion brand. (2023, December 31). AIM2Flourish. https://aim2flourish.com/innovations/stylishly-sustainable-a-social-movement-through-a-fashion-brand

Sugandini, D., Susilowati, C., Siswanti, Y., & Syafri, W. (2020). Green supply management and green marketing strategy on green purchase intention: SMEs cases. [JIEM]. *Journal of Industrial Engineering and Management*, *13*(1), 79–92. DOI: 10.3926/jiem.2795

Sun, Z., Liu, L., Johan, S., & Zhao, L. (2024). FinTech Adoption and Corporate Greenwashing: A Technology Affordance Perspective. *British Journal of Management, 36*(3), 978–1002. DOI: 10.1111/1467-8551.12879

Suroso, D. S. A., Setiawan, B., Pradono, P., Iskandar, Z. S., & Hastari, M. A. (2022). Revisiting the role of international climate finance (ICF) towards achieving the nationally determined contribution (NDC) target: A case study of the Indonesian energy sector. *Environmental Science & Policy, 131*, 188–195. DOI: 10.1016/j.envsci.2022.01.022

Sustainability Directory. (2025, April 1). What are common challenges for SMEs when implementing ESG reporting practices? Sustainability-Directory.com. Retrieved July 31, 2025, from https://sustainability-directory.com/question/what-are-common-challenges-for-smes-when-implementing-esg-reporting-practices

Sustainable Materials. (n.d.). Nike.com. https://www.nike.com/in/sustainability/materials

Switzerland, W. (n.d.). Integrating ESG factors into financial models for infrastructure investments: Guidance note. World Economic Forum.

Syamsudin, S., Imronudin, I., Utomo, S. T., & Praswati, A. N. (2017). Corporate governance in detecting lack of financial report. *Jurnal Dinamika Manajemen, 8*(2), 167–176. DOI: 10.15294/jdm.v8i2.12757

Tackling Vulnerability in the Informal Economy. (2019). In the Development Centre studies. DOI: 10.1787/939b7bcd-en

Tambe, P., Cappelli, P., & Yakubovich, V. (2019). Artificial Intelligence in Human Resources Management: Challenges and a Path Forward.[·. *California Management Review, 61*(4), 15–42. https://mitsloan.mit.edu/ideas-made-to-matter/productivity-paradox-ai-adoption-manufacturing-firms. DOI: 10.1177/0008125619867910

Tassinari, A., & Maccarrone, V. (2020). Riders on the storm: Workplace solidarity among gig economy couriers in Italy and the UK. *Work, Employment and Society, 34*(1), 35–54. DOI: 10.1177/0950017019862954

Team, I. (2024, January 30). Sustainable footwear brand Neeman's reports Rs 69 crore revenue in FY23; Losses stood at Rs 34 crore. *Indian Startup News*. https://indianstartupnews.com/news/sustainable-footwear-brand-neemans-reports-rs-69-crore-revenue-in-fy23-2407612

Teece, D. J., Pisano, G., & Shuen, A. (1997). Dynamic Capabilities and Strategic Management. *Strategic Management Journal, 18*(7), 509–533. DOI: 10.1002/(SICI)1097-0266(199708)18:7<509::AID-SMJ882>3.0.CO;2-Z

Testa, F., Pretner, G., Iovino, R., Bianchi, G., Tessitore, S., & Iraldo, F. (2021). Drivers to green consumption: A systematic review. *Environment, Development and Sustainability*, *23*(4), 4826–4880. DOI: 10.1007/s10668-020-00844-5

Thakor, A. V. (2020). FinTech and banking: What do we know? *Journal of Financial Intermediation*, *41*, 100833. DOI: 10.1016/j.jfi.2019.100833

The Economist. (2023). Digital transformation and sustainability: Climate change and economic development.

The importance of sustainability in Business | HBS Online. (2019, November 6). Business Insights Blog. https://online.hbs.edu/blog/post/business-sustainability-strategies

The Payments Association. (2024). *How payments companies can integrate ESG into their business models and the benefits of doing so*. https://thepaymentsassociation.org/article/how-payments-companies-can-integrate-esg-into-their-business-models-and-the-benefits-of-doing-so/

Thottoli, M. M., & Thomas, K. V. (2023). 'The impact of web marketing on corporate social responsibility (CSR) and firms' performance'. *Rajagiri Management Journal*, *17*(1), 37–51. DOI: 10.1108/RAMJ-03-2021-0022

Tirole, J. (2017). *Economics for the Common Good*. Princeton University Press. DOI: 10.2307/j.ctvc77hng

Tolliver, C., Keeley, A. R., & Managi, S. (2019). Green bonds for the Paris agreement and sustainable development goals. *Environmental Research Letters*, *14*(6), 64009. DOI: 10.1088/1748-9326/ab1118

Tranfield, D., Denyer, D., & Smart, P. (2003). Towards a methodology for developing evidence-informed management knowledge by means of systematic review. *British Journal of Management*, *14*(3), 207–222. DOI: 10.1111/1467-8551.00375

Tseng, M. L., Wu, K. J., Hu, J., & Wang, C. H. (2018). Decision-making model for sustainable supply chain finance. *International Journal of Production Economics*, *205*, 30–36. DOI: 10.1016/j.ijpe.2018.08.024

Tsoncheva, G. (2014). Measuring and assessing the quality and usefulness of accounting information. Izvestia – Journal of the University of Economics – Varna, 58(1), 52–64.

Turner, M., & Houston, P. (2009). Going green? Start with sourcing. *Supply Chain Management Review*, *13*(2), 14–21.

Tursunbayeva, A., Pagliari, C., Di Lauro, S., & Antonelli, G. (2021). The Ethics of People Analytics: Risks, Opportunities, and Recommendations. *Personnel Review*, *51*(3), 900–921. DOI: 10.1108/PR-12-2019-0680

Tyron, L. (2024). How Blockchain Revolutionizes Supply Chain Tracking for ESG and Corporate Accountability. Medium. Retrieved from https://medium.com/@adelstein/how-blockchain-revolutionizes-supply-chain-tracking-for-esg-and-corporate-accountability-0deea5bcc4dc

UNEP. (2021). UNEP's digital initiatives for sustainability.

UNEP. (2024). *Digital Finance for the Planet: Accelerating Climate Action through FinTech.* United Nations Environment Programme.

United Nations Development Programme (UNDP). (2025a) Egypt Accelerator Lab. (2025, July 24). Mapping global signals for fintech in green sectors: agriculture, energy, and sustainable tourism. UNDP. https://www.undp.org/acceleratorlabs/blog/mapping-global-signals-fintech-green-sectors-agriculture-energy-and-sustainable-tourism

United Nations Development Programme (UNDP). (2025b, May 7). THE POTENTIAL GROWTH AND FUTURE TRENDS OF GREEN SUKUK AS A TOOL FOR SUSTAINABLE FINANCING. https://www.undp.org/sites/g/files/zskgke326/files/2025-05/undp-kfh-green-sukuk-tool-for-sustainable-financing.pdf

United Nations Environment Programme (UNEP). (2023). Adaptation Gap Report 2023: Underfinanced. Underprepared. Inadequate investment and planning on climate adaptation leaves world exposed. DOI: 10.59117/20.500.11822/43796

United Nations Environment Programme Finance Initiative (UNEP FI). (2024). *From Disclosure to Action: Advancing Climate-Related Financial Disclosures in Emerging Markets*. UNEP Finance Initiative.

United Nations. (2015). *Transforming our world: The 2030 Agenda for Sustainable Development.*

United Nations. (2015). Transforming Our World: The 2030 Agenda for Sustainable Development.

Uyar, A., Wasiuzzaman, S., Kuzey, C., & Karaman, A. S. (2022). Board structure and financial stability of financial firms: Do board policies and CEO duality matter? *Journal of International Accounting, Auditing & Taxation*, *47*, 100474. DOI: 10.1016/j.intaccaudtax.2022.100474

Vachon, S., & Klassen, R. D. (2008). Environmental management and manufacturing performance: The role of collaboration in the supply chain. *International Journal of Production Economics*, *111*(2), 299–315. DOI: 10.1016/j.ijpe.2006.11.030

Van Niekerk, G., & Ponelis, F. (2024). Strengthening Law Enforcement to Address White-Collar Financial Crime in South Africa's Private Sector. Potchefstroom Electronic Law Journal/Potchefstroomse Elektroniese Regsblad, 27. DOI: 10.17159/1727-3781/2024/v27i0a17141

Vanderklift, M. A., Herr, D., Lovelock, C. E., Murdiyarso, D., Raw, J. L., & Steven, A. D. L. (2022). A Guide to International Climate Mitigation Policy and Finance Frameworks Relevant to the Protection and Restoration of Blue Carbon Ecosystems. *Frontiers in Marine Science*, *9*(July), 1–14. DOI: 10.3389/fmars.2022.872064

Vargo, S. L., & Lusch, R. F. (2004). Evolving to a New Dominant Logic for Marketing. *Journal of Marketing*, *68*(1), 1–17. DOI: 10.1509/jmkg.68.1.1.24036

Varsha, V. R. (2024). Digital platforms and ESG integration in sustainable finance. *International Journal of Finance & Economics*, *29*(1), 115–132.

Verhoef, P. C., Broekhuizen, T., Bart, Y., Bhattacharya, A., Dong, J. Q., Fabian, N., & Haenlein, M. (2021). Digital transformation: A multidisciplinary reflection and research agenda. *Journal of Business Research*, *122*, 889–901. DOI: 10.1016/j.jbusres.2019.09.022

Veronica, S., & Bachtiar, Y. S. (2005). The role of corporate governance in preventing misstated financial statements. Jurnal Akuntansi dan Keuangan Indonesia, 2(1), 159–173.

Vishnevsky, V. P., Harkushenko, O. M., Zanizdra, M. Y., & Kniaziev, S. I. (2021). Digital and green economy: Common grounds and contradictions. *Science and Innovation*, *17*(3), 14–27. DOI: 10.15407/scine17.03.014

Visser, W. (2008). Corporate Social Responsibility in Developing Countries. In Crane, A. (Eds.), *The Oxford Handbook of Corporate Social Responsibility* (pp. 473–500)., DOI: 10.1093/oxfordhb/9780199211593.003.0021

Vives, X. (2019). Digital disruption in banking. *Annual Review of Financial Economics*, *11*(1), 243–272. DOI: 10.1146/annurev-financial-100719-120854

Waage, S. A., Geiser, K., Irwin, F., Weissman, A. B., Bertolucci, M. D., Fisk, P., Basile, G., Cowan, S., Cauley, H., & McPherson, A. (2005). Fitting together the building blocks for sustainability: A revised model for integrating ecological, social, and financial factors into business decision-making. *Journal of Cleaner Production*, *13*(12), 1145–1163. DOI: 10.1016/j.jclepro.2004.06.003

Walker, K., & Wan, F. (2012). The harm of symbolic actions and green-washing: Corporate actions and communications on environmental performance and their financial implications. *Journal of Business Ethics*, *109*(2), 227–242. DOI: 10.1007/s10551-011-1122-4

Warren, P. (2020). Blind spots in climate finance for innovation. *Advances in Climate Change Research*, *11*(1), 60–64. DOI: 10.1016/j.accre.2020.05.001

Whelan, T., Atz, U., Van Holt, T., & Clark, C. (2021). ESG and financial performance: Uncovering the relationship by aggregating evidence from 1,000 plus studies published between 2015 – 2020. NYU Stern Center for Sustainable Business & Rockefeller Asset Management. https://www.stern.nyu.edu/sites/default/files/assets/documents/NYU-RAM_ESG-Paper_2021%20Rev_0.pdf

Williams, A. (2024, August 20). Guide to sustainable business practices in 2024. https://blog.shorts.uk.com/. https://blog.shorts.uk.com/sustainable-business-practices

Williamson, O. E. (1981). The economics of organization: The transaction cost approach. *AJS; American Journal of Sociology*, *87*(3), 548–577. DOI: 10.1086/227496

Winner, L. (1980). Do artefacts have politics? *Daedalus*, *109*(1), 121–136.

Wood, A. J., Graham, M., Lehdonvirta, V., & Hjorth, I. (2019). Good gig, bad gig: Autonomy and algorithmic control in the global gig economy. *Work, Employment and Society*, *33*(1), 56–75. DOI: 10.1177/0950017018785616 PMID: 30886460

Woollard, R. F., & Ostry, A. S. (2000). *Fatal consumption: rethinking sustainable development*. UBC Press.

World Bank. (2022). The Global Findex Database 2021: Financial inclusion, digital payments, and resilience in the age of COVID-19.

World Bank. (2023). *Blended Finance for Climate Action: A Progress Report*. World Bank Group.

World Bank. (2025, February). Labeled Sustainable Bonds Market Update February 2025. The World Bank. https://thedocs.worldbank.org/en/doc/cd82b4033281dab2cb1a1c71eeb691e4-0340012025/original/Labeled-Bond-Quarterly-Newsletter-Issue-No-10.pdf

World Bank's Policy Response to the COVID-19 (Coronavirus) Pandemic: Promoting the Use of Digital Payments in Russia. (March 09, 2020), https://www.worldbank.org/en/country/russia/brief/covid-19-response-digital-payments-russia

World Commission on Environment and Development. (1987). *Our common future*. Oxford University Press.

World Economic Forum. (2023). Digitalization and Sustainable Development Goals: Global trends.

Xue, J., He, Y., Xu, H., & Gong, Z. (2023). Under the ecological label policy: Supply chain Heterogeneous product innovation strategies for green marketing. *Journal of Cleaner Production*, *428*, 139370. DOI: 10.1016/j.jclepro.2023.139370

Xu, L., & Solangi, Y. A. (2023). Evaluating the impact of green bonds on renewable energy investment to promote sustainable development in China. *Journal of Renewable and Sustainable Energy*, *15*(5), 055901. Advance online publication. DOI: 10.1063/5.0161387

Xu, N., Kasimov, I., & Wang, Y. (2022). Unlocking private investment as a new determinant of green finance for renewable development in China. *Renewable Energy*, *198*, 1121–1130. DOI: 10.1016/j.renene.2022.07.037

Yan, C., & Tan, Q. (2023). Has the level of green finance development improved carbon emission performance?—Empirical evidence from China. *MDE. Managerial and Decision Economics*, *3891*(6), 3485–3499. Advance online publication. DOI: 10.1002/mde.3891

Yang, H. (2024). Advancing sustainable development through financial innovation and investment. The Frontiers of Society. *Science and Technology*, *6*(1). Advance online publication. DOI: 10.25236/FSST.2024.060111

Yang, X. (2020). FinTech is promoting the development of green finance in China. In *Proceedings of the 4th International Seminar on Education Innovation and Economic Management*.

Yoshino, N., Rasoulinezhad, E., & Taghizadeh-Hesary, F. (2021). Economic impacts of carbon tax in a general equilibrium framework: Empirical study of Japan. *Journal of Environmental Assessment Policy and Management*, *23*(01), 2250014. DOI: 10.1142/S1464333222500144

Younas, A., & Kassim, A. A. M. (2022) 'Measuring Corporate Social Responsibility by Constructing an Index: An Empirical Evidence from Oman', In Eurasian Business and Economics Perspectives: Proceedings of the 35th Eurasia Business and Economics Society Conference (pp. 231-244). Cham: Springer International Publishing. DOI: 10.1007/978-3-030-94672-2_14

Younas, A., & Kassim, A. A. M. (2023) 'Exploring the Impact of Corporate Social Responsibility on Leverage of Listed Companies in Oman', In Global Economic Challenges: 6th International Conference on Banking and Finance Perspectives, Cuenca, Spain (pp. 39-53). Cham: Springer International Publishing. DOI: 10.1007/978-3-031-23416-3_4

Younas, A., Kassim, A. A. M., & Bhuiyan, A. B. (2021). Construction of corporate social responsibility (CSR) disclosure index and its practices by listed companies in Oman. *American International Journal of Economics and Finance Research, 3*(1), 57–68.

Younas, A., Muthuraman, S., Al Darmaki, A., Khan, F., & Kassim, A. A. M. (2023). Empirical Review of Measuring Corporate Social Responsibility in the Sultanate of Oman. *Artificial Intelligence, Internet of Things, and Society, 5*(0), 167–177. DOI: 10.1007/978-3-031-43300-9_15

Yurisandi, T., & Puspitasari, E. (2015). Financial reporting quality – Before and after IFRS adoption using NiCE qualitative characteristics measurement. *Procedia: Social and Behavioral Sciences, 211*, 644–652. DOI: 10.1016/j.sbspro.2015.11.091

Zaheer, A., Singh, A., & Mishra, K. K. Reepu, and Vardari, L. (2024), "The Future of Alchemy: Emerging Trends and Technologies Metaverse in Insurance – A Virtual Customer Experience", Taneja, S., Kumar, P., Reepu, Kukreti, M. and Özen, E. (Ed.) Data Alchemy in the Insurance Industry, Emerald Publishing Limited, Leeds, pp. 133-152. DOI: 10.1108/978-1-83608-582-920241021

Zamawe, F. C. (2015). The implication of using NVivo software in qualitative data analysis: Evidence-based reflections. *Malawi Medical Journal : The Journal of Medical Association of Malawi, 27*(1), 13–15. DOI: 10.4314/mmj.v27i1.4

Zampese, E. R. D. S., Moori, R. G., & Caldeira, A. (2016). Green marketing as a mediator between supply chain management and organizational performance. *RAM. Revista de Administração Mackenzie, 17*(3), 183–211. DOI: 10.1590/1678-69712016/administracao.v17n3p183-211

Zerbib, O. (2019). The effect of pro-environmental preferences on bond prices: Evidence from green bonds. *Journal of Banking & Finance, 98*, 39–60. DOI: 10.1016/j.jbankfin.2018.10.012

Zhang, S., Anser, M. K., Yao-Ping Peng M., & Chen C. (2022). Visualizing the sustainable development goals and natural resource utilization for green economic recovery after COVID-19 pandemic. *Resources Policy.* December 13, 103182. .DOI: 10.1016/j.resourpol.2022.103182

Zhang, P., Yang, X., Chen, H., & Zhao, S. (2023). Matching Relationship between Urban Service Industry Land Expansion and Economic Growth in China. *Land (Basel), 12*(6), 1139. DOI: 10.3390/land12061139

Zhang, X., Xiu, G., Shahzad, F., & Duan, Y. (2021). Optimal financing strategy in a capital-constrained supply chain with retailer green marketing efforts. *Sustainability (Basel), 13*(3), 1357. DOI: 10.3390/su13031357

Zhang-Zhang, Y., Rohlfer, S., & Rajasekera, J. (2020). An eco-systematic view of cross-sector FinTech. *Sustainability (Basel), 12*(21), 8907. DOI: 10.3390/su12218907

Zhao, X., Benkraiem, R., Abedin, M. Z., & Zhou, S. (2024). The charm of green finance: Can green finance reduce corporate carbon emissions? *Energy Economics, 134*, 107574. 10.1016/j.eneco.2024.107574. DOI: 10.1016/j.eneco.2024.107574

Zhou, X., & Cui, Y. (2019). Green Bonds, Corporate Performance, and Corporate Social Responsibility. *Sustainability (Basel), 11*(23), 6881. DOI: 10.3390/su11236881

Zhu, Q., Sarkis, J., & Lai, K. (2018). Confirmation of a measurement model for green supply chain management practices implementation. *International Journal of Production Economics, 111*(2), 261–273. DOI: 10.1016/j.ijpe.2006.11.029

Ziolo, M., Bak, I., Cheba, K., & Spoz, A. (2020). Sustainable business models of enterprises - actual and declared activities for ensuring corporate sustainability. *Procedia Computer Science, 176*, 1497–1506. https://creativecommons.org/licenses/by-nc-nd/4.0. DOI: 10.1016/j.procs.2020.09.160

About the Contributors

Dharmendra Singh is an Associate Professor (Finance) at Modern College of Business and Science, Muscat (Oman). He possesses rich professional experience of over 25 years in the field of finance. He holds a Ph.D. (Finance), professional certifications like Certified Financial Planner (CFP), an associate diploma (life insurance) from the Insurance Institute of India, and a CFA from ICFAI. He has published more than 51 articles & research papers in ABDC, CABS, and Scopus Q1-ranked international and referred journals. He has 1949 citations, h-index 20, and i10-index 27 in google scholar. He has authored and published five edited books on contemporary subjects in finance with renowned publishers and these books have been included in the Scopus database. His research areas include banking, corporate finance, entrepreneurial finance, and financial markets. He has conducted training programs in collaboration with CMA, Oman, as well as in multiple universities as well as outside Oman. He also serves as a reviewer for high rank journals. He is a member of the Financial Planning Standard Board (FPSB), the Indian Econometric Society, and the Insurance Institute of India.

Rene Y. Paquibut is Head of the Department of Institutional Research and Quality Assurance at the Modern College of Business and Science (MCBS), Oman, and an active researcher in business ethics, sustainability, circular economy adoption, artificial intelligence ethics, and higher education quality systems. He has held academic and quality-assurance leadership roles in the Philippines, the United Arab Emirates, and Oman, and has served as an external reviewer for national accreditation and audit bodies. His scholarly work examines the psycho-social foundations of sustainable consumption, the intention–action gap in circular economy adoption, technology adoption and trust, and governance frameworks in higher education. He has published and edited peer-reviewed articles and book chapters and regularly presents at international conferences in business, management, and education. His research integrates theoretical development, systematic literature reviews, and empirical analysis, with a strong focus on policy relevance and institutional impact, and is supported by ongoing collaborations across Oman, the Philippines, and the United Arab Emirates.

***

Vineeta Agrawal holds a Doctorate in Microfinance, MBA and M.Com. Currently, She is working as an Associate Professor at JSPM University, Pune. She has rich experience in Academia for more than fifteen years. Her area of teaching interests are Economics and Finance. She is also examiner for Ph.D. thesis evaluation and viva at multiple institutions . She has presented research papers in various national and international conferences and her research work is published in journals of repute including Scopus, Springer and Web of Sciences. She frequently writes articles and opinion pieces on contemporary international and national issues. Her articles have also published in different newspapers and websites.

Swati Bhatnagar currently serving as an Asst. Professor in the Marketing Department at New Delhi Institute of Management, she is a B.Sc. (Hons) graduate from Hindu College, Delhi University and did her MBA from ICFAI Business School, Gurgaon. She is a Ph.D from Delhi Technological University and did her research on the topic of Distribution Channel Conflict in the FMCG Sector. She is also UGC NET qualified. She has cumulative experience of more than 22 years. She has corporate experience with Birla Sunlife & ICICI Prudential AMC Ltd where she was instrumental in revenue generation from the Banking channel and worked with global banking giants like ABN AMRO Bank, HDFC Bank ICICI Bank, and Kotak Mahindra Bank. She transitioned to academics and worked at Amity Business School for more than 12 years before joining NDIM. Her deep domain expertise lies in advance selling techniques, GTM strategy, Omnichannel Management, and Service Marketing.

Bushra – Associate Professor, Jagan Institute of Management Studies, Rohini, Delhi This is Dr. Bushra, currently serving as an Associate Professor at Jagan Institute of Management Studies (JIMS), Rohini, Delhi. I hold a PhD in Behavioural Finance and am UGC NET (Management) qualified. My academic background includes an MBA in Finance, M.Com, B.Com (Hons), and B.Ed., which collectively form a strong foundation in the disciplines of finance, commerce, and education. With over 15 years of teaching experience, I have been engaged in delivering a wide range of subjects in the areas of finance and accounts. My core areas of interest include Behavioural Finance, Financial Management, Accounting, and Investment

Analysis. I am passionate about blending theoretical knowledge with practical insights to enhance student learning and engagement in the classroom.

Jaya Gupta is a Professor of OB and HRM at BIMTECH and has been spearheading the AACSB accreditation activities at BIMTECH. Having been actively involved in national and international accreditations and rankings at BIMTECH, she has over 29 years of rich experience in Management Education, training and research. She has been an active researcher and has successfully published articles in reputed international journals. She has conducted Management Development Programmes and training workshops at mid and senior management levels in the area of time management, work life balance, conflict management, stress management, healthy mind and healthy body, etc, for leading organizations such as NTPC, IIFCO, Power Grid, ISB Goldman Sachs 10,000 Women Entrepreneur project etc. She has been part of the interview panel as HR expert for the selection of Probationary Officers for UCO Bank. She has successfully completed certification in Talent Management by T.V. Rao Learning Systems and a Certificate Course on People Analytics from XLRI, Jamshedpur.

Ramya H P holds an MBA in finance and is pursuing a Ph.D. in investments from VTU. Currently, she works as an assistant professor at the Department of Management Studies at DSCE, with 16 years of experience. She has conducted workshops and seminars on topics such as financial management using Excel, financial accounting and taxation, and financial statement analysis, and has presented and published research papers in various national and international journals. Additionally, she is trained in personal finance, data processing using Python, taxation, financial modelling, trading strategies, portfolio optimization using the Markowitz model, and investment management. She is also an AICTE-nominated innovation ambassador for the Institute Innovation Council.

Siriyama Kanthi Herath is an Associate Professor of Accounting at Clark Atlanta University's School of Business (CAU) and was a Renwick Faculty Fellow at New York University's Stern School of Business in 2022. She earned a Bachelor of Commerce Honors and an MBA from the University of Colombo in Sri Lanka, as well as a Ph.D. and a Master of Commerce Honors in Accounting from the University of Wollongong in Australia. She worked at the University of Lynchburg, Georgia State University and Georgia Institute of Technology before joining CAU. Dr. Herath worked in Australia at the University of Wollongong and Western Sydney University and in Sri Lanka at the University of Ruhuna and the University of Colombo. She has contributed over 70 publications to a diverse range of journals. She has published 17 book chapters with coauthors. She is a Distinguished Toastmaster and served as the President and served as an Area Director from 2020 to 2021 in Georgia, United States. She possesses the TESOL Professional Certificate from Arizona State University. Dr. Herath is the Editor-In-Chief of the Asian Journal of Economics and Business and Global Journal of Accounting and Economy Research.

Anand Jaiswal is an Assistant Professor in the Department of Management Studies at the TERI School of Advanced Studies, New Delhi. He holds a Ph.D. in Industrial Management from the Indian Institute of Technology (BHU), Varanasi, along with an MBA and a B.Tech. He is certified professional in Blockchain, Lean Six Sigma, and Project Management. With over 18 years of diverse experience spanning academia and industry, Dr. Jaiswal previously served as an Associate Professor in the Operations and Supply Chain Management Department at the New Delhi Institute of Management. He actively engages in training and capacity building program and has delivered sessions at institutes like IOCL, HPCL, GAIL, IITs, and also international universities and organizations such as Pennwest University, USA. He has also carried out several funded government and corporate projects in the areas of sustainability, environmental assessment, and supply chain management.

Nitendra Kumar received a Ph. D (Mathematics) from Sharda University, Greater Noida, India and a Master of Science (Mathematics and Statistics) from Dr Ram Manohar Lohia Avadh University, Faizabad, India. Currently, he is working as an Assistant Professor at Amity Business School, Amity University, Noida with interests in Wavelets and its Variants, Data Mining, Inverse Problems, Epidemic Modeling, Fractional Derivatives Business Analytics, and Statistical Methods. He has more than 10 years of experience in his research areas. Dr Kumar has published many research papers in reputed journals and also published 6 books on engineering mathematics. He contributes to the research community by undertaking various volunteer activities in the capacity of editor for two edited books and guest Editor of reputed journals.

K. K. Mishra is a Professor of Marketing in the Department of Management at Chandigarh University, Unnao, Uttar Pradesh, India. He has published 119 research papers in Scopus-indexed journals and book chapters, and has contributed to national and international conferences. He has five patent rights and three copyrights. He has 26 years of experience in teaching and research. He has supervised two PhD scholars. He has twice qualified for the UGC NET in Management. He has received the Best Faculty Award three times from the Indian Institute of Materials Management, National Headquarters, Mumbai, in 2009, 2016, and 2018, respectively. He has been conferred the Best Paper Award for the paper titled "Harnessing AI: Unveiling Educators' Intentions and Synergy in Education", presented at the 8th International

Conference on Information System Design and Intelligent Applications (ISDIS 2024) in Dubai, UAE, in 2024. He has chaired technical sessions of international conferences organised by the Indian Institute of Materials Management, Mumbai, in 2016 and 2018, and OP Jindal University, Raigarh, in 2022 and 2023.

Sushma Murlie has been working with Presidency University since 2025. She has a teaching career of 29 years, she has taught in various colleges in the NCR region, including NDIM, JIMS, SRISIM, and Asia Pacific school of management. She has a postgraduate degree in chemistry from Delhi University, an MBA from Pune University, and Ph.D. from GSSIP. She has published papers in Scopus-indexed ABDC journals and has attended various international conferences. Her current areas of interest include developing teaching cases and researching in the domain area of Sustainability and Public Policies. In her previous stint, she worked with a chemical manufacturer in the product development of specialty chemicals. Currently taking courses on general management, HRM, and Business law.

Pawan Pant is working as an Associate Professor of Management at the University School of Business, Chandigarh University, Mohali, Punjab. He has published eight research papers, including one in a national and one in an international journal. He has 11 years of teaching experience and worked as an Assistant Manager (Purchase) at Pacific Industries Ltd., Udaipur (Rajasthan), for one year. His area of specialisation is Economics. email: pawanpant04@gmail.com,

Pushpalata Patil is currently working as an Assistant Professor, JSPM University. Prof. Patil has 15 years Academic Experience with 7 year Pharma Industrial Experience.

Swati Priya is working as an Associate Professor at the Dept. of Humanities and Professional Communication, BBDNIIT, Lucknow, Uttar Pradesh, India. Her specialisation area is Rural marketing. She has qualified for UGC NET in Management and has 14 years of teaching experience. My research focus is on marketing. I have published various research papers and book chapters in reputed journals and presented them in conferences.

Ishrat Rasool is an academician, researcher, and author specializing in accounting, finance, healthcare management, and the integration of emerging technologies into business and healthcare practices. She is currently serving as Assistant Professor in the Department of Hospital Management and Hospice Studies at Jamia Millia Islamia, New Delhi, where she teaches Financial, Cost and Management Accounting, Business Research Methodology, Quantitative Techniques, and Data Analysis. Her teaching and research focus on blending theoretical knowledge with practical applications, preparing students and scholars to undertake evidence-based and analytical decision-making. Before entering academia, Dr. Rasool gained professional experience as a Financial Analyst at EXL Service, contributing to global projects in mergers and acquisitions, corporate restructuring, financial performance evaluation, and deal analysis. This background allows her to combine academic rigor with industry relevance in her research and teaching. Dr. Rasool has an extensive record of publications in SCOPUS- and Web of Science–indexed journals, covering diverse themes such as financial inclusion, mergers and acquisitions in the Indian pharmaceutical sector, consumer behavior during economic shocks, cryptocurrency adoption, and rare disease management policy. She is the author of Financial Accounting Concepts & Applications and has contributed to several edited volumes. Her scholarly engagement extends to presenting research at numerous national and international conferences, including those focused on financial inclusion, sustainability, entrepreneurship, innovation, FinTech, and AI-driven financial decision-making. She has also actively participated in workshops and faculty development programs on business analytics, research methodology, financial statement analysis, structural equation modeling, and sustainable development, organized by leading institutions such as IIMs, IITs, and international universities. In recognition of her academic contributions, she has been awarded the Hamdard National Fellowship. She also serves on editorial and advisory boards, reviews for reputed journals, and contributes as an organizer and convener in academic events. Her current research interests focus on the intersections of finance, technology, and healthcare, particularly in advancing sustainable, inclusive, and innovation-driven economic and healthcare models.

Kanhaiya Singh, a seasoned Banker turned as an Academician began his academic journey in 2002 and associated with the Birla Institute of Technology & Management, (BIT, MESRA, Ranchi) at its Noida Center and later he joined as Professor at FORE School of Management, New Delhi. He has conducted good number of MDPs in the area of Finance and Cost Accounting, published good numbers of research papers. Prof. Singh has participated in International Faculty Development Programs and presented research papers in the International conferences abroad. He also headed Financial Markets Research Center in collaboration with University of St. Thomas, USA at GLA University. Prof. Singh is presently associated with GL Bajaj Institute of Technology & Management as Professor-Emeritus and also Adjunct Professor at Jamia Hamdard (Deemed University) New Delhi. He carries with him a long experience in academics and industry. 12 research scholars awarded PhD under his supervision at Birla Institute of Technology & Management, Jamia Hamdard and GLA University and 5 more are in process of submission. He is empaneled as an expert for evaluating PhD

Thesis in five universities. He is also on the review panel of different International Journals including Emerald. He has published text books on Commercial Bank Management and Strategic Cost Management with Wiley and Tata Mac and also contributed contents to Corporate Finance Book being published by Wiley, USA. He has guided several research projects of PG students.

Poonam Singh has been serving as an Assistant Professor at the School of Commerce, Manav Rachna International Institute of Research and Studies since August 2023. With over 5 years of teaching experience in Commerce and Finance, she earned her Ph.D. in 2018 and secured Net/JRF in management in 2010. Driven by a passion for teaching, she actively engages in research, boasting a record of 4 research papers in various Scopus Indexed Journals, 1 in an ABDC journal, and 3 in non-indexed journals. She has also contributed two book chapters, a case study, and a book while publishing two patents. Dr. Singh has participated in numerous national and international conferences, FDPs, and workshops.

Azmee Zaheer is an Assistant Professor at the University School of Business, MBA department, Chandigarh University, Gharuan, Punjab. She has completed her PhD and MPhil in Management from Babasaheb Bhimrao Ambedkar University (A Central University), Lucknow, Uttar Pradesh. She received a Gold Medal for her M.Phil's exemplary work. She has four years of research experience, 3.5 years of corporate marketing experience, and 1.5 years of academic marketing experience. She has also contributed to various research journals, including Scopus, Web of Science, UGC Care, and Edited Books, and has participated in multiple national and international seminars. ORCID ID: https://orcid.org/0000-0002-6281-2608 Azmee.zaheer@gmai.com

Index

A

B

C

D

E

F

G

I

M

O

P

Q

R

S

T

www.ingramcontent.com/pod-product-compliance
Lightning Source LLC
LaVergne TN
LVHW062326300926
849161LV00007B/1589